# Money Secrets
# of the Rich

'John Burley's no-nonsense approach to money management has given us the inspiration and discipline we needed to regularly invest a portion of our money. In the last eight months we have accumulated $5,500 in managed funds ... and we don't miss the money that we are investing. The step-by-step methods that John teaches make it easy for anyone to get started!'

ADAM & KATH EDWARDS, BRISBANE QLD, AUSTRALIA

'We knew we wanted to be financially free but we were lost in a maze of poor advice and misinformation. John's principles and specific techniques created a clearly defined path to the goal.'

MALCOLM & FIONA LINSELL, MELBOURNE VIC, AUSTRALIA

'Who better to learn the secrets of the rich from than a multi-millionaire? I made the decision to not be middle-class any more and now, with the help of mentor programs and John's advice, in just 10 months I am well positioned to achieve my goal of financial independence (I have more than 40 positive cash flow properties!). Yes, with the lessons contained in this book and hard work you can do it too, whatever your circumstance.'

STEVE MCKNIGHT, MELBOURNE VIC, AUSTRALIA

'John Burley's *Money Secrets* program completely blew the lid off our conventional ideas on the rich and how they build their wealth. With two financial degrees in the family, and a father who was a bank manager, we were brought up to be reasonably "financially savvy" – at least we thought so. But John's simple principles showed us we really had no idea. He teaches you how to build a foundation of wealth, which then gives you the confidence to fast-track your investments. Since completing the program 10 months ago we have turned our finances around by $17,000. But best of all we feel *in control* of our money and can see ourselves being completely debt-free next year.'

BRIAN & ELIZABETH YATES, BRISBANE QLD, AUSTRALIA

'After months of searching for the answers to financial freedom, we were inspired into immediate action by John Burley's *Money Secrets* program. Within 6 months we had purchased a positive cash flow investment property and accumulated over $8,000 in our Automatic Investment Program. All this has been achieved by following a simple formula and without hardship.'

CAROLE STALEY, MELBOURNE VIC, AUSTRALIA

'Within just a few months of receiving John's information we now have two properties earning a passive income and we have purchased a business that is rapidly growing. It is an absolutely fantastic feeling, receiving cheques in the mail rather than bills! Financial independence is now a real and achievable goal. John's teachings are life-changing.'

KAREN & RUSSELL DORLANDT, PERTH WA, AUSTRALIA

'JB gives you the ABC on how to become wealthy on a regular income. *Money Secrets* is a must read for all those who want to teach their children the benefits of investing and producing a *lifestyle*. With John's information and some get-up-and-go we have acquired more than 30 positively-geared properties in just over six months!'

TONY BARTON, MELBOURNE VIC, AUSTRALIA

'John Burley is a man to be held in high esteem. His *Money Secrets* program has changed not only the way I think about money but has given me practical solutions to reduce debt and increase cash flow substantially. Using his methods I will wipe out my $200,000 debt in 18 months and turn two negatively-geared properties into cash flow producing deals with a conservative 40% return. Thank you John for changing my life from a downward-spiralling debt burden into an ever increasing financially successful future.'

DAVID WOOD, ADELAIDE SA, AUSTRALIA

'Fantastic stuff! We wish we were taught this in school. In less than 12 months using John's *Money Secrets* program, we have created a significant AIP, reduced our expenses by more than 30%, become debt-free (*including our home*) and are increasing our passive income using John's real estate cash flow strategies. Unbelievable. Thanks John.'

MICK & JANE HAGARTY, BRISBANE QLD, AUSTRALIA

'John Burley's *Money Secrets* program has completely changed the way we handle the subject of money and our financial lives. Not only has it taught us how to become and remain debt-free, but also it has enabled us to transform our lives from that of regular employees to property investment business owners. Within the space of six months we have set up a solid investment plan and have purchased eight positively-geared properties.'

PAUL & TRACEY VERSCHUUREN, BRISBANE QLD, AUSTRALIA

'An amazing collection of extremely practical and useful wealth-building tools. Essential for anyone wanting integrity in their wealth-building adventures. Outstanding! Thanks John.'

KEVIN SCHWAGER, NEWCASTLE, AUSTRALIA

'The most important information I've learnt in the past 10 years is what I've learnt from John Burley. He thinks like no other individual! I have been consistently *amazed*, amused and enlightened by everything he teaches. And unlike any other trainer, he shows you how to *do*, not only how to think.'

KATE HOSIE, SYDNEY, AUSTRALIA

'John Burley, hands down, is the best communicator of financial concepts that I have ever heard. His ability to simply explain the complex is unsurpassed. Not only that but his ideas of creating wealth are right on! If you are interested in improving your financial situation, learn from the best and invest in yourself. Buy into John's information now!'

THOMAS BENTLY, COLUMBUS OH, USA

'Learning *Money Secrets* wealth habits should be taught to everybody at school. I will certainly be sharing this information with my children to give them a head start in life.'

DR IAIN FERGUSON, B.D.S., M.MED.SCI, D.ORTH. R.C.S., MELBOURNE VIC, AUSTRALIA

'John, where were you when I was digging a financial hole for myself? If I had access to John Burley's *Money Secrets* program several years ago, I would have saved myself a world of financial disaster. Don't just stand there and take my word for it, buy this book and empower yourself financially.'

SHAWN DERRICK, WELLSVILLE NY, USA

'John teaches the 95% of the people who don't know how to manage money, what the other 5% know. With this information you can be in command of your life.'

DAVID D'AMICO, PONTE VEDRA FL, USA

'This *Money Secrets* program taught our family how to save up to $100 a day! Finances is not my favourite topic. However, seeing and receiving the financial rewards by learning to handle our finances differently has been very beneficial and hopeful to me. We look forward to becoming better educated and financially smart and to pass this gift to our children.'

KATE RIEGEL, BATAVIA NY, USA

'*Money Secrets* was a revelation. The simple and multiple ways of improving your money management and then the next step up to being a Level Five investor were presented in a most enlightening way. I would highly recommend this man's ideas to anyone who wants to be financially independent.'

CHRIS BAILEY, WAGGA WAGGA NSW, AUSTRALIA

'John Burley's *Money Secrets* program has had a dramatic impact on our lives! We now have a high level of awareness, and know exactly where our money is going. We make conscious choices to use surplus money to create further wealth! We are excited by the prospect of watching our money grow automatically every month! John's program has served to clarify our plan and direction for the future, and has instilled in us the importance of educating our young children about the principles of money and wealth creation. We now welcome the challenge and excitement of creating further financial and personal wealth in our lives!'

DENNIS & ANGELA PERIN, BRISBANE QLD, AUSTRALIA

'John Burley's insights and knowledge are exceptional. His ideas and information are truly new and enlightening. Since attending and following his programs I have wiped out *all* my consumer debt, and started my asset portfolio … John showed me how!'

ANTONY COMANOS, SYDNEY NSW, AUSTRALIA

'John Burley's program is a brilliant tool to financial success and freedom. His down-to-earth ideas allowed me to track down where my money was going, what I needed to do to change this and how to start an investment program. Before John's program, I did not invest because I could not understand financial jargon, and I was scared to trust. I now can confidently find the good investments for my money. I have channelled $15,000 of my funds into profitable investments that grow every month from the savings I make by managing my money effectively. I am debt-free and intend to stay that way. I am in control of money I earn, money I spend and money I invest. Before I was vague and uncertain about my financial future. Now my financial future is bright and predictable. What is most important is: I now have confidence in what I am doing thanks to John's brilliant program.'

SINAN KORAY, SYDNEY NSW, AUSTRALIA

'I never knew how out of control my finances in my own business and personal budget were. I thought I was doing really well, but after reading *Money Secrets* and listening to John's tapes, my mental attitude and finances have increased dramatically!'

ELIZABETH KIRIAKIDIS, MELBOURNE VIC, AUSTRALIA

# Money Secrets of the Rich

## Learn the *7* steps to financial freedom

## John R. Burley

### with Bruce Whiting

### Contributing Editor Simon Hall

TREASURE CHEST UNLIMITED, INC.

ISBN 1-929238-00-2

This publication is designed to provide accurate and authoritative information in regard to the
subject matter covered. It is sold with the understanding that the publisher is not engaged in
rendering legal, accounting, or other professional service advice. If legal advice or other expert
assistance is required, the service of a competent professional should be sought.

The authors and publisher specifically disclaim any responsibility for liability, loss or risk,
financial, personal or otherwise, that is incurred as a consequence, whether directly or indirectly,
of the use and application of any of the contents of this book. Throughout the book readers are
encouraged to take responsibility for their own lives, financial and otherwise, which
responsibility, by definition, extends to their reaction in all facets to the contents of this book.

This book references many Internet sites that may be of interest and assistance to readers. The
authors and publisher make no representation or warranty of any sort with respect to the
value, accuracy or completeness of the information contained on any of these Internet sites,
and specifically disclaim any liability for any information contained on, or omissions from these
Internet sites. References to the Internet sites in this book shall not be construed to be an
endorsement of the Internet sites, the companies represented by the Internet sites, or of the
information contained thereon, by the authors or publisher. The same disclaimer applies to the
use of telephone numbers throughout this book. Readers shall in all circumstances determine
and be responsible for their own use of these Internet sites and telephone numbers as provided
to assist readers by the authors and publisher. Readers must be able to take ultimate
responsibility for all their decisions in relation to all the information contained in this book or
such information, in the final analysis, can be of little long-term use.

Cover Design by Insync Graphics
First Edition printed 2000
Reprinted 2001 (twice)
Published by Treasure Chest Unlimited, Inc.
Distributed in Australia by Pow Wow Events International (612) 9923 1699
Printed by Griffin Press

*This book is dedicated to my family. To my wonderful wife Shari and my great children John, Jr. and Danielle.*

JOHN R. BURLEY

# Contents

---

**PART TWO**

Know thy enemy: eliminating financial traps
– saving money

---

**PART THREE**

The magic of financial freedom

# Editor's Preface

As you commit to undertake the *Money Secrets of the Rich* program, please understand that there is no theory within this book, only tried and true information and experiences distilled. There are certainly no quick fixes or magic wands, potions or earth-shattering revelations. There is simply the unglamorous wisdom of ages, seasoned with the modern and unmistakable quality of one of America's foremost investment minds and practitioners, John R. Burley.

I have come to know John as a great friend and a man who is an inspiring example of the triumph of the courage and the commitment it takes to chart a better course, a course for success and prosperity. He stands in elite and rare company as one of the finest wealth-creating minds and technicians on our planet today and as your navigator and companion through the turbulent waters of knowledge financial. His commitment to your best interest is unparalleled. He has proven this on his many visits to Australia since April 1997. I assure you that within the pages of *Money Secrets of the Rich* you will find a step-by-step path to financial prosperity that is at once breathtakingly original in its simplicity and eminently powerful in its implementation.

'What lies behind us, and what lies before us are small matters compared to what lies within us.'

**RALPH WALDO EMERSON**

Jim Rohn, noted American business philosopher, author and lecturer has described in his book *Seven Strategies for Wealth and Happiness*, one of the best ways to ensure success: 'Watch what successful people do. Why? Because success leaves clues. Watch how the successful man shakes the hand of someone else. Watch how the successful woman asks questions. People who do well *own* the habits of success. They create patterns of winning behaviour just as the struggler creates patterns of losing behaviour.'

John has done more than leave clues for us, he has provided a detailed map setting out the methods required for achieving the same degree of success that he has achieved, but without the hardships. As P.T. Barnum said in his often-delivered speech, *The Art of Money-Getting*, '…happy is he who by listening to the experience of others avoids the rocks and shoals on which so many have been wrecked.'

For the last three years I have been watching and successfully applying the investment techniques that John applies and teaches. This is primarily how I came in 1999 to be available for the opportunity to edit and contribute to his book; by being open to the possibility to listen, to learn, to make changes and to persist with them.

As John speaks to you from the pages of *Money Secrets* he does so from the heart, knowing where you are and where you want to go because he knows each location with intimate experience. The muscle of his message is genuinely delivered with passionate sincerity because he is at all times focused on *your* financial well-being. I do not make such ostensibly 'fluffy' claims lightly. Nor am I prone to bouts of sentimentality, or hero worship. I just know these things for a fact. I can honestly say that it was John's qualities of integrity and his boundless energy for helping others that first impressed me when I saw him speak at that 1997 Australian seminar. The information he offered, his inspiring teaching manner and the fact that he had the runs on the board to back himself were fairly impressive too.

Remember at all times as you undertake this program that we are not advocating a reduction in your lifestyle. On the contrary, we are seeking to improve your quality of life on every page. The message may at times, by virtue of its content, appear unglamorous and thus unattractive when seen through 21st century consumer-jaded 'get me there at the speed of light' eyes. I recommend you slow down to the speed of the information in order to best take it in, and look long and hard at what it will do for you and your family.

> 'If this world affords true happiness, it is to be found in a home where love and confidence increase with the years, where the necessities of life come without severe strain, where luxuries enter only after their cost has been carefully considered.'
>
> **A. EDWARD NEWTON**

The *glamour* of achieving financial independence through the practice of habits of financial responsibility and competence, of living debt-free and within one's means, and of retiring wealthy, is always, in the final score, 100% determined by the individual. There is much elegance and glamour to living such a life, if one cares to see it, despite what the science and art of modern consumerism tell us daily. Most precious of all, however, there is peace and happiness. There is sleeping well and worry-free, and there is pride and honour that radiates from building and maintaining true stewardship of your own affairs. There is Freedom!

You will glean from the pages of *Money Secrets of the Rich* that this Financial Freedom is achieved by a combination of:

- keen self-awareness and self-discipline;
- a certain mastery of certain knowledge;
- decisiveness and taking positive action on decisions;
- hard work, resilience, determination and perseverance;
- patience and faith (positive attitude);
- quiet reflection;
- the passing of time.

I do encourage you at all times as you progress along the road to *Automatic* Financial Freedom to remain aware that, although *Money Secrets of the Rich* is certainly one of the best navigational tools you could have with you on your journey, it is *you* who are nonetheless still in the driver's seat at all times. I only tell you this to alert you that you will be inevitably faced with the very human temptation to nod off at the wheel at critical moments.

To avoid potential 'wrecks' I encourage *you* to *own* the material that you are learning (through practice and experience), review it constantly and know that by force of your decisions, combined with conducive action, and a little reflective quiet listening (not flurry and noise), you *will* achieve a prosperously altered state of (financial) reality. This has been my experience over the last three years. I know that it can be yours too.

Congratulations on your commitment to creating *Automatic Financial Freedom*!

*Simon E. Hall (Ed) BA(Syd), LLB(UNSW)*

'To laugh often and much;
To win the respect of intelligent people
and the affection of children;
To earn the appreciation of honest critics
and endure the betrayal of false friends;
To appreciate beauty;
To find the best in others;
To leave the world a bit better,
whether by a healthy child,
a garden patch or a redeemed social condition;
To know even one life has breathed
easier because you have lived;
This is to have succeeded.'

RALPH WALDO EMERSON (1803–82), *What is Success?*

# Introduction

I have not always been financially successful. Like many people reading this book, I once struggled from month to month trying to make ends meet. I can clearly recall a time, in the not too distant past, when my decision as to where I went shopping was based primarily upon which store was still stupid enough to give me credit.

I often lived beyond my means and on many occasions struggled to pay my bills on time. Although I appeared (based on my lifestyle) to be doing well, the reality was that I spent much time worrying about money and my financial situation. I was 29 years old, newly married and planning on becoming a father in a couple of years, but despite my well-above-average income, I was broke, in debt and going nowhere fast. I spent many sleepless nights lying in bed worrying about the truth of my financial situation.

Up until the age of 29 I had focused most of my energy and time learning how to make *more* money. I had the belief (which I know now to be false) that if I could just make *more* money everything would work out. I came to realise that just wasn't true. My income continued to go up but my situation never really changed. The only real difference from when I was younger (and earning less) was that I now had a whole lot more debt and financial responsibilities (burdens). Sure I had nice things (flash cars and a big house), but they also came with big payments. I did not want to give up my nice lifestyle, but I did want to get out of the trap of just getting by.

> 'Of all the advantages which come to any young man, I believe it to be demonstrably true that poverty is the greatest.'
> **JOSEPH G. HOLLAND**

I realised that things had to change. That *I* had to change. That I had to stop living the way I had lived all of my life. I knew that if I did not change how I *thought* about and *dealt* with money that my situation would never really get any better, despite the level of my *income*. In short, I decided to take on new *financial responsibility* for my own life.

I realised that just making more money was not the answer. I had to learn how to properly *manage* my money. And I had to learn how to create *assets* that would create *wealth*. My plan was to develop a system that would allow me to maintain my lifestyle while freeing me from money worries and traps. **To do this I needed to develop assets that would provide me with cash flow to live off for the rest of my life!**

> 'All growth depends upon activity. There is no development physically or intellectually without effort, and effort means work. Work is not a curse; it is the prerogative of intelligence, the only means to manhood, and the measure of civilization.'
> **CALVIN COOLIDGE**

For the next 10 solid years I made it my mission to locate and study all the information I could find on the subject of money: making it, keeping it, spending it and investing it. I read, listened, studied and attended seminar after seminar. I talked with as many rich people as I could. I developed, experimented and took action. And through effort, trial and error and a lot of learning experiences, I developed a step-by-step system for becoming rich.

**By age 32 I was in a financial position to be able to retire!**
*I was in a position to be able to live off the positive cash flow from my investments, and if I so desired, never have to work again!*

*Money Secrets of the Rich* provides you with the system I used (and thousands of my students have used) to obtain financial freedom and security. It is a sure-fire system to riches. And it's easy to do. Simply read a chapter and follow the action steps. In just a few days you will have learned all you need to achieve **Automatic Financial Freedom**! This book shows everyone, regardless of their current financial situation, how to move from a life of financial stress, worry, and disappointment, to one of freedom, abundance and true financial independence. Welcome to the world of **Automatic Financial Freedom** that awaits you.

In *Money Secrets of the Rich* I share with you what the rich do to become rich. You will learn the proven **7 Steps to Automatic Financial Freedom** (the *7 Money Steps of the Rich*). This is not philosophy or theory. It is the essence of my 20+ years of financial experience, experience gained 'down and dirty' in the 'real world'. Everything you need to know is laid out in simple, easy-to-follow steps.

The idea for this book has been in my head for several years. For me, reading financial books was often a frustrating experience. It seemed that in most cases the books did one of two things. Either the author told a great, motivating story that made me realise that I had to do *something*, I just wasn't clear *what*. Or the book was filled with tons and tons of (technical) information that often confused me and almost always gave me so many new questions (and doubts about what to do) that rather than start taking action I felt I needed to do even *more* research.

I always wondered why somebody didn't just tell you about the subject and then tell you *what* to do. Isn't that why we buy financial books, to get answers and be given a direction to follow?

The path to Financial Freedom is not the complicated or difficult journey that most have been taught to believe. The main reason so many people struggle financially is because they have never been taught a proven system for becoming rich. This is what *Money Secrets of the Rich* provides. A hold-your-hand, step-by-step system to lead you on your way to **Automatic Financial Freedom** In *Money Secrets* we give you the **Who, What, Why, When, Where and How** of money. We provide you with the names, phone numbers and website addresses of the people and companies you need to contact to properly take care of your money. We cover everything from getting started to the advanced investment techniques used by the super traders and investors of the world. And we do this all in an easy-to-follow format with action steps at the end of each chapter to lead you safely to take control of your financial life.

'By whatever basis human desires are classified, the promise of an abundant life covers virtually all. To the spiritual, it suggests escape from futility; to the sensuous it calls up visions of luxury; to the defeated it is a dream of success.'

**CADMAN**

But who am I, a Yank born and raised in California and residing in Phoenix, Arizona for the last 10 years, to be instructing Australians on how to become financially free and secure?

Since April 1997 I have been making regular visits to Australia, studying your economy, businesses, tax, real estate and entrepreneurial opportunities. Not surprisingly, I have found more similarities than differences between our two countries: our dreams of home ownership and comfortable retirement; of providing for our families; and of doing something worthwhile with our lives. Our support of a 'fair go' and rewards for hard, honest work. And our passions for sport and the outdoors, for family and friends, good food and good wine (beer!)–you bet!

I first started working with Aussies and Kiwis at seminars in the US and internationally as far back as 1993. In 1997 I had the opportunity to make my first visit to Australia. My friends Robert and Kim Kiyosaki were heading to Sydney to do a seminar for Pow Wow Events International (Robert is the best-selling author of *Rich Dad Poor Dad, The Cash Flow Quadrant* and *Rich Dad's Guide to Investing*).

Since Robert and I had enjoyed teaching together on several occasions (at each other's seminars) he asked me if I would join him in teaching a seminar in Australia on 'The Secrets of Professional Investors'. I said I'd love to. The seminar was such a tremendous success that Pow Wow asked me if I would return to do a series of events later that year. Since my family and I had enjoyed the visit so much I jumped at the chance to return.

This has expanded into my spending a little over two months each year (one sixth of my yearly life) in the Land Down Under.

I have now taught and shared my information during six national speaking tours with more than 10,000 Aussies and Kiwis. I have conducted more than a dozen 'Automatic Wealth' weekend education seminars and 20+ evening events on 'Winning the Money Game'. Australia has become a very special place in my and my family's life, and for this privilege I must thank Robert and Kim for their gracious invitation for that first trip.

As I was nearing completion on the US version of *Money Secrets of the Rich*, the challenge was then put forth to create this Australian version. With the assistance of my two Australian mates, co-author Bruce Whiting (chartered accountant, managing partner of MGI Wamstekers), and contributing Editor, Simon Hall (lawyer, director of Lightning Ridge Enterprises), we completed the task. We produced a book that provides solutions to people's financial problems.

Extensive market and field research was conducted prior to completing the fully rewritten Australian version of *Money Secrets of the Rich*. We worked extensively with some of Australia's best tax planners, accountants, lawyers and investors, and met with hundreds of highly successful entrepreneurs. During this time I learned how to do what I do in the US, under Australian rules and laws. The research my team and I conducted on your economy, businesses, tax, real estate, investment and entrepreneurial opportunities revealed many similarities between our two countries. This makes sense since both of our economic and legal systems have their basis in English Common Law. We did find differences, but we also found experts to translate them from US to Oz.

And so I can confidently say that with the extensive help of my Australian friends, the information in *Money Secrets of the Rich* is spot-on for you, the Australian reader. The many graduates of my Australian seminars are doing all of the techniques in this program for obtaining Financial Freedom right now, today, in Australia.

So rest assured that I am in touch with the Australian investment landscape and tuned in to the *Australian Dream*. I have even managed to start speaking properly... no worries!

Countless people have shared with us that after completing the *Money Secrets of the Rich* program they consider it to be *essential* reading for anyone seeking financial success in the 21st century. Some of their testimonials appear in the front of the book. Some of their results, shared throughout the book, are nothing short of astounding.

As *you* begin this program I want to commend you for doing what so many others will not, stepping forward and taking action to improve your life. My sincere thanks for the trust you have placed in me by investing in this book. And my congratulations on the success, prosperity, financial freedom and security that this book will help you acquire.

I trust that one day we can meet. Until then please contact me and tell of your many successes (www.johnburley.com).

Thank you and God Bless.

*John R. Burley*

## PART ONE

# Recognising and breaking old habits – Finding Financial Freedom

'You see but you do not observe.'
SHERLOCK HOLMES (BY ARTHUR CONAN DOYLE)

'I finally know what distinguishes man from the other beasts: financial worries.'
JULES RENARD

'We all have two choices: We can make a living or we can design a life.'
JIM ROHN

# The Seven Levels of Investor

'If you reach for the stars, you might not quite get one, but you won't end up with a handful of mud, either.'
LEO BURNETT

What type of investor are you? Have your investment experiences been positive, negative or mixed? Would you like to know why you get the results (positive or negative) that you get when you invest? Of course you would!

Good news. I am here to tell you why you get the results that you do! Over the past 20 years, I have devoted myself to the study of money. I have driven myself to know exactly how it works and why. I have read every book, watched every video, and listened to every tape I could find on the subject. Over that same period, I have interviewed, counselled, and trained thousands of people in relation to the practices of wealth-building.

During my in-depth study of what I refer to as the **'Money Game'**, I made a startling discovery. Despite the many and varied personality types in the world, there are really only seven basic types (or levels) of investor. And while it is common for an

'Obstacles cannot crush me
Every obstacle yields
to stern resolve
He who is fixed to a star
does not change his mind.'

**LEONARDO DA VINCI**

individual to drift a little from one investor type to another, most people will stay fixed at one level for their entire lives. The bad news is that they are often 'stuck' at a level which prevents their financial success. The good news is that anyone, with a little effort, including you, can easily upgrade their investment skills.

The first step to upgrading yourself is to identify what type of investor you really are. Knowing this will give you a clear awareness of why you get (or do not get) the investment results you desire. With this new awareness you can adopt (or maintain) the attitudes required for your desired level. You can then invigorate this awareness with appropriate action, to give yourself the results you so richly deserve.

---

**To summarise**: The first step in the process of change is *Awareness*. Awareness of where you are and where you want to go. The second step is to adopt the *Attitude* of the people whom you would like to emulate (model). The third step is to take positive *Action*.

---

Always carry with you the **Three As**: *Awareness*, *Attitude* and *Action*. I have found that when people are off-track, it is because one of the Three As is not being properly applied.

As stated, the great thing about your investor type is that it can be easily changed. So as you read on, do not despair if you are currently one of the lower levels of investor. You can always upgrade to a higher level. Think of the process as an *evolution*. All of us begin at the bottom and progress upwards. The key to your own progress, or evolution, is to first determine where you are and where it is you want to go.

People often get caught up in the 'I need to make more money' trap. In fact, your income actually has very little to do with your ability to obtain Financial Freedom. Let me be clear, the **Seven Levels of Investor** have *nothing* to do with your income. Rather, they relate to what you do *with* your income. I know people who make millions of dollars per year who are financial failures (I know, I agree this is ridiculous, yet true). I also have a graduate of mine who is a multi-millionaire yet he never made more than $18,000 a year from his job.

**Remember, it's not how much you make, but rather what you keep and what you do with it.**

**So don't get hung up on your income. Concentrate instead on putting money aside into investments that will grow!**

As you read through the Seven Levels of Investor I want you to know that at various times in my life I have been at every single one of these levels. It was only as my knowledge increased that I was able to upgrade myself to where I am today. Thus, at some point in the descriptions of each level you may recognise yourself and the people in your life. I recommend that you write down to the side of the page who you know in each level and also where *you* currently are. It will really help you to open up your awareness.

Here now are the **Seven Levels (Types) of Investor**.

## LEVEL ZERO: THE NON-EXISTENT

*(This first Level of 'Investor' actually does not exist as an investor. They are Level Zero.)*

This type of investor is the **Non-Existent**. These people live their financial lives with their heads in the sand like ostriches. They essentially have no investments or savings. They are completely unconscious or oblivious of money matters in general and their

For a FREE TAPE

*"Investment Strategies
of the Rich"*

Call 1300 550 240

'...the taxes are indeed very heavy, and if those laid on by the government were the only ones we had to pay, we might more easily discharge them; but we have many others, and much more grievous to some of us. We are taxed twice as much by our *idleness*, three times as much by our *pride*, and four times as much by our *folly*, and from those taxes the commissioners cannot ease or deliver us by allowing an abatement.'

**BENJAMIN FRANKLIN**

'Empty pockets never held anyone back. It's only empty heads and empty hearts that do it.'

**NORMAN VINCENT PEALE**

'You can't build a solid, substantial house with decayed planks, no matter what kind of a veneer is put over their rottenness.'

**BENJAMIN FRANKLIN**

spending habits in particular. Their financial lives are so completely mismanaged that they do not even qualify for the simplest credit products and so, ironically, though their financial outlook is bleak, they are often in a better financial position than the person for whom credit is all too easily available.

When asked what their problem is, they will invariably state that they just don't make enough money. That if they just made more money, they would be OK. The fact is that in many cases they are now 'starving' on what they 'dreamed' they could make five years ago.

These people fail to see that the problem is not necessarily their income (or lack of it) but rather their **Money Habits**.

## LEVEL ONE: THE BORROWER

*(Also not, technically speaking, an investor.)*
As implied above, the **Borrower** is often in a far worse financial position than the Non-Existent, though his or her potential for change may be greater. The Borrower often has very high debt.

Borrowers spend all that they make and more besides. What they know how to do best is consume. When they have money, it gets spent. At best, they 'survive' on a month-to-month basis. Their solution to a money crisis is to either attempt to spend their way out of it or to take on more debt, oblivious of both the short and long-term consequences of their actions. Their idea of 'financial planning' is to get a new VISA card or MasterCard, or to refinance their home in order to buy more things on credit.

Similar to Non-Existent investors, Level One Borrowers refuse to see that the problem is not necessarily their income (or lack of it) but rather their Money Habits. I personally know of one individual who was making more than $3 million a year and yet still was a Level One.

Our Money Habits (what we do with our income) are far more important than the level of income we make, or do not make, in any given year.

Borrowers often get themselves caught in a vicious cycle of spiralling debt, coming to believe that their situation is hopeless, and as a result, giving up all hope. They usually live in complete financial denial. Unless they are willing to change, their financial future is bleak and they are accelerating towards oblivion.

## LEVEL TWO: THE SAVER

The third type of investor is the **Saver**. The Saver usually puts aside a 'small' amount of money on a regular basis. The money is generally deposited into a very low-risk, low-return vehicle such as a cheque account, savings account, money market account or term deposit. If this person has a personal superannuation fund, it is usually held with a bank or insurance company.

Savers usually save to consume rather than to invest (i.e. they save for a new TV, stereo, etc.). They are very afraid of financial matters and are unwilling to take any risks. Even when shown that in today's economic environment, cash investments give a negative return (after inflation and taxes), they are still unwilling to alter their investment habits.

The Saver's idea of an 'aggressive' investment is to start an insurance-style savings plan or buy whole-of-life insurance (a horrible investment that almost no individual should ever do– I will tell you why later.) From my years in the business, I can tell you that the insurance industry loves this type of person because they can prey on their conservatism and deep-seated need for 'security' and make *huge commissions* in so doing.

> 'The drifters slip along until they float into some quiet by-water, or they go over the falls – and that is the end of them. Ambition is something more than *looking* at the point you want to reach. Ambition is taking off your coat and pulling and dragging you boat up the stream.'
>
> **HENRY S. FIRESTONE**

Although the strategy of *saving* worked well for my grandfather (way back in the first half of the last century when inflation was low and the temptation to consume was minimal), it no longer works in today's economic environment.

We need to face the facts: the days of old are gone. No longer do we work for the same company all of our lives and then retire with a nice pension (as was commonplace throughout the 1950s, 1960s and 1970s). And unlike people retiring in the middle and towards the end of the 20th century, few people working today will retire to live in the same home (mortgage-free) that they've lived in for the majority of their working lives.

> 'Money is like ... an arm or a leg. Use it or lose it.'
> **HENRY FORD**

In addition, at the end of their working lives, my grandparents' generation were able to receive the benefit of pensions and/or retirement plans that were almost fully funded by the Federal Government or the employee's respective companies (versus today's plans that are almost entirely directly employee-funded). And they benefited from health care plans that for the most part were paid for by the Federal and/or State governments or the companies. All these benefits of old were provided with only nominal contributions required by the employee.

Thus, for them, the strategy of saving for the long term worked well. Over the course of their lives, by diligently saving (without investing) and only paying cash (except for modest borrowing to buy their home), they were able to live comfortably when they retired.

Would the same be true today? Very doubtful. Let's look at the six main reasons for this:

1. **Inflation** – Over the last 20 years inflation has proven to be very irregular. The luxury days of counting on bank interest rates to keep up with inflation are over.

2. **Consumption** – Throughout the world, consumption has exploded. The last two generations have become the 'ultimate consumers', eating up much of the money they should have saved for retirement. Unbelievably, the average US 'baby boomer' (born between 1940 and 1960) had less than $2,000 saved towards retirement at June 2000.

3. **Income taxes** – The 'average' family loses between 20 and 40%+ of their lifetime earnings to Local, State and Federal

governments in the form of direct and indirect taxation.

4. **Social security** – When Federal Government social security programs were originally set up, a large percentage of the population contributed to the funding of these programs compared to a relatively small percentage of the population drawing benefits from them. There was plenty of money to fund the programs. Today this is not the case. The government does not allocate any of *your* taxes and isolate them in a special account for *your* retirement. Of total government outlays, about 21% is allocated to social security income support programs of which 46% is spent directly on retirement income for pensioners. And the percentages are growing. It is predicted that a slowing rate of growth and an ageing profile are likely to characterise the Australian labour force over the period to 2016. Make no mistake, the government is keenly aware that they cannot continue to fully fund retirement and the introduction of compulsory superannuation shows its clear intention for the individual to take responsibility for his or her own retirement.

5. **Increased longevity** – People are living longer and requiring extra funds to sustain their lives beyond their retirement age. Conversely, employment opportunities for older citizens to extend their working age (at their current pay level) and provide for their longer retirement are diminishing for social and skills-related reasons.

6. **Higher cost of housing** – Housing costs for the average family, within city environments where employment opportunities are available, have risen dramatically in relation to the wages offered by that employment. It takes the average family many more years to pay off their home than it would have taken for their grandparents with a similar quality of life.

Because of the above factors, unless Savers have already saved enough for their 'golden years', they are destined for financial mediocrity. Their retirement will require family, government, and employer subsidies (if available) just to provide the basic essentials for survival.

## LEVEL THREE: THE PASSIVE INVESTOR

The fourth type of investor is the **Passive Investor**. These investors are aware of the need to invest and usually add to their superannuation fund by making employee contributions. Sometimes they even have outside investments in managed funds, shares, and bonds.

'Opportunity, for most of us, doesn't knock just once; she raps a continual tattoo on our doors. The pity is that much of the time we're either too preoccupied to hear or too lethargic to answer.'
**BENJAMIN F. FAIRLESS**

Generally speaking they are intelligent people. They are part of the two-thirds of the population that we call the 'middle-class'. However, when it comes to investing they are **Financially Illiterate**. The Passive Investor falls into three typical categories, as follows.

### A. THE 'GONE INTO A SHELL' PASSIVE INVESTOR

The **'Gone into a shell'** category is comprised of people who have convinced themselves that they do not understand money and never will.

They will say things like:
- 'I'm just not very good with numbers.'
- 'I'll never understand how this [blank] investment works.'
- 'I'm just too busy to follow everything.'
- 'There's too much paperwork.'
- 'It's just too complicated.'
- 'I prefer to leave the money decisions to the professionals.'

They then follow up these comments with the following types of rationalisations:
- 'But that's OK because I have a great accountant.'
- 'My stockbroker picks all my investments for me and she's a pro!'
- 'We have a great financial planner.'
- 'I have the best financial adviser in town, I don't need to understand everything that's going on. He's a great guy.'
- 'The personnel department at work handles everything, it's fine.'

The excuses and justifications go on and on. All designed to relieve them from having to take responsibility for their own money... and future.

Due to their beliefs, they have very little idea where their money is invested or why. These investors blindly follow the market like sheep and then squeal (a lot like pigs) before running to their own slaughter. Professional traders actually commonly refer to this type of investor as 'PIGS' because of this behaviour.

> 'He who tries to seize an opportunity after it has passed him by is like one who sees it approach but will not go to meet it.'
> **KAHLIL GIBRAN**

> The most amazing consequence of their blind following of the farmyard mentality of investing is that over the last decade or so (1987–2000), during the greatest Bull Market in history, these 'investors' have *literally* amassed *no* net returns on their investments!

## B. THE 'IT CAN'T BE DONE' PASSIVE INVESTOR

The **'It can't be done' Passive Investor** has determined that all investments involving more than the most basic research by the investor, and promising more than bank interest rates of return, are beyond them and 'can't be done' by other than the most 'gifted', 'lucky' or 'connected' business people, 'corporate highflyers' or 'shady wheeler-dealers'.

They truly believe that high rates of return on investments are impossible, probably illegal or available only to the chosen few. They believe that the knowledge and skills required to even recognise such investments is beyond *them*, in their present circumstances.

This type of passive investor's usual defence to demonstrations of successful investing by friends or high-profile investors is that the successful investors knew something that they could not possibly have known. They will also claim that they are not privy to the same opportunities or resources that the successful investor uses to make their investments so profitable. What a convenient justification.

Typically you will hear them state, right in the face of irrefutable evidence to the contrary, that the successful investment strategy they have just heard described in complete detail, cannot be successfully or indeed legally undertaken in their state or by them in their particular circumstances or financial position. They are very willing to defend their position to the death while their friends, the higher-level investors, continue making great investment after great investment. It seems often as if they take some form of perverse delight in thinking that they are right by trying to poke holes in *well-proven* investment opportunities.

'The little fishes of the sea,
They sent an answer
back to me.
The little fishes' answer was
"We cannot do it, Sir,
because—"'
**LEWIS CARROLL**
**(Through the Looking Glass)**

It is common for these people to whinge and complain about missing out on investment opportunities (after the fact), as if some barrier other than their own psychology (in regard to investing) was to blame for them missing out.

I do have compassion for this type of investor, but let me be frank. The bottomline is that these people are *cowards*. Often vocal, they are quick to try to bring others down… to their level. Because they are afraid, and unwilling to gain the knowledge they need to invest successfully, they choose instead to 'shoot down' and criticise others in an attempt to make themselves, and their beliefs on investing, right.

My advice is to spend as little time and effort as possible (discussing money or investments) with these people. When they see you moving forward, their natural tendency is to put you down and try to convince you of all of the 'reasons' why you can't do it.

The reason they do this? If the people around them become financially successful, they believe that this makes them wrong. And thus in their minds it makes them losers. As a form of self-preservation, they instinctively strike out to pull down all who are trying to escape the 'Rat Race'.

So avoid discussing matters of finance with these people at all costs (and if your spouse or significant other happens to be one of these people, please don't argue with him or her). Let them be right in their own minds for the time being. Just go out there and prove them wrong by becoming a successful investor. When you 'show them the money', maybe then they will begin to come around to your way of thinking. Again though, if positive results *still* fuel their negative fires, don't waste your time and energy trying to put the fires out, you will probably only succeed in fanning them.

**Bottomline:** Don't ever let the **'It can't be done' Passive Investor** take away from you the opportunity to become or continue to be a successful investor.

## C. THE 'VICTIM' PASSIVE INVESTOR

The **'Victim'** is the third category of Passive Investor. Like the people who have 'Gone into a shell' or those who fight for the truth of 'It can't be done', they are intelligent people. However, these investors have no *Principles* or *Rules* for investing. They impulsively buy high and (in a panic) sell low. They look at the share market about the same way as they look at a Las Vegas craps table. It's all just luck. Throw the dice and pray. They are endlessly searching for the 'secret' to investing. Continually looking for new and exciting ways to invest.

My good friend Dr. Van K. Tharp, the trainer of traders who was featured in the book *Market Wizards*, teaches many of the world's elite investors in shares, futures and other derivatives markets. He calls this behaviour 'the pursuit of the Holy Grail'. For 'Victim' Passive Investors this pursuit occurs, usually with repeated failures (and without accompanying behaviour changes), as a consequence of superficial and quick reliance on others for what investments to buy and sell, and how to buy and sell them.

> 'Most people would succeed in small things if they were not troubled by great ambitions.'
> **HENRY WADSWORTH LONGFELLOW**

With stars in their eyes distorting their view of investment opportunities, 'Victim' Passive Investors believe that finding the 'Holy Grail' is all about striking gold somewhere in the outside world, through some amazing new investment that they were quick enough to recognise and jump into. They are always searching for the secret to investing outside themselves, rather than within by changing their unsuccessful behaviour.

Because they are not afraid of risk (far from it, they actually find risk exciting and often actively pursue it), they are easy 'marks' for brokers. They often fall for investment telemarketing schemes, direct mail 'opportunities' and the 'hot' offerings in newspapers and magazines.

'In all games the difference between the amateur and the professional is that the professional plays the odds, while the amateur, whether he realizes it or not, is among other things a thrill seeker. Investment, too, is part a science and part a game, and just as in poker, you need to sort out your motives.'
**JOHN TRAIN**

They are quick to jump into: initial public offerings (IPOs or floats); commodities and futures trading; 'penny dreadful' mining, gold, gas and oil stocks (and other low-probability/high-risk mining ventures); ostrich farms; wine growing; timber and tea-tree plantations; and every other risky, trendy, exotic or 'tax-effective' investment known to mankind. They love to use 'sophisticated' investment techniques such as margins, short-sells, puts, calls, warrants and other options, without proper knowledge of exactly what it is they are committing to or the *real* investment risks.

These people are easily the worst investors the planet has ever known. Always trying to 'hit a six', they usually 'fall flat on their face' in a big way. When asked how they are doing, they will always state that they are 'about even' or 'a little bit up'. The truth is that they have lost money. Many times and often in huge amounts.

'Victim' Passive Investors lose money more than 90% of the time! They will never discuss their losses but will *always* brag about their big win during the 'Wheat Drought of '97'. Despite the rarity of such wins they will eagerly keep coming back for more (like Bart Simpson to a hot-wired cupcake – Bzzz Ow!).

'I don't think you have to chase success, but you do need to slow down enough to let it catch up to you.'
**RICHARD CARLSON**

They believe that all they need is just one 'big one' to be on easy street. Society refers to this person as an 'incurable gambler'. I call them a 'financial failure'.

Dr. Tharp describes these people – the pursuers of the Holy Grail of instant success based on hitting some magic formula or investment opportunity – as people who fail to appreciate their own 'ability to think and be unique'. These people jump into any and all investment schemes, sufficiently convinced by the sales pitch of the investment representative to shut down their own inner wisdom and instincts long enough to hand over their cheques.

Always searching for the 'Holy Grail' in entirely the wrong place, they run around so fast that their inner abilities and powers of independent thought cannot catch up with them long enough to show them, as Dr. Tharp best puts it, that 'People make money by finding themselves, achieving their potential, and getting in tune with themselves so that they can follow the flow of the market.'

## LEVEL FOUR: THE AUTOMATIC INVESTOR

When you reach the level of **Automatic Investor**, your investment success is assured. You are truly on the path to Financial Freedom.

Automatic Investors are clearly aware of the need to invest. However, unlike Passive Investors, they are *actively* involved in their investment decisions. They have a clearly laid out *written long term plan* that will enable them to reach their financial objectives.

'Money, which represents the prose of life, and which is hardly spoken of in parlors without an apology, is, in its effects and laws, as beautiful as roses.'
**RALPH WALDO EMERSON**

They follow **The 7 Money Steps of the Rich**. The seven powerful Money Steps of the Rich allow anyone to achieve *Automatic* **Financial Freedom**. Each step is a simple *action* step that Level Four Automatic Investors must *always* follow when managing their money.

---

### The 7 Money Steps of the Rich

1. Paying Yourself First
2. Reinvesting Your Investment Returns
3. Receiving Level Four Automatic Investor Rates of Return
4. Knowing What Your Money is Doing
5. Adopting the Automatic Money System
6. Financial Competence (Intelligence and Responsibility)
7. Avoiding Debt and Living Debt-Free

*Financially successful people follow the Seven Money Steps of the Rich. Religiously!*

Over the course of this book you will learn each of them and how to easily put them into action to produce financial results that will astound you. Excited? Read on!

Make no mistake; these people are not what you would think of as glamorous big-time investors. Far from it. It is doubtful that they invest in futures, mining and oil, or gold shares, or any other 'exciting' investment vehicle. They are unlikely to be interested in speculation, and if they are, will only speculate with small percentages of their total investment capital (less than 5%) with clearly defined parameters to minimising losses (risk).

Rather, these people have adopted the same type of intelligent long-term approach as used by investors such as Peter Lynch of Fidelity's Magellan Fund fame (one of the largest and most successful mutual funds in history) and Warren Buffett (the world's best investor and one of the wealthiest men in the world).

'To invest successfully over a lifetime does not require a stratospheric IQ, unusual business insights, or inside information. What's needed is a sound framework for making decisions and the ability to keep emotions from corroding that framework.'
**WARREN BUFFETT**

The approach is to keep investment *simple*. Invest in equity positions (such as shares or managed share funds) that realistically provide the opportunity for rates of return of 12%+ over the long term.

Level Four Automatic Investors are not concerned with what the 'in crowd' is doing. They look for a 'good story' and then invest via a systematic **Automatic Investment Plan (AIP)**. They do not get fancy. They rarely use options or margin accounts or any of that other stuff that the 'sophisticated' money managers use. They just buy good shares, proven managed funds or other solid investments and hold them for the long term. And they do so without overcommitting themselves.

They are the people living next door to you driving the three-year-old used Ford (I strongly recommend you confirm this by reading *The Millionaire Next Door* by Thomas J. Stanley, Ph.D. and William D. Danko, Ph.D.).

I know that you are probably not yet convinced. You are thinking: 'Come on John, let's be realistic. You're saying all I have to do is invest in a good growth managed fund on an Automatic Investment Plan (AIP) and I'll become rich? No way!' If that's what you are thinking, let me give you an example of what this simple strategy can do for you.

If you had given Warren Buffett $10,000 just 30 years ago, today you would have **$68,417,563**! That's not a typo, that is over *68 million dollars*! If you had given him $200 a month in an AIP, starting 30 years ago, today you would have **$47,165,321**! And if you had done both, given him $10,000 plus the $200 a month, today you would have a tidy **$115,582,885**!!

## COMPOUND INTEREST – THE EIGHTH NATURAL WONDER OF THE WORLD

Never again question the power of money invested over time. This power is known as **Compound Interest**. According to Albert Einstein, compound interest is the 'Eighth Natural Wonder of the World' and the most powerful thing he ever encountered (including the atom). With as little as $100–200 a month, you too can *unleash the power of Compound Interest* and become a millionaire over time. All you need to do is become an Automatic Investor.

If you are not yet an Automatic Investor, become one as fast as you can. Read on and take notes. (If you are already at this level, congratulations! You have already unleashed the power!)

'If, in order to succeed in an enterprise, I were obliged to choose between fifty deer commanded by a lion, and fifty lions commanded by a deer, I should consider myself more certain of success with the first group than with the second.'
**SAINT VINCENT DE PAUL**

We will talk in greater detail in Chapter 3 about the **Automatic Investment Plan (AIP)**. For now, simply set out a plan of how much you will need a month for how many months (at a realistic rate of return) to get you to where you want to go.

> rstand that a long-term **Automatic**
> **Plan (AIP)** (in concert with the debt and
> ction techniques you will soon learn) will
> provide you with all the money you will need to retire
> wealthy. Your understanding and acceptance of this reality
> is critical to your financial well-being.

**As stated before: at Level Four, keep it simple. Don't get fancy. Avoid the 'sophisticated' investments (until you gain proper knowledge). Stick to owning shares in solid companies and proven growth managed fund investments. Do not attempt to outsmart the market.**

You can find out the most successful and best performing managed funds in Australia from managed fund rating and analysis companies. Try for example, Investor Source at www.personalinvestment.com.au, or *The Australian Financial Review Weekend Edition.*

Stop waiting for the 'big deal'. Get into the Game. If you are just beginning, start with small deals (like managed funds). You can always move up to a bigger game, but you can never get back the time (and money) you lost by waiting for that elusive and illusive big deal. It is the life-changing habits represented at first by these smaller investment decisions and initiatives that are the true 'Holy Grail' of the Level Four Automatic Investor. They are your foundation.

'The centipede was happy quite,
Until a toad in fun
Said "Pray, which leg goes after which?"
That worked her mind to such a pitch
She lay distracted in the ditch
Considering how to run.'

If you don't have an AIP, my firm advice is to start today. Contact a proven managed fund like the ones listed in Chapter 3 and begin putting away money for yourself (even if it's just $100 a month). Many funds even offer no-commission (brokerage) joining deals if you do so via one of the many broker mechanisms offered currently on the Internet (such as Direct Access through www.brw.com.au or www.yourprosperity.com.au).

The longer you wait, the harder it will be for you to become financially successful. The difficulty becomes exponential too, like compound interest in reverse! So get going! Every month you will enjoy a compounding sense of achievement while your assets grow.

## LEVEL FIVE: THE ACTIVE INVESTOR

The top two levels of investor are reached by only a very small percentage of the people on planet Earth. Contrary to what most people (who don't have money) believe, you do not have to become a Level Five or Level Six Investor to become wealthy. But you do at least have to master the habits of a Level Four Automatic Investor.

The **Active Investor** is the sixth type of investor. This is the level where hundreds of my students are. These people have become highly successful private investors, on either a part-time or full-time basis.

'Procrastination is a total barrier to the acquisition of purposeful action. Nothing should be put off until another time, not even for a few minutes. That which ought to be done now should be done now. This seems a little thing, but it is of far-reaching importance. It leads to strength, success, and peace.'
**JAMES ALLEN**

'There are few ways in which a man can be more innocently employed than in getting money.'
**SAMUEL JOHNSON**

Under no circumstances whatsoever should you forego upgrading yourself to the Level Four Automatic Investor because you are sure you can become a 'big-time investor'. I have personally seen friends take this approach and the results have been disastrous. If you want to become a Level Five or Level Six Investor, that's great. I will even teach you the *Principles* and *Rules* involved (later in the program). You must become a Level Four Investor first. You must not skip this stage. Remember the golden rule of Level Four: **If you skip you will trip!**

For further information on educational investment products and upcoming training seminars, contact Pow Wow Events International; on 1300 550 240 or in Sydney on (612) 9662 8488; at www.powwowevents.com.au

Level Five Active Investors understand that to move to this level they must become very clear on their **Principles** and their **Rules** for investing. Their vehicle of choice might be real estate, discounted paper, businesses or shares. Their investments may vary but their *Principles* and *Rules* seldom do.

These investors *actively* participate in the management of their investments. They consistently strive to *optimise* performance while *minimising* risk. It is normal for Active Investors to have long-term annual rates of return of 20–100%+. They intimately understand money and how it works.

A major distinction they have made is that:

> **Rich people**
> **work hard to have their money work hard**
> **while**
> **poor/middle-class people**
> **work hard for money.**

Level Five Active Investors become very wealthy. Their main working focus is on increasing their assets and thus their cash flow. Their money philosophies vary dramatically from those lived by the poor and middle class; rather than investing what is left of their money *after spending*, they believe in spending what is left of their money *after investing*. This shift in perspective is a fundamental one for the budding millionaire.

## LEVEL SIX: THE CAPITALIST

The seventh and final type of investor is the **Capitalist**. Few people in the world ever reach this level of investment excellence and fewer still manage to remain there.

> 'The surplus wealth we have gained to some extent at least belongs to our fellow beings; we are only the temporary custodians of our fortunes, and let us be careful that no just complaint can be made against our stewardship.'
> **JACOB H. SCHIFF**

Capitalists have two principle motivations with regard to investing: to be a *good steward* of their money (while they are living); and to *create a Legacy* (to continue after they are gone). To fulfil these two motivations, they apply the bulk of their money to the task of

making more money. These people are the 'movers and shakers' who
have propelled many western nations to become economic and
industrial powerhouses.

These are the Rockefellers, the Kennedys, the Fords, the
Carnegies, the J. Paul Gettys, the DuPonts, the Ross Perots, the
Bill Gateses, the Rupert Murdochs and the Frank Lowys. These
great Capitalists have provided more jobs, more homes, and more
financial benefit to the world than all the poor people who ever
lived combined.

Consider for example Australia's second-
richest man, Frank Lowy, the driving force
behind the mighty Westfield empire for 40
years. If you had invested $1,000 (around
$9,500 in 2000 dollars) with Westfield
Holdings in 1960 and reinvested all
dividends and taken up all rights issues and
bonus offers, not only would you would
have enjoyed 40 consecutive years of profit
increase, you would also now be sitting on
more than $90 million for your trouble!

'A hundred times every day I
remind myself that my inner
and outer life depend on the
labors of other men, living and
dead, and that I must exert
myself in order to give in the
same measure as I have
received.'
**ALBERT EINSTEIN**

These great Capitalists also contribute
hundreds of millions (if not billions) of
dollars to causes and charities throughout
the world. The Rockefeller Foundation,
for example, generates more money for
charitable distribution from its

'It requires a great deal of
boldness and a great deal of
caution to make a great
fortune; and when you have
got it, it requires ten times as
much wit to keep it.'
**MEYER ROTHSCHILD**

investments *each* year than the Gross Domestic Product (GDP)
of many third world countries (US$177 million in 1999). And
it *never* spends its capital.

In fact, the charter of the Rockefeller Foundation stipulates
that it must 'spend at least 5% of the market value of its
investment portfolio each year on grant programs and
supporting activities. Investment returns must be sufficient to
offset grantmaking of at least 5% per year plus the rate of
inflation.' The foundation was worth $3.8 billion at the end of
fiscal 1999. If you are interested, have a look at their website at
www.rockfound.org and see what the foundation is worth today
and some of the programs they support.

Here is an extract from the Rockefeller Foundation website current at July 2000 which shows both their philanthropy and long-term (Level Four) rock-solid investment focus:

'No person was ever honored for what he received. Honor has been the reward for what he gave.'
**CALVIN COOLIDGE**

'Some men see things as they are and say "Why?" I dream of things that never were, and say "Why not?"'
**GEORGE BERNARD SHAW**

The Foundation's endowment was $3.8 billion at year-end 1999, a beneficiary of double-digit investment returns for the fifth straight year. The Foundation's return was 21.5 per cent in 1999; investment returns for the past five years were 19.1 per cent per year. From 1995 through 1999, the endowment has increased by $1.7 billion, after providing for record-level grantmaking and related expenditures of $700 million during this five-year period. Since inception (1913), the Foundation's grantmaking has totalled more than $11 billion in 1999 dollars.

The Finance Committee periodically reviews the portfolio's commitment to each asset class and establishes a policy portfolio with target allocations. The Foundation rebalances to policy targets as markets move but does not make frequent tactical shifts in asset allocation. The long-term asset allocation targets are U.S. equity 35 per cent, international equity 22 per cent, bonds 22 per cent, real estate 10 per cent, private equity 10 per cent and cash reserves 1 per cent.

**Bottomline: Capitalists** not only create large amounts of wealth, they invariably also create vast legacies of innovation, efficiency, economic prosperity, employment opportunity and philanthropy, thereby greatly increasing the standards of living for hundreds of millions of people throughout the world every year. Are you the next great Level Six Investor, the next great Capitalist?

---

## CHAPTER 1 ACTION STEPS REVIEW

1. Identify what level investor you are. Today, I am a Level _____ Investor.
2. Adopt the long-term investment approach of Peter Lynch and Warren Buffett.

3. Work out how much cash flow you require a month and how much capital you will need for that cash flow in order to retire comfortably.
4. Commit to learning and applying the *7 Money Steps of the Rich*.
5. If you are not already there, upgrade yourself to a **Level Four Automatic Investor** right now.

## CHAPTER 2

# Committing to your Financial Goals

'A journey of a thousand miles must begin with
a single step.'

ANCIENT CHINESE PROVERB

'It is a nuisance that knowledge can only be acquired by
hard work.'

W. SOMERSET MAUGHAM

The most important step to achieving total Financial Freedom
is your 100% *commitment* to completing this *Money Secrets of
the Rich* program. At the end of each chapter you can expect to
spend anywhere from a couple of minutes to one hour on your
assignments. That's all it will take. Just think, in less than 30 hours
you will be applying the *Money Secrets of the Rich* to your life and
be well on your way to *Automatic* **Financial Freedom.**

Right now, commit *in writing* to completing the entire
program. Many people complete the program in far less than 30
hours. Others spend the full 30 hours or indeed several days. It
does not really matter how long you take as long as you take the

right amount of time for *you*. What matters is that you complete the program in its entirety. I know that your desire for control of your financial life will motivate you to complete the tasks required in this program. If you find yourself tempted to skip or gloss over certain chapters or tasks, take a good look at your reasons for this approach and check that they are indeed serving you on your road to Financial Freedom.

'I knew a wise man that had it for a by-word, when he saw men hasten to a conclusion. "Stay a little, that we may make an end the sooner."'
**FRANCIS BACON**

'... remember that the moment you reduce the statement of your desire, and a plan for its realization, to writing, you have actually taken the first of a series of steps, which will enable you to convert the thought into its physical counterpart.'
**NAPOLEON HILL**

**Suggestion:** Get together with like-minded close friends or family members to complete the program for added team motivation.

We begin this program by determining your *Financial Goals*, in **_writing_**. This first step is so easy that you may be tempted to skip it. *Don't*. It is my experience that one of the biggest differences between those people who are financially successful and those people who are not, begins with this critical first step.

Repeated studies have demonstrated that having *written financial goals* dramatically increases your motivation for and thus achievement of financial success. Take a minimum of 30 minutes to sit down with your partner (if applicable) to discuss your financial situation. Ask yourself the following questions:

- **'What do I want to achieve in the next 30 days?'**
  Be realistic when you answer this question.
- **'On a scale of 1 to 10 where is my commitment level?'**
  Be honest with yourself when you answer this question.

---

Then ask yourself these four essential questions:

1. 'What are my dreams?'
2. 'What are my goals?'
3. 'What are my values?'
4. 'What strategies should I use?'

Qualify your answers to *each* of the above questions by also giving serious thought to the following:

## WHY? WHEN? HOW?

When you know what you truly want, why you really want it, when you want it, and how you are going to get it, the rest is easy. Take this first project very seriously. Once you have made these commitments, the rest is simply a matter of determined implementation of the *Money Secrets of the Rich* program (your road to *Automatic* Financial Freedom).

In fact, many students have found that by genuinely making a commitment to knowing *what* they want, *why* they want it and *when* they want it, the matter of *how* they go about getting it almost takes care of itself. Make these decisions and make a genuine commitment towards bringing them to life. You must *decide*.

The important point here is to *commit* to the *decision* to start, though you may not be entirely sure of the *how*. Be open-minded enough to realise that much of what you thought you *knew* about money before beginning this program may not be serving you, and that what you are currently unsure of will become clearer once you get started. So make the commitment to your goals. This is what my friend Simon Hall refers to as 'the infinite power of decisions'. It will all fall into place once you commit and take action. The power is in the *commitment* and not in the *details*. I will provide you with most of the details here in the *Money Secrets* program. So relax and enjoy the journey.

> 'Success is not to be pursued; it is to be attracted by the person you become.'
> **JIM ROHN**

> 'If a man begin with certainties, he shall end in doubts; but if he will be content to begin with doubts, he shall end in certainties.'
> **FRANCIS BACON**

---

Other questions to consider:
- 'What do I really want to accomplish with my life?'
- 'What is my purpose?'
- 'Where do I want to live?'
- 'What type of *lifestyle* do I want?'

- 'What have I always dreamed of doing?'
- 'What "toys" would I like to have for myself and my family?'
- 'How much income each month (cash flow) do I need to meet my current needs? My future needs? My retirement needs?'

## WHAT WILL IT TAKE FOR YOU TO BECOME FINANCIALLY FREE?

The answer to this question depends entirely upon your lifestyle.

'Abundance is in critical ways a state of mind.'
**SUZE ORMAN**

When you run the numbers, assume that your money will earn 10% per annum. For example, the earnings (interest) on $1,000,000 would provide $100,000 a year, or $8,333 a month. Decide for yourself how much money you need to enjoy life and to do the things you passionately want to do.

Your final task for Chapter 2 is: calculate how much money *you* require in order to live comfortably. Start with your monthly income.

**Monthly income required** _____

Multiply this number by 12 to calculate your required *annual* income.

**Annual income required** _____

Now multiply this annual figure by 10. This will give you the total investment capital you will need to satisfy your financial objectives.

**Total investment capital required** _____

# STOP!
## If you have not completed this first step <u>in writing</u> DO NOT PROCEED ANY FURTHER!
## GO BACK!

**Please note:** If you are unsure of the meaning of any words I use, *please* consult a dictionary or financial reference manual. Do not proceed (Do not pass go, do not collect $200!) without maintaining a clear understanding of each concept at the time it is presented. Without this clarity, you will be unable to make the best use of your valuable time. You will make better use of that time by getting clear on words, phrases and concepts when they arise. Although I have attempted throughout the text to provide comprehensive and clear information, some of the material may prompt you to refer to other resources to better your understanding. Take the time to remove any confusion.

**Surf the net for glossaries:** Some dictionaries and manuals are available on the Internet, such as:
- Directory of Investment Terms at
  www.moneymanager.com.au;
- Australian Stock Exchange glossary at
  www.asx.com.au;
- Association of Superannuation Funds of Australia at
  www.superannuation.asn.au.

---

## CHAPTER 2 ACTION STEPS REVIEW

1. **Commit in writing** to completing the *Money Secrets of the Rich* program.
2. Spend a minimum of 30 minutes writing down your **Financial Goals**.
3. Using the simple formula provided, determine how much investment capital (money) you require to become financially independent.
4. Congratulate yourself for taking the first big step towards *Automatic* **Financial Freedom**.

## CHAPTER 3

# Money Step #1 –
# *Paying Yourself First*

'... if you would have a faithful servant, and one
that you like, serve yourself.'

BENJAMIN FRANKLIN

This chapter will be a breeze! All you have to do is hop on
the Internet or make one telephone call! Today is the day
you will set your investment program on autopilot. Today you
are going to learn and take your first new **money step**.

## MONEY STEP #1 – *PAYING YOURSELF FIRST*

The first **money step** is to always *Pay Yourself First*. This does
not mean going to the shops and buying a new shirt or
television. That is not paying yourself, that is paying somebody
else. After all, how much real value do you actually receive
from that shirt or television ten or 20 years from now?
Absolutely none!

*Paying Yourself First* means investing your money so that it can
grow for *you*. This is a very powerful concept. For example, did
you know that $1,000 invested at 15% compounded will be

worth $19,962 in just 20 years? That's almost a 20-fold increase in value.

---

The best method for *Paying Yourself First* is via an **Automatic Investment Plan (AIP)**. This is simply any program whereby money is withdrawn automatically and regularly from your pay or your cheque (or savings) account and invested on your behalf.

---

## THE ADVANTAGES OF AN AUTOMATIC INVESTMENT PLAN (AIP)

- It's easy to set up.
- You only have to 'think' about it once.
- It is simple and painless.
- It's hassle-free.
- It is fun to watch the account grow.
- Your investment account has more money added to it every month.
- Your *asset* column grows automatically.

Like many other Level Four Investors, I have generally preferred setting up an **Automatic Investment Plan (AIP)** linked to investment in the share market (either shares directly, managed funds, or unit trusts).

'If you want to build a realistic retirement nest egg, you have to marry the stock market as soon as you can and stick with it for the rest of your life.'
**JIM JORGENSEN**

The share market, like no other readily accessible and uncomplicated investment vehicle, has produced compounded returns averaging more than 14%+ over the last 45 years! (S&P 500). Very few other investments offer the benefits associated with ownership of shares over the long term. And although historical performance is no guarantee for the future, for the Level Four Investor, when starting out, a basic share market–type investment offers the easiest opportunity for entry into investing and long-term growth.

There are two simple steps involved in starting your **AIP** process:

1.  Decide at what level of sophistication you should begin.
2.  Contact the appropriate broker or managed fund company for the necessary forms.

## STARTING YOUR AIP

Most people will fall into one of five categories of investor comfort (i.e. experience/confidence/sophistication) with regard to commencing their initial AIP. Decide which approach best suits you and commence and manage your AIP accordingly.

1.  You are very experienced with investing (and probably already make a significant portion of your income from trading shares or other investment vehicles). You manage your investment decisions on a regular basis, without the assistance of a full-service broker, probably preferring to use a discount or online broker for your trading.

     *All you need to do is contact a broker for an AIP form. It is important, when trading for a living, to avoid the two major pitfalls many business owners fall into: not paying themselves first; and overpaying their taxes. By separating a portion (10%) of your business income (from your trading) and diverting it into an AIP you are consciously achieving the separation of business and investing that is vital to the Level Four Automatic Investor.*

     You could either focus on select blue-chip stocks for your AIP in the style of Warren Buffet, or simply continue to trade, as you do in your business, but also in your *separate* AIP account. *The point to understand here is the importance of the separation of money between you (your AIP) and your trading*

'If you are trying to preserve purchasing power, it's better to be an owner than a lender. That's why, in the long run, common stocks are your best protection. In terms of purchasing power, the worst thing you can own is cash. You can't play safe with cash. If you want to play safe, put it into something that is genuine, something that has fundamental earning power and value – such as real estate or common stocks... I believe you are safer with common stocks than with cash.'
**JOHN TEMPLETON**

'Diversification is a protection against ignorance. [It] makes very little sense for those who know what they're doing.'
**WARREN BUFFETT**

*business. If you are successfully trading, do not stop, just add the separation to make sure you Pay Yourself First as well.*

2.   You are sufficiently experienced with investing (though not a trader) to be able to pick your own stocks, to manage your monthly investment decisions, without the assistance of a full-service broker.

*Use a fully automated online or discount broker to trade shares, access market information and manage your portfolio for much less than the cost of full-service brokerage.* Watch out for the conditions and any hidden charges that may apply to the transactions and end up costing more than you first thought (e.g. some online brokers advertise low rates but they are for market orders only, not the limit or stop orders, which most successful investors use). Here is a sample of some of the discount brokers you can try and brokerage rates for trades up to $10,000 online and by phone, and for frequent trades online:

- E★Trade Australia at www.etrade.com.au or 1300 658 355. $10,000 online – $32.95 each trade. $10,000 by phone – $71.45 each trade. Frequent trades online – $19.95 each trade up to $20,000 provided more than 20 trades a month.
- Commonwealth Securites at www.comsec.com.au or 131 519. $10,000 online – $31.60 each trade. $10,000 by phone – $54.60 each trade. Frequent trades online – $19.95 if you hold a Commonwealth Investment Account with a balance of at least $5,000.
- Quickbroker at www.quicken.com.au or 1800 555 330. $10,000 online – $21.89 each trade. $10,000 by phone – $53.90 each trade. Frequent trades online – no frequent trader discounts.
- Sanford Securities at www.sanford.com.au or 1300 360 892. $10,000 online – $27.45 each trade. $10,000 by phone – $43.95 each trade. Frequent trades online – no frequent trader discounts.
- TD Waterhouse at www.tdwaterhouse.com.au or 1300 360 359. $10,000 online – $16.30 each trade

at market (not limit). $5,000 by phone – $53.20 each
trade; $15,000 – $64.30. Frequent trades online – 10%
rebate on total trades if more than 15 trades a month.

- Your Prosperity at www.yourprosperity.com.au or
  1800 062 061. $10,000 online – $21.80 each trade.
  $10,000 by phone – $53.90 each trade. Frequent trades
  online – no frequent trader discounts.

Keep abreast of new entrants in the market, particularly
the other larger banks who now also offer competitive rates
and services (ANZ Etrade; NAB online trading; Westpac
broking; and St. George Quicktrade). You can fully compare
and contrast the various broker offerings on
www.brokerchoice.com.au or by checking *The Australian
Financial Review Weekend Edition* which usually prints the
latest Brokerchoice tables.

As rates, terms and conditions change, you should
continually watch and update your understanding of what
is on offer. Some online brokers also offer other services for
a fee, such as news, research, charting and analysis. Premium
services are also usually available.

Starting an Automatic Investment Plan (AIP) is the first
and most important step on your path to financial
independence. In my opinion, these brokers are convenient,
flexible and most importantly, charge low commissions. I
receive no compensation, commission or inducement of any
description from any financial company I recommend. My
recommendations are based upon my independent research of
investment products and performances.

3. You are sufficiently experienced with investing and want to
   pick your own shares, to manage your monthly investment
   decisions, but with the assistance of a broker.

   *Call your broker and request an AIP (direct debit/payroll
   deduction) form. If you don't already have a good broker you can
   start with those brokerages listed above who also provide varying
   degrees of full-service broking or contact other leading brokers who
   you can research at www.brokerchoice.com.au.*

4. You want to invest wisely without having to take the time to select individual shares/investments and thus you would rather spread your exposure across a selection of investments where your **AIP** money is placed for you by fund managers.

    *In the US I recommend Vanguard. It's Index 500 Fund has outperformed over two-thirds of all managed funds over any annual period in the last 40 years. For any 10-year period the fund has outperformed more than 90% of the 'professional' fund managers. Currently there are few managed funds in Australia offering index funds. This will change. In Australia I recommend Equity Trustees (EQT) and Vanguard Investments Australia. They both offer the considerable benefits of no application and withdrawal fees and very low MERs (Management Expense Ratios of around 1% p.a.). Equity Trustees also offers a regular contributions plan from $100 a month once you have made your initial investment of $5,000, with an MER of 1.1%. The EQT Australian Equities Fund primarily invests in the Vanguard 100 Australian Shares Index Fund so it is a way of investing with Vanguard with an AIP (contact Equity Trustees on 1300 55 55 11 or www.eqt.com.au to request a prospectus). Whilst Vanguard Investments Australia does not offer an automatic investment plan for regular additional contributions, once you have set up an investment in one of their index funds (minimum start-up of $5,000) you can then use their BPAY service to contribute amounts of $1,000 regularly throughout the year. The even lower MERs and the larger range of index funds might make this BPAY option appealing for the diciplined investor (contact Vanguard on 1300 655 101 or www.vanguard.com.au to request a prospectus). (MLC MasterKey Unit Trust is currently the largest retail player in the index funds market in Australia (57% of the funds invested) and offers an AIP attached to an Australian shares index fund, BUT they do charge fees of around 5% for all contributions.)*

Vanguard 500 Index rose 1,849% in the 17 years between 1982 and 1999. Last five years: 207%.

5. You want to invest in a managed fund but your budget will not currently stretch to provide the minimum entry and monthly contribution amounts required for the AIP facility with that fund. *Begin by saving the start-up amount in your bank*

*account and thereafter commit to regular contribution amounts to the fund until such time as you are able to generate the minimum monthly debit amount required to activate and sustain an AIP facility with the fund.*

Various top managed fund managers allow initial investments of $500 to $1,000 plus an AIP contribution of just $100 a month. Try NRMA Personal Investment Trust (on 132 976 or www.nrma.com.au); Colonial First State Managed Investment Funds (at 131 336 or www.colonial.com.au); Mercantile Mutual Investments Trusts (on 133 665 or www.mercantilemutual.com.au); MLC MasterKey Unit Trust (on 131 831 or www.mlc.com.au); AMP (on 133 888 or www.amp.com.au). Many of these funds now allow initial applications and contributions to be made online (using BPAY).

If you want to research the performance and investment terms, conditions and fees of funds, there are plenty of information resources available:

- in the newspaper (like *The Australian Financial Review Weekend Edition,* which lists performance tables);
- in popular investment magazines;
- on the Internet, where you can apply or invest directly (online) through fund brokers and avoid or be refunded initial brokerage fees (entry fees) – these services are offered on sites such as:
  - www.yourprosperity.com.au (or on 1800 062 061);
  - www.investorweb.com.au, which has 177 managed fund prospectuses online;
  - www.comsec.com.au, Funds Direct service which compares more than 220 funds with rebates on entry fees;
  - PI Direct Access (1800 047 745) via a number of websites such as www.personalinvestor.com.au (or on 1800 809 091), the Business Tools section of www.brw.com.au, and www.tradingroom.com.au.

> 'Some people see the future as something that will eventually roll along to them, just like a train pulling into a station. They wait hopefully for this train to bring them what they wish for... But the future is not like this. Just as our present is the result of our past, so our future will be the result of our present. Every minute of every day we are weaving threads that will make the cloth of the future.'
>
> **ANNE SPENCER PARRY & MARJORIE PIZER**

If you could afford to buy *this* book, you can afford at least $100 a month to guarantee your financial future. No excuses. Take action now. Make your decision and make that one phone call.

---

**Bottomline: Decide which AIP approach best suits you, then take that first step and make that phone call!**

---

**Note**: Automatic Investment Plans are given different names by different companies, including *regular contributions plans*, *regular investment plans*, *regular savings plans*, *easy investment plans* and *automatic monthly investment facilities*. So don't worry what they call it, just do it!

Decide how much money you wish to invest each month. I strongly recommend that you place a minimum of 10% of your *gross* income into your AIP. If necessary, start with less and 'crank it up' on a regular basis as your circumstances allow. Fill in the form required for this amount of money to be automatically withdrawn each month from your pay or bank account. The company you choose will provide you with a **direct debit authority** for a regular contribution from your bank account, or a **payroll deduction authority** for a regular contribution from your pay. You simply fill in the forms and they do the rest.

If you have decided to invest through a managed fund then you will have to make a decision regarding which fund, when your application forms and prospectus arrive. There are hundreds of managed funds covering different asset classes and providing a wide range of expected risks and returns. Most managed funds are unit trusts which allow you to access investments you cannot afford on your own such as large commercial properties, diversified share portfolios, overseas investments, bonds and mortgages. You should choose a fund that suits your objectives, risk profile, performance expectations and investment time-frame.

These decisions are entirely up to you. If you are unsure of your preferences at this point, don't worry. By the time you complete the *Money Secrets* program you will be in a position to make an informed decision based on your investment objectives.

## THE POWER OF *PAYING YOURSELF FIRST*

This first **money step** will make you richer, right now. Each and every month you will own more assets (shares) and fluctuating share prices will not concern you because your investment strategy is for the long term. Your regular contribution amount will buy as many or as few shares each month as the fluctuating market prices allow (you are using the *dollar-cost averaging* method for buying shares), and you will rest easy knowing that you are building your wealth every month. *Paying Yourself First* is the most important money step required for financial success.

## YOU *WILL* MAKE $1,000,000+ IN YOUR LIFETIME!

Making over $1,000,000 in your lifetime is not difficult. If your family earns just $25,000 a year, you are already certain millionaires. How is that possible? Because $25,000 x 40 years (approximately the minimum wage multiplied by the minimum working years for the average Australian) = $1,000,000. The question is not whether you can make $1,000,000+. You will. The question is whether you can *keep* $1,000,000!

The first money step of *Paying Yourself First* via an Automatic Investment Plan (AIP) will provide you with at least the $1,000,000 again that you would make through your lifetime's work. If you retain just 10% of what you earn and invest it, and reinvest the returns, your money will all by itself produce your entire lifetime's earnings!

This claim can be easily demonstrated using the example of the $25,000-a-year millionaire: 10% of $25,000 is $2,500; $2,500 a year is $208 a month; $208 a month for 40 years invested at just 9.08% will produce $1,000,000!

You read that correctly! An investment of just 10% of your earnings will easily produce an amount of money equivalent to that which you earned over the course of your entire lifetime. All you have to do is live off the earnings and enjoy your wealthy

> 'If you want to become wealthy… you must have your money work for you. The amount you get paid for your personal effort is relatively small compared with the amount you can earn by having your money make money.'
> **JOHN D. ROCKEFELLER**

> 'What you are now comes from what you have been, and what you will be is what you do now.'
> **THE BUDDHA (SIDDHARTHA GUATAMA)**

retirement as a millionaire (living on $90,800 a year every year generated from that same rate of 9.08%)!

**Do not delay!** Every dollar that you contribute to your AIP will increase your wealth. This money step is incredibly powerful. Starting now, your money will grow every day. That is all money does. When left alone to compound, money grows: if you let it work! I cannot overstate the personal enjoyment my family has experienced reviewing our various investment statements and watching our assets increase every month, month after month.

## THE BROKEN AIP

Okay, so if the power of an AIP over the long-term is so obvious and it is so easy to implement, why doesn't everybody do it? Let's be realistic. We have all heard of the idea that we should pay ourselves first, that we need to put some money aside for the future. Then why don't most of us do it? Most of us try to 'budget'. We want to put some money aside for savings and investing every month, don't we? Of course we do. We know that we have really tried, don't we? Then why hasn't it all happened like we wanted it to? What is it that is not working with our budgets?

I have spoken to thousands of people who have told me the same things. No matter how hard or how many times they try, they just never manage to get ahead. They always seem to run out of money before they run out of month. No matter how much money they make, there never seems to be enough to do more than pay the bills and just get by. What is really scary is I hear the exact same 'story' from people making $10,000 a year to people making $600,000 a year!

That's right $600,000! I once worked with a man who consistently earned in excess of $600,000 a year and he was still always broke. How is that possible, you ask? Simple. He did what most people do. He spent all the money he made and then some. And like so many other people he had virtually no investments. Like so many others he never managed to have any money to put aside at the end of the month. His budget just never seemed to work. Does this sound familiar?

## THE DOOMED BUDGET

Most budgets are doomed to fail. Very few work for the long term. Why? They are too much like a quick-fix 14-day diet plan! The plan works for the first 14 days but then after that we all too easily fall back into our old habits again. Conventional budgets usually break down for two main reasons: the arrival of an unplanned 'emergency' which completely 'blows' the budget; and the lack of determination to actually stick to the budget in the first place. You give up on your budget and on your own ability to see it through. It just seems too tough, right?

With the **Automatic Investment Plan (AIP)** you will accumulate a large independent source of riches very quickly without relying on strict budgets, new sources of income or on dogged determination. And best of all, you can start today.

## DO YOU FIND IT DIFFICULT TO SAVE?

If you are anything like most people, you find it difficult to save and easy to spend. Most people start out trying to save with the best of intentions. The story goes something like this: 'Darling, it sure would be great to save a deposit for a new home. We get paid every other week. Let's really do it this time. Let's take $200 out every time we get paid and put it aside for the future. What do you say?' Of course, your partner says, 'Great, let's do it.'

> 'In the middle of difficulty lies opportunity.'
> **ALBERT EINSTEIN**

In theory, this couple could set aside $5,200 a year for investing. That money, combined with their **return on investment**, should provide them with the deposit for the home of their dreams in a relatively short period of time. In reality, what really happens to this budgeted $200 from each pay packet? Life gets in the way, doesn't it? The car breaks down, someone gets sick, they need a new TV, etc. The list is endless. One thing that is *guaranteed* is that you can always expect unexpected expenses!

The truth is that from the outset this couple made it very difficult for themselves to save. They did not make a commitment to (automatically) save. Instead they made a *wish*.

And without action, wishes rarely come true. They needed to use a system that is conducive to saving, one that is 'saving-friendly'. A system that only requires one decision and then *voila*, everything is taken care of automatically!

## SOLUTION: USE THE GOVERNMENT'S PLAN

Yes, that's right, the Federal Government is an excellent role-model for how to set aside money to become rich. Every time you get paid the government automatically takes money from you in the form of pay as you go (PAYG).

The government automatically takes (withholds) a huge chunk in the form of taxes (up to 48.5% marginal tax including Medicare levy). Why do they take the taxes this way? Because they realise what would happen if everybody was required to come up with the money later to pay their taxes on June 30. Very few could afford to pay because their budgets would not have allowed for it. The government would be shut down due to lack of money and all the politicians and bureaucrats would be out of a job (no comment on whether this would be a good or a bad thing!). Of course, the government prevents this from ever happening by requiring you to automatically pay your taxes via PAYG.

Why don't you use the same strategy the Australian Tax Office (ATO) uses to confiscate some of your hard-earned money for yourself?

---

**Bottomline:** Do to yourself what the ATO does to you. Deduct a percentage of your wage or salary from your pay (or bank account) and invest it automatically in your favourite investments.

---

## TYPES OF AUTOMATIC INVESTMENT PLANS (AIPS)

1. **Payroll deductions.** Check with your company's accountant or payroll officer and ask them to explain what your company offers in this area. Some companies even offer 'free money' in the form of matching your own contributions. One drawback is that sometimes the

investment options are quite limited. If the company offers free money though, it is probably worth any limitations!

2. **Superannuation fund.** Your employer must pay a minimum of 8% of your salary or wage into superannuation on your behalf. Find out if you can enter into a 'salary sacrifice' arrangement which allows you to reduce your gross salary and add the sacrificed amount to your superannuation fund AIP. If your company offers this, jump on it. Not only will your investment be automatically taken from your pay, the contribution will be tax-deductible and all the earnings will grow at a concessional tax rate. In addition, many companies will offer 'free money' in the form of matching contributions. Check this with your employer. Note that there are age-based limits to the amount of superannuation contributed and watch out for the 15% superannuation surcharge.

3. **Individual Automatic Investment Plan.** This is the same plan that we discussed earlier in this chapter, the only distinction being that you do it yourself, rather than through your employer.

> 'What the fool does at the end, the wise man does at the beginning.'
> **ENGLISH PROVERB**

4. **Self-employed superannuation.** If you are self-employed you can increase your savings by putting money into an approved superannuation fund. All earnings are subject to a maximum of 15% tax and 10% in the case of capital gains. You get a tax deduction for the first $3,000 of your contribution per annum, plus a 75% tax deduction for contributions over $3,000 (figures current for 2000–01 financial year).

In Chapter 16, I reveal more about superannuation funds and my eight tips for choosing the right fund. In the meantime you might look at the Association of Superannuation Funds of Australia website at www.superannuation.asn.au which has fact sheets, an interactive calculator and a dictionary of terms.

## START NOW, NOT LATER...

You must start now. Procrastinating can be very expensive. Let me demonstrate what I mean. If a 25-year-old woman invests $100 a month at 15% for 40 years she would have $3,101,605 at age 65. If this woman waited for 10 years till age 35 to get started she would have an extra $12,000 ($100 x 12 months x 10 years) of spending money during that 10 years, but how much would that failure to start cost her in the long run? *$2,409,277!*

That's right. By waiting until age 35 to start she would end up with only $692,328 at retirement instead of $3,101,605!

'If you don't want to plan for success and happiness, what right do you have to worry about non-success and unhappiness? If you're not planning where you want to be, what reason or excuse do you have for worrying about being nowhere?'
**TOM HOPKINS**

**Question:** Does she really need that $100-a-month extra spending money? Based upon my work with thousands of people, my experience tells me the answer is an emphatic *no*! After a couple of months she would not even notice that the money is gone. It just goes into her **AIP**.

**Question:** Do *you* really need that $100-a-month extra spending money? After a couple of months, would *you* even notice that it was gone (into *your* **AIP**)?

## CASE STUDY: TIFFANY, THE 18-YEAR-OLD FUTURE MILLIONAIRE

Here is the story of a good friend of mine. Her name is Tiffany. When she started investing she was 18 years old. She worked in my office part-time while attending a local community college. She knows that I am financially successful. While she worked in my office, I talked to her about the idea of her starting an Automatic Investment Plan (AIP).

I showed her how for just $100 a month invested she would be a millionaire at age 50. She wasn't crazy about not having the $100 a month (she wanted to buy more CDs and maybe save for a new car), but she really liked the idea of automatically becoming a millionaire by age 50. So she committed to do it. I would take the money directly from her pay (so she wouldn't be tempted to spend it). I agreed to show her a good managed fund in which to invest her money (US Vanguard Index 500 Fund).

Two months later she came to me and told me that she needed the money back. She said, 'I promise I'll start back up, but I need the money to go on vacation to Texas with my friend.' We had a long talk, the bottomline being I told her, 'No. You made a commitment and I think you should keep it. What do you think?' From her answer, I knew she was not happy about it, but she agreed to leave the money there.

Now, a few short months after wanting to shut it down, she is extremely excited about her **AIP**. I am proud to report that she is sticking it out. She now has over $2,000 in her account. This amount grows every month with her faithful **AIP** contribution of $100. She is well on her way to becoming a millionaire.

Here is the kicker. When she started she was a 'normal' 18 year-old. She was earning $US460 a month. And she is going to be a millionaire. She managed to find a way to afford the $100 a month. How about you? Why not let this 18-year-old from Glendale, Arizona be your role-model? If Tiffany can afford to do it, so can you. Be like Tiffany, be a millionaire!

## THE TWO KEYS TO FINANCIAL SUCCESS FOR THE LEVEL FOUR AUTOMATIC INVESTOR

1.  The first key is to develop a systematic investment plan (the **AIP**). If you want to learn more on this subject I highly recommend you read *The Richest Man in Babylon* by George Clason.

    > 'Once begun, a task is easy: half the work is done.'
    > **HORACE 20-6 BC**

2.  The second key is to ensure that the money *Receives Automatic Investor Rates of Return*. I will show you how this is achieved in Chapters 4 and 5.

Have you already completed the **AIP** assignment? If so, congratulations! If not, *do it now*! The cost of delaying is far too great.

## SURFING AND PHONING FOR INFORMATION AND TIPS

When researching your share investments it is a good idea to gather as much independent information as you can. The

Internet is an invaluable source of such information. Check out the free share information content at financial markets and information sites such as:

- www.afsd.com.au (the Australian Financial Services Directory);
- www.tradingroom.com.au; www.afr.com.au (*The Australian Financial Review* websites);
- www.investorweb.com.au;
- www.sharesdaily.com.au (*Shares* magazine website);
- www.yourprosperity.com.au (or on 1800 062 061);
- www.nevward.com.au (Selector's List from Neville Ward Direct, featuring 4 and 5 star rated managed funds using data and ratings by Morningstar, or on 1300 139 319);•
  www.asx.com.au (the Australian Stock Exchange, or on 1300 300 279);
- www.centrelink.com.au (or on 136 357);
- www.fpa.asn.au (the Financial Planning Association of Australia).

If you are just starting out and would prefer to put your AIP money into a managed fund, but would like to practice your own share investing skills, try some simulated trading at: the Australian Stock Exchange website at www.asx.com.au; E★Trade website at www.etrade.com; or Equity Café at www.equitycafe.com.au. These sites and others offer virtual trading contests with prizes for the largest gains. Sometimes there are charity sharemarket games you can enter.

---

## CHAPTER 3 ACTION STEPS REVIEW

1. Follow **Money Step #1** – *Paying Yourself First* and decide which investor comfort level suits you with regard to commencing your initial **Automatic Investment Plan (AIP)**. Decide which *type* of AIP to use to best support your investor comfort level.
2. Call a broker firm (or managed fund company) to request an application (or prospectus) for an AIP and to open a client account (if applicable to your investment comfort level).

3. Decide the amount of money you want to automatically invest each month (via an **automatic direct debit** from your bank account, or an **automatic payroll deduction** from your pay).

4. Start out with an amount that works for you. Do not become so over-zealous that you set yourself up for failure. Most people should start at 10% of their gross income. (You can always increase the amount later.)

5. Conventional budgets rarely work. Don't make the mistake of pretending that you will deposit the money at the end of the month. Set up the AIP to automatically deduct directly from your bank account or your paycheque at the beginning of each month. Don't take any chances with your financial future.

6. If you don't wish to actively manage your own AIP, start your AIP by calling a managed fund like NRMA Personal Investments Trust 132 976; Colonial First State Managed Investment Funds 131 336; or Mercantile Mutual Investments Trusts 133 665; MLC MasterKey Unit Trust 131 831; AMP 133 888; Equity Trustees 1300 55 55 11. Or surf online at the sites like www.yourprosperity.com.au to see how you can reduce brokerage fees or avoid them altogether.

7. Remember the high cost of procrastination.

---

**Feedback:** We would love to hear of your successes (and any learning experiences) in researching, setting up and maintaining your AIP.

Please contact Prosperity Training Inc. in the US on (623) 561-8246 (intl.) or through www.johnburley.com

---

## MORE FREE ONLINE INVESTOR EDUCATION

- www.personalinvestment.com.au (similar to magazine with plenty of tips);
- www.mymoney.com.au (about investment, shares, retirement, banking, insurance);

- www.ozemail.com.au (stock market guide);
- www.investorweb.com.au (portfolio tracking and investment information);
- www.yourprosperity.com.au (share and fund trading, portfolio service);
- www.tradingroom.com.au (*The Australian Financial Review* website);
- www.egoli.com.au (Shaw Stockbroking research reports, archives, news and analyst comments, float information and feature articles);
- www.spiwatch.com (trader tips);
- www.synaptic.com.au (Australian share prices);
- www.baillieu.com.au (daily market reporting);
- www.guppytraders.com.au (share trading education and resources);
- www.cob.ohio-state.edu (a mass of financial web links throughout the world);
- www.stockwatch.aust.com (daily share prices);
- www.brokerchoice.com.au (compares brokers and provides market information);
- www.afsd.com.au (free stockwatch Australian Charting service);
- www.abc.net.au/news/business/chart (charts ASX shares);
- www.validea.com (teaches stock analysis techniques based on methods of or investment gurus such as Peter Lynch and Benjamin Graham);
- www.yourbroker.com.au (information about stockbrokers, trading and the markets).

## CHAPTER 4

# Money Step #2 – *Reinvesting Your Investment Returns*

'Money is a guarantee that we may have what we want in the
future. Though we need nothing at the moment it ensures the
possibility of satisfying a new desire when it arises.'

ARISTOTLE

Money Step #2 – *Reinvesting Your Investment Returns* is critical to your long-term financial success. Many investors start out on a good path. They set up the **Automatic Investment Plan (AIP)**. They watch their investment account grow. Everything is working exactly like it should. Then it all comes to a grinding halt when they sabotage the entire program by 'stealing' the earnings, to consume.

The main concept behind the Automatic Investment Plan (AIP) is to follow Money Step #1 which is *Paying Yourself First*. By prematurely spending the earnings, you remove the power of **Compound Interest** and shoot yourself right back to being a Level Zero, Non-Existent.

Remember, Money Step #1 – *Paying Yourself First* only works effectively as a *long-term* plan. Am I saying you must never spend the money generated by your AIP? Of course not. I am saying you need to look at investment from a *long-term* point of view. Putting aside the money for a couple of years will not change your life. However, contributing to your AIP until the earnings can support your lifestyle, will. This is why it is critical that you also follow Money Step #2 and *Reinvest Your Investment Returns.*

The most exciting thing about applying this money step is that it will allow you to retire early and wealthy with very little effort. All you have to do is allow your money to fulfill its only purpose: to make more money.

> That's right, all money knows how to do is make more money. So leave your money alone and let it produce offspring (more money). Then let its offspring produce more offspring, and so on and so on and so on. This is all your money knows how to do, so invest it and then leave it alone until you are ready to live off the earnings.

The beauty of this program is that you can create hundreds of thousands (or millions) of dollars, and thereby live an abundant, luxury-filled retirement without ever having to touch the principal. Leave your AIP money alone until you are ready to live off the fruits of its labour. Avoid the temptation to tap into the money for consumption purposes. Do not fool yourself: small leaks can easily turn into gushers, and once tapped most AIPs run dry. People who prematurely tap into their AIP, I am afraid, will be relegated to being a Level Zero, Non-Existent.

'Reinvesting your dividends in a stock mutual fund is the glue that holds your financial plan together.'
**JIM JORGENSEN**

'"Will you walk a little faster?" said a whiting to a snail, "There's a porpoise close behind us, and he's treading on my tail."'
**LEWIS CARROLL (Alice's Adventures in Wonderland)**

If the companies you invest in pay dividends and offer dividend reinvestment plans, participate in them. They are usually offered to shareholders with no or discounted brokerage and transaction costs.

I spoke in Chapter 3 of the power of compounding, of *Reinvesting Your Investment Returns*, and I speak of it again in Chapter 23. In fact, this theme is a constant one throughout the

*Money Secrets* program. Without the power of compounding over time, of your investments earning *returns on their returns*, over and over again, your journey towards Financial Freedom is made with the handbrake firmly on. If you leave a measly little dollar alone invested at 10% for 10 years it becomes $2.59. This is without extra investment of capital, two-and-a-half times its original size. In 200 years, $1 compounded at 10% becomes $190 million dollars, all by itself.

> 'If you have not acquired more than a bare existence in the years since we were youths, it is because you either have failed to learn the laws that govern the building of wealth, or else you do not observe them.'
>
> **GEORGE S. GLASON**

If this is the power of compounding over time, imagine the power of compounding (Money Step #2), combined with regular contributions (Money Step #1), and above 10% average annual rates of return (Money Step #3)! Imagine the power of Money Steps 1, 2 and 3 combined!

**Make the conscious decision right now to become rich!** Do not violate the *Seven Money Steps of the Rich*. Live by and follow Money Step #2 – *Reinvesting Your Investment Returns*. If you ignore Money Step #2, it is just like killing the offspring. Enjoy your future prosperity.

---

## CHAPTER 4 ACTION STEPS REVIEW

1. Commit to **Money Step #2** and *Reinvest Your Investment Returns*.

> 'A faithfully kept program of savings and conservative investments can give you more money and a better life than that of your neighbors who spend everything they get. This is probably the oldest financial advice in the world, but there are some things you can't improve on.'
>
> **JANE BRYANT QUINN**

## CHAPTER 5

# Money Step #3 – *Receiving*
# *Level Four Automatic Investor*
# *Rates of Return*

'The world is not transformed from one day to the next, and the average investor makes less money with his brain than what in chess is called his *Sitzfleisch*, or patient rear end.'

JOHN TRAIN

As a **Level Four Automatic Investor** your objective is to earn a minimum of 12–15% return on your investments. I am not talking about for a year or two, but for the *long term*.

This is actually much easier than it sounds. For example, did you know that the S&P 500 Index (500 of the largest companies in the US) has grown an average of 14.5% p.a. for the last 45 years? In fact, over the last 20 years it has averaged 19% growth a year! And over the last five years, 28%! In Australia the All Ordinaries Index has grown an average of 10% a year for the last 10 years.

And for the last five years (to June 30, 2000) the All Industrials price index has risen an average of 11.1% a year which, when you add what is known as the accumulation index (the effect of reinvesting dividends), produces an average return of 18.3% a year. The compounding power of reinvested dividends is vital to the long-term success of your investment plan (dividend growth for industrial companies in Australia over the last seven years has been 8.4% a year). (Figures from *The Australian Financial Review*, August 2000.)

A major key for the Level Four Automatic Investor is *patience*. Don't try to get rich quickly. Go for *solid long-term equity positions*. There are many managed funds that produce long-term returns of 12–15%+. Earlier I shared some of those with you. Later I will show you several ways that you can earn much higher rates of returns as a Level Five Investor.

As mentioned in Chapter Four, the effects of compounding rise exponentially when we add a regular contribution (Money Step #1) *and* above 10% average rates of return. If you want to see the difference that a higher return makes to an initial investment even *without* regular additional contributions, simply apply the **Rule of 72**. If you divide 72 by your expected rate of return you will determine the number of years it will take for your investment to double. The higher rate of return makes a difference (for example, at 10% it takes 7.2 years for your money to double, while at 18.3% just 3.93 years).

Whether you are investing directly or via a managed fund in 'blue-chip' Australian companies, you will find that most of these industrial companies offer dividend reinvestment plans and, as stated earlier, if you are a shareholder you should participate fully in these plans to maximise the compounding potential of your dividend returns.

Level Four Automatic Investors understand that they will have to spend some dedicated time actively managing their investment portfolios. How much time? Stanley and Danko in *The Millionaire Next Door* state that 'prodigious accumulators of wealth' spend an average 8.4 hours a month researching and managing their money and investments versus 'underaccumulators of wealth' who spend only 4.6 hours. Isn't it worth an additional four hours a month to be

> 'The person who makes a success of living is the one who sees his goal steadily and aims for it unswervingly.'
> **CECIL B. DE MILLE**

wealthy? Of course it is! And with *Money Secrets of the Rich* as your guide, you are certain of success.

Stanley and Danko also found that 'People who become wealthy allocate their time, energy and money in ways consistent with enhancing their net worth' and that there was a 'strong correlation between investment planning and wealth accumulation'. The irony is that although the non-wealthy spend more time worrying about their financial situation than do the wealthy, they spend very little time actually doing anything about it. That time could be so much better spent on investment planning and money management. I strongly recommend you read Stanley and Danko's book for inspiration. Now let's move on.

> 'It is not enough to take steps which may some day lead to a goal; each step must be itself a goal and a step likewise.'
> **GOETHE**

## SURFING FOR OTHER FINANCIAL INFO NEWS AND GENERAL INTEREST

- www.investmentwarehouse.com.au (managed and direct funds);
- www.investmentlink.com.au (portfolio information);
- www.county.com.au/dict.htm (dictionary of investment terms);
- www.facs.gov.au/invest/chklist.htm (government checklist for investing);
- www.thegroup.net (investment research and technical analysis);
- www.btfunds.com.au (managed fund manager site);
- www.yourbroker.com.au (details on the trading 'experience');
- www.investorweb.com.au (general financial information);
- www.au.finance.yahoo.com (local and financial newslinks to other sites);
- www.floatnews.com.au (upcoming floats on market);
- www.vanguard.com (managed fund performance);
- www.money.ninemsn.com.au (personal finance and investment information);
- www.moneyweb.com.au (online calculators, links to other sites);

- www.equitycafe.com.au (news, charts and profiles);
- www.yourprosperity.com.au (clear information on managed funds);
- www.sharesdaily.com.au (investment, shares and market information);
- www.moneyinpractice.com.au (investment and general financial information);
- www.armchairmillionaire.com (general interest investment information).

**For young investors:** In the United States there is a youth membership available in the National Association of Investors Corp. They have recently launched a new program for the under 18s. 'In today's world, young adults are using credit cards more frequently, taking out loans for education and leasing or financing automobiles and homes with little or no background in personal finance or investing,' Robert O'Hara, vice-president of NAIC said when the program was announced. 'We need to better equip young people with financial knowledge early to make educated choices throughout their lifetime.' The program features a low-cost investment plan that provides investments for as little as $10–20 a month with a special adult-minor (custodial) account.

Nothing like this appears to be available in Australia as yet, but it can't be far away. Schools sometimes offer contests and programs sponsored by banks and there is the Young Achiever's business scheme. The Australian Stock Exchange organises a Schools Share Market game each year (www.asx.com.au or 1300 300 279).

## CHAPTER 5 ACTION STEPS REVIEW

1. Commit to **Money Step #3** and *Receive Level Four Automatic Investor Rates of Return*.

# Money Step #4 –
## *Knowing What Your Money is Doing (Part I)*

'Economy is half the battle of life; it is not so hard to earn
money as to spend it well.'

CHARLES SPURGEON

This is a *very* important chapter. In this chapter you will begin to learn **Money Step #4 –** *Knowing What Your Money is Doing*. You are now going to learn the fundamentals required to run your family's finances like a successful public company. You will be astounded at how easy this is. The results will amaze you. This one easy step can liberate hundreds of extra dollars from your pay-cheque every month for you to invest. So many of my students have told me that this one step provided them with more money than any other part of the material, so read on and learn Money Step #4.

## MONEY STEP #4 - *KNOWING WHAT YOUR MONEY IS DOING*

Most people have very little idea where all their money goes. What they do know is that they do not have enough of it. And when they take a quick snapshot of their financial situation they know they should have more money left than they do.

If you are like I used to be (with my personal finances) your situation probably looks something like this: ➔➔➔ Money comes in and it all goes out. ➔➔➔ None (or next to none) is left at the end of the month.

And if you ever take the time to sit down and figure out what you really spend your money on you would probably find that there *should* be money left over each month. For example, monthly income was $4,000, yet the fixed monthly expenses – such as taxes; housing (mortgage or rent, utilities, maintenance, etc.); food; car; insurance; debts (credit cards, personal loans, etc.); entertainment and recreation; clothing; medical; school and child care; and miscellaneous (haircuts, laundry, etc.) – was only $3,200. Thus you should have $800 left over, but in fact you have none. This is the financial reality for most families.

'To be mistaken is a misfortune to be pitied, but to know the truth and not to conform one's actions to it is a crime which Heaven and Earth condemn.'
**GIUSEPPE MAZZINI**

And this is the main problem with how most families manage their finances. They don't know where the extra $800 a month goes. They are not actively and consciously tracking their money and thus, by the end of the month, it is all gone.

What all individuals and all families should do is run their personal finances in a way similar to that of a public company.

Think about it. How long would a public company survive if it could not account for 10–50% of its income each month? That's what most families lose every month: 10–50% of their income gone. Spent. Not sure on what, but it is gone anyway. This is because most families do not follow Money Step #4 – *Knowing What Your Money is Doing.*

Just imagine for a moment how this would go over in the business world. You are the CFO (chief financial officer) and are about to make your monthly financial report to the CEO (chief executive officer) of the company. The conversation would go something like this: 'Hi boss. I've got great news! Last month we took in $1,000,000. I know where we spent $700,000 of it but there is none left.' How long do you think you would keep your job? How long do you think the company would stay in business if it continued to manage its money in this way? The answer to both questions is, *not long*.

So, you (and your family) need to adopt a simple system that will allow you to run your personal finances in a manner similar to any successful business (although it is nowhere near as complicated). Let's get started.

The first task required for Money Step #4 – *Knowing What Your Money is Doing* is to take a detailed 'snapshot' of your current financial situation. You do this by completing a **Cash Flow Statement** and a **Balance Sheet**. In this chapter we will complete the Cash Flow Statement and next chapter the Balance Sheet.

> 'When a man's affairs are not going well, he hates to study the books and face the truth. From the first, the men who managed the Standard Oil Company kept their books intelligently as well as correctly. We knew how much we made and where we gained or lost. At least, we tried not to deceive ourselves.'
>
> **JOHN D. ROCKEFELLER**

## THE CASH FLOW STATEMENT

The **Cash Flow Statement** is an analysis of your income and expenses, or an **income/expense** *tracking* exercise. Only by tracking where it is that your money is really going can you reallocate the extra dollars to invest. You will achieve this by actively and conscientiously tracking your income and expenses via the Cash Flow Statement.

Take a look at the Cash Flow Statement at the back of this chapter. We will complete it together. The first section is the **income** section. The second is the **expense** section. (I suggest you make a few photocopies of the page before you fill it in.)

I strongly recommend that you involve *every* family member in this process. This includes (if applicable) your partner and children. Get things out on the table where everybody can see what is really going on. If you are the main breadwinner, you might be pleasantly surprised just how supportive your partner and family can be when they know the family's *true* financial situation.

So, breadwinner, time to top acting like your parents. Speak openly and honestly to your partner and children about the family's financial situation. If it's bad, they probably already know. You will be surprised how much they will help you. So pull together as a family on your path to Financial Freedom.

## THE INCOME SECTION

Go first to the income section of the Cash Flow Statement. Start filling it in with last *month's* records. For most people this is a fairly easy section to complete. We are trying to establish an accurate picture of your average monthly income. So take some time to make sure you include *all* your income. Although we are only concentrating on your income over the last month in this initial exercise, you may find it easier (in order to arrive at an accurate monthly average figure) to have a look at the whole of the last year's income (and divide it by 12). If you are a regular salary and wage earner with few investments at this time, last month's income should be accurate enough. Here is a brief list of typical sources of income to prompt you:

*'Problems are only opportunities in work clothes.'*
**HENRY J. KAISER**

- Salary or wages from your job or business;
- Commissions, bonuses or royalties;
- Pensions or superannuation income – this would include benefits from the government and private sector;
- Other government allowances such as child-care benefits and family assistance;
- Workers compensation, disability or income protection insurance income;
- Child support, or child maintenance payments;
- Dividend and investment income – this would include income from shares, bonds, real estate, loans, term deposits, and interest from cheque and savings accounts;
- Trust fund(s) income;

- Miscellaneous income – this would include income from a part-time business, one-time income (inheritance, lottery, etc.) or income from the sale of assets;
- Children's income – children are part of the family; I strongly believe that as parents it is our responsibility to ensure that our children develop proper financial intelligence, so please make sure you involve your children.

Sometimes income does not come in on a monthly basis. Dividends or a year-end bonus would be examples of this. Self-employed business owners also often have irregular personal income. If you have this type of income simply break it into an estimated monthly amount. Please remember to be conservative. Avoid the mistake of overestimating what the year-end bonus or commission will be for the year, pre-spending the money (not yet earned), and ending up in a very bad position when that big cheque does not arrive.

So, although I believe in being optimistic, I prefer surprises in regard to money to be good ones not bad ones. From hard-won experience my advice is to shoot for the stars and record commissions and bonuses. However, plan for these amounts to be normal (conservative) and be pleasantly surprised when you do actually receive extra money rather than being caught short, not having enough money to pay for all that things you already bought.

## THE EXPENSE SECTION

Now go to the expense section of your Cash Flow Statement. Start again with last *month's* records. Categorise and total all your monthly expenses. Dig out your bank statements (and cheque stubs) and credit card statements. It is important that you be as specific as possible. Just writing down 'American Express: $400' isn't going to cut it. You need to itemise each expense by category. For example, the American Express statement might show 'Food – Lunch at the club: $25', 'Clothing – David Jones: $200', etc. We are trying to establish an accurate picture of your average monthly expenses, so again, take some time to do this properly so that you include *all* your expenses.

Remember to include any expenses that have been automatically deducted from your pay or your bank account. These could include: superannuation contributions; AIP contributions; or health, car, home and contents or life insurance premiums.

When you total the entries from your bank statements and credit card statements, you will probably discover that your expense section total is much smaller than your income section total, leaving you with a huge surplus. Before you get too excited, remember that although the surplus is real on paper, the money is *gone*. After all, it's not as if it is sitting in the bank.

> 'A foundation must first be laid...It must receive the greatest care, and be made stronger than any other part.'
> **JAMES ALLEN**

What you need to do now is get the family to brainstorm to try to remember the missed expenses. Do you buy things with cash? If so, how are the expenses accounted? How do you pay for your food? Meals when you eat out? Allowances? Petrol? Fast food? Video rentals? Get busy to determine as accurately as possible where your money *really* goes on a monthly basis.

Look at the income and expense sections again. If you can account for all but 10–15% of your expenses you are doing well. You now have a fairly accurate analysis of your spending patterns. Later I will show you how to become more precise. However, if you still don't know where a large portion of your money is going (and not surprisingly, many people don't), you need to begin a **Money Tracking Program (MTP)**.

I know when I first started tracking our expenses my wife and I realised that we did not know where over 20% of our money was being spent. We agreed to develop a Money Tracking Program (MTP). It is really a very simple exercise.

All you have to do is write down every single cent you spend for a period of 30 days. For me, I wrote down my expenses in my DayTimer™ Planner during the day as they occurred (it is very important to track *while* you are spending, not later that night or at the end of the week). My wife Shari put a little notepad in her wallet to jot her expenses down as she went. We recorded everything – from lunch at the deli, to cans of soft drink at the local takeaway. By the end of the month we had accounted for *all* our money. The expenses that we did not feel were justifiable we eliminated, reduced or changed (more on that to come).

If you need to track your expenses then do so with an **MTP** for the next 30 days and then return to this chapter to accurately complete your Cash Flow Statement.

---

The next step is to make a similar assessment of your income and expenses for previous months. Record these expenses for the past year. Remember to look for items like council and water rates, insurance policy renewals, and car registrations. Now you will be able to make any required changes to your Cash Flow Statement based on your annual income and expenses (some of you may have already done this to produce an accurate monthly income and expense figure).

You are now experiencing Money Step #4 – *Knowing What Your Money is Doing*. If you are like I was, this is the first time you have *truly* taken a look at your cash flow situation. Some of my family's expenses and spending habits made us sick. We felt a lot of frustration about our old ways. And although we realised that we couldn't get back all that wasted money, we could certainly keep the income from now on.

Now that you have determined your *true* expenses, what you need to do next is take a look at your spending *patterns*. For most people there is some obvious waste that can be eliminated immediately. Most people also find expenses that can be

> 'I earn that I eat, get that I wear, owe no man hate, envy no man's happiness, glad of other men's good, content with my harm.'
> **WILLIAM SHAKESPEARE**
> *(As You Like It)*

greatly reduced with just a little bit of effort. Many people also discover (when they really look at it from an annual basis) that they buy a lot of 'stuff' that they don't really need and never really wanted!

You will be able to recognise, quantify and compare the categories where you do and those where you do not spend your money. This understanding will give you the power to decide how to reallocate your money to give you the most satisfaction. You are now automatically becoming a better consumer by adhering to this money step.

## THE CASH FLOW STATEMENT INCREASES YOUR STANDARD OF LIVING

This exercise is in no way designed to *reduce* your standard of living. Far from it. It is designed to *increase* your standard of living while at the same time 'freeing' money for investment (in your **AIP**) and for **debt reduction**. Here are a few typical examples of what students have said after completing this exercise:

- 'It's not all my partner's fault. We both needed to re-evaluate our spending habits. Now we fight less.'
- 'I knew I spent a lot of money on clothes. But I had no idea it was so much. Now I purchase less and I only buy items that are on sale.'
- 'When we looked at the maintenance, insurance, and lease cost we decided we no longer wanted the expensive luxury car. I now get far more pleasure driving a nice car and knowing that I'm paying off my mortgage 20 years earlier!'
- 'I no longer automatically spend all the money in my pocket. I now know that it's OK not to buy something.'
- 'The first time I go into a store I don't buy anything. Instead I write down what I want and how much it costs. Then, if I still want it the next day I see how I can work it into my budget. By stopping impulse buying of non-essential items, I freed up over 20% of my income for debt reduction and investment.'
- 'I always ask for a discount. Always. At my dentist, at the mall, at the petrol station. Always. And most people give me one.'
- 'I found by using coupons and waiting for sales I could "save" thousands of dollars per year.'
- 'We followed your advice and made our kids a part of the program. They have a budget just like Mum and Dad. By not asking for everything they saw they ended up getting the "nice" things they "really" wanted. Now, we're not broke.'

- 'I'm now aware how "easy" it is to spend. I had a problem and this project made me aware of it. I stopped and now I'm on my way.'

Later I will show you more specific ways to organise your personal or family finances. For now, make sure that you have included the whole family in the **income/expense** tracking exercise. Please remember to include your children in this process.

Again, as a parent it is *your responsibility* to teach your children the *Money Secrets of the Rich*. If you don't teach them about money then they will (in all likelihood) live their financial lives similarly to how you used to live yours. So please, teach your children about money. Let them understand the consequences of expenses. Get them involved. In most cases you will be surprised how willing and happy they are to be part of the process and to help.

---

**Hot tip**: If you receive a pay rise or a lump sum of money, pretend it never happened! That's right, try pretending you never got the money! Instead of running out to spend the money, try delaying the urge for instant gratification. Put all or most of the money into your AIP and/or debt reduction. This extra money can greatly accelerate your path to riches. You've managed without this extra money all this time. You can manage without it just a little longer, can't you? This is your opportunity for permanent financial gratification. Just think how wonderful it will feel watching your AIP jump into hyper-growth mode! You will enjoy the benefits of this decision for the rest of your life.

---

If you have not already done so, turn to the **Cash Flow Statement** in the back of this chapter and complete it. Please remember that this is a positive step that you are taking for you and your family. Now is not the time to blame others for your or the family's current financial situation. Here are the 'house rules': no arguing; no fighting; no bickering; no finger-pointing; no accusations; no name-calling; no shaming; no grabbing the guilt; no martyrs; no justifying; and no blaming.

Do this exercise with tolerance, maturity and love. You are washing the slate clean and committing to a new start. Maintain this spirit throughout the exercise. If you become stressed, take a break and some deep breaths. Go for a walk. Do what it takes to maintain a fresh and positive attitude throughout the process. It will make all the difference. You and your family are worth the extra time and effort involved.

The purpose of this exercise is to produce an accurate diagnosis of your current financial health in relation to your standard of living. As stated, this all starts with examining your records for one month and having the courage to be honest with yourself and your family.

---

## CHAPTER 6 ACTION STEPS REVIEW

1. Develop **Money Step #4 – *Knowing What Your Money is Doing***.
2. Treat your personal finances as you would those of a public company.
3. Complete the **Cash Flow Statement**.
4. If you cannot account for more than 85% of your monthly income, starting today and for the next 30 days, begin a **Money Tracking Program (MTP)** and record whatever you spend money on, no matter how small.
5. Even if you have managed to account for within 10–15% of your monthly expenditure, without tracking it, track it anyway for the experience and distinctions the exercise will provide you.

## CASH FLOW STATEMENT

### Income

Gross salary/wage              $_____

Interest/dividends             $_____

Commissions                    $_____

Net rental income              $_____

Miscellaneous                  $_____

**Total income**               $_____


### Fixed Expenses

Income tax                     $_____

Home loan(s)                   $_____

Car loan(s)                    $_____

Personal loan(s)               $_____

Credit card(s) minimums        $_____

Land rates                     $_____

Insurances                     $_____

Super contributions            $_____

AIP                            $_____

Miscellaneous                  $_____

**Total fixed expenses**       $_____


### Variable expenses

Food                           $_____

Transportation                 $_____

Clothing/pers. care            $_____

Entertainment/holiday          $_____

Medical/dental                 $_____

Utilities                      $_____

Charitable giving              $_____

Miscellaneous                  $_____

**Total variable expenses**    $_____


**Total expenses**             $_____

## CHAPTER 7

# Money Step #4 – *Knowing What Your Money is Doing* (Part II)

'Do a balance sheet of your own, and then find ways to turn your minuses into pluses. In the entrepreneurial game, that balance sheet is going to reflect your batting average. An upswing in assets should generate enthusiasm for further improvement. If the liabilities have crept ahead, you'll be able to identify these areas of chronic weakness and take the necessary steps to keep them in check.'

VICTOR KIAM

In this chapter we are going to determine your financial **net worth**. This is accomplished by completing the **Balance Sheet** (located at the end of this chapter). First we will tabulate the current value of all your **assets** (house, car, investments, etc.). Then we will tabulate your outstanding **liabilities** (mortgage, car loan, personal debt, etc.). The difference between the two totals is your financial *net worth*.

It is important to do this exercise so that you can gain a clear understanding of where you are now. I realise that for most people the idea of filling out **Cash Flow Statements** and **Balance Sheets** is about as enjoyable as having a tooth pulled. I also realise that some of you may have slightly glossed over the last chapter and be tempted to do the same for this chapter if the findings were/are not favourable (i.e. you confirmed the fact that you are broke).

If you don't feel like doing this assignment then that is exactly the reason you *must* do it. Here is the truth: people who do not want to do this exercise (or refuse to) feel that way because they are a Level Zero. They are the financial Non-Existent. If that is where *you* are, it is time to pull your head out of the sand (like the proverbial ostrich) and get involved in your own future. It's your life and this is important. I would not ask you to do this assignment if it wasn't *vital* to your Financial Freedom. ***Stop being a passive, uninformed and irresponsible bystander in your own financial life***.

My sincere apologies if the previous paragraph did not apply to you.

> 'If you don't experience dark clouds, rain and storms there is no way of measuring sunshine.'
> **SIR JAMES HARDY**

> 'When you dissemble sometimes your knowledge of that you are thought to know, you shall be thought, another time, to know that you know not.'
> **FRANCIS BACON**

When you compile your Balance Sheet avoid the tendency that many people have to make the numbers look better than they really are. If you place a higher value on the assets than they are really worth you are distorting the picture of your true net worth. The only person you will be fooling is you. Don't do it. List the value of all items as honestly as possible. Ask yourself: What would they be worth in a garage sale in today's market? That is their true value. (Again, I suggest you make a few photocopies of the pages before you fill them in).

## WHAT IS AN ASSET AND WHAT IS A LIABILITY?

As my good friend Robert Kiyosaki, author of *Rich Dad, Poor Dad*, enjoys pointing out, an **asset** is something that *feeds you* (provides income), and a **liability** is something that *eats you* (an expense). If it does not *feed you*, then it is not an asset. If it costs you money, then it is a liability (an expense). No arguments. Accept it! This concept is seriously misunderstood by most people. Particularly by many bankers, financial planners, bookkeepers and accountants.

Unfortunately, when you apply this definition of an asset to most of what you 'own' and think of as assets, you will realise that very little can be categorised as assets at all. For example, does your living-room furniture feed you? Other than the odd potato-chip crumb or coin? No! So it is not really an asset. Let's review what items would be traditionally considered assets.

## FIXED ASSETS

- House/unit. **Please note**: I have a philosophical problem with including your house in the asset column if it is encumbered with a mortgage. If your mortgage payment is more than fair market rent, then your house is currently eating you. I know what people say, 'It's an asset because it appreciates in value.' This may be true. However, if you are not accessing the asset's income value then it is not a true asset in the strict sense of the definition. However, for now, you may consider your house an asset.
- Second home. Same as above.
- Other (land, investment property, etc.).
- Business and other equipment.

## INVESTMENT ASSETS

- Bank accounts (savings, cheque, transaction, term deposit and cash management/money market).
- Life insurance policy cash value (current surrender value, not projected value).
- Superannuation funds.
- Insurance savings plans.
- Shares.
- Managed funds.
- Bonds.
- Futures.
- Business interests.
- Collectibles (only with legitimate resale appraisal and willingness to sell).
- Miscellaneous (notes receivable, other equities, etc.).

## MOVEABLE ASSETS
- Vehicles (keep in mind the running and depreciation costs).
- Boats/planes (keep in mind the running and depreciation costs too).
- Collectible artwork (only with legitimate resale appraisal and willingness to sell).

The last type of asset is classified by the catch-all description of 'other assets'. My *financial opinion* of these items is that they have no real *financial value* in your life. For example, you may have spent $10,000 on clothing. However, if you died tomorrow, what would your clothes sell for at a garage sale? That is what they are worth, and even then the clothes still only have 'financial value' *after* you are dead.

My wife once asked me, 'What about my diamond engagement ring, isn't it an asset?' My answer, 'No.' Why not? Because it does not *feed* her. It provides her no *financial value*. Further, although the ring itself does have a true 'monetary value', that value could only be realised by selling it. She is never going to sell it even if she does manage to trade me in on a newer model! Therefore, her ring has no value on her *true* Balance Sheet.

I have observed many people who have tried to fool themselves by including the following type of items/numbers in their asset column:

| | |
|---|---|
| Clothing | $ 20,000 |
| Furniture | $ 50,000 |
| Jewellery | $ 25,000 |
| Household appliances | $  9,000 |
| Stereo | $  3,000 |
| TV | $  2,000 |
| **Total** | **$109,000** |

Let's be realistic. These items are not assets. They do not *feed* you. You are not going to sell them. Even if you did sell them you would have to sell them for their depreciated 'market value', not what you paid for them. And the reality is that after you sold them, you would just use the money (plus some more money) to buy something new.

'Other assets' are what my dear friend Keith Cunningham refers to as *doodads*. They are nice, they are fun, but they have very little 'financial value'. So, for the purposes of this exercise, all 'other assets' are to be given a total value of $1,000 only. No more, no less. Call it a grand and move on. Here is a partial list of such 'other assets'.

'He that wants money, means, and content is without three good friends.'
**WILLIAM SHAKESPEARE**
*(As You Like It)*

'...silks and sattins, scarlets and velvets...put out the kitchen fire.'
**BENJAMIN FRANKLIN**

## OTHER ASSETS

- Furniture
- Tools
- Appliances
- Jewellery
- Clothing
- Stereo/TV
- Cameras
- China/silver
- Sports equipment
- Other

In most cases your 'valuable' 'other assets' are only worth 10–50% of what you paid for them. If you do not believe me, check the classified ads in the newspaper, because that's where you would find a buyer. If you check with pawnshops, second-hand goods retailers, estate buyers or auction houses remember to ask for the price they would give you, not the price at which they would resell it. That is what it is worth. Regrettably most people will find that many of their prized possessions have relatively low resale value. This information should provide you with five valuable lessons:

1. Only buy consumer goods on which you are willing to accept an instant loss of 25–75% of your money. I'm not saying you shouldn't buy things. I'm just saying you should make sure you really, truly want them first.
2. Never consider consumer purchases to be *investments*.

3. Avoid consuming impulsively (particularly on high-ticket items like cars, stereos, TVs, etc.).
4. When you do buy, select items of high quality that tend to retain their value.
5. Alternatively, buy someone else's prized possessions for 10–50 cents on the dollar. Let them take the huge loss of value. Turn the tables and buy your *doodads* from your local classified ads or auctions. You will be amazed at what you will find.

## LIABILITIES

Now that you have completed the Asset section of the Balance Sheet, it is time to fill in the Liabilities section. Again, what is a liability? A liability is anything that generates an expense or cash outflow. Here are examples of items that would be considered liabilities.

1. First mortgage, second mortgage or equity line of credit.
2. Personal loans.
3. Business loans.
4. Car loans.
5. Credit and charge cards (MasterCard, VISA, store cards, etc.).
6. Unpaid taxes.
7. Any other outstanding (unpaid) debt.

## CALCULATING YOUR NET WORTH

Total your liabilities and deduct them from your assets. Make sure you are sitting down while you do this! For many people the total is actually a negative number. This means that they actually have more financial liabilities than assets. Their house may be filled with all kinds of *doodads* but they are actually broke. If you fall into this category do not despair. Before you are finished reading this book you will not only learn how to reduce your expenses 20–50% without affecting your *lifestyle*, but you will also learn how to become a great investor. Plus, you will learn how to become completely debt-free.

> '... at a great pennyworth pause a while.'
> **BENJAMIN FRANKLIN**

In the next chapter we will outline the immediate steps that can be taken to turn a negative net worth position into a positive net worth one. To turn a financial situation around 180 degrees!

---

## CHAPTER 7 ACTION STEPS REVIEW

1. Further develop **Money Step #4 – *Knowing What Your Money Is Doing***.
2. Determine the value of all your 'valuable' **assets**. Remember the *doodads* rule.
3. Determine your total **liabilities**.
4. Determine your **net worth**.
5. **Congratulate yourself!** You made it. For most people, the last two chapters are the most challenging of the entire *Money Secrets of the Rich* program.

'Everyone has setbacks. This is a normal fact of life. And when you have more than one in a row, as sometimes happens, it can be very discouraging. If you allow it to be so, it can take the life out of you. But you should always remember that even so, you still have a lot of rebound left.'

**NORMAN VINCENT PEALE**

## BALANCE SHEET

### Cash assets/cash equivalents

Cheque accounts    $ _____

Savings accounts    $ _____

Term deposits    $ _____

Life insurance cash values    $ _____

Cash management accounts    $ _____

**Total cash assets**    $ _____

### Invested assets

Art collection    $ _____

Coin/stamp collection    $ _____

Superannuation    $ _____

Shares    $ _____

Bonds    $ _____

Managed funds    $ _____

Real estate    $ _____

Partnerships    $ _____

Other    $ _____

**Total invested assets**    $ _____

### In-use assets

Residence    $ _____

Cars    $ _____

Personal property    $ _____

**Total in-use assets**    $ _____

**Total assets**    $ _____

### Liabilities

Credit cards    $ _____

Car loans    $ _____

Home loans    $ _____

Personal loans    $ _____

Miscellaneous loans    $ _____

Investment loans    $ _____

**Total liabilities**    $ _____

**NET WORTH (total assets minus total liabilities)**    $ _____

# Turning your old *doodads* into cash!

'Luxury is the first, second and third cause of the ruin of the republics. It is the vampire which soothes us into a fatal slumber while it sucks the life-blood of our veins.'

PAYSON

That's right. In your garage, wardrobe, attic, basement, storage-unit and throughout your house, you have money just waiting to be liberated. Possibly lots of money, just sitting there, *unemployed*. An asset is only an asset if it *feeds* you so why not convert some or all of the *doodads* that you no longer need back into hard cash? That's right, sell your *doodads*. Put an ad in the paper and hold a good, old-fashioned garage sale.

---

**Make your garage sale an 'estate sale', 'private property sale', or 'business equipment liquidation sale'**

---

By upgrading the name of your sale from a 'garage sale' you can often dramatically attract more buyers and better prices. If you have bigger items like a motorcycle, TV, dining-room setting, etc., run ads in the weekend newspapers directly advertising those items. Remember to use the local newspapers, and the very popular *Trading Post* (in paper format from your newsagent or www.tradingpost.com.au). Many supermarkets also have community bulletin boards where you can advertise for free or a minimal fee. They are very effective for such sales.

## PASSIVE ASSETS

A **passive asset** is an asset that produces no income. Vacant land would be a classic example. Another type of passive asset would be a boat or a caravan/motor-home. Not only do these types of passive assets depreciate in value, they can also eat away at your current income (and strictly speaking, according to our 'eat me' definition of an asset, should not be considered an asset at all). If you have passive assets from which you do not receive benefit (from either regular personal enjoyment or financial gain), consider selling them and reallocating the money to a **performing asset**.

> 'Too many people spend money they haven't earned, to buy things they don't want, to impress people they don't like.'
> **WILL ROGERS**

The cost of owning items like a boat, caravan/motor-home or recreational vehicle (RV) often makes it better to rent the items instead (unless they are truly used on a consistent basis). For example, I can rent a $90,000 motor-home for a couple of weeks (anytime I want to) for less than $200 a day. Yet, if I owned the motor-home, I would have to pay for the loan, the maintenance, the registration, the insurance, etc. Unless I use this 'big-ticket item' frequently, I am much better off renting on an as-needed basis rather than owning. The same strategy applies to a boat that is infrequently used.

Now don't get me wrong. My intention is not to lower your standard of living. It is just the opposite in fact. If you own a boat, caravan/motor-home or RV and you truly make good use of it, then by all means, keep it. If you do not use it as often as you should or as often as you originally intended, for it to make even remote economic sense to own rather than periodically rent, then consider selling it and putting the cash to work for you.

Do you have belongings sitting gathering dust in a rented storage unit? Why? When was the last time you saw them? Are you even sure what's in there? How much hard earned money each year are you paying to rent the storage space? $500? $1,000? Why? If it's been in storage for more than a year, the odds are pretty good that you don't need it and will never use it again. Convert it back to cash. Take the *fleeting parting pain* for the *long term earning investment gain*!

Many people find that this technique, repeated every few years as life priorities change, produces hundreds, if not thousands or tens of thousands of instant investment dollars.

## CHARITABLE CONTRIBUTIONS

If you don't want the associated hassles of selling your disused items, or cannot easily find buyers, simply give them away! That's right, give the stuff away! Donate the items to your favourite worthwhile charity, such as the Salvation Army, your local church, St Vincent de Paul, Red Cross, or the Smith Family.

Imagine all the room you will have in your wardrobes and garages once you get rid of all that old stuff! If the items are less than one year old you can usually claim them as a deduction when you lodge your income tax return. Itemise your donation (and estimate its current 'retail market value' from newspaper ads or thrift shop prices) and obtain an official receipt for the items when you donate them. In my family we make it a practice to go through our wardrobes and garage every December (the month the personal tax year ends in the US) and donate all that old stuff to our favourite charities. By doing this we get to help worthy causes, reduce our taxes, and free up space around the house.

'Surplus wealth is a sacred trust which its possessor is bound to administer in his lifetime for the good of the community.'
**ANDREW CARNEGIE**

'I have tried to teach people that there are three kicks in every dollar: one, when you make it – and how I love to make a dollar; two, when you have it – and I have the Yankee lust for saving. The third kick is when you give it away – and it is the biggest kick of all.'
**WILLIAM ALLEN WHITE**

## CHAPTER 8 ACTION STEPS REVIEW

1. Practice **Money Step #4 – *Knowing What Your Money is Doing*** and sell all *doodads* that you no longer need or want.
2. Sell all **passive assets** that are no longer wanted or fully utilised.
3. Put the extra cash straight into your **AIP**.
4. Donate all that you do not sell to your favourite worthy charity, such as the Salvation Army, your local church, St Vincent de Paul, Red Cross or Smith Family.

## CHAPTER 9

# Money Step #5 – *The Automatic Money System*

'Budget: a mathematical confirmation of your suspicions.'

A.A. LATIMER

I know that for a 'money system' to work for the average family it must be simple to understand and more importantly, convenient to use. Many families attempt to set up budgets to control their expenses. Rarely do these budgets work for the long term. Generally they lead to nothing more than fighting within the family and the complete destruction of the family's finances (and often relationships). In short, for most people budgets only bring failure.

It is fairly easy to understand why this happens. I know myself that I never cared for budgets. Probably for the same reasons most people don't. Here are some of the complaints I have heard about budgets:

☒ They're too restrictive and limiting.
☒ They reduce my options.
☒ Too complicated.
☒ They don't work.
☒ Just too much effort.
☒ They take away my freedom.

☒ Too hard to follow.
☒ They set you up for failure.
☒ They cause arguments within the family.
☒ They are not fair.
☒ The reality of my poor management is not something I
   really want to face.

The list goes on and on. You probably have a few extras of your own to add.

Simply stated, a budget should be just a mechanism, a conduit through which to monitor, achieve and maintain financial goals (those you established in Chapter 2). It should be your *servant* and not your *master*. 'Should' being the operative word!

I disliked budgets so much that I tried (for many years) to see if I could find a legitimate reason for not doing one. I spend a great deal of time studying financial subjects. I read a couple of books a week and listen to tapes and attend seminars all the time. So I figured if I could find just one example of a successful company that for the long term did not have financial controls I would have it made. I would be able to get out of doing the dreaded budget.

After several years it became obvious that there was not *one* example of a successful company or entity that for the long term ignored such things as *financial statements* and *budgets*. (And no, the government is not a successfully run entity!).

So I was stuck with the 'cold hard facts'. To obtain long-term Financial Freedom I had to develop and implement a *system for managing my money*. But it had to be different than a normal budget. This new system would contain the following characteristics:

☑ Easy and fun to follow;
☑ Not take up a lot of time;
☑ Provide freedom for fun consumption;
☑ Be simple and not require me to have to watch every
   penny all of the time;
☑ Give immediate results (that 'instant gratification' thing);
☑ Have no more than a handful of steps (say, five);
☑ Produce a chunk of money invested somewhere that

would eventually provide enough cash flow for me to live on for the rest of my life without having to work;

☑ Be able to pay off all my consumer debt within a reasonable period of time;

☑ Allow me to donate money to my favourite charity;

☑ Provide true long-term Financial Freedom;

☑ Be set up so that once it got going I could forget about it and just let it go (in other words it needed to be Automatic).

In summary, what was needed was a true *Money Secret of the Rich*. So allow me now to introduce the next money step.

## MONEY STEP #5 – *THE AUTOMATIC MONEY SYSTEM*

> *The Automatic Money System* equals fun and freedom!

When I introduce **The Automatic Money System** to students attending my seminars I begin by asking them how they feel about budgets in general. After the groans and complaints subside, I tell my students that I agree with their budget sentiments.

In fact, I tell them that when it comes to budgets I am the *Anti-Financial Planner*. I tell them that 'budgets suck' and that they can now tell everyone they know that a financial authority (that's me) told them that 'budgets suck' and that they should feel free to list all the reasons that were mentioned earlier as to exactly why budgets suck so much. It's a lot of fun.

Everyone then stands up and we rally together in a few resounding and cleansing choruses of 'budgets suck!' – fists punching the air. This is a fun and useful exercise to help purge all the old psychological notions of what a budget means to your lifestyle. It helps clear out all the negative expectations and experiences of how much work and how complicated a traditional budget is to implement and follow.

'Budgets are not merely affairs of arithmetic, but in a thousand ways go to the root of prosperity of individuals, the relation of classes and the strengths of kingdoms.'

**WILLIAM E. GLADSTONE**

Today you have the opportunity to cleanse yourself of all those old negative thoughts of the budget being something that works *against* you, not *for* you. On the count of three, stand up, pump your fist in the air and let out a loud cheer: 'budgets suck!'

One... Two... Three... budgets suck! Right! Feel better? Good. Now get ready to move into the 21st century. Time to adopt a new mindset on budgets and prepare to embrace *The Automatic Money System!*

*The Automatic Money System* equals fun and freedom. The first thing you do when preparing your *Automatic Money System* is place as much emphasis on the income, savings and investing sides of the equation as you do on the expense side. This is *your Automatic Money System*, so have fun with it. There is no need to sacrifice all the things you want. Leave yourself some room for fun.

## THE FIVE-STEP AUTOMATIC MONEY SYSTEM

**Money Step #5** – *The Automatic Money System*, itself has five simple, powerful steps to lead you to your Financial Freedom:

1. **Automatic Investment Plan (AIP).** An automatic investment of at least 10% of your (gross) income that systematically increases your wealth every month. Throughout the world, students share with me that they don't even notice that this money is gone. The reason, they used to just spend it anyway. Try it for yourself. (The AIP was fully covered in Chapter 3).
2. **Debt Terminator Plan (DTP).** A contribution of at least 10% of your (gross) income that systematically reduces your debt every month. This one step (fully covered in Chapter 23) will have you *completely debt-free in 3–7 years (including your house and car(s))*;
3. **Charitable Giving Plan (CGP)** (or *tithing*). A contribution of at least 10% of your (gross) income as part of the responsibility and reciprocity associated with creating and being a good steward of wealth\*;
4. **Debt Avoidance Lifestyle Strategies (DALS).** Living by such strategies as only paying cash and maintaining tough

restrictions on the use of credit cards (and consumer credit for consumption). DALS are comprehensively covered in Chapter 10;

5. **Spending the Rest (PARTY).** The flexibility to spend all the rest of your money on whatever you want!

**In summary:** It truly is just that simple. Learn to live on 70% of what you make and you will become rich. What you do with the other 30% will make it so: take 10% for your **Automatic Investment Plan (AIP)**, take 10% for your **Debt Terminator Plan (DTP)**, and take 10% for your **Charitable Giving Plan (CGP)**.

Now I know that some of you are thinking, 'John there is no way I can do this. I couldn't even figure out how to do the 10% for the AIP and now you want another 10% for the DTP and another 10% for the CGP. I just can't afford it.'

> 'A man who both spends and saves money is the happiest man, because he has both enjoyments.'
>
> **SAMUEL JOHNSON**

For those who are in this predicament I understand. I've been there myself. My advice? Start *now*! Even if it is just a few per cent to each one, start *now*! Then, start increasing it a little bit every month until you are there. It may take a while but do not lose your momentum. **Start now**!!!

I also know that some of you are thinking: 'Come on John, this isn't a *Money Secret of the Rich*! Rich people don't really do stuff like that.' For those of you who feel that way I recommend you read the following excerpt from the book *Kids and Cash*, by Ken Davis and Tom Taylor:

### ROCKEFELLER RULES

'John D. Rockefeller, Jr. was certainly not trying to save money when he decided to pay an allowance to his five sons.

According to son Nelson, "We got 25 cents a week, and had to earn the rest of the money we got." To earn part of that extra money he raised vegetables and rabbits… "We always worked," said Nelson. All the boys were required to give 10% of the income to charity, to save 10%, and to account for all the rest. They had to balance their account books every month and to be able to tell what happened to every penny. Nelson went on to serve as Governor of the state of New York

> for many years, and ultimately became the Vice President of the United States. One of his brothers, David Rockefeller, Chairman of the Chase Manhattan Bank, says, "We all profited by the experience – especially when it came to understanding the value of money."'

So unless you are in a better financial position than the Rockefellers, my advice to you is to follow their advice (Rules). If it is good enough for the Rockefellers it is good enough for you. Go get started.

As we have seen, this five-step 'budget' is not really a budget at all, but rather an Automatic System. For most people, Money Step #5 – *The Automatic Money System*, will be very simple and painless to implement. For those people who are currently very overextended and/or living way beyond their means, this is a money step that will need to be eased into gradually.

It is achievable, regardless of your income and your current level of expenses. For some it may require serious adjustments to lifestyle, on the income side and/or on the expenditure side, before it will properly function. For others, it will merely require some minor adjustments. I assure you however (regardless of your present financial situation), that once implemented, *The Automatic Money System* will improve your *quality* of life, albeit for some people at the *temporary* expense of an extravagant life *style*.

---

**This system works. I have thousands of students throughout the world who have achieved the carefree existence of semi-retirement simply by following the five simple steps of *The Automatic Money System:*** They add to their wealth via their AIP each month; they eliminate their debt each month (as described fully in Chapter 23); they practise charitable giving; they pay cash for consumables and live within their means (by avoiding consumption debt); and they really enjoy spending the rest of their money!

If you are among those people who require serious changes to make *The Automatic Money System* work, then take encouragement in the knowledge that by undertaking this program you have already begun to make those changes happen. Whether or not you act on those intentions is entirely up to you. It is your choice. Decide here and now to go through the short-term pain of change rather than the enduring pain of financial ruin.

> 'People's feelings about themselves change when they change the way they handle their money. Once they begin treating their money with respect, their self-respect shoots up as well.'
>
> **SUZE ORMAN**

The rest of this chapter will assist you in implementing the elements of *The Automatic Money System* in the easiest manner possible:

## START WITH THE EXPENSE SECTION

Most people have better success starting with the **expense** section of the Cash Flow Statement (from Chapter 7) than with the **income** section. This is because for the average family it is easier to *reduce expenses* than *increase income*. The objective here is to *simplify* your life, not make it more complicated by trying to increase your income just yet. (However, we do show you from Chapter 24 onwards how to dramatically increase your income.)

Go back to your Cash Flow Statement. Thoroughly go through your expenses. While looking through the old receipts you will probably notice many purchases from which you received little pleasure. Many people also find that they often pay for services, without even (consciously) thinking about it, that are in many cases unnecessary.

In looking back over expenses you will most likely notice a trend: the tendency to spend money unconsciously (without even thinking). Look at your 'unconscious spending' and knock out the purchases that are unnecessary. I will also show you from Chapter 10 onwards many techniques for significantly reducing the costs of your existing 'essential' expenses.

If you are like most people you are probably very surprised how much money you actually pay each year in interest charges.

Just think how different your financial statements would look without *any* of your money being spent on interest!

In Chapter 23 you will learn how to get yourself out of debt forever. The plan is so easy to follow that it will enable the 'average family or individual' to be *completely debt-free in 3–7 years (including the house and car(s))*. For now, resolve firmly to stop using consumer credit, even if it means dramatically altering your current lifestyle spending habits.

There is no joy keeping up with the Joneses when they are accelerating backwards at breakneck speed! That debt will eventually kill you. It is a black hole that will suck you in and take you completely out of the Money Game.

Speaking of the Money Game… why not play a homespun version of that yourself…

## THE HOMESPUN 'MONEY GAME'

This 'Money Game' is really quite simple. Get everybody together around the kitchen table. Bring your completed Cash Flow Statement. Get some play money (from any old board game). Count out the amount of money that equals the family's monthly income. Put it in the centre of the table. First subtract the taxes (in all likelihood the family's biggest expense). For emphasis you might want to burn this tax money or throw it into the rubbish bin (your children may better appreciate the value of your hard-earned cash when they see so much of it going up in smoke!).

'That money talks
I'll not deny.
I heard it once:
It said "Goodbye".'

**RICHARD ARMOUR**

Next, go through your expenses one by one and remove the corresponding amount of money from the centre of the table. Make little piles that represent the various expenses that are listed in the expense section of your Cash Flow Statement: AIP; food; utilities; transportation; housing, etc.

Eventually you will be finished pulling money from the centre of the table. What is left is the family's *discretionary* income. Brainstorm together on how this discretionary income might be best (better) utilised. Ask questions. What would happen if we used it to pay off the car faster? What expense(s) would we have to eliminate to be able to go to Hamilton Island on holiday this year? Do we really want to spend $100 a month on video rentals? As the questions continue the family will begin to make distinctions and better understand what the family's 'true' financial situation is. Have fun with it. Reduce *expenditures* and increase *income*.

## COMPUTERISE!

If you are reasonably computer literate I highly recommend that you use one of the many personal finance programs available. Quicken and Microsoft Money are two good ones that my family and I have used. These programs allow you to budget, itemise your expenses, store all your income tax information, track your investments, do online banking, and much more.

> 'Success is getting up one more time than you fall down.'
>
> **ANON**

Personally I have found Intuit's Quicken to be a very powerful and user-friendly program. These and other personal similar programs are available at most office supply or computer/electronics stores. You can

> 'The greatest mistake you can make in life is to be continually fearing you will make one.'
>
> **ELBERT HUBBARD**

contact Quicken customer service on 1800 674 888 or through www.quicken.com.au. You can buy Quicken Personal for less than $90; Quicken Personal Plus for less than $110; or Quicken QuickBooks for small to medium businesses starting at less than $220. Alternatively, you may want to try Microsoft Money 2001 for less than $65 or Money 2002 Deluxe for around $100. Call 132 058 or log on to www.microsoft.com.

## RED FLAGS!

As you get started on your *Automatic Money System* expect to make some mistakes during the process. As Lee Iacocca says, when referring to making decisions, 'you shouldn't get too old over them' if they are not all perfect. Be prepared to be flexible. Try to plan for some unexpected expenses. Double-check your entries to ensure you don't overlook a quarterly, semi-annual or annual expense. In the beginning of the process, always expect the unexpected.

Be consistent and keep the family involved at all crucial times. The biggest budget problems usually result from lack of family involvement. Many times I have seen one of the parents take off like the Lone Ranger and attempt to manage everything by themselves. This usually involves just one person setting up the *new* financial program and inflicting the finished product on the entire family. Often this is followed by a stern lecture, finger-pointing, yelling, fighting and screaming.

I implore you not to go about implementing your new financial system in a solitary or a confrontational way. Please remember the 'house rules' we discussed earlier for these meetings. You need to work together as a team, not separately. So remember, the dictator approach may work for the short-term but for real long-term success the whole family needs to be welcomed and involved in the process from the beginning.

You must also have the family involved for two *specific* reasons. First, you need their *help*. With everybody involved the potential to leave out certain expenses or income sources from the equation is greatly reduced. Second, if left out of the planning process, family members may resent your sudden imposition of the new spending rules. If they do not fully understand the reasons for change then they are far less likely to cooperatively surrender any expenditures to ensure the success of the system. I recommend you bring the family together to play the Homespun 'Money Game', described earlier.

'A man with a surplus can control circumstances, but a man without a surplus is controlled by them, and often he has no opportunity to exercise judgment.'

**HENRY FIRESTONE**

Avoid impulse buying/spending. The most important risk to your new *Automatic Money System* is the tendency to spend without thinking. Later in the program I will provide you with several Debt Avoidance Lifestyle Strategies (DALS) to eliminate impulse buying/spending.

The key to your new *Automatic Money System* is to use your money in a logical, beneficial manner. Learn to apply discipline towards your money. Buy only that which you truly want. And yes, you can still go out and buy 'stuff'. A little instant gratification isn't going to kill you. A lot almost certainly *will* kill you *financially*. Where needed, strive to use more control.

In essence, your *Automatic Money System* is designed to facilitate stress-free financial control. It should be a great source of information and guidance, as well as providing *workable* restrictions in relation to your spending habits. Remember, this system was designed to make your life fuller and more enjoyable. Stick with the system and you will soon reap the benefits of true long-term Financial Freedom.

## START TODAY!

Money Step #5 – *The Automatic Money System*, will carry you to riches and abundance. Remember the five steps: AIP; DTP; CGP; DALS; and PARTY!

1. **AIP** – invest 10% of your gross income via your Automatic Investment Plan.
2. **DTP** – invest 10% of your gross income via your Debt Terminator Plan.
3. **CGP** – contribute 10% of your gross income via your Charitable Giving Plan.
4. **DALS** – implement the Debt Avoidance Lifestyle Strategies.
5. **PARTY** – spend the rest and enjoy it!

## FINANCIAL SYSTEM SURFING

The Internet provides many useful and free financial management sites that offer financial calculators designed for helping you with insurance, loans, investing, retirement and budgeting calculations. Three of the best multi-purpose sites:

1. Money Web at www.moneyweb.com.au provides free financial calculators as well as other financial guides.
2. Quality Software Australia at www.softwareaustralia.com.au has financial calculators for financial planning;
3. MoneyCentral at www.moneycentral.msn.com.

There are also many Internet sites offering free trial budgeting software that will assist those people who initially want a little more formal assistance in reforming their budget habits. Here are two:

- http://info.apnpc.com.au which has a personal expense journal, budgeting software and accounting ledger, which you can try before you buy.
- www.microsoft.com/money lets you have a free trial of Money 2000 Business and Personal software.

---

\* I also talk in Chapters 21 and 22 about the third element of *The Automatic Money System*: Charitable Giving (generosity). I know several hundred people who are millionaires. With the exception of one person, they *all* firmly believe in Charitable Giving. I know that personally I give without the expectation of return. However, my experience has been that the more I give, the more I receive. Personally, I believe I get back more than a hundredfold for everything that I give.

As described above, I believe that the act of regularly contributing part of your wealth to charitable purposes (at least 10% of your gross income) is just as vital to achieving Financial Freedom and living an abundant life, as any of the other steps of *The Automatic Money System*. I truly believe that generosity of money, time and spirit are all gifts which when given unconditionally, always return to the giver in far greater magnitude, and in multi-faceted forms. To me, such generosity is a necessary part of adopting the mindset of the *money attractant* person for whom abundance and success, not scarcity and failure, are the destined order of things in this world. My advice: be sure to follow this step. I believe it is critical and part of the responsibility of accumulating wealth. More on the value of generosity in Chapters 21 and 22.

For further understanding of how money works I highly recommend Robert Kiyosaki's games CASHFLOW™ (versions 101 and 202) and CASHFLOW For KIDS™ available in Australia/New Zealand through Pow Wow Events International on 1300 550 240, in Sydney on (612) 9662 8488; or through www.powwowevents.com.au.

---

## CHAPTER 9 ACTION STEPS REVIEW

1. Adopt **Money Step #5 – *The Automatic Money System***.
2. Record all your **expenses** and **income** with the help of your family.
3. Use 'real-world' numbers. Be conservative. Let any financial surprises be in your favour, not against you.

4. Keep the whole family involved.
5. Play the Homespun 'Money Game' with your family.
6. Avoid the **red flags**: being discouraged by mistakes; unexpected expenses; the Lone Ranger syndrome; failure to involve the whole family; and impulse buying.

**CHAPTER 10**

# Money Step #6 – *Financial Competence (Intelligence and Responsibility)*

## How to reduce your *cost* of living 20–50% without reducing your *standard* of living

'Get to know two things about a man – how he earns his money and how he spends it – and you have the clue to this character, for you have a searchlight that shows up the innermost recesses of his soul.'

ROBERT JAMES MCCRACKEN

**F**inancial Competence (Intelligence and Responsibility) is actually quite simple to achieve. All it consists of is adhering to 'common sense' **Money Habits** in your day-to-day money decisions. Let's begin with shopping habits.

If you are like most people, you have a certain tendency to spend money impulsively. For some it causes only minor financial problems. For others it becomes like a disease. These latter people

'Prosperity is too apt to prevent us from examining our conduct: but adversity leads us to think properly of our state, and so is most beneficial to us.'
**SAMUEL JOHNSON**

'Be not made a beggar by banqueting on borrowing.'
**THE BIBLE (ECCLESIASTICUS)**

often become very depressed over how far they have sunk into debt. They feel very bad about their high monthly payments but when they try to escape from their worries for a while, where do they usually end up? At the shopping mall again!

To distract themselves from their money problems and make themselves feel better they will go shopping! Ah, the healing power of whipping out the plastic and buying whatever they want! Now they feel they are real 'movers and shakers'. They have credit cards. They have consumer clout. They have the power and the freedom to buy anything! Then they get home. And they feel worse than ever. Not only did they buy something they didn't need, but now they are even further in debt. What can they do to stop this feeling? What can they do to numb this pain? Maybe go for a drive? To the mall!!!

If this scenario sounds all too familiar to *you*, I implore you to take control of your impulsive spending habits immediately. If you cannot do it on your own, seek professional help. I am not joking. You have a 'compulsive shopping disorder'.

A person with compulsive shopping problems is very similar to the person who keeps overeating because they are depressed about being overweight; or the alcoholic who keeps drinking because they are depressed about their drinking problem; or the drug addict who keeps taking drugs while desperately wanting to stop.

A credit counsellor would be a good first step for anyone who believes that their debt payments are beyond their own ability to manage. Money Care financial counselling service is a confidential, free-of-charge service operated by the Salvation Army. They can determine the cause of the problem, prepare a budget from the information provided, monitor an agreed monthly budget and speak with creditors to explain the situation and seek an extension of time to rectify it. In Sydney their contact number is (02) 9633 5011 (Parramatta); for Brisbane (07) 3222 6642; and for Canberra (02) 6247 3635.

Creditline financial counselling also offers a free service for those with debt and other financial problems. Immediate advice is given for urgent problems. Telephone 1800 808 488 (in Sydney (02) 9951 5544) or visit their website at www.wesleymission.org.au/centres/creditline (email at creditline@wesleymission.org.au).

For people who believe that their (or someone else's) debt crisis is symptomatic of deeper psychological problems there are various organisations which can assist people to work through the issues. For example: St Luke's financial counselling service, on 1800 626 617 or at www.stlukes.org.au; and South Pacific Private Hospital which runs clinics for behavioural addictions, on 1800 063 372 or at www.spph.com.au.

There is much information available in the public domain to assist people in the use and management of credit, and their rights in relation to credit providers and collection agencies. Here are some good places to start:

- Australian Consumers' Association at www.choice.com.au. You can subscribe to their magazine *Choice*; it includes issues and reports regarding your rights as a consumer, money issues and other interesting consumer information. Or you can write to their consumer information team for help or advice at Australian Consumers' Association, 57 Carrington Rd, Marrickville NSW 2204 ((02) 9577 3399);
- Most State Governments provide consumer information and protection of consumer rights. For example, New South Wales has the Department of Fair Trading (www.fairtrading.nsw.gov.au or 1800 451 301); Consumer Credit Legal Centre on (02) 9212 4111 which has free legal advice on borrower's rights, credit/debt problems or bankruptcy issues; Victoria has the Financial and Consumer Rights Council at www.vicnet.net.au or (03) 9699 9710; South Australia has the Citizens Advice Bureau at www.citizensadvice.sa.gov.au or (08) 8212 4070.
- Trade Union and industry organisations usually have free consumer information. For example Incolink at www.incolink.org.au or on 1800 337 789 provides financial and consumer advice and counselling.
- Obtain a copy of your own official credit history from Credit Advantage Ltd. This is a free service if you are prepared to

have a copy of your file sent to you by mail within 10 days, or
$16.50 (incl. GST) if you require it within 24 hours. Write to
Credit Advantage Public Enquiries, PO Box 964, North
Sydney, NSW 2059 or contact them on (02) 9464 6000 or at
www.credref.com.au. You must supply your full name,
residential address, date of birth and driver's licence details.

You should also be aware that debt-collection agencies may
not legally:
- threaten or abuse you;
- use obscene language;
- advertise on any correspondence with you that they are a
  debt collector;
- inform anyone at all that you owe money;
- contact you at your home or place of work if you have
  instructed them not to.

If considering bankruptcy as a last resort, first consult your solicitor
or accountant. A good guide to bankruptcy is available at
www.vicnet.net.au. Bankruptcy is something that must be
considered very carefully before making a final decision.

## AVOID PAY-DAY LENDERS AT ALL COSTS

Slipping through the cracks of the Uniform Consumer Credit
Code (set up to protect consumers from unfair lending
practices), is a new breed of lenders known as 'pay-day lenders'.
These essentially unregulated lenders target people who are
unable to manage until pay-day and lend them small sums of
money for exorbitant fees. Because the loans are for less than 62
days they remain outside the Credit Code. Usually charging
around $22 every 14 days for every $100 loan, these 'services'
work out to be around 70 times more expensive than using a
credit card (more than 1000% interest if calculated on an
annualised basis). Pay-day lenders should be avoided at all costs.

Now review the techniques below. The first nine are
particularly helpful to the impulsive/compulsive spender. These
techniques should form part of your **Debt Avoidance Lifestyle
Strategies (DALS)**, part of your *Automatic Money System*.

## 25 FINANCIAL COMPETENCE PURCHASING TECHNIQUES

These **25** *Financial Competence* purchasing techniques are designed to reduce unwanted spending and enhance your ability to buy the items you really want at substantial discounts.

1. **Stop before you buy.** Leave the store, go home and think about it overnight. That's right, sleep on it. If you are worried that the item might be sold before you return, ask that it be held overnight. When you get home write down the cost of the item, how you can pay for it (without the use of credit), and what value you are going to receive from the purchase. If you do this the odds are good that by morning you will have decided not to go ahead with the purchase. If you do still want it, *and* you can afford it, by all means buy it and enjoy it. If not, don't buy it. In using this technique, you will avoid 'buyer's regret'.

   > 'It is easier to resist at the beginning than at the end.'
   > **LEONARDO DA VINCI**

   > 'In squandering wealth was his peculiar art:
   > Nothing went unrewarded, but desert.
   > Beggared by fools, whom still he found too late:
   > He had his jest, and they had his estate.'
   > **JOHN DRYDEN (*Absalom and Achitophel*, 1681)**

   Be aware that impulse buying is generally emotionally motivated. By disciplining ourselves to ignore and thus delay the initial impulses, most of the time we will not want to purchase the items later. Be aware of the emotional origins of impulse buying. Try to recognise any insecurities (stresses and fears) you may have associated with not purchasing an item or with purchasing only one of two or more competing items (like choosing between two pairs of shoes or between three T-shirts). As I just said, the easiest way to accomplish this is to go home, write everything down that you want to buy and then sleep on it. I call this technique 'stay away buy!'

2. **When you go shopping or 'browsing', try leaving your wallet and cheque book at home.** Revel in the power of being able to look without having to shop. Marketers are brilliant at making you think you need everything you see. The stores are set up to compel you to think you are unable to live without something that 15 minutes earlier you didn't even know existed. Have fun with this knowledge. Some

people even keep a journal of all the 'stuff' they thought they wanted and how much it would have cost. They then congratulate themselves on all the money they saved. Take on the challenge and beat the retailers at their own game!

3. **Be aware of the persuasion techniques ('weapons of influence') used to get you to spend more.** Typical techniques are: exploiting the stereotype of 'expensive = good' by inflating prices to make an item seem desirable and/or then discounting it to make it seem a bargain for its quality; the 'contrast principle' whereby an expensive or overpriced item is presented and/or sold first in order to lessen the perceived cost and increase the saleability of subsequent cheaper presented items, or options; or the scarcity technique whereby items are marked 'For 5 days only' or 'A limited time only' or 'Limited edition', etc. These are just a few of the many influence techniques described by Robert Cialdini in his groundbreaking book *Influence, The Psychology of Persuasion*. Be aware of these techniques.

4. **Take your name off catalogue mailing lists, telephone lists and email lists.** Catalogues provide unnecessary temptations and telephone solicitations can be very persuasive. To stop catalogues: contact the distributors and request your name be removed from their lists. Next, have your name removed from most mailing lists, telephone and email lists by writing to Australian Direct Marketing Association, Reply Paid 38, PO Box 464 Kings Cross 1340 or www.adma.com.au.

5. **Don't buy over the telephone from the unknown.** Say 'No thank you' to *every* unknown telephone solicitation. Never give out your credit card number over the telephone. If you are familiar with the company and you really want the product, then make the *Financially Competent (Intelligent and Responsible)* decision as to whether or not you can truly afford the item and whether or not you can delay (sometimes indefinitely) the purchase of the item. Always say 'NO' to in-home demonstrations of products. The mark up for in-home, telephone solicitation, and door-to-door sales is usually between 100 and 500%. This means you pay 2–5 times more

than you should. And always say you are 'just browsing' whenever you are approached by an eager sales assistant in a store.

6. **Always think about the value of the purchase versus the effort required to earn the post-tax dollars you are about to spend.** In other words, is the value you are going to receive truly worth the time and effort you put in to make the money?

7. **Invest instead of consuming.** Whenever you are *tempted* to consume but manage to avoid it, why not add the money you saved to your **AIP** account? From month to month this can really add up. Also, do what I have been doing since my teens. Every night I drop my loose change into a jar. When it is full I cash it in. When I was younger I of course spent the money. However, today I just add it to investments. This easily turns into hundreds of dollars each year.

8. **Get rid of your ATM card.** The average person pays around $100 a year for avoidable ATM fees. This money could be working for you. The ease of access to the money is the real 'evil' of an ATM card. How often do you take out amounts of $40 or less? Was this withdrawal for planned or unplanned spending? Many people will use the ATM three to five times every weekend. For what? To get money to buy things they do not need and for which they have not budgeted.

> 'Oh money, money, money
> I'm not necessarily one of
> those who thinks thee holy,
> But I often stop to wonder
> How thou canst go out so fast
> when thou comest in so slowly.'
> **OGDEN NASH**

This is one convenience you can live without. In fact, you used to, remember? In the days before the ATM when you planned your spending better. The days before you got your first credit card, when you only paid cash for everything!

9. **Keep a written record of every time you spend money for a minimum of 30 days.** Do this in concert with your *Automatic Money System* and make sure you record a description of each item and what it cost. People find that by first 'thinking purchases through' they usually spend a lot less money.

10. **Never pay full retail price for anything!** Paying full retail price is lunacy. After all, everything goes on sale eventually. Heed the advice of the great capitalist J. Paul Getty, 'I buy my straw hats in the winter.' The message: make your purchases based on when the prices are the lowest (i.e. snow skis are cheapest in December, swimming suits are cheapest in June). Become *Financially Competent*. Be an Intelligent and Responsible consumer. Promise yourself that you will do your best to never pay retail again.

11. **Consider buying shares in solid public companies that offer real value to your lifestyle by way of shareholders discount schemes.** Check out the minimum share parcels required for shareholder benefits in some of the best examples:

   • Coles Myer – offering between 2.5 and 10% discounts on merchandise at outlets in the Coles Myer organisation including: Myer; Grace Bros; Kmart; Coles supermarkets; e.colesmyer group at www.colesmyer.com.au; Fosseys; Katies; Liquorland; Officeworks; Red Rooster; Pick 'n' Pay Hypermarket; Target; Tyremaster; World 4 Kids and Bi-Lo. Currently requires ownership of 500 shares (shareholder discounts not available to new shareholders registered after Oct 11, 2000, pending full review of the scheme; minimum parcel requirements also likely to rise to 1,000 for eligible shareholders).

   • David Jones – offering similar discounts to Coles Myer for all purchases made on the David Jones charge card. Currently requires ownership of 2,000 shares.

   • National Australia Bank, ANZ, Westpac, Bendigo Bank and Bank of Queensland all offer both offer features such as no account service fees, bonus interest on term deposits, discounts on fees for other bank products and lower interest rates on home and personal loans for shareholders.

   • Foster's Brewing, Brian McGuigan Wines, Blackmores, Amalgamated Holdings; Rebel Sports, OPSM Protector, BRL Hardy, Gowing Bros, Queensland Tourism Industries, Mirvac, Village Roadshow and Petaluma all offer shareholder benefits.

Check out the complete list of such companies and the discounts offered for share ownership on the Internet at:
- www.rtrfm.iinet.com.au/~tighe/discount.htm;
- www.shares.aust.com/frame.asp?page=/newsadmin/ stories/shares/19991001/3585.htm.

12. **Always ask for a discount!** You will be amazed at the results. At a retail shopping centre recently I received a 15% discount on an old-fashioned teddy-bear for my daughter. The item wasn't on sale, I just asked the manager for a discount. She offered 10%. I countered with 20%. The result, a 15% discount. Over the length of your lifetime, these types of discounts on everything you purchase would make you rich all by themselves.

Ask for discounts even on items you don't conventionally associate with discounts. Ask for the 'cash price' on higher-ticket items. Sometimes a retailer will wish to avoid credit card commissions and bank processing charges or will be short of cash and will offer a substantial discount for cash payments.

13. **When dealing with goods and services purchased through quotation never pay the amount of the original quote.** I can assure you, there is almost always room in the bid for negotiation. If you are contracting work out, always ask, 'Is this your best price?' Then, stop talking. Let the contractor talk. Usually they respond with some kind of a discount. Whatever the discount offered, tell them you would feel much better if they could double it. Then say nothing. Prepare to be amazed at their response. Then ask them if that is their 'cash price'.

> 'Annual income twenty pounds, annual expenditure nineteen nineteen six, result happiness. Annual income twenty pounds, annual expenditure twenty pounds ought and six, result misery.'
> **CHARLES DICKENS (David Copperfield, 1850)**

I have done in excess of 800 real estate transactions over the last 10 years and as a consequence, have contracted out a lot of work. I have seen this technique work over and over again for my wife, my office staff, and myself.

14. **Tell sales staff or contractors that your spouse or boss won't let you buy anything unless it's on sale or you get a discount.** My wife, Shari, has become an expert at

doing this. She has said that the more times she tries it the more fun and challenging it becomes to get even better deals. Whatever she is shopping for, her final strategy is to tell the seller that her husband never lets her buy anything unless it's on sale. It almost always works. She also uses this technique to get even more discount on an item that has already been discounted. I tell sellers the same thing (only in reverse).

15. **Reduce your food costs by 20–40%.** First, when you go grocery shopping, if possible use discount coupons. Shrewd shoppers know that this technique puts a whole lot more food on the table for their dollar. Second, base your main course selections (meat, poultry, etc.) on sale items. Decide on your menu at the market based on what is on sale or as you read the sale advertisements in the newspaper. By doing this you will always eat well without great expense.

16. **Buy household items when on sale.** As stated before, everything goes on sale eventually. When it's on sale, purchase in bulk what you will need at least until the next time it goes on sale. For example, buy laundry soap in bulk containers from wholesalers, store it in the garage and decant to smaller containers for use in the home as needed.

17. **Use 2-for-1 coupons.** When you dine out, use 2-for-1 coupons whenever possible. In most communities there are 'Dining & Entertainment' discount books available. Don't buy them all. Just the one(s) you will really use. Carry the coupons in your purse or wallet so you always have them when you need them. Also, restaurants often offer the same 2-for-1 deals in the Friday and Saturday newspapers.

18. **Buy goods from the classified ads.** Have you looked at the classifieds lately? I am constantly amazed by the number of ads that offer merchandise for 10–50 cents on the dollar. I have purchased several quality items from the classified ads. Example: a two-month-old US$4,500, Italian leather, sectional couch for US$1,400. The sellers had a beautiful house (10,000+ square feet with six fireplaces) and in the husband's opinion, his wife had no taste for decorating. So, he hired a 'decorator' to redo the whole interior. Bless her, the 'decorator' decided this gorgeous couch clashed with the

'motif'. Today, that couch clashes with the fireplace in my living room (just kidding, it looks great). I bought it for less than one-third of its retail value. How would you like to purchase a $6,000, solid-oak desk and credenza for $550? Or, how about a large wide-screen, surround-sound television for $650? I did both, from the classifieds.

Most major newspapers now list their classified sections online and sites such as the following can be a great source for pre-owned or discounted goods (factory or display seconds, etc.) via posted (negotiable) price or via auction:

- www.tradingpost.com.au;
- www.bidorbuy.com.au (use as buying guide or low-bid items);
- www.gofish.com.au (use as buying guide or low-bid items);
- www.ebay.com.au (use as buying guide or low-bid items);
- www.sold.com.au (use as buying guide or low-bid items)

19. **Use the Internet in general to value shop retail goods and services before you commit to buying them.**
    Following on from technique 18, the Internet can be a great source for new goods (as well as for used/factory/display seconds). When shopping for goods and services such as mobile phones or phone plans, electronics, travel or bank services, etc., good websites can offer pricing guides and/or goods and services at significant discounts to full retail:

- www.webtrader.com.au (buying guide for all types of goods);
- www.tradingpost.com.au (use as buying guide or to buy);
- www.phonechoice.com.au (use as buying guide or to buy);
- www.bankchoice.com.au (part of the www.infochoice.com.au suite of sites run by infomediary Infochoice Limited, providing comparative pricing and product information on a wide range of financial and telecommunications products and links businesses to consumers);
- www.choice.com.au (Australian Consumers' Association CHOICEOnline site that provides consumer articles and reports on particular goods and services)
- www.myfinance.com.au (for comparing telephone rates);

- www.bidorbuy.com.au (use as buying guide or low-bid items);
- www.gofish.com.au (use as buying guide or low-bid items);
- www.bestbid.com.au (use as buying guide or low-bid items);
- www.ebay.com.au (use as buying guide or low-bid items);
- www.sold.com.au (use as buying guide or low-bid items).

Also, some of the goods offered on secure retail Internet shopping sites can offer real value and may even save you transport money if goods are delivered to your door in sufficient volume. Check out:

- www.greengrocer.com.au;
- www.ninemsn.com.au;
- www.looksmart.com.au;
- www.shopfast.com.au;
- www.au.shopping.yahoo.com;
- www.wineplanet.com.au;
- www.dstore.com.au;
- www.wishlist.com.au.

Always remember not to fall for the glossy lure these sites may have to spend beyond your original intentions on impulse buys, thereby cancelling out any of the savings you may have received on your essential purchases. Be disciplined in your use of them and only use them if they offer true value. Become fully informed about Internet retailing by reading the ADMA Online Marketing Guidelines at www.adma.com.au and Shopping on the Internet Facts for Consumers by the Department of Communications, Information Technology and the Arts (DCITA) at www.dcita.gov.au/shoponline.

**Charity Hint:** As part of your Charitable Giving Plan (CGP) which you are including as part of your *Automatic Money System*, check out www.free2give.com.au. This site links to many reputable online retailers which have committed to passing on small percentages of what you spend on their sites, to your selected charities. You pay no more for the products because the retailers are happy to relinquish small amounts of profit for the goodwill and extra business generated.

20. **Check out garage sales and opportunity (thrift) shops.** You can often find high-quality, little (or never) used items for 10–20 cents on the dollar. And in the case of opportunity shops or thrift stores, your money will also be supporting good causes.

21. **Consider permanently or at least temporarily giving up or reducing a vice (e.g. smoking, drinking, gambling, sweets and chocolates) or reducing a luxury item or service.** You will be surprised how easily you can live without these items or services. Just think how proud you will be of yourself for your stoic resisting of these indulgences. How often do you actually use that $3 a month phone service like Call Forwarding or Caller ID and how often do you actually read the gourmet-cooking magazine you have on subscription that you could easily read at the library?

> 'Many estates are spent in the getting,
>
> Since women for tea forsook spinning and knitting,
>
> And men for punch forsook hewing and splitting.'
>
> **BENJAMIN FRANKLIN**

22. **Spend half as much as usual during the holidays.** Many people over-spend on Christmas, only to regret it for the next several months. If you find yourself in that position, ask yourself one question: 'Would my family and friends really want me to buy these gifts for them if they knew the financial hardship it will cause me?' The answer is 'No!' (If the answer is 'Yes', then you *definitely* know you don't want to buy the gifts.) Either way you cannot lose if you are willing to impose unemotional discipline on your holiday spending habits. Use a little of what the great industrialist Bernard M. Baruch called 'reliance on one's own cold detached judgment of the economic facts' when shopping for presents so that you don't let your emotions run away with you.

23. **Your children do not need every toy in the world.** The amount of toys a parent gives a child is not a testament to the amount of love the parent has for the child. Children know this. They do not need your money. They need your time, love, patience and guidance. If you generously provide these non-material gifts they will readily forgive you your resistance to their fleetingly impassioned pleas for all of the latest toy sensations.

Question to parents: How often do your children really play with all the toys they got last Christmas? Don't spend money on them in an effort to compensate them for the time you don't spend with them. Spend the time with them instead. Spend the time and watch the investment grow. Spend the money and watch your kid's future slow. After all, the spirit of such times as Christmas is to give of yourself, not of your wallet.

Suggestion to parents: Limit the time your children watch television and thus their exposure to powerfully suggestive commercials for all the latest toys they cannot possibly live without.

24. **Travel discounts.** If you would like to save up to 50% on your holiday, try travelling the week before or after peak season. The weather is still good, the prices are just much lower. We have travelled to Mexico, Hawaii, the Caribbean, Australia and the South Pacific several times for 30–50% discounts because we were willing to wait a week or two. Call airlines and hotels six months in advance, on their 1800 number, to find out when their prices change. You may also look at joining 'Fly Buys', which rewards shoppers at certain stores with award points that can be exchanged for a range of gifts including free flights and accommodation. Be careful only to buy using the *Financial Competence* spending techniques. Membership of Fly Buys is free. You can contact Fly Buys Service Centre on 13 11 16, by mail to Reply Paid AAA4114 PO Box 833, South Melbourne 3205, or on www.flybuys.com.au. Frequent flyer programs may also be of benefit if you travel regularly by air.

Check out some of the online travel sites which often have amazing specials and/or allow you to bid on airfares, accommodation or package deals:

- www.travel.com.au;
- www.travelshop.com.au;
- www.holidays.com.au (complete with 'summer holiday' music!);
- www.priceline.com (large US site with great deals/auctions);
- www.travelocity.com (large US site with great deals/auctions);
- www.harveyworldtravel.com.au;
- www.travelmate.com.au (auctions and 'smart-trip' functions for planning a trip. Also has daily updated Caltex and Ampol petrol pricing for your suburb);
- www.traveland.com.au;
- www.flightcentre.com.au;
- www.bidorbuy.com.au; www.sold.com.au;
- www.gofish.com.au;
- www.lastminute.com.au.

25. **Use Bargain Shopping information**. Consult your local *Bargain Shoppers Guide* (if your state has one). Check out www.bargainshoppers.com.au.

**Bottomline**: if you need to acquire any major (or minor) item look first in the paper, at a garage sale, opportunity or second-hand goods store, or on the Internet... *not* at the shopping centre. To reiterate, I often see items that have never been used, still in the box, for 50 cents (or less) on the dollar.

## 50 FRUGAL IS AS FRUGAL DOES TIPS

Over the course of my seminars I have been able to gather from students many cost-saving tips for daily living where the watched pennies take care of the pounds. Here is a short-list taken from tips compiled at seminars held in Australia in 1999 and 2000 (some tips listed were already covered in our 25 techniques). You may add more of your own.

> 'I would rather have people laugh at my economies than weep at my extravagance.'
> **KING OSCAR II OF SWEDEN**

- Buy clothes, electrical goods and linen wholesale at factory outlets, reject shops or seconds stores.
- Take your own lunch to work instead of buying takeout. Save $10 a day.
- If you drink bottled water buy a filter for $100, which you will recoup in four weeks.
- Shop around a little for petrol prices, midweek prices are usually lower.
- Read Consumer Advocate magazines.
- Use the discounts on the 'shopper dockets'. This program is developed for your local area, e.g., dry cleaners, 2-for-1 meals and movies.
- Buy small business items at discount shops rather then office supply stores.
- Investigate discount phone carriers for calling interstate and overseas.
- Be aware of when you use your mobile, different times have different rates.
- Use compact fluorescent light globes which last around eight times longer than conventional globes and save around $60 a year in electricity for each globe.
- Turn off appliances at the wall outlet to stop standby power drain and seepage, particularly when you go away. Check your major appliances such as computers and televisions for their standby power rate (anything above about two watts is high).
- Use voucher books. They give you discounts and 2-for-1 deals.
- Do your research on travel, consider using Internet travel sites which can offer huge savings on advertised specials or when you win a low bid, or opt for stand-by travel.
- By furniture and kids toys at garage sales.
- Maintain and service your car to reduce breakdowns.
- Conserve electricity and water. Turn down heating or air-conditioning.
- Turn down the temperature on electric hot water systems and/or opt for off-peak service.
- Buy shares in companies which offer retail discounts on merchandise for stockholders.
- Go to the movies on discount days and times or buy books of

movie tickets.
- Buy cinema tickets in books of ten.
- Use recycled cartridges for your office and home printers.
- Instead of making multiple copies from a laser printer, print one copy and then photocopy others. A laser printer costs 3¢ per page and a photocopy costs 0.3¢/page.
- Borrow books first from the library instead of or before buying them and sell your used books.
- Try to make your telephone calls off-peak.
- Download software from the Internet where available to try before purchasing.
- Double-check all bills before paying.
- Women and beauty products – try the supermarket brands as they have the same ingredients.
- Women – go to the beauty and hairdressing schools for cheap treatments.
- Eat fruit and vegetables that are in season. Grow your own vegetables, herbs and flowers.
- Shop at the returns section of a department store. You can buy returned products for 20–70% of retail.
- The local library has free community information for upcoming activities, especially for the kids.
- Check the *Trading Post* for free items that you would otherwise buy.
- Avoid carrying loose change, which tends to get spent. Carry larger notes which you may resist breaking for impulse 'small change' items.
- Check restaurants that allow you to bring your own wine.
- Brew your own beer at home.

'Give every man thine ear, but few thy voice;
Take each man's censure, but reserve thy judgment.
Costly thy habit as thy purse can buy,
But not expressed in fancy; rich, not gaudy;
For the apparel oft proclaims the man...
Neither a borrower, nor a lender be;
For loan oft loses both itself and friend,
And borrowing dulls the edge of husbandry,
This above all: to thine own self be true,
And it must follow, as the night the day,
Thou canst not then be false to any man.'
**WILLIAM SHAKESPEARE** (*Hamlet*)

'At the end of each day, you should play back the tapes of your performance. The results should either applaud you or prod you.'
**JIM ROHN**

- Do your grocery shopping once a week instead of impulsively and unplanned and use pre-prepared lists.
- Before planning your weekly meals, look at the supermarket ads in the paper to see what is on special that week. There will always be specials to attract you into the supermarket. Shop just before closing to obtain the last-minute clearance specials.
- Buy generic and in-house brand grocery lines when quality is the same, such as for flour, sugar and salt. Try other items and see if they are as good as brand name product.
- Leave the kids at home when shopping.
- Install push-button automatic light switches in walkway areas.
- Car pool – drive slower! Ride your bike or walk instead of driving.
- Buy at the end of the season for clothing sale discounts.
- Consider home sharing/swapping for your holidays.
- Use auto sprinklers in off-peak times.
- Wash clothes in cold water and fix dripping taps.
- If eligible, obtain discount card for seniors.
- Join a barter card club.
- Ask for a decrease in your rent, etc., if you pay early.
- Form a babysitting club or buying club, buy in bulk and share.
- Form a buying club with family, friends and neighbours and buy items such as pet food, toilet paper, domestic cleaning products and laundry powder in bulk and share. Check out co-operative buying sites such as CoShopper.com at www.coshopper.com.

---

## CHAPTER 10 ACTION STEPS REVIEW

1. Commit to exercising **Money Step #6 – *Financial Competence (Intelligence and Responsibility)*.**
2. Beware of and actively avoid *impulse spending*.
3. Put into action the 25 *Financial Competence* purchasing techniques.

## CHAPTER 11

# Review I –
# The Foundations Are Laid

'If you would be powerful, pretend to be powerful.'
HORNE TOOKE

'Some relaxation is necessary to people of every degree,
the head that thinks and the hand that labors must have
some little time to recruit their diminished powers.'
BERNARD GILPIN

**C**ongratulations! You have made it a third of the way through! You are well on your way to Financial Freedom. Know that the steps you have taken to this point are ensuring that you and your family achieve the prosperity you so richly deserve. Revel in your accomplishment, because you have already done what less than 5% of the population has done, or likely will ever do. You have taken the steps required to provide yourself and your family with true Financial Freedom.

Take some time to review where you have come from and where you are going. Review the last ten chapters:
• What have you learned?
• Which assignments were the hardest for you?
• Which ones helped you the most?

- How much money have you saved so far?
- In what ways do you have a better 'handle' on what you are doing?
- How do you feel better about yourself and your money management?
- How much money will be in your **Automatic Investment Plan** at the end of the year? In five years? In ten years? In 20 years? At retirement?

'Waste of time is the most extravagant of all expense.'
**THEOPHRASTUS**

'To be able to fill leisure intelligently is the last product of civilisation.'
**BERTRAND RUSSELL**

'Yesterday is not ours to recover, but tomorrow is ours to win or to lose.'
**LYNDON B. JOHNSON**

'Anyone who has ever been faced with the task of objective self-evaluation will agree that, while not pleasant, it was enlightening. Once you have completed your self-examination, you must be willing to change your thinking and behaviour to that which is more beneficial. Old habits die hard and change is tough, so you must discipline yourself until the new behaviour becomes old habit. The whole process is one of getting mentally tough with yourself in the short run to make it easier on yourself in the long run.'
**JACK COLLIS AND MICHAEL LEBOEUF**

After you have completed your review and answered these questions, you can catch up on any assignments you may have not yet completed.

Then take some time to rest and let all that you have done and learned so far sink in and embed itself in your mind. Slow down enough to let all the information and the insights you have gained catch up with you. Review your goals!

Remember to employ yourself to your own best advantage. Take time out on a regular basis to focus on your personal financial success. This does not mean that you cannot take time out to just relax or have fun. It simply means that when you do, make sure your relaxation time is benefiting you in developmental ways wherever possible (i.e., relaxation becomes reflection and meditation).

The more time you spend learning to enhance your situation the more confidence you will have to bolster yourself against the trials of life, financial and otherwise.

Have fun, enjoy the rest and review and I will join you in the next chapter. And again, my congratulations to you on your significant accomplishments to date.

## CHAPTER 11 ACTION STEPS REVIEW

1. Review the first ten chapters of the *Money Secrets of the Rich* program for *Automatic* **Financial Freedom.**
2. Answer the questions listed above.
3. Catch up on any assignments missed.
4. Rest and reflect.

'He started to sing
As he tackled the thing
That couldn't be done,
And he did it.'
**EDGAR A. GUEST**

## PART TWO

# Know thy enemy: Eliminating financial traps — Saving money

'In short, the way to wealth, if you desire it, is as plain as the way to market. It depends chiefly on two words, *industry* and *frugality*, that is, waste neither *time* nor *money*, but make the best use of both.'

BENJAMIN FRANKLIN

'When prosperity comes, do not use all of it.'

CONFUCIUS

**CHAPTER 12**

# When and how to refinance your home

'The time to repair the roof is when the sun is shining.'

JOHN F. KENNEDY

In this chapter we continue working on **Money Step #6 –** *Financial Competence (Intelligence and Responsibility)*. It is critical that you begin implementing as many *Financial Competence money habits* as soon as possible. Last chapter we examined a variety of small and medium-sized steps that you can take to improve your **bottom line** – how much money you have at the end of the month. Do not ignore those steps simply because you think they are not worth the effort. They are all significant when added together and will produce much momentum for you on the road to Financial Freedom.

'... a small leak will sink a great ship... '
**BENJAMIN FRANKLIN**

The **25** *Financial Competence* **purchasing techniques** you learned in Chapter 10 will *literally* save you thousands of dollars each year. Always remember, it is usually the combined effect of the *little* expenses that has the *greatest* impact. Not of the big expenses. Think about it for a minute. How many big expenses do you have? Not many. Yet, you have many little expenses eroding your wealth each and every day. Ignore them at your financial peril. I urge you to apply as many *Financial Competence* purchasing techniques as you possibly can.

Having said that, we are going to concentrate over the next couple of chapters on some of your big expenses. We will target expenses such as your *mortgage* and your *car*. Would you like to significantly reduce your mortgage payment? Would you like to learn how to buy your next car for a minimum of 20% below wholesale? Then read on, because in the next couple of chapters you are going to learn some big *Money Secrets of the Rich* that can save (and even make) you tens of thousands of dollars!

In western nations we are conditioned that *we need to pay more to get more*. That precept may seem logical. In fact it is, for the companies selling you products! It is an assumption that sits at the very foundation of advertising. Robert Cialdini, in his book *Influence, The Psychology of Persuasion*, has called this the 'expensive = good' stereotype, just one of the many 'weapons of influence' advertisers use when marketing their products.

Advertisers 'package' products with all the 'bells and whistles', inflate the prices, and then put 'SALE' tags on them. As normal consumers we are taught to believe that these products are the best because of their high original prices. Then, we are induced to buy them because they are 'on sale'. We often conclude that it is a waste of time to shop around and compare other items to the 'high-quality' sale items. It is too much of a hassle.

I believe that people are also often intimidated by their own lack of knowledge about many products, and consequently allow salespeople and advertisers to act as their experts, their authorities. Unfortunately, ignorance is not bliss. It is expensive.

## REFINANCING YOUR HOME

Since late 1992, home mortgage rates have dropped consistently and dramatically. Today, in 2001, rates are still under 8%. Despite these rates of 6–8% being available for the last five years, figures from the Bureau of Statistics (current at August 2000) show that only 15% of Australian borrowers who would have benefited from a lower interest rate have actually refinanced! Why is this rate so low? Why have the remaining 85% of homeowners who would have benefited from refinancing to a lower rate not done so? (Australia's refinancing rate is even lower than that in the US and UK, where around 34% and 29% of respective borrowers have refinanced in recent years to take advantage of the lower interest rates.)

I believe that many people think it is too *difficult* to refinance. They are afraid of and do not want to pay the accompanying costs. They associate refinancing with starting over on a new loan and thus they baulk at doing it so that they don't 'waste' the years of payments they have already made. Often they have a mental block on how the numbers actually work. Possibly they are also intimidated by the lenders and are afraid to fully investigate the options.

And believe it or not, sometimes people are simply embarrassed to admit that their payments are too high and that they need to either reduce their payments or move to a smaller house. I have even known some families who have told me that they thought it would be easier to just sell their house, rather than to refinance it. The diagnosis – **Level Zero Non-Existent** thinking. The old 'Jam-the-head-in-the-sand-and-hope-the-problem-goes-away' solution.

'Opportunity has power over all things.'
**SOPHOCLES**

The **Automatic Investor** solution is to contact a finance broker or banker (ask a friend who has recently purchased or refinanced a home for a reference) to find out what your monthly payment would be if you refinanced. In most cases, if you purchased your home prior to 1993 you can reduce your mortgage payment 20–30%! The lender can even add the costs of refinancing to the new loan.

If you are worried about 'losing' all the years you have paid in (almost all of which is interest anyway) then investigate a 15- or 20-year mortgage. If your interest rate is 8% or higher, you should be able to convert your existing 25-year loan (at today's low rates) to one of these popular shorter-term loans, and still have a slightly lower monthly payment.

You may also have a fixed interest rate loan that you took out some years ago which has a high interest rate compared with today's rates. The banks typically want to charge you a high penalty if you elect to refinance to a cheaper loan – don't be put off from doing the sums. In the long run it could still be cheaper to refinance now (even with the penalty) and take advantage of loans with financiers who offer lower rates than to stay with the lender you are now using. (The home loan lending market has become so competitive in recent years that you may find any refinance penalty to be entirely negotiable when the lender is faced with losing your loan business if they enforce the penalty.)

And remember to shop around beyond simply a cursory review of the major bank offerings. According to Cannex surveys (current to Dec 2000), none of the major banks had a variable rate home loan in the top 20 products available.

**Bottomline**: If your home interest rate is over 8%, contact a banker or finance broker immediately to investigate refinancing your home. I know of families who have lowered their monthly payments by more than $500! Surely that is worth the 'hassle' of calling? A good rule of thumb is that if you save enough each month to recoup the costs of refinancing within two years or less, then it is a worthwhile deal. Do not be put off by all the hype surrounding recent interest rate rises from investigating your refinancing options.

You cannot afford to sit still when interest rates are low. Avoid the tendency not to investigate beneficial changes to your existing financial circumstances. This tendency to be complacent

'And out of the delusion that life is a battle that may be lost by a false move grows, I have noticed, a great love for regularity. Men fall into the half-alive habit. Seldom does the cobbler take up with the new-fangled way of soling shoes, and seldom does the artisan willingly take up with new methods in his trade. Habit conduces to a certain inertia, and any disturbance of it affects the mind like trouble... It could almost be written down as a formula that when a man begins to think that he has at last found his method he had better begin a most searching examination of himself to see whether some part of his brain has not gone to sleep. There is a subtle danger in a man thinking that he is 'fixed' for life. It indicates that the next jolt of the wheel of progress is going to fling him off.'

**HENRY FORD**

is indicative of living by money habits that are not *Financially Competent (Intelligent and Responsible)*.

## SURF OR PHONE FOR REFINANCING QUOTES

There are an increasing number of lenders, mortgage brokers and quote and referral services available online (also by phone) for the savvy shopper of original home loans, refinancing and home equity loans. In the US, more than 70% of home loans are organised through a broker, and this trend is catching on in Australia. Many web-based lenders, with lower processing overheads, can offer lower rates and fees for loans than traditional lenders.

The majority of sites include a range of services such as calculators, guides to the different available loan products and loan originators, and online applications. Here are some popular ones for you to check out:

- iSAY at www.isay.com.au will find you the best mortgage by comparing over 100 loans and it will even email you later if the new mortgage is bettered by enough to make it worthwhile changing again (iSay *Trigger Point* service). It receives identical commissions from lenders regardless of which mortgage it recommends; callback service if you leave email address on site.

- Mortgage Choice at www.mortgagechoice.com.au has a loan repayment calculator, stamp-duty calculator and deposit planner. You can examine many different loans and apply for loans online; 1800 646 789.

- Home Loans at www.homeloans.com.au has a mortgage calculator, repayment calculator and an extra repayment calculator. You can examine different loans and apply for loans online; 13 38 39.

- eChoice at www.echoice.com.au is an excellent mortgage broker site that offers to find you the best mortgage for your needs. It also has a buyer's guide and calculators; callback service if you leave email address on site.

- Mortgage Store at www.mortgagestore.com.au compares various home loan options, provides an individual needs analysis and independent assessment service; (02) 9460 3233.

- BestBid at www.bestbid.com.au works like an auction site, where lenders bid for your home loan business.
- The Mortgage Bureau at www.tmb.com.au has home loan information, compares all major lenders and has branches throughout Australia; 1800 505 530 or (02) 6550 1055.
- E-LOAN at www.eloan.com.au includes a free subscription service, enables you to compare your current loan, finds the right loan for you and has calculators, information and online applications; 13 30 50.
- Lenders On Line at www.lendersonline.com.au (Telstra.com service) has online home loans (more than 50), mortgage advice, loans consumer news, legal information and services, and loans glossary; 1800 426 022.
- Loans at www.loans.ninemsn.com.au has online tools such as money finder, repayment calculator and home loan simulator. There is information, loan comparisons and online applications (via eChoice).
- MyFinance at www.myfinance.com.au home loan comparisons and general home loan and finance information.
- CANNEX *Pollfax* service provides up-to-date financial (rates) data via automatic fax (*PollFax* on 1902 935 661 for *Mortgages* three-page survey faxed at $0.83 a minute, costing about $2.85); www.cannex.com.au/surveys.
- There are other sites with good calculators and reckoners such as:
  - www.homedirect.com.au/loans/reckoner.html;
  - www.drsref.com.au/finance.html;
  - www.fpa.asn.au/calculators/main.calculator.frame.html.

Most major Sunday newspapers also provide comprehensive guides to the best mortgage rates available. Specific magazines such as *Mortgage Magazine* are also excellent reference sources – check out what is on offer at your local newsagent.

**Warning**: Be careful of applying too quickly for loan approval, even if you are encouraged to do so by the many brokers or lenders (either online or on the phone). You should only make your application once you have shopped around and decided which lender is offering the best deal for you. The reason I caution you here is because (unbeknown to most people), each time you make an application for credit ('accommodation') you receive a notation on your credit report. The more applications you make the more 'marks' you will have possibly working against you on your credit report (particularly if you apply for larger amounts than the lenders are willing to accommodate). This could damage your credit and prejudice your application at an important time. So only complete the application process when you have made your final decision on the loan that is best for you.

The Financial Services Consumer Policy Centre also recommends that you compare all online offerings thoroughly before picking one and making an application. The Australian Consumers Association has issued a checklist for evaluating a mortgage broker:

- Find out which lenders the broker represents.
- Find out what qualifications and experience the broker has.
- Ask for references and to speak to other clients.
- Make sure the broker carries professional indemnity insurance.
- Find out what commissions the broker receives from the lenders.
- Make sure the broker is offering a range of products.
- Make sure you understand what fees and charges are payable on the loans you are offered.
- Ask for the Comparative Lending Rate of different loans (to gauge the long-term costs of the loans).
- Don't rely totally on the broker – make sure you fully understand the products being offered.

You could also check out your own credit file before applying so that you know exactly what the lender will see when processing your application. As we mentioned in Chapter 10, obtain a copy of your own official credit history from Credit Advantage Ltd. This is a free service if you are prepared to have a copy of your file sent to you by mail within ten days, or $16.50

(incl. GST) if you require it within 24 hours. Write to Credit Advantage Public Enquiries, PO Box 964, North Sydney, NSW 2059, or contact them on (02) 9464 6000 or on the net at www.credref.com.au. You must supply your full name, residential address, date of birth and driver's licence details.

---

## CHAPTER 12 ACTION STEPS REVIEW

1.  Practice **Money Step #6 – *Financial Competence (Intelligence and Responsibility)*** by considering refinancing your home at a lower interest rate if your current interest rate is 8% or above. Do the research. Make the effort.

## CHAPTER 13

# Getting the Best Home Loan

'Happy he who like Ulysses has made a great journey,
Or like that man who won the Fleece,
And then came home, full of experience and good sense,
To live the rest of his time among his family.'

JOACHIM DU BELLAY (*Les Regrets*)

In Chapter 12 we discussed the possibility of *refinancing* your home. What if you are purchasing a *new* home? What kind of mortgage should you use? There are three basic types of home loan: the **variable rate loan**, the **fixed rate loan** and the **interest-only loan**. There are also new loans which are hybrids of the three, allowing borrowers to switch from one loan type to the other. Which one of these is best and when and why should you choose it?

Please keep in mind that this chapter looks at loans for your personal residence only. Investment property borrowing is something we will consider more in the context of Chapter 26, though the points made in relation to the **home equity loans** in this chapter are important for that topic.

Regardless of the type of loan you choose there are some features you should make sure you have in any home loan that you choose:

✔ It should allow *additional* repayments to be made at any time (without penalty) which immediately reduce the principal owing.

✔ It should have low or no monthly or ongoing fees.

✔ It should be *daily reducing* whereby payments made come off the principal on the days the payments are made.

✔ It should not have any early payout fees or penalties.

✔ It should not treat the *principal* and *interest* components of payments separately in any way.

## VARIABLE RATE LOANS

This is Australia's most popular style of loan. It is sometimes called a **standard variable loan**. As the name suggests the interest rate can vary over time, depending on market forces. Usually the variable rate is based on Reserve Bank official rates and will not change unless there is an official rate change.

The **variable rate loan** offers the advantage of being very flexible, allowing you to pay off the loan quicker by making additional payments without penalty. If official interest rates fall, your repayments will also come down. The greatest disadvantage is that if interest rates rise, so will your repayments. Many people will recall 1985 when official interest rates peaked at a little over 20%. This type of loan would certainly be a major burden if rates ever return to those levels.

Some financiers allow the loan interest rate to be capped. With a capped loan, an upper limit is set on how high the loan rate can go while no limit is set on how low it can go. A capped loan interest rate is usually higher than a variable rate loan interest rate (you pay for the 'insurance').

Lenders are fond of variable rate loans. Why should they, the lender, bear any of the risk, when they could pass all of the risk onto you, the borrower? By shifting the full responsibility for the normal fluctuations of interest rates (which are essentially just a reflection of inflation) onto the borrower, the bank passes all of the risk on to the borrower as well. Then if inflation takes off, the banks are covered because the borrower pays the higher rate, up to the *cap* on the loan. Your house will be worth more (because of inflation) whether or not you can afford the new, much higher house payment. The lender is not too concerned if you cannot keep up the payments. If they have to foreclose, they will invariably be able to resell the property for at least the amount of your loan. And if they do take a small loss on the loan this is a business expense which they can easily live with. They are more than compensated by profits from other borrowers and by their own efforts to re-lend the money realised from the mortgagee sale (foreclosure) in a new mortgage with new origination fees, etc.

> 'Nay, take my life and all; pardon not that: You take my house when you do take the prop That doth sustain my house; you take my life When you do take the means whereby I live.'
> **WILLIAM SHAKESPEARE**
> *(The Merchant of Venice)*

Always remember, when a financial institution creates a new product (and then heavily markets it), the idea is generally in their best interests, not yours. They are looking for any possible way to profit (from your financial incompetence and/or ignorance). For lenders, variable rate loans are a dream come true. Good profits today, without the risk of losses tomorrow.

A trend developing as a result of heavy competition in the loan market is the *introductory* or *honeymoon rate* loan. These are so named because the customer is offered a low interest rate in the first year or two of the loan, after which the loan reverts to a variable rate loan. When interest rates are, say, 7.8%, it is possible to get an introductory rate for as little as 5.8%.

The advantages of these low *teaser* rates are that they let you get used to making regular mortgage payments and in some cases you can reduce the loan much more quickly if you make higher repayments during the honeymoon period. When the honeymoon period ends though, repayments will increase and you may find your loan contract has penalties if you want to refinance within a certain time period.

Another of the biggest traps in variable rate loans with an introductory rate is there may be hidden (or difficult to calculate) additional ongoing fees and charges after the honeymoon period. In some Australian states, legislation is being introduced whereby the financier must advise you of the loan's 'AAPR' or true interest rate. The AAPR of a loan is a standard calculation which takes into consideration the interest rate and the upfront and ongoing fees over the first seven years of the loan, thereby allowing you to assess the 'true' cost of the loan and compare it to other available loans.

In the case of introductory loans, the AAPR of a 5.8% honeymoon rate can be as high as 7.6%! This may be higher than what you could find by shopping around for the best variable rate from the outset.

## FIXED RATE LOANS

These loans allow you to fix the interest rate for a set period, normally between one and five years. After the set period, most **fixed rate loans** either revert to variable rate loans or allow you to roll them over for another set period at a new fixed interest rate.

Usually a fixed interest rate loan is between 1.5% and 3% higher than a variable rate loan. If you choose a fixed rate loan you have assurance that your repayments will remain the same regardless of how much interest rates *rise* during the set period.

However, you will not be entitled to any reduction in your repayments if interest rates *fall*.

Fixed rate loans can be ideal where your income is also fixed or your budget stretched such that increased payments caused by rises in interest rates would be difficult for you to handle.

Many lenders in Australia are now looking at offering fixed rate loans for longer set periods along the lines of mainstream home financing products available in the US (where 15- and 30-year fixed rate loans are the norm). I have some students who have received 10, 15 and 20-year competitive fixed rate loans in Australia for investment properties (more on this in Chapter 26). So if this appeals to you, make sure you shop around. And remember, if you don't ask, you don't get.

## INTEREST-ONLY LOANS

For this type of loan you do not make any *principal* repayments. You only pay the *interest* on the loan. The advantage of this loan is that your regular payments are lower because you are not repaying the principal. **Interest-only loans** are generally used for short-term borrowing or property investment and are not a popular way to purchase a home for the long term. If you are only paying the interest you are of course not reducing the principal and therefore also not reducing the repayments.

## HYBRID LOANS

There are a number of different alternatives to the above basic loans and many more coming on the market, with financiers eager to create new ways to extract as many dollars from the consumer as possible.

The main types of hybrid loans are as follows:

- **Split (or combination) loans** – this is where you can divide your loan into two parts, fixed and variable. You are effectively having an each way bet, hedging yourself against rises or falls in interest rates. This type of loan can provide a blend of interest rate, security and repayment flexibility.

- **Mortgage-offset (or all-in-one) loans** – some financiers let you offset your mortgage with the account you use for personal banking transactions. This means you can deposit all your wages/salary or other income in one account to more dramatically reduce your mortgage and then draw-back from the credit balance to pay your expenses from that account. With 100% mortgage-offset, each dollar deposited into the account, for as long as it is offset against the loan balance, saves you interest. If used properly this type of facility also has the added benefit of causing you to spend less money each month because you are less inclined to unnecessarily draw-back money 'out of the equity in your home' to spend elsewhere.

    However, the potential advantages of this type of facility are, for some people, not properly utilised. The temptation to re-spend or draw down the 'equity' in the home via the ready and easy access to the line of credit can become all too strong.

    While these types of facilities can offer great benefits, they are designed in such a way that if you fall for temptation (by continually tapping the easily available equity money in your home), you may quite possibly *never* pay off your loan.

Make sure that if you use one of these mortgage-offset facilities that you take advantage of all the benefits and avoid falling victim to the temptations. Remember that the test of true *Financial Competence (Intelligence and Responsibility)* is to keep the lender's rules working in your favour so that you come out on top.

**Bottomline:** Be *Financially Competent (Intelligent and Responsible)*! Research and understand the types of loans available and do not agree to a particular loan without first completing your due diligence. Shop around. Talk to a minimum of five mortgage brokers, bankers or non-bank mortgage originators. The home lending business has become very competitive, but you will not receive the full benefits of this increased competition if you do not ask questions and make the lenders compete for your loan business. If you have Internet access, try the listed lenders, brokers and information/software sources suggested at the end of Chapter 12.

Take care to know your rights. The Consumer Credit Code requires credit providers to tell you your rights and obligations under any credit arrangement. They are required by law to truthfully disclose all relevant information about your arrangement in a written contract, including interest rates, fees, commissions and other information which in the past was often hidden. If they fail to do this, the law provides for significant penalties.

At the end of this chapter we list a few more financiers who offer a range of products, although the list could be almost endless! So do your research and happy borrowing.

## HOME-EQUITY LOANS

People often ask me my opinion of **home-equity loans**. These loans are typically a line of credit, much like an overdraft, secured by your home. They became extremely popular during the 1990s. You can redraw against the line of credit up to the original amount borrowed. Many people use them to pay off existing consumer debt, buy 'luxuries', pay for holidays, or to invest. However, it has been my experience that most people do not fully grasp the 'double-edged sword' effect this type of financing creates.

Originally, the home-equity loan was created for people to borrow money to improve their home. This in turn would (in theory) increase the value of the home, thus providing the lender with greater security, and the borrower with greater equity. Today, this original practice has become severely distorted.

Home-equity lines of credit have been widely advertised as an easy way to get money at a relatively low cost (to consume or pay off other debt). They are promoted as the 'loan for all purposes'. The main selling points are the lower interest rates (generally lower than unsecured personal and investment loans) and the fact that you can 'benefit from releasing' the increasing equity in your own home.

Because these loans are secured by the equity in your home, they are very easy loans to obtain, and lenders know that the last loans or debts homeowners will default on are the ones tied to their homes. If the borrower does default, the lender has the home as collateral. The terms for these loans are almost as favourable as those for a standard variable rate loan. Home-equity loans are themselves usually variable rate loans that are set up in much the same way as the standard variable rate home loan.

---

## The selling points of home-equity loans

1. Low interest rates.
2. Flexible payment schedules.
3. Low establishment costs.
4. Easy qualifying. Often your home equity and proof of satisfactory income is enough.
5. Money available now (all you need is equity).
6. No pre-payment penalties.
7. Flexibility. Money is available via a line of credit or a straight loan.

Although home-equity type loans are a very attractive and easy source of money, they should be given very serious thought. The consequences of default are much more serious than those associated with default on an unsecured loan (such as a credit card). With a home-equity loan, if you fail to pay, you lose your home. With an unsecured loan, you simply face debt-collection action. For the disciplined and competent **Level Five Active Investor**, the home-equity loan can be a possible source of low-risk investment leverage. If proper money habits are not followed however, the result of this ready access to extra leverage, secured by your home, can be catastrophic.

**If you use a home-equity loan to consolidate and pay off other debt you could just end up making your financial situation even worse!**

Why do I say that? After all, wouldn't it be better to pay off high-interest, non-deductible debt with a low interest loan? Logically, yes. In the real world, no. Here is why. Lets say that you have $20,000 in credit card and personal consumer debt (*doodads*) and the monthly payments are really starting to add up but you would like to go shopping for Christmas presents.

By taking out an additional loan on your home, you could 'consolidate' your bills into one new low payment and (maybe) even have some cash left over to go shopping. Sounds great, doesn't it? Here you are behind the proverbial 'eight-ball' in debt and now the equity in your house can come to the rescue and save you. The diagnosis is however, that if you want to use the equity in your house to pay off bills, then you are probably financially doomed.

The reality is you will still have your credit cards and the ability to run up your balances (to the limit) all over again. My observations have demonstrated to me time after time that if you pay off your credit cards with a home-equity loan, and retain the cards, you are in trouble. Invariably you will revert to using the credit cards all over again.

## The drawbacks of home-equity loans

1. Mortgage is placed on your home.
2. Ease of availability. These loans are so easy to get you may overlook the potential dangers.
3. Easy qualifying. All the lender wants is your equity.
4. If you cannot pay, the lender can foreclose. They have very little risk.
5. Restriction of your credit. Home-equity lines of credit are generally reported to credit reporting agencies and will appear on your credit statement whether or not you have accessed the money.
6. Scams. There are a lot of very dubious loan products in the market. Often lenders will charge exorbitant interest rates or they will add thousands of dollars in fees onto the loan.
7. Foreclosure on the collateral – your home (if you default).

A year or two later, most people who have used a home-equity loan to pay off debt are in a far worse position than when they started. Not only do they have an additional debt on their house but now the credit cards are maxed-out again. The loan they initiated to save themselves has facilitated their sliding into worse levels of debt.

**Be realistic and honest. If poor money habits have put you in the situation where you think you need a home-equity loan to pay off debt, what is going to change, once you use the home-equity loan, to prevent you from going further into debt as a result?**

### NEVER USE A HOME-EQUITY LOAN FOR...

1. **Holidays.** What sense does it make to be still paying for a holiday five to 15 years after it occurred?
2. **Luxuries.** Never pay for a pool or spa-bath (highly depreciative improvements), boat, furniture or other luxury

equipment with the equity in your home.

3. **Debt consolidation.** As discussed, it is a rare person who has the discipline not to use their credit cards again. If you are considering debt consolidation, I strongly recommend that you cut up and then permanently cancel the credit cards. If you are not willing to (permanently) cancel your credit cards then you should *never* take out a home-equity loan.

4. **Investments in shares, bonds, etc.** No-one can reliably predict the future. There is no such thing as a sure investment. Do you really want to gamble your home on such speculation? Many people have placed this bet and lost big time. Examples: Gold in the mid-1980s was $US800 an ounce and seemed to have nowhere to go but up; the share market in September of 1987 was invincible (you were told to bet the ranch, or your house); the late 1990s dotcom share boom through to March 2000 where *everyone* was making money on IPOs and tech stocks (until the savage April correction where many Level Three Passive Investors lost 20–75% of their money). **Do not risk your home and your family's stability on these types of investments.**

5. **Loans to friends or family.** No matter how good the story or business opportunity sounds, never borrow money on your house to lend to someone else. If the borrower is coming to you it probably means everybody else has already said no. Do not lend the money and ruin the relationship. Besides, you need your money for your own future and they *will* manage without it. Keep it. If you still want to lend to friends or family, I recommend you look at the loan as a gift, not as a loan. Do not ever bank on getting the money back because many times you will not.

> 'It is better to give than to lend, and it costs about the same.'
> **SIR PHILLIP GIBBS**

6. **Income taxes.** This is an expense that should already have been paid. Negotiate a payment plan directly with the ATO. A home-equity loan should not be a bail-out tool unless your actual life *depends on it.*

7. **Everyday expenses.** These expenses should never be paid for via a home-equity loan. If you cannot afford it, you do not need it. Reduce your expenses instead.

**Exceptions:**
- If you have really and truly changed; *and*
- You have set up your *Automatic Money System*; *and*
- You are following all of **The 7 Money Steps of the Rich**; *and*
- You have (permanently) closed your non–emergency-use carry-over balance credit card accounts (by writing to the companies); *then and only then*
- Possibly consider the shortest-term debt-consolidation loan available.

**Condition:** Do not lower your total monthly debt payment.

**Translation:** If you are now paying $500 a month in consumer debt, continue to pay a minimum of $500 a month on your home-equity loan. If you are not willing to do that, again you are just kidding yourself. **Never ever use debt consolidation loans for the purpose of lowering your payments**. Use them to lower the interest rates and pay off the debts faster, not prolong them. Utilise the loan to beat the banks at their own game.

> 'Money is in some respects like fire – it is a very excellent servant but a terrible master. When you have it mastering you, when interest is constantly piling up against you, it will keep you down in the worst kind of slavery.'
>
> **P.T. BARNUM**

**Consumer debt will burn you alive if you let it. Do not fuel the consumer debt fire with a home-equity loan.**

## ONLY CONSIDER USING A HOME-EQUITY LOAN FOR...

1. **Home improvements that will truly add resale value to your home.** Improvements such as badly needed bathroom and kitchen renovations, carports or garages, basic landscaping or vital maintenance work. In such cases the home-equity loan is undoubtedly your cheapest form

of funding, but make sure you increase your overall payments to offset your larger debt balance and pay it off sooner rather than later.

2. **Investment in a money-making business or other cash-positive form of investment.** This could be your existing successful business or another genuine business opportunity. Prior to taking out the loan, apply the *Money Secrets of the Rich* that you have learned in this book to the business in the same way you are applying them to your life. Check the numbers out thoroughly. Do not be emotional. Stick to the bottom line. Never borrow money on your home to invest in an *unproven* business. And remember: Never, never borrow money on your home to 'invest' in a friend's or relative's business! If you do, the money is likely to be gone forever!

> 'Drown thyself not to save a drowning man.'
> **ENGLISH PROVERB**

3. **Financing a car.** If you must buy a car and you need to finance it (for no more than three years), you could use a home-equity loan to finance the car so long as you do not break the rules previously discussed.

4. **Debt Consolidation.** Only use a home-equity loan for debt consolidation in the strict circumstances described above. If you are not prepared to get rid of the credit cards, maintain your total monthly payments and adopt the other habits of the financially successful, do not do use a home-equity loan for debt consolidation.

Having satisfied all the *Financially Competent (Intelligent and Responsible)* criteria for considering taking out a home-equity loan, then make sure you call or surf for quotes. See the list of lenders, brokers and information/software sources near the end of Chapter 12. E-LOAN, for example, provides broking online for home-equity loans at www.eloan.com.au or on 13 30 50.

## MORTGAGE INSURANCE

Mortgage insurance is designed to offer the lender protection against financial loss if a borrower defaults on mortgage payments. Most lenders require this insurance on all new loans with less than 20% deposit.

Mortgage insurance is normally a one-off upfront payment. Remember, it is designed to protect the lender in the case of default, not you. It is costly and should be avoided wherever possible.

## FIRST HOME BUYERS

If you are a first home buyer, yet to undertake what will likely be the largest financial commitment of your life, it is well worth fully researching all the options available to you. The First Home Owner Grant Scheme is a Commonwealth–State government initiative consisting of a $7,000 one-off grant. To quote from the NSW Office of State Revenue website (www.osr.nsw.gov.au), the scheme is 'designed to assist first home owners in offsetting the impact of the GST on the purchase or building of their first home.' This grant is available in every state and territory of Australia.

In addition to the grant, some states have enacted further assistance schemes for first home buyers. In NSW, for example, there is the First Home Plus Scheme which 'provides exemptions and concessions on transfer (stamp duty) and mortgage duty.' For a house in a metropolitan area, the first $200,000 of the purchase price would be entirely stamp duty-free and then discounted on a sliding scale up to $300,000. Check out what is on offer in your state or territory.

## SURFING OR PHONING FOR QUOTES

For further information on home loans refer to the various online calculators and referral services listed in Chapter 12. Some of the major lending institutions' websites and information phone lines also contain useful information:
- ANZ at www.anz.com or 1800 035 500;
- Citibank at www.citibank.com.au or 13 35 35;
- Colonial at www.colonial.com.au or 13 18 18;
- Commonwealth at www.commbank.com.au or 13 22 24;
- NAB at www.national.com.au or 13 13 12;
- St. George at www.stgeorge.com.au or 13 35 55;
- Westpac at www.westpac.com.au or 13 19 00.

As mentioned in Chapter 12, some of the best sites for online mortgage brokers are:

- www.isay.com.au or callback service if you leave email address;
- www.echoice.com.au or callback service if you leave email address;
- www.eloan.com.au or 13 30 50;
- www.mortgagechoice.com.au or 1800 646 789;
- www.lendersonline.com.au; 1800 426 022;
- www.bestbid.com.au.

And don't forget your state or territory Treasury Office if you are a first home buyer:

- ACT at www.revenue.act.gov.au or (02) 6207 0029;
- NT at www.nt.gov.au or (08) 8999 7949;
- NSW at www.osr.nsw.gov.au or (02) 9685 2187; 1300 130 624;
- Vic at www.sro.vic.gov.au or 132 161;
- QLD at www.osr.qld.gov.au or (07) 3404 3956;
- SA at www.treasury.sa.gov.au or (08) 8226 3750;
- Tas at www.tres.tas.gov.au or (03) 6233 3465;
- WA at www.wa.gov.au or (08) 9262 1100.

---

**Warning:** Heed the warning from the previous chapter about applying too quickly for loan approval, even if you are encouraged to do so by the many brokers or lenders (either online or on the phone). Remember what we said about possibly 'damaging' your credit report by making multiple applications for loan 'accommodation'. So only complete the application process when you have made your final decision. Get a copy of your credit report to help you be fully informed about where you stand prior to making an application, from www.credref.com.au.

## CHAPTER 13 ACTION STEPS REVIEW

1. Practice **Money Step #6 – *Financial Competence (Intelligence and Responsibility)*** when considering a home loan. Determine your requirements and then research the available products for the one that best suits your needs.
2. Get quotes from at least five lenders prior to making a decision.
3. Only use a **home-equity loan** if it makes realistic financial sense in relation to your present financial habits.
4. Avoid mortgage insurance whenever possible and/or check out the terms of your existing mortgage insurance: if it is more than a one-off payment and you are eligible to do so, cancel it.
5. Check out the mortgage choices you have available to you via the Internet online information services and mortgage brokers.

## CHAPTER 14

# Buying your next car for a 20–50% discount

*'Any color – so long as it's black.'*

HENRY FORD

(on the choice of colour for the Model T Ford)

Several years ago I used to think it was 'cool' to purchase a *new* car. There's that invigorating 'new car smell'. The status, the prestige, the power! It sure feels great driving off the lot in a 'brand new' car.

Then the painful reality of the purchase sets in. The *payments* (for five years) and the *depreciation* take the shine off the purchase (that brand new car is worth 20% less the moment it leaves the dealer's yard).

Today, I cannot think of any good financial reason for anyone to justify buying a new car. For most people it is the worst possible investment they could ever make. And yet, it is an 'investment' that most people do make (or aspire to make).

As a general rule, the more expensive the car, the more you will overpay. The dealers consider that if you can afford to spend $30,000–40,000 on a car, you won't miss another $2,000 tacked on for their profit margin! And they are right. Many people are actually embarrassed to quibble over the price of an expensive car. They believe that it is beneath them to suggest that a price is too high, or even to question it. Remember the old saying: 'If you have to ask the price, you can't afford it!'

Salespeople in the luxury car business often exploit this attitude (insecurity) to intimidate their customers. My advice is to *never* worry about offending the salesperson or about what they might think of you. Let's get this in perspective. You are buying a car, not asking for a character reference for membership of the local country club.

So what *should* you do? For a start, get out of the showroom! There is no worthwhile benefit to buying a brand new car. You will overpay at least 20% for the 'privilege'.

Do what so *many* rich people do: buy a late-model used car with a few thousand kilometres on the dial. These days you can easily buy a car that is two years old that is still under full new car warranty. If you absolutely have to have the 'new car smell', go to the carwash and have them *detail* your car. You can actually have the car impregnated with synthetic new car scent if you want to! I hear Kmart carries the full spray-can range!

What would happen if you bought a used car? For a start, you would have several thousand dollars left in your pocket. What about the emotional consequences? Will it reduce your standard of living if you buy a slightly used car? Will your friends and neighbours laugh at you? Will you get fired from your job? Will your spouse leave you? Will your dog bite you more often? Will your hair fall out faster? The answer is a resounding NO!

If you would like some added inspiration on the advantages of buying a used car instead of a brand new car then consult *The Millionaire Next Door* by Thomas J. Stanley and William D. Danko. The authors conclude after 20 years of extensive research that the 'typical' millionaire pays under US$25,000 for a car and that 37% of millionaires buy their cars used.

Stanley and Danko also discovered that, although they may drive nice cars, 'typical millionaires' usually spends less than 1% of their net worth on a motor vehicle as compared to non-millionaires who routinely spend a minimum of 30% of their net worth on a car purchase.

I understand the feeling of pride that accompanies the purchase of a brand new car, along with the 'new car smell'. That feeling wears off very quickly... but those high payments sure don't. Keep in mind that a car is just a hunk of metal and plastic on rubber wheels. I have owned several expensive luxury and sports cars and they were all very expensive lessons. The money I spent for those cars is all gone, and so are the cars. I don't want the cars back, but I would love the money lining my pockets again.

## BUYING A USED CAR

Today there are more low-mileage, high-quality used cars available than ever before. The major reason for this? The Australian car industry has been opened up to the world with reduced tariffs on new cars and at the same time the finance industry has been deregulated. And with the removal of sales tax (and introduction of 10% GST instead), new car prices have moved even lower. As new car prices continue to fall and levels of consumer credit rise, new cars will be purchased at an unprecedented level. The more new cars there are sold, the more competitive and available the deals become in the *used* car market.

By purchasing a used car you can instantly reduce the original sticker price of the car by 20–30%. And since the dealers need to sell these vehicles to make room for even more trade-ins, the discounts can be even bigger.

A popular way to buy a used car is through the classified ads in the weekend newspapers or weekly publications such as the *Trading Post*. The Internet is also becoming very popular for buying and selling used cars privately. I consider the used car market a *buyer's* market, so never believe you have to pay the prices initially suggested by sellers. Negotiate! If they won't, there are plenty of other sellers around. Check out Internet sites like:

* www.drive.com.au (used cars, valuations, car classifieds);
* www.motorama.com.au (used car valuations, one-stop shopping);

- www.carnet.com.au (used car specials, free classifieds and Red Book search function); 136 134;
- www.webtrader.com.au (buying guide for all goods including used cars);
- www.tradingpost.com.au (classifieds for all goods including used cars can be used as a buying guide);
- www.carpoint.com.au (ninemsn.com.au site with used car sales, articles and general information);
- www.motomarket.com.au (tips and information on buying used cars);
- www.myfinance.com.au (links to Auto Group Ltd ex-fleet pre-auction applications www.auto-group.com.au);
- www.eauto.com.au;
- www.carsales.com.au;
- www.sold.com.au;
- www.gofish.com.au;
- www.autobytel.com.au (buying guide and service);
- www.choice.com.au (CHOICEOnline site that provides consumer articles for buying a used car).

**Warning:** When visiting a website with the intention of buying a used car, do not be lured by the slick marketing on the site into buying a new car instead. According to a recent survey conducted by carsales.com.au, 17% of people who visited their site with the serious intention of buying a used car, ended up buying a new one. Sort out your intentions clearly before going online, in the same way as you would before attending a dealership.

While there can be disadvantages to buying a used car privately, such as no statutory warranty and no guarantee of title to the car, the government provides safeguards to protect the consumer. For example, in some states you have the peace of mind of a REVS check, which for around $10 allows you to search a government database to determine whether the car is encumbered and therefore if you will receive legal title when you buy it:

- For NSW, ACT, NT, WA you can telephone REVS on 1800 424 988 or (02) 9600 0022.
- Other states have VSR (Vehicle Security Register) on (03) 9348 1222 for Vic, (07) 3246 1599 for Qld, 13 10 84 for SA and (03) 6233 5201 for Tas.

Your state motoring organisation can also inspect the used car you want to purchase for a fee of around $90. Contact them as follows:
- NSW (NRMA) on 13 21 32 or www.nrma.com.au;
- Vic (RACV) on 13 19 55 or www.racv.com.au;
- Qld (RACQ) on 12 19 55 or www.racq.com.au;
- SA (RAA) on (08) 8202 4610;
- WA (RACWA) on (08) 9421 4444;
- Tas (RACT) on (03) 6232 6300;
- NT (AANT) on (08) 8981 3837.

Rental agencies are another great source of used cars. Many people reject this idea by immediately thinking of how they treated the last rental car they rented. Dad played Indy 500 race-car driver, the dog got sick in the back, etc. Sure there are horror stories that accompany rental cars, but most people drive them somewhat respectfully. Moreover, most rental agencies have their own service departments that keep their cars well maintained. Because of this service record, a used rental car is often one of the best-condition used vehicles you can buy.

Most large rental agencies have a facility through which they sell their rental cars. These cars seldom have more than 40,000 kilometres on the speedometer and invariably come with a new car warranty still in force. Always ask your mechanic to check the car first before you buy it. Hertz, Budget and Avis can inform you of what stock is available. Before you buy, I recommend you rent the car for a weekend. It is a great way to fully test-drive a car you will have to live with for many years to come.

I am now going to teach you how to buy a car for 20–40% below wholesale! To do this you need to deal in cash. Follow the plan and your next car can be a 'hot' car for cents on the dollar!

## BUYING A CAR AT AUCTION

Vehicle auctions are the best way available to buy cars at or well below their wholesale prices. Auctions are usually organised by private auction houses on behalf of individuals, government departments, finance companies (usually repossessions), company liquidators, car franchises and larger public companies.

Many people are afraid to buy at auctions because of a perception that auctions deal in suspect property. Auction houses are, however, usually responsible for ensuring that no monies are owing and that no other parties can claim financial interests in the vehicles they sell. Many provide express facilities on-site (REVS hotlines) for checking the encumbrances on the vehicles. The mechanical state of the cars may be harder to reliably gauge without the assistance of your mechanic or the NRMA/RACQ, etc. I strongly recommend that you always get an inspection and written report done on any car you are interested in, prior to bidding. I must say though that I feel a lot safer at an auction with *my* mechanic, than at a used car dealership with the *dealer's* mechanic.

Auctions are where most used car dealers go to stock their inventories. Do not be intimidated by this fact. If you buy a car for $50–250 more than a dealer is prepared to pay, then you just got the car deal of a lifetime. Remember, when the dealer is buying they are expecting to add at least 20% mark-up on resale to consumers like you.

Auctions take place all over the country and the opportunities can be incredible. Many of my students buy cars for 10–50% below wholesale costs. In fact, at the seminars I conduct, there is usually always at least one person (and often many more) who has bought, either for personal use or resale, a car at an auction. I once had one student who bought a two year-old van with around 30,000 kilometres on the clock, in perfect condition, for $750!

## WHOLESALE AUCTION SOURCES

Great buys can be found at auctions for all sorts of merchandise. At most auctions there are usually no minimum or predetermined reserve prices for the items on sale. This means that if the competition is thin you can really clean up. Over the years I have acquired a tremendous amount of property at auctions, both personal and real estate. The easiest places to find out about auctions are the classified ads. Look under the headings 'Auctions' and 'Autos'. Auctions can also be found through many other sources (often more lucrative). Contact these organisations or search these locations to see what they have for sale, or if they have any upcoming auctions:

- Auction houses (check out the Yellow Pages, newspaper advertisements and the Internet);
- Classified advertisements (particularly weekend newspapers);
- Australian Customs (particularly for seized goods);
- Finance companies (repossessions);
- Local council/municipal departments (try your local newspapers);
- New car franchises (selling ex-demonstrators and 'rep' cars);
- Public companies (such as Telstra, banks);
- Rental companies (large car fleets usually only retaining latest models);
- State and Federal government departments (cars usually less than 40,000 kilometres or two years old);
- Unclaimed property (e.g., railways).

You will find that there are many sources for auctions. Most government departments can be located by looking under the 'Government' section of the Yellow Pages directory. In addition to cars, you can literally buy anything, from jewellery to aeroplanes, boats and houses to computers. If you can name it, then it is sold at auctions. Usually for between 10–60 cents on the dollar.

After you have located the auction, the next step is to do what is called *market research*. Study the classifieds in your local newspapers and the *Trading Post*. This will give you a 'feel' for what the low retail/high wholesale market price is in your area for the vehicle in question. The next step is to get a copy of the Red Book (see www.redbook.com.au or www.carnet.com.au) or Glass's Guide (see www.glasscar.com.au). These publications show both mean retail and mean wholesale prices for all makes and models of vehicle. These are established values as set by actual car sales to, and by, car dealers. Glass's Guide also has Cartalk, an advice and pricing service on 1902 212 574, but this phone service charges around $7.75 a minute.

Let these publications serve as 'value' guidelines going into an auction. Keep in mind that your objective is to always buy well below wholesale. Be patient, there are always phenomenal deals just waiting for you.

Each auction you attend will be a little different. Always check by phone, the week before, to find out the 'rules to the game'. How much deposit is required? (usually 10% or $500 at the fall of the hammer). Is it an all-cash sale? Is financing available? How long do you have to bring in the balance of the cash? When do you get possession? Remember to call your insurer as soon as you win the bid. As auction cars are generally not covered by statutory warranties and generally you cannot test-drive them, you must always have the cars checked by a qualified mechanic prior to bidding.

If you are worried that the dealers have too much of an advantage, consider this: it is *you* who has the advantage. Your purchase is the *final* sale. The dealers are just the middle-people. You can pay just a little above a dealer and get the buy of a lifetime. The dealers cannot. They have resale margins to consider. Remember to bid based on the wholesale price guide, not retail.

Only buy a car at auction if you can get it for at least 20–30% below the wholesale value. Any more than that and you are over-paying. Again, be patient, there is always another auction around the corner. Be prepared to walk away from any auction without a car if the deal is not truly wholesale. This is the discipline of the *Financially Competent (Intelligent and Responsible)* person.

## EIGHT STRATEGIES FOR AUCTION SUCCESS

1. **No emotions.** Many people have a tendency to get very excited at auctions. They want to be the winner. They want that car. It's their 'dream' car. They decide to bid a little higher, then a little higher. Before they know it, they just paid retail, in cash, at a wholesale auction. Do not get

emotional. There will always be another car.

2. **Take a mechanic to the auction to preview the car.**
It might cost you $50 an hour, but it is money well spent.
Go to the auction early and decide which cars you are
interested in ahead of time. Have the mechanic meet you
there. Do not argue with him, he's the expert. You are
paying him for his advice. Follow it. If he says no, it's no.
Go to the next car.

3. **Never pay more than 70–80% of wholesale value.**

4. **Never be the person who starts the bidding.** The
only bid you want to make is the winning bid. Every bid
you make moves the price up. Be patient and disciplined.

5. **Write down your parameters and know your top
bid before the auction begins.** Top investors always
determine how high they will bid before the bidding starts.
If the price goes too high they drop out. I have seen several
people violate how much they said they would pay, before
the auction. Don't do it! Decide your top-dollar bid and
stick to it.

6. **Do not be intimidated by the auctioneer.** Some
auction houses will try to persuade you to bid more than
you want to. Don't fall for that. Also, even today, some
auctions illegally 'run up' the bid. Don't get sucked in,
remember the rules. Be smart.

7. **Know the rules of the auction before it starts.** Get
all the auction information prior to the start. This should
eliminate unwanted surprises.

8. **It's OK not to win.** If you do not win a bid, that means
you did not overpay. Remember, there is always another
auction right around the corner.

## EXTRA INCOME

A great money-making strategy is to re-sell the car you just
bought. Put an ad for just below average retail in the *Trading Post*,
Sunday newspaper or on one of the popular Internet car sales
sites. If someone bites, you just made a quick couple of thousand
dollars. If they don't, you still have the car you wanted. The
lesson is, why not *always* have your car for sale? If you like the

idea of auctions to buy your own car, why not turn it into a part-time business. I have several students who have done just that. If you have done it once you can do it again, better!

## NINE STRATEGIES FOR BUYING A NEW CAR

If you still insist on buying a new car rather than a used one, make sure to follow these nine strategies:

1. **Never buy a car the first time you see it.** You will be far too emotionally motivated on this first occasion and will almost always overpay. The car is not going anywhere. They will give you the same deal next week. So leave. Plan your strategy and come back ready to negotiate. And stick to your guns.

2. **Don't get sucked into the 'We can only do this deal today.'** If they tell you that, they are full of you know what.

3. **Contact a service to help you.** There are several:
   - Car Search Motor Vehicle Brokers, which can source cars based on your specifications, on 1300 650 890 or at www.car-search.com.au;
   - National Car Search brokers source and negotiate deals, financing and insurance on (02) 9456 5500 or at www.carsearch.com.au;
   - Motomarket has a comprehensive website which provides names of dealers in your area and loads of interesting information at www.motomarket.com.au;
   - MyFinance brokers at www.myfinance.com.au source and negotiate deals, financing and insurance.
     Most of the websites listed earlier in this chapter for buying a used car also provide new car buying services including:
     - www.drive.com.au;
     - www.motorama.com.au;
     - www.carnet.com.au; 136 134;
     - www.autobytel.com.au; carpoint.com.au; carsales.com.au.

4. **Demand the price** *in writing* **on the dealer's stationery.** This lets them know two things: 1) You are going to 'shop the price'; and 2) that they cannot take

advantage of you. This will encourage them to give you
their best price right out of the barrel.

5. **Dealers often make more profit from the options
   than the car.** The last new car I bought was a sport utility
   vehicle way back in 1992. I negotiated and ordered the car
   without all the options from the dealer. My savings were
   substantial: dealer price for stereo system $1,900; my price
   $450; dealer price for electronic sunroof $2,000; my price
   $860; dealer price for optional body-moulding and pin-
   stripes $1,200; my price $300. A total saving of $3,490 by
   adding the options myself in the after-market. That's more
   money than the dealer made from the entire car sale.
   Lesson: it is usually much more cost-effective to buy
   options in the after-market, not from the dealer.

6. **Credit life insurance.** This is a phenomenal rip-off. Never
   buy it on anything. If you do, you are paying 500–800%
   more than if you had bought a term life insurance policy
   for the same purpose. On a car, this option can add between
   6 and 10% to your payment. Never do it. Never!

7. **Extended warranty from the dealer.** Extended
   warranties on cars can be a good idea. However, did you
   know that you don't have to accept the extended
   warranties the dealers want you to buy? The dealers make a
   great commission when they sell you *their* product. As for
   insurance, you should always shop around for the best deal,
   and make sure you read the fine print. Some extended
   warranties are far too restrictive, particularly when it comes
   to the types of repairs covered, the level of servicing
   required and who can carry out the services.

8. **Financing.** Before you agree to the financing the dealer
   offers, check in advance with your local finance broker,
   credit union or bank. They can almost always beat the
   dealer's standard rate. The main reason: finance companies
   pay car dealers a commission for each deal. They then have
   to charge the customer a higher loan rate to cover these costs.

   Go online where lower transaction costs tend to allow
   lenders, such as those in Chapter 12, to offer lower interest
   rates and more favourable terms on car loans. Such

financiers/ brokers (e.g. www.eauto.com.au) will often pre-approve a loan application before you go shopping for the car, allowing you the extra bargaining power that comes with having finance ready to do the deal on the spot.

9. **Negotiate a *cash price*.** Always negotiate for the lowest *cash* price from the start. *Always* settle on the price *before* you let a dealer think you need to finance the purchase. If you don't, they will invariably try to focus on the 'monthly payment'. After all, there's no difference if you finance for four years or five years, right? Wrong! Before you know it, you will have overpaid, and you will be stuck with those 'low monthly payments' for many years to come.

Remember, I really don't think you should *ever* buy a new car. But, if you must, follow my strategies and you will still save a lot of money.

## FINANCE FOR YOUR CAR

If you must finance you car purchase, it is wise to understand the different types of credit available. This information is very similar to what you learned earlier for refinancing your home. There are three main ways to finance your car purchase.

### LEASING

Leasing is mainly used for business purposes and in most cases for new or late-model cars. There are two types of leases:

1. Finance leases – monthly payments are made to a finance company and equity is built up in the car. The term is usually for three to five years with a 'residual' payment at the end between 30 and 50% of the original price. The financier retains legal title throughout the lease, and after the final lease and residual payments are made, title to the car is transferred to the lessee. The lessee is responsible for insurance, registration and maintenance of the car.

2. Operating leases – monthly payments are made as with the finance lease, but no equity is built up in the car. Usually the financier is responsible for insuring, registering and maintaining the car.

For business purposes, monthly payments are tax-deductible. If you decide to lease your vehicle for business purposes make sure to first shop around for the best rates. Start with www.bankchoice.com.au for up-to-date comparisons of the best car lease products, or www.auto-group.com.au (Auto Group Ltd car site with information about car leases, a finance calculator; glossary of terms, and online applications for two finance providers).

## HIRE PURCHASE

Hire purchase is popular with consumers and commonly available from finance companies and banks. Car dealers sell hire purchase financing and receive commissions from the financier. With hire purchase the purchaser retains ownership of the car although the financier may take a lien over it. Monthly payments are made over three or five years and usually the loan is fully paid out by the end of the period. For business, only the interest portion of the hire purchase is tax-deductible although the car can also be depreciated for tax purposes.

National Car Search brokers financing deals on (02) 9456 5500 or at www.carsearch.com.au (a useful site for comparing the various finance options available to the car buyer).

## PERSONAL LOANS

A personal loan is usually more expensive than leasing or hire purchase and is arranged by your bank or credit union. Monthly repayments are made and the loan is paid off in up to five years. The car is not generally used as security.

The important issues with regard to a personal loan are the interest rate and the term of the loan. As with all finance products, it pays to shop around. Don't just take the first finance deal offered to you. Obtain at least three quotes and you could reduce your monthly payments by up to 30%!

Financiers are great at confusing people. They may quote you a low interest rate but charge extra fees for brokerage and therefore make your monthly payments higher than the interest rate would have first indicated. They may extend the period of the loan so that the monthly payments *appear* lower. On a lease, they may raise the residual value to *actually* make the monthly payment lower, but the kicker is in the much bigger payout required at the end of the lease.

For a comparison of rates or for online calculators, have a look at:

- www.lendersonline.com.au;
- www.carpoint.com.au (finance calculator information);
- www.eauto.com.au (has details about car loans and a loan calculator);
- National Car Search brokers financing and insurance deals on (02) 9456 5500 or at www.carsearch.com.au;
- MyFinance brokers financing and insurance deals at www.myfinance.com.au.

There is a growing trend in Australia for new car manufacturers to offer consumer leasing. This practice is commonplace in the US. This type of lease is really nothing more than a long-term rental. If you take up a lease with the manufacturer you are merely deluding yourself. You are in reality just paying rent on somebody else's car.

From my experience in the US, the selling points of leasing from the manufacturer are that: monthly payments are less because you do not retain equity; the deposit is less (if not nil); you can upgrade cars more often; sometimes there is a guaranteed future value; and, if used for business, the lease (rental) payments are tax-deductible.

In comparison to leasing from the manufacturer though, the advantages of *buying* a quality *used* car are that: it will be much cheaper than leasing one; lease payments never stop while loan payments are usually completed in three to five years; and there are no charges for excessive wear and tear which can occur with a leased vehicle. Of course, if you must finance your car purchase, buying a used car (with a loan rather than on a lease) allows you to buy better, cheaper and to shop around.

On your next car purchase try this: Buy a nice used car, one that you can afford in no more than 36 (monthly) payments. If the car requires more than 36 payments (i.e., to keep the payments affordable), then that car is too expensive for your current budget. Look for a more reasonably priced car. Then after the car is paid for, set up an Automatic Investment (Car) Plan. Put your usual payment directly into this account so that when you need your next used car you can pay for it in cash.

## RENTING YOUR NEXT CAR!

Yes, that's right! For some people it makes much more financial sense to actually rent rather than own or lease a car! Many rental car companies will rent you a great car for between $1,200 and $2,000 a month. That means you have a car with the only expense being petrol. No maintenance. No repairs. No insurance. And you can always exchange the vehicle for a different one to suit changing needs and cost priorities.

If, for example, you are a travelling salesperson who clocks up thousands of kilometres a month then long-term renting may be preferable to leasing or buying. You will avoid the huge depreciation and additional maintenance associated with owning a heavily used car.

Before you consider long-term renting, check the rules! Make sure that you are properly insured.

---

## CHAPTER 14 ACTION STEPS REVIEW

1. Practice **Money Step #6 – *Financial Competence (Intelligence and Responsibility)*** by saving thousands on your next car purchase by buying used.
2. Research auctions in your area. Auctions are an incredible opportunity to not only *save* thousands of dollars, but to *make* thousands of dollars. Follow the **Eight Strategies for Auction Success**.
3. If you insist on buying new, follow the **Nine Strategies for Buying a New Car**.
4. If you must finance your car, be informed when you do.

# CHAPTER 15

# Cutting your bank fees to the bone

'A sound banker is not one who foresees danger and avoids it, but one who, when he is ruined, is ruined in a conventional and orthodox way so that no one can really blame him.'

JOHN MAYNARD KEYNES

When you were growing up, if your childhood was like mine, most of your parents' financial lives revolved around one bank: the family bank. Most families were loyal to the one institution and considered their local banker a trusted friend. Almost all the family's financial transactions were handled by that one (basic) bank: saving; chequing; home loans; personal loans and Christmas club accounts. Your parents probably helped you open your first savings account there. They very likely even got their first credit card there. It was a simple time. All you had to do was go to one place to take care of your every financial need.

In today's world this simplicity is no longer financial reality. Many services such as savings, personal loans, investments, etc., can be handled much more efficiently by other financial institutions. That being the case, why do you now need a bank at all?

The answer: you need a bank because banks have one essential service that is difficult to obtain elsewhere. They offer all-purpose transaction accounts (providing cheque facilities). In addition, although it is a 'double-edged sword', they offer widespread access to your cash via automatic teller machines (ATMs).

(Stay tuned, because recent rumblings by the Australian Competition and Consumer Commission (ACCC) and the Reserve Bank indicate that moves to open up the major banks' cartel stranglehold on transaction banking are on the cards.)

For the time being though, the *key* factors when considering one bank over another should still be the costs of a transaction account and the costs of using the ATM services. By taking the time to compare charges from one institution to another you should be able to save yourself several hundred dollars each year. That is what we are going to do in this chapter, show you how to shop for a bank.

Banks that also trade as publicly listed companies (i.e. all the major ones) have one main purpose: to make a profit for their shareholders. And this profit is derived from you, the customer. Banks generate a tremendous amount of money from what is called 'the spread': the difference between what the bank pays you (interest) for the use of your money and what they charge somebody else (interest) for the use of the same money (in reality *your* money). In other words, they pay you (usually 0–5%) for the use of your money and then lend it to somebody else for much higher interest.

'What is robbing a bank compared with founding a bank?'

**BERTOLT BRECHT**
*(Die Dreigroschenoper)*

Banks also generate huge profits by charging you fees for your account and ATM usage. Isn't it interesting that banks charge you (via ATM and other account-keeping and transaction fees) for the right to access your own money? And finally, they sell you investments (often with high commissions and/or fees).

One thing to keep in mind is that it does not matter whether an institution calls itself a bank, credit union, building society or friendly society. Although there are internal infrastructure differences, more often than not these differences have no material impact on you as a customer. A credit union is a special kind of bank formed by people who have a common bond, such as a shared workplace, profession, or even homeowners' association, but it is for the most part still a bank.

The Australian Prudential Regulation Authority (APRA) is responsible for the prudential regulation of banks, credit unions, building societies and special service providers. Under APRA's new prudential supervision guidelines, there are now **depositor protection rules**. While depositor priority arrangements have always applied to banks, now depositors are given *first* claim on the assets of banks, credit unions, building societies and special service providers in the event of financial difficulty.

## CREDIT UNIONS

Doing your banking at a credit union will usually save you money. Credit unions tend to offer lower priced services and rates on personal loans and pay higher rates on savings accounts than do ordinary banks. They are usually non-profit organisations, simply operating to provide services to members. In Australia there are currently 255 credit unions with more than 2,000 branches and agencies. More than 3.5 million Australians currently have all, or part, of their financial services requirements met by credit unions.

Because of the advantages, I recommend, if possible, that you join a credit union rather than use a bank. Before you sign up though, make sure the credit union offers all the services you require. Many do not have their own ATMs (something I actually view as a hidden benefit); however, credit unions combined provide access to around 8,800 ATMs, which is one of the largest networks in Australia. In addition, those credit unions who provide larger networks of their own ATMs generally charge a little more for this service than the banks do.

If the minor inconveniences do not bother you, you should definitely enquire whether you are eligible to join a credit union. These days it is usually very easy to qualify for membership. For example, if you or a relative work for Federal or State government; a community homeowners' association; certain employers, trade or professional associations; a church, club or civic organization; or have a relative who is a member of a credit union, you are probably eligible for credit union membership.

Finding a credit union is as easy as looking up the Yellow Pages directory or checking whether your workplace or profession is represented by a particular credit union. Some credit unions advertise regularly in newspapers, on television or on radio. If you are in any doubt about which credit union to join, telephone the Credit Union Movement on 13 11 28. Or try their website www.cu.net.au, which also has a credit union locator service to find the one which best suits your needs.

## BUILDING SOCIETIES

The main difference between building societies and credit unions is more one of historical purpose than one of modern function. Building societies were originally established as a self-help mechanism to provide pooled sources of money for lending to their members to build houses (they were known as *terminating* societies and when your number came up you got your loan). They in turn developed into larger lending institutions and became *permanent* societies with an expertise focused on home-loan lending and customer service. They are uniformally co-operative and like most credit unions, are non-profit organisations operated for the benefit of their members.

These days building societies offer full banking services though their branch networks tend to be concentrated in regional centres outside the state capitals. There are currently around 17 different building societies Australia-wide, with the largest operations in NSW in cities like Newcastle and Wollongong.

Because of their origins, building societies tend to be highly customer-focused and because they are mutuals (owned by their members), their fees are typically lower in accord with the principles of a mutual. They also tend to have lower income-to-cost ratios and as a result still seem to have an edge over credit unions in the home lending market.

Because credit unions used to operate with fairly strict 'common bond' membership requirements, and thus relied for business on their captive memberships who could not join other credit unions, they tended not to develop as efficiently as many of the building societies did. They typically focused on the higher margin types of lending, like personal loans, and became highly specialised in these areas, passing the spread benefits on to their members via higher bank account interest rates and lower fees. Building societies competed instead in the wider banking market head-on with the banks, primarily for the home lending market. Consider the success of the St. George Building Society and you will get some idea of how successful some building societies have been in this niche.

If you want more information on building societies and the services they offer, telephone the Australian Association of Permanent Building Societies (AAPBS) in Canberra on (02) 6281 1588, or visit their website at www.aapbs.com.au.

## COMMUNITY BANKS

Of recent times, in response to the growing groundswell against banks caused by regional branch closures and higher bank fees, community banks are enjoying a growing popularity. The number of community banks, currently 26 in four states, is expected to double each year for the immediate future. The most well-known of these would be Bendigo Bank, which focuses on providing branch services in regional areas of Victoria to compensate for major bank branch closures in those regions.

Obviously the main limitation of community banks is their current small market presence (watch for strategic mergers between similarly motivated groups in the future to address this limitation). This will not be a problem if you live in a region where a community bank is the major or only banking presence. Community banks (not surprisingly) are very customer-focused and their fees are very competitive. Unlike other banks, they usually exist primarily to serve the interests of their customers, not the interests of their shareholders. The only word of caution when considering a newly established or perhaps very small player in the community banking game, is to make sure the organisation is managed well enough to be around for more than the short term (your funds would not be at risk but you may be greatly inconvenienced by a closure).

## BANKS

Most banks pay about the same interest as each other on transaction accounts. The important distinctions between banks have more to do with the fees you pay for services and the minimum balances required or maximum transactions allowed to avoid such fees. The biggest challenge most people face is to find a bank that does not require you to maintain a high minimum balance to obtain free transaction account services.

If you do not maintain a minimum balance, usually between $500 and $5,000 (depending on the bank), most banks charge a monthly account-keeping fee for operating the account, usually between $2 and $6. In addition, you may be charged for any transactions you make over a set free limit depending on the types of transactions and whether they are over-the-counter or electronic. For example, you can be charged around $2 for an over-the-counter withdrawal or around 70 cents for an electronic withdrawal which is over your allowable transaction limit. 'Excess' ATM service charges range from 50 cents if it is your bank's ATM up to $2.50 if it is another bank's ATM. Some banks even charge for deposits.

Most people don't realise how quickly these fees add up. Surveys suggest the average transaction account costs between $120 and $500 a year depending on the service you require and the bank you use. With careful planning and preference for electronic banking, it is not difficult to halve these costs and also improve the service you currently receive.

What does *your* bank charge each month? Is there a withdrawal charge after a certain number of withdrawals? What other fees are there? What is the minimum balance required to avoid all fees? If you don't know, call (now!) and find out. Or better still, most banks are on the Internet so you can compare their fees, services and requirements online.

You need to research each bank and see which offers the best deal for your requirements. Make sure you understand the fine print. Ask yourself the following:

- Do I *need* a cheque book, credit card and ATM access?
- Are over-the-counter services required?
- What is my expected minimum account balance?
- How many transactions do I need each month?
- Do I need electronic services such as EFTPOS, phone and Internet banking?
- Can I organise direct debit and telephone transfers?
- If I am a pensioner or student, can I take advantage of the bank's special deals?

Then check the Yellow Pages directory, search the Internet and speak with your friends and co-workers to determine the best bank, credit union or building society for you. Not surprisingly, I have found that local credit unions, building societies or smaller regional banks are generally more interested in this type of retail customer business than the 'big boys' are.

## SURF FOR RATES AND VALUE BANKING PRODUCTS

- *Personal Investor* magazine has an interesting interactive tool to help you find the best bank for you, at www.personalinvestor.com.au.
- For a list of available banks the Australian Financial Directory at www.afsd.com.au is also a good start. It has a national index of banks, building societies and credit unions.
- While set up for a different purpose, the Australian Institute of Banking and Finance has an interesting website if you want to know more about the different banks, regulations and services. They also have a finance dictionary. Their website is at www.aibf.com.au.
- Bankchoice at www.bankchoice.com.au has various levels of information on bank rates and charges. It provides the different government charges on bank deposits and withdrawals, as well as including other items such as calculators and interest rates. It also compares other financial products such as credit cards and loans. Bankchoice is part of the www.infochoice.com.au suite of sites run by infomediary Infochoice Limited.

- BestBid at www.bestbid.com.au works like an auction site, where lenders bid for your transaction account business.
- Australian Consumers' Association CHOICEOnline website which provides articles/reports on banking products at www.choice.com.au.
- CANNEX *Pollfax* service which provides up-to-date financial (rates) data via automatic fax (*PollFax* on 1902 935 665 for automatic *Financial Institutions Hotlines/Websites* two-page survey faxed at $0.83 a minute, costing about $1.90); www.cannex.com.au/surveys.
- If you are concerned with your bank's credit worthiness, Thomson Financial Bankwatch provides a *Global Rating Coverage* and research on banks throughout the world at www.bankwatch.com.
- In Australia there is a banking ombudsman who handles claims and disputes between customers and their banks. It is administered under the Australian Banking Industry Ombudsman Scheme. The ABIO will usually request that you attempt to resolve the dispute yourself before approaching them. Call 1800 337 444 (9613 7333 from metropolitan Melbourne) or visit their informative website at www.abio.org.au.

## SIX WAYS TO REDUCE YOUR TRANSACTION ACCOUNT AND/OR CHEQUE ACCOUNT COSTS

1. **Know what formula your bank uses to calculate the minimum balance when determining account fees.** Avoid institutions that use what is called the **minimum daily (or monthly) balance method**. This system requires you to maintain the minimum balance every single day in order to get free transactions. If your balance drops below the minimum for even one day, you will be charged a fee. Only do business with a bank that uses the **average daily balance method**.

   With the average daily balance method the bank adds up your daily balances and then divides that total by the number of days in the billing cycle to get an average figure. For example, if your bank's balance requirement is $1,000 and your account dips below that a couple of times in a billing cycle, you will not be penalised as long as your average balance is at least $1,000. This simple difference in the method of determining your minimum balance can be the difference between no-fee versus high-fee transactions. Average daily balance method is the only way to go.

2. **Check if your bank allows you to 'link' accounts to meet balance requirements.** Some institutions insist that you keep a minimum amount of money in your transaction account (exclusively) in order to get free transactions. Others allow you to combine or 'link' accounts to qualify for the minimum and receive the free transactions. The combination of accounts might typically include: cheque account(s); savings account(s); and term deposits. For most people the 'combo deal' is the best deal. You may also consider consolidating accounts where linking is not possible or the requirements are too restrictive.

   Be mindful though when you link accounts to a cheque account because under many present state government tax rules all withdrawals (whether via cheque, ATM, EFTPOS, etc.) made from cheque accounts or accounts *linked* to cheque accounts attract BAD tax (Bank Account Debits Tax). Banks will not usually make this effect of linking certain accounts clear to you. Depending upon your monthly level of withdrawal activity the BAD taxes can often outstrip any penalties you may be incurring from breaching minimum balance requirements in your 'unlinked' transaction account. BAD taxes are slated for removal on July 1, 2005 as part of the tranche of GST-related tax reforms (not something I would *bank* on). (Another GST-related reform: FID (Federal Institutions Duty) is scheduled to be removed from July 1, 2001, so this is good news for reducing your transaction account costs.)

3. **Avoid face-to-face transactions.** It is much more cost (and time!) effective to bank electronically. Use ATMs (within fee-free limits), EFTPOS (sensibly), and telephone banking and Internet banking (via your personal computer).

The banking industry suggests each transaction costs them $1.60 if handled over-the-counter, 50 cents for telephone banking and 10 cents for Internet banking. They are willing to pass *some* of these cost savings on to you.

4. **Limit transactions.** Consider alternatives to writing a large number of cheques or making frequent withdrawals via ATM or EFTPOS. Keep in mind that many banks offer you a number of free transactions, but if you exceed that number the fees start to become hefty. If you can control your credit card habits, it is possible to pay the majority of your bills using the card and then pay the card off each month with one transaction (by cheque, telephone or Internet banking). All that said, if you can limit the number of transactions, finding an account which is cheaper but has a lesser number of free transactions is the way to go.

5. **Avoid interest-bearing transaction accounts that require you to maintain high minimum balances.** Transaction accounts that pay interest, usually termed 'Advantage Saver' or similar, *sound* like a good deal. However, most banks require a high minimum balance (typically $1,000–$2,500). If you fall below the minimum at any time in the month, you are zapped with the monthly service charge. The interest rate paid on these accounts is pitiful. These accounts are simply marketed to induce you to open the account believing that you will earn interest, instead of paying greater fees. Always remember, if the bank came up with the idea (and markets it like crazy), it is generally in *their* interests, not *yours*.

6. **Consider share ownership as a means of reducing or eliminating fees.** Provided the investment also makes sense on wealth-creation grounds, you might also like to consider an investment in a minimum qualifying parcel of shares in a bank that offers shareholder banking benefits. Two of the best are ANZ and NAB, which both offer features such as no account service fees; extra interest on term deposits (usually .25%); and discounts on variable rate home loans, personal loans and other bank products.

## FIVE POWERFUL TECHNIQUES TO MANAGE YOUR TRANSACTION ACCOUNT AND/OR CHEQUE ACCOUNT

After you have found a no-cost or low-cost transaction and/or cheque account, you must make sure you manage it wisely. If you don't, you may quickly find yourself with such surprises as $20 bounced-cheque charges, and overdrawn accounts. Here are techniques that will help you avoid the 'extortion' fees that banks charge for irregular account balances. Follow these five techniques and you will have total control of your transaction accounts (and be *Financially Competent (Intelligent and Responsible)* as a result). The first two are primarily for people with cheque accounts but nonetheless provide useful information for all people with any types of transaction accounts.

1. **Balance your bank account (and cheque book).** I know that I used to dread this almost more than a trip to the dentist. At the time I was not sure why, I just knew that I didn't like doing it. The reason? I did not know how to do it. And that ignorance (*Financial Incompetence*) was expensive, because like many of you, I have paid my share of bounced-cheque charges.

   You need to balance your cheque account to avoid the bounced-cheque charges and to track how much money you have. Even if you are rich enough to keep so much money in your cheque account that you never have to worry about covering all the cheques you write, you must still learn how to balance your cheque book. Otherwise, you are out of control. Know your own balance because often the bank will charge you an extra fee if you request a statement of balance in addition to the regular monthly statement.

   The other main reason to balance your cheque book is that banks often make mistakes. Over the years, I have personally found tens of thousands of dollars in errors made by my banks. (Strange how they always seem to find the errors in their favour, but they never seem to find the errors in my favour. Can you relate to this?) It helps to keep your cheque stubs (the place in your cheque book where you are supposed to record all deposits and withdrawals) at all times.

You can record details of cheques the minute you write them, deposits right after you make them, and ATM transactions (withdrawals or deposits) on the spot. If your company deposits your wages into your transaction account, remember to enter that deposit on your cheque stubs every payday as well.

If you need help balancing your cheque book, first look at the back of your bank statement: many banks provide useful worksheets that can help you keep your cheque book in order. If you still do not understand how to do it, get over the embarrassment and call the bank to set up an appointment to have someone help you figure it out. If your transaction account is so messed up that there is no way to ever figure it out, close it and open a new account. Make a fresh start. (Be sure to leave enough money in the old account to cover any outstanding (unpaid) cheques). Open the new account with the bank you find that offers you the best deal.

2. **Computerise your bank account and cheque book.** As I mentioned previously, setting your finances up on a computer program, such as Quicken, will automate the entire process. You still have to enter all transactions (deposits, cheques and withdrawals), but you no longer have to worry about the arithmetic. The computer will do it for you. If you are using Internet banking, many institutions offer the ability to download your financial details to financial management software.

3. **Pay your bills electronically or by telephone.** An efficient way to keep your transaction account balanced is to pay your bills (and transfer funds) electronically or by telephone. Such arrangements will save bank fees as well as provide efficient control and management for your transaction accounts. This can be done in four ways:

   a) **BPAY** – There are more than 900 companies including telephone, electricity and water companies which accept BPAY and this number is growing by more than 30% each year. BPAY allows you to:

- pay all your bills in one telephone call or Internet session;
- avoid waiting in queues;
- choose a payment date that suits *you*;
- save time and expense;
- pay from cheque, savings or credit card accounts.

Most banks, building societies and credit unions now offer the BPAY service.

b) **Internet banking** – Internet banking allows you to:
- view account, credit card and home loan balances;
- view transaction details for the past 18 months;
- transfer funds between linked accounts;
- obtain e-cash from your account and shop on the Internet;
- download financial information to help you balance your account.

c) **Telephone banking** – Telephone banking (which you would use for BPAY services), can also be used for checking account balances and recent transactions, and for transferring funds from one account to another (cheque, savings or credit). You have to register for telephone banking and you are given an access number (just like you are for ATM access).

d) **Credit card payments by phone** – As mentioned earlier, if you can control your credit card habits, it is possible to pay the majority of your bills over the phone using your credit card and then pay the card off each month with one transaction (by cheque, telephone or Internet banking). This can also be a good idea for racking up those rewards or frequent flyer points.

4. **Set up a salary account.** Many institutions let you deposit your salary into your home loan account as part of a standard variable loan (not just for home-equity loans). This allows your salary to be offset against the home loan balance and as your home loan interest is calculated on a daily basis, reduces your interest on the loan.

5. **Do not rely on the ATM or bank to keep track of your transaction account balance.** Many people make the mistake of checking their ATM balance (or calling the bank for their balance) to find out how much money they have left in their transaction account. The problem with this strategy is that neither the bank nor the ATM knows how many cheques, and for what amounts, you have outstanding (cheques you have written that have not been cashed yet).

## ✗ THE EVIL ATM ✗

Today's young adults, Generation X and the younger baby boomers, have become addicted to the ATM. Remember a few years ago when the banks offered the wonderful new ATM service for free? After all, banks are there to help you, just like the government. Trusted friends. They told you about the safety of not carrying a lot of cash. They told you about the convenience. They told you about 24-hour banking service. (And now of course we have the latest scourge of EFTPOS, which we take for granted in the same way, which this year doubled in dollar usage).

You could withdraw or deposit money at will, without hassle. You could even borrow money from your credit card or pre-arranged line of credit. They even set it up so you could pay credit card and loan payments. All for free. Our bankers, our good friends, right? Well, guess what? The free days of the ATM are over, aren't they? You are already paying some ATM fees, aren't you? And since deregulation, fees for bank services are still expanding, aren't they?

Your friends at the bank can charge, in essence, whatever they want for ATM use! That means you could pay 50 cents to $3 an ATM transaction! This is huge money for the banks. This is why they worked so hard to get so many people addicted to the ATM. Do you know that the average ATM card holder uses his or her ATM card six times a month? And not always at their own bank! That could be an extra $3–18 a month, each customer, for the bank (depending upon free transaction limits and use of other bank ATMs). Multiply that by the millions of people who have an account with an ATM card. How exciting! (If you have shares in a bank or an ATM that is.)

My advice is if you use an ATM card: **STOP!** The banks set you up, got you addicted with the free service and are now closing in for the kill. They know you will continue using the ATM even with the obnoxious fees. Why? Because they know they can count on the average person being *Financially Incompetent* or at the very least lazy. They want your money. They set you up on purpose. Do not fall for their trap. Break your addiction to the ATM.

If you still insist on using ATMs, I recommend you clearly understand the fee structures. You need to ask yourself if the convenience is worth the cost. Right now, some banks allow you a set number of free withdrawals a month. Others charge you a 'small' fee if you use the ATM at one of *your* branches. If you use another institution's machine (such as a CIRRUS network machine), you will pay an extra fee to the other institution plus an extra fee to your bank. The total transaction fee is usually somewhere between $2 and $3. That is a fairly large fee for a 'quick cash' withdrawal of $40 (the $40 quick cash is the most commonly used ATM option). The banks know that with extra branch closures you are more likely to use another bank's ATMs and incur that $2 fee for doing so, rather than to discipline yourself to manage accessing your money better.

How does it feel to pay a transaction charge of 5–10% for the 'privilege' of withdrawing your own money? Remember, the average ATM user visits an ATM six times a month. Many people use them much more often. How many times a month do you use an ATM? What fees are you paying now? Are you prepared to continue paying those fees or are you ready to give up (or reduce the use of) your ATM card? When I started getting those 'little charges', I stopped using ATMs entirely. Look at your transaction account statements and find out how much you paid for ATM use in 1997, compare it to 1998, then 1999 and 2000. Is the annual figure trending upwards, dramatically? Expect that trend to continue *ad infinitum*.

The ATM is a horrible (and expensive) way to track your money. There is a reason a 'quick cash' withdrawal of $40 is the easiest transaction. Firstly, you will keep coming back (more fees) and secondly, it makes it almost impossible to track your money which leads to more bounced cheques and… surprise surprise… more fees. Sound a little sinister?

The final big problem with the ATM is that it makes your money too easily available for impulse shopping. I have a friend who uses the ATM two to five times every weekend. The result: a good time that he can't remember, and no money on Monday. If you have a hard time controlling money, use of ATMs can quickly erode your finances. For many people the shiny plastic card is just too tempting. Like chocolate, you will use it if it is in the house. Do not get an ATM card if you haven't the discipline to use it wisely (sparingly).

Remember, the biggest ATM charge is when you use another bank's machine. Currently many banks charge $2 or more each transaction. These charges *will* rise. Beware.

---

**New strategy:** Never use the ATM again (unless it is free). If you cannot do that, then commit to using the ATM no more than once a week. If you need to keep withdrawing more cash, you need to re-evaluate your budget. Either you need to start the week with more cash, or you need to spend less. Figure out what you need each week (in cash), then promise yourself that once you run out, you will not get more. This strategy will help you become ***Financially Competent (Intelligent and Responsible)*** in your spending habits.

---

## BANK SAVINGS OPTIONS

Banks offer three basic types of savings options. The returns are, at best, dismal for all types. Other than for short-term saving needs or to maintain a minimum balance, I do not recommend any of them. And never confuse a bank savings account with an *investment*. It is not. In fact, a bank savings account loses money (after taxes and inflation).

Let's say you put $10,000 in a money market (or cash management) account. The account pays 4%. That means at the end of the year you would have made $400. Now comes the taxman, who gets about 30%, that's $120. Next comes inflation, on average about 3.6% a year, that takes away $360 of the original spending power of your $10,000. The end result is you now have the spending power of $9,920 ($10,000 + $400 − $120 − $360). With that said, here is some information on the three savings vehicles banks offer:

1. **Savings accounts.** These are nothing more than your basic accounts for saving. They require very little money to open and are totally liquid. They can be used as part of your minimum balance requirements. They pay the worst possible interest rates.

> 'I know you wouldn't think of putting fresh asparagus in the back of a drawer and eating it three months later, and yet otherwise sensible people do take sizable amounts of money and pretty much let it rot.'
> **MISS PIGGY**

2. **Money market (or cash management) accounts.** These accounts usually pay slightly higher interest rates than the basic savings accounts. They usually require $1,000–$2,500 to open and are totally liquid. They can be used as part of your minimum balance requirements.

   Don't waste your money in these accounts simply for the purposes of meeting minimum balance requirements. Put your money to work in real investments. Do not let it dissolve in the bank. If you must hold cash in a money market or cash management account at least check if you are getting the best deal by comparing the rate to those offered by other banks and financial institutions (check *The Australian Financial Review Weekend Edition* or CANNEX *PollFax* service via automatic fax on 1902 935 662 for Cash Management Accounts two-page survey faxed at $0.83 a minute, costing about $1.90);

3. **Term Deposits.** Term deposits usually pay fixed interest rates for fixed periods of time (usually 90 days to 10 years). They usually require at least $1,000 to open. Money is liquid, however, there is an interest penalty (no principal penalty) for early withdrawal. They may be used as part of your minimum balance requirement. If you must hold cash in a term deposit make sure you are getting the best rate (again, check *The Australian Financial Review Weekend Edition*

or CANNEX *PollFax* service via automatic fax on 1902 935 660 for *Term Deposits* two-page survey faxed at $0.83 a minute, costing about $1.90). Look for interest rate bonuses for online term deposits from institutions such as AMP Banking and ING Direct.

**Bottomline:** *These accounts are not investments.* They are simply vehicles for holding cash. If you need a place to park your cash, park it with a non-bank financial institution such as a merchant bank or stockbroker cash management account. You will earn more and have the money ready to invest when an opportunity comes along.

## BANK-SOLD INVESTMENTS

In the last few years, banks have started selling managed funds and acting as if they are 'financial planners'. Many people falsely believe, because they purchase units in a managed fund at a bank, that the investments are bank guaranteed. They are not. Bank-sold managed funds are loaded, meaning that you pay big commissions for no reason. You would be much better off buying through one of the no-commission (or low-commission) managed fund brokers or directly from the top managed fund companies themselves as discussed in Chapter 3.

**Bottomline:** Never buy 'investments' from a bank.

'Remember, what you are doing is giving your money to somebody else to hold on to, and I think that it is worth keeping in mind that the businessmen who run banks are so worried about holding on to things that they put little chains on all their pens.'
**MISS PIGGY**

**Learning tools for kids:** Check out the US website www.kidsbank.com for a site that teaches children about saving, money and banking in an animated environment. It includes information on savings, interest, and cheque accounts and the history of money as well as a bulletin board where money-related questions can be asked. The site is provided by Sovereign Bank.

*Pocket Pal* is an interactive Australian program for children, containing a cheque book (which must be balanced) and a credit card (which charges interest). Income tax must be paid and and budgeting and saving is taught as part of teaching kids good financial habits early in life. It is available by mail order on 1800 898 435 for $39.95 and comes with a 30-day money-back guarantee.

## CHAPTER 15 ACTION STEPS REVIEW

1. Practice **Money Step #6 – *Financial Competence (Intelligence and Responsibility)*** by shopping around for a bank that offers you free transactions and waives other fees if you maintain a low minimum monthly balance in your transaction account (or combination of accounts). This will save you hundreds of dollars a year.
2. If possible and practical, sign up with a credit union, building society or community bank to minimise your banking costs.
3. Consider the advantages of the various electronic banking methods.
4. Follow the **Six Ways to Reduce Your Transaction Account and/or Cheque Account Costs**: know the minimum balance conditions; link accounts if advantageous to maintain minimum balances; avoid face-to-face transactions; limit transactions; avoid high minimum balance accounts; and consider share ownership of banks that offer shareholder banking benefits.

5. Apply the **Five Powerful Techniques to Manage Your Transaction Account and/or Cheque Account**: balance your bank account and cheque book; computerise your bank account and cheque book; pay your bills electronically or by phone; use a salary account; and do not rely on the bank to keep track of your account.
6. Avoid the **Evil ATM** whenever possible. If you must use it, limit yourself to once a week maximum.
7. Keep as little money as possible in the bank (minimum required for free transactions). The rate of return is horrible. **A bank account is not an investment. Put your money to work.**
8. **Never buy investments from a bank.** The advice is often poor and the loads (sales charges or commissions) are usually high.

## CHAPTER 16

# How to increase your pay to the max

'The slave has but one master; the man of ambition has as many as there are people useful to his fortune.'

JEAN DE LA BRUYENE

If you work for an employer, there is a good chance you are not maximising the employee benefits and taxation advantages you probably have available to you.

In this chapter we will maximise your pay-packet power by:
- examining benefits that your employer may provide (including fringe benefits, some subject to tax and some not);
- retirement planning via superannuation, preferably with the support of your employer;
- claiming personal tax deductions in your tax return.

If you are self-employed or a business owner, you should review this chapter very carefully so you understand the basics. When we review self-employed and business owner benefits, your knowledge of this information will be essential for maximising your own pay-packet power.

## POTENTIAL EMPLOYEE BENEFITS

The first thing to do is request a copy of your employee benefits handbook or ask your employer what benefits are available. Yes, I know this sounds about as much fun as having another tooth pulled (remember we already pulled one in Chapter 7). Read on though, because this single act could make/save you thousands of dollars a year.

Now for a quick lesson about fringe benefits and the tax payable by your employer on the value of some benefits provided to you. Fringe benefits tax (FBT) was introduced in 1986 as an attempt by the government to stop benefits being provided tax-free by employers to employees. With continual amendments to the FBT legislation the tax office has been quite successful in removing many previously tax-free benefits.

' "Take some more tea," the March Hare said to Alice, very earnestly. "I've had nothing yet," Alice replied in an offended tone, "so I can't take more." "You mean you can't take *less*," said the Hatter: "It's very easy to take *more* than nothing."'
**LEWIS CARROLL (*Alice's Adventures in Wonderland*)**

More recent FBT changes mean the value of fringe benefits are included on your group certificate and although you are not taxed on these (because your employer has already been), they are taken into account by government departments for purposes such as determining the extent of social security benefits, child maintenance payments administered by the Child Support Agency and taxation surcharges such as the Medicare levy or superannuation guarantee levy.

Some employers will allow you to package your salary and reduce your paycheque by the corresponding amount of the benefit and the amount of FBT payable. The FBT is effectively equal to the top rate of personal tax so to obtain a benefit is not tax-effective for you if the employer reduces your pay by the amount of FBT that they have to pay.

However, there are some benefits which don't attract as much FBT as you would pay in personal tax if you were to purchase those benefits personally, and there are some fringe benefits which don't attract FBT at all! The key is to find them.

There is a trend for 'smart' employers to look for ways to retain good employees by packaging salary into a number of components to give the employee maximum benefits, without increasing the employer's overall employment costs. These employers may also pay FBT for providing some benefits where they have an interest in looking after the employees' welfare and other interests. Read on and I will give you some examples where FBT is:

- fully payable on fringe benefits;
- partially payable on fringe benefits;
- not payable on fringe benefits.

## EMPLOYEE BENEFITS WHERE FRINGE BENEFITS ARE FULLY TAXED

**Health insurance.** Sometimes employers want to ensure that employees and their families are well cared for in the event of illness or accident and will pay private health insurance premiums as well as the associated FBT. Even if you are required to pay part of the premiums, it is probably a better deal, possibly much better than the insurance you would get on your own. Review Chapter 17 on health insurance before finalising any decision on this.

**Life insurance.** This might be offered by an employer. You may have your salary reduced by the FBT but this could still be well worthwhile if the employer can obtain discounted premiums.

**Savings plans.** These are not fringe benefits I usually like, but are fine if the amounts are paid as your **AIP**. The effect of your employer paying into your AIP where your employer deducts the FBT from your salary works out the same as if you paid it yourself after tax, provided you are in the top tax bracket. In any case the arrangement may offer benefits by forcing a more disciplined approach to investing in an AIP.

## EMPLOYEE BENEFITS WHERE FRINGE BENEFITS ARE PARTIALLY TAXED

The main fringe benefit available to employees in this category is the car. You are probably aware that many salary packages allow a car to be included and this can be beneficial, particularly if you are in the top tax bracket. This is because the FBT, though payable, is normally *concessionally* treated. There are two usual ways the FBT on a car can be calculated:

1. **Statutory formula method.** This is where the car is assumed to be 100% private. Depending on the number of kilometres travelled and the car's age, the cost price of the car is multiplied by a 'statutory fraction' provided by the ATO. This provides an *assumed fringe benefit* amount. I find that if you are in the top tax bracket and you travel more than 15,000 kilometres a year, even if the car has no business use, it can be advantageous to have a car as part of your salary package.

2. **Operating cost method.** This is where you complete a log book for the car to determine the percentage of business use. The private use of the car multiplied by the running costs of the car will determine the amount of the fringe benefit provided to the employee. Note: a log book needs to be completed for 12 weeks in a manner prescribed by the ATO. Ask for details from your employer and complete it exactly as set out.

Please also take heed of the chapter on buying a car. If you then still decide to buy a car through your salary package, your employer may be entitled to a fleet discount and other rebates from the car manufacturer or distributor that make your purchase more appealing.

## EMPLOYER BENEFITS WITH NO TAX ON FRINGE BENEFITS

You can have a bit of fun here. Typically, if you qualify for a personal tax deduction for something, but your employer happens to pay for it instead, then no FBT is payable. This can sometimes help your cash flow or your employer may be able to get a better price through its buying power or network. Examples of this include:

- interest expense on an income-producing loan (e.g., loan on a rental property);
- education, including self-education, where there is some relationship with your employment or income;
- income protection insurance.

There are also a number of other fringe benefits which, if paid by your employer, are exempt from FBT. Examples include:

- work-related items such as mobile phones (when primarily used for employment purposes), protective clothing, briefcases, laptop computers, electronic diaries, computer software or tools of trade;
- employee share plans;
- membership fees and subscriptions, including corporate credit cards, airport lounge memberships, but not sporting or social clubs (and certainly not annual frequent flyer membership fees unless you want your frequent flyer points taxed as a fringe benefit);
- newspapers and journals;
- child care provided at the employer's premises;
- car parking where the employer provides parking (not at a commercial car park) and the business income is less than $10 million per annum;
- compassionate travel paid for an employee to visit a seriously ill close relative or in the event of a death;
- minor benefits – infrequent and irregular bonuses, etc., that are less than $100;
- relocation expenses where your employer requires you to relocate (these expenses include home sale and purchase costs, travel, furniture removal, utility disconnection and reconnection fees);
- superannuation benefits (which are included as a separate topic later in this chapter).

There are also some employers who are *exempt* from FBT legislation. These include religious institutions, public benelovent institutions and some international bodies (rare). So if this applies to you, have a very close look at maximising your salary package with fringe benefits.

## RETIREMENT PLANNING

By law your employer must contribute to a superannuation fund on your behalf unless you are aged over 70 or receive a wage of less than $450 a month. The minimum contribution amount is 8% of salary and wages which rises to 9% from 1 July 2002 onwards. Salary and wages are defined as 'ordinary time earnings'.

As part of your salary package, your employer may contribute more than the minimum contribution required by law. Sometimes you may be able to negotiate a 'salary sacrifice' whereby your employer contributes more towards your superannuation and reduces your payable salary accordingly. This means you contribute larger amounts of superannuation without paying personal tax and your employer does not pay fringe benefits tax on this amount. If you were to make voluntary superannuation contributions post–paycheque, you wouldn't get any tax deduction, although you might be entitled to a small tax rebate (for example, if you contributed superannuation for a non-working, or low-income, spouse, you may be entitled to a tax rebate of up to $540 a year).

There are limits on what your employer can contribute each year to your superannuation and still receive a tax deduction. These are based on age and for the 2000–01 tax year are:

| Age in years | Deduction limit |
| --- | --- |
| Under 35 | $11,388 |
| 35 to 49 | $31,361 |
| 50 and over | $78,445 |

The self-employed person can get a 100% tax deduction for the first $3,000 of superannuation contributions and a 75% tax deduction for amounts in excess of this, subject to the age-based limits.

So, which superannuation fund should you choose? Check the options with your employer. Some want you to use their own, others will allow you to choose any fund. It can pay big time to shop around on this front.

I find the decisions involved in superannuation very much like contributing to an AIP, so choosing the right *superannuation* fund is very much like selecting the right *managed* fund. They are usually the same types of companies. It constantly surprises me that many astute financial people ignore their superannuation simply because they don't make the contribution directly themselves. It's as if it isn't really their money, simply because it hasn't passed directly through their hands. This attitude is just plain Level Zero ostrich thinking. Well-invested superannuation money can provide you with bountiful rewards.

## EIGHT TIPS FOR CHOOSING THE RIGHT SUPERANNUATION FUND

1. **Read the information booklets (prospectuses) supplied by the funds.** Make sure you understand what they are offering.
2. **Don't choose a fund just because a salesperson talks you into it.** Salespeople usually receive commissions and they could be biased towards those funds offering the largest commissions.
3. **Determine the nature of the benefit the fund will give you upon retirement.** There are two main types of benefit:
   - *Defined benefit* – where the retirement benefit is fixed, usually a multiple of your final average salary.
   - *Accumulation fund* – your retirement benefit depends on the amount contributed and the success of the investment strategy.

   Most funds are now accumulation funds, which offer less security than defined benefit funds because they are subject to the usual fluctuations of the performance over time of the investment vehicle (shares, bonds, money markets, property trusts). Defined benefit funds however, are less popular these days because they are typically valued based on the length of time an employee spends with the *one* employer.
4. **Examine the fund investment strategy.** The fund's information booklet (prospectus) usually allows a degree of flexibility for where the funds are invested, typically letting you have a choice of high risk (e.g., growth funds in shares and property) or low risk (e.g., capital guaranteed or capital stable in bank deposits or interest deposits). Balanced funds which have a mix of shares, property, cash and fixed interest are sold as medium risk. If you are close to retirement you

might opt for a lower-risk strategy to protect the assets you already have.

5. **Watch those fees and charges.** Like all investment products, fund managers love to extract money from you in subtle ways. There are a range of types of fees and charges including:
   - contribution fees (up to 5% of amount contributed);
   - asset fees, based on your fund balance (these are usually referred to as 'management fees' and included in what is often referred to as the Management Expense Ratio – MER); could be up to 1.5% of your fund assets, charged annually;
   - performance fees based upon the performance of the fund over and above a certain level (e.g., over 10% p.a.);
   - trustee and custodial fees (usually included in the overall MER);
   - establishment fees (one-off fees for starting the fund);
   - rollover fees when you swap your assets between investments in the same fund;
   - entry and exit fees when you change funds (these can be as high as 5% of assets held in the fund).

   Do your sums. Calculate the possible fees you might be paying based on a standard amount and compare each fund from there. The difference over your working life in higher fees and charges could add up to tens of thousands of dollars. So when possible, opt for competitive plans with lower fees and charges.

6. **Review current and past performance.** Look at who is managing the fund. Has it performed consistently? What about the past three or five years? Remember that superannuation is a long-term investment, so don't just look at the past six– or 12–month performance figures. Evaluate performance based upon expectation for the longer term.

7. **Consider any additional benefits.** For example, many funds offer life insurance as part of the fund. Life insurance paid by your superannuation fund is tax-deductible, whereas if you pay it yourself it is not. Examine the coverage offered. Review the chapter on life insurance and make sure that you don't end up with the wrong type or indeed the wrong amount of coverage.

8. **Think about whether you can manage your own superannuation fund.** It is possible to have your own self-managed fund whereby you administer and control your own fund entirely and are responsible for your own investment strategy. I recommend this approach only for Level Five and Level Six Investors.

As part of your decision-making process, take a look at the Association of Superannuation Funds of Australia website (www.superannuation.asn.au) which provides fact sheets, an interactive calculator and a dictionary of terms. Also, the Australian Securities Insurance Commission (ASIC) has various publications to protect you, such as *Don't Kiss Your Money Goodbye*. Call ASIC on its infoline 1300 300 630 or visit its website at www.asic.gov.au.

## WHAT DO I DO NOW?

Once you have selected the right fund and determined the appropriate investment strategy, the real question is whether you should contribute *more* to your superannuation than the amount your employer is already contributing.

The main advantage of superannuation is of course its tax-concessions. Monies contributed to superannuation are tax deductible for your employer. However, the superannuation fund must pay a 15% tax on your contributions. If you earn over $78,209 (for the 2000–01 year) then the tax on your contributions rises by 1% for each thousand dollars above the $78,209, to a maximum total of 30% tax if your salary is $94,966 or higher. This is known as the **superannuation guarantee levy**.

Once your funds are invested, the fund is taxed at 15% on income generated and 10% on capital gains. This is significantly less than the level of tax payable if the income was generated in your own name.

The main disadvantage of superannuation is that your money is indeed locked away until retirement and, with a few strict exceptions, *cannot* be removed. Also, the government will never stop tinkering with your superannuation money and although there are great tax concessions now, with the many billions now invested in superannuation, who's to say what new tax-grabbing ideas the government will come up with before you retire!

As a general rule, I recommend that you get your other financial affairs in order before making large additional contributions to your superannuation plan. Once you have your debt under control, you can treat additional contributions to superannuation as part of your AIP, particularly where you are able to make those contributions via a salary sacrifice arrangement with your employer.

## PERSONAL TAX DEDUCTIONS

The final strategy for getting the most out of your pay cheque is to consider whether there are any tax deductions you can legally claim in your *personal* tax return.

My advice is first to always use the best tax adviser (agent, accountant) you can afford. Don't try to do your own tax return, thinking you can save a few dollars in professional fees, unless you are absolutely certain you are claiming everything you legally can and completing your return properly. I have heard countless stories of taxpayers completing their own returns for years, then (usually by luck) meeting with a tax adviser who knows the tax law and claims additional tax deductions or even where there has been incorrectly over-declared investment income, enabling the taxpayer to receive refunds of thousands of dollars. So take the time to look around to find a good tax adviser.

Always use a tax adviser whom you can trust. While you should always seek value for money, do not shop for the cheapest deal in this situation. You will get what you pay for! The better tax advisers rarely (if ever) discount their fees. They have ample work from those who know their value and professionalism.

The most critical part of claiming tax deductions is **substantiation**. I say this because although you might have a great tax deduction, without the documentation it cannot be claimed. Usually substantiation requires written evidence of the expenses being claimed, a diary entry in some situations and in the case of travel, a travel diary. The extent of the expenses determines the necessary level of substantiation.

On top of the substantiation requirements, before you can claim a deduction, you must ensure the expense is incurred in gaining or producing **assessable income**. It cannot be an expense which is of a private, capital or domestic nature. There have been volumes written on what expenses are deductible and thousands of cases between the ATO and taxpayers. The verdicts are at best confusing and that is why I always recommend getting the best professional advice you can afford.

The ATO has released various rules (taxation rulings) for particular trades, professions and industries. The rulings do not carry the weight of being actual law but are nonetheless working guidelines. Remember the ATO wants to limit your claim and the rulings are thus very conservative. To go against the rulings, however, is always a good start to attracting an audit and possibly a day in court.

Without going into specific deductions for specific areas of employment, here are general deductions which might be appropriate for you in your current situation:

- technical and trade books, journals;
- gifts and advertising (for example, those who generate commissions and give incidental presents or need to promote themselves);
- telephones, including mobile phones;
- income protection insurance;
- tax adviser fees and related costs to manage your income tax affairs;
- home office expenses;
- self-education expenses;
- travel (*not* home to work and return, but work to work);
- compulsory uniforms, protective clothing and occupation-specific clothing;
- laundry and dry-cleaning expenses for tax-deductible clothing only;
- fitness expenses (when fitness is a condition of employment);
- conventions and seminars (including travel and accommodation);
- car, bridge/motorway tolls and car-parking expenses.

Don't forget that the above are *general* deductions and to claim such expenses will depend on:
- the nature, extent and type of your trade, profession or employment;
- substantiation requirements.

The best approach is to interview your tax adviser before the end of the financial year, discuss with them your employment situation and seek their guidance on what can be claimed and the types of records you must keep for substantiation purposes.

Whatever types of benefits your employer or the tax law offers you, they are bound to accelerate you towards your goals of true financial independence. Benefits must be seized and invariably cannot be of advantage to you outside certain windows of available opportunity. Act now, become fully informed and get your remuneration working at its highest pitch.

> 'Gather ye rosebuds while ye may,
> Old Time is still a flying,
> And this same flower that smiles today,
> Tomorrow will be dying.'
> **ROBERT HERRICK**

---

## CHAPTER 16 ACTION STEPS TO REVIEW

1. Practice **Money Step #6 – *Financial Competence (Intelligence and Responsibility)*** by obtaining a copy of your company's employee benefits handbook or talk to your employer and determine what benefits are available.
2. Consider any salary-packaging opportunities with your employer which may be of advantage to you.
3. Take an interest in your superannuation fund and follow the **Eight Tips for Choosing the Right Superannuation Fund**.
4. Make the decision whether you should contribute additional amounts to your superannuation fund.
5. Maximise your personal taxation deductions by selecting the right tax agent and keeping the right substantiation documents.

## CHAPTER 17

# What type of health, income protection and trauma insurance do you really need?

'Now, here, you see, it takes all the running you can do, to keep in the same place. If you want to get somewhere else, you must run at least twice as fast as that!'

LEWIS CARROLL (*Through the Looking-Glass*)

The concept of insurance is one where you take on a small guaranteed loss (the premium) as substitution for the possibility of a larger uncertain loss (the peril). The greater the possibility of a potential loss, the greater the cost of the insurance.

Insurance first started as a way of sharing the risk between a group of people. Remember the stories of how a village used to come to the aid of a fellow farmer who had lost his home in a fire? At no cost, the whole village would pitch in to rebuild the house. Without the help of the community, the farmer would have suffered a tremendous loss, possibly even be ruined. There was no repayment, only the understanding that the assisted farmer would pitch in to help when someone else was in trouble. Those 'good old days' were the last time insurance was either cheap or primarily non-profit. Today, insurance is easily one of the largest and richest industries in the world.

Just how big is the insurance industry, you might ask? Well, today the insurance industry is bigger than all the banks, brokerage firms and restaurants combined! Although the growth of the *industry* has been stupendous over the last 100 years, the basic insurance *concept* has not changed. The sole purpose of insurance is to replace the large unpredictable potential loss with the combined smaller guaranteed losses of many people.

> ''Twas brillig, and the slithy toves; Did gyre and gimble in the wabe; All mimsy were the borogoves, And the mome raths outgrabe.
>
> "Beware the Jabberwock, my son! The jaws that bite, the claws that catch!"'
>
> **LEWIS CARROLL**
> **(Through the Looking-Glass)**

I worked for several years in the life, disability and health insurance industry. I was a top producer for one of the top 10 insurance companies in the world. I was trained by my company and sent out to 'help' people. I truly believed in my product and I *knew* in my heart that I was helping people. It was only well after leaving the industry and reflecting on all that I had since learned about money that I realised that I had not necessarily helped as many people as much as I thought I had.

**It is very important that you understand that the main purpose of an insurance company is not to help people.** The main purpose of an insurance company is to make the largest profit possible. I am not saying that your insurance agent is a bad person. Far from it. My personal experience has shown me that most agents truly believe in their products. In fact, I found that most career insurance agents are people of high integrity and ethics. What I am saying is that agents have been trained by their companies to market (sell) as much insurance as possible for as much premium as possible.

The insurance industry makes billions of dollars a year and has many millions of customers. And while insurance is certainly a necessity, many people overpay and take out coverages that they never really need. Let's be realistic about this. Insurance is big business and the main purpose of an insurance company (like any other company) is to make as much money as it possibly can. And insurance companies don't go broke paying out claims (although some have gone broke because of mismanagement and poor investments).

In the previous chapter we discussed maximising the power of your pay cheque where the main emphasis was on benefits available from employers for everything from insurance to retirement planning and superannuation, to salary packaging and fringe benefits. I understand, however, that many employees or self-employed people receive limited or no benefits from their employment other than those they are provided by law (such as workers' compensation insurance and superannuation). So, over the next few chapters I am going to show you how to handle your insurance needs on your own.

First I will show you how you can save hundreds (if not thousands) of dollars a year on your annual insurance expenditure. And exactly how health, income protection, trauma, home and home contents, car and miscellaneous insurance products work. This information should dramatically change how you take care of your insurance needs.

## HEALTH INSURANCE

If you are seeking to be *Financially Competent (Intelligent and Responsible)* you must be able to understand and select the right level of health insurance for your lifestyle and situation. An individual policy can often be expensive, but if you know what you are looking for and do some research, you will find a good policy for a reasonable price.

Your main goal is to find coverage that will help you pay for a major medical problem. Policies that cover other contingencies may be prohibitively expensive. You may find it wisest to pay for routine medical services with your own money (self-insure) and rely on health insurance only to protect you in case of major medical event or catastrophe.

Australia operates a two-tiered healthcare system:
1.  A universal health insurance scheme known as Medicare;
2.  A 'voluntary' facility for providing private funding of hospital care and ancillary services, provided by private health funds.

Since the introduction of Medicare in 1984, the costs to the government (read 'taxpayer') of providing universal healthcare have risen dramatically and are a major burden. This escalation in costs has further accelerated in recent years because of a trend by Australians to move away from being privately insured in preference to using the public system.

Various initiatives have been recently introduced by the Federal Government to make private health insurance more attractive to the uninsured and thus relieve the mounting pressure on the public healthcare system. The initiatives operate as either positive or negative incentives to induce people to the private sector or repel them from the public. To date, they consist of:

* 30% private health insurance rebate available for those with hospital cover, ancillary cover or combined cover;
* lifetime health cover whereby premiums are frozen at a lower level for those entering private health cover at an earlier age;
* additional tax through a 1% Medicare surcharge levy if your income is above a certain level and you don't carry private health insurance.

Healthcare provision remains a very political and sensitive necessity for administrators to manage as the delivery of services and the allocation of resources continually changes. One thing is fairly certain though: the cost to the community does not ever really reduce in real terms. Did you know, for example, that the average private health insurance policy in the year 2000 represents about 8% of the after-tax average weekly wage?

So health insurance is an expense that begs to be managed very judiciously by the *Financially Competent (Intelligent and Responsible)* person. I will explain the public and private healthcare models and their related incentives (and disincentives), and give you some tips on how you can save big dollars on your health insurance costs, ensuring that you maximise the benefits available to you.

## MEDICARE

This is Australia's universal health insurance scheme which is compulsorily funded via the Medicare levy and other federally imposed taxes. Every Australian and New Zealand citizen, or person with a permanent residency visa for Australia, is eligible for Medicare. It provides access to:

- free treatment as a public patient in a public hospital;
- free (or subsidised) treatment by some general practitioners (GPs) and most specialists, plus limited dental and optometry services.

For in-hospital services, if you are a public patient in a public hospital, you receive treatment by those doctors and specialists nominated by the hospital. Care and treatment, including after-care treatment is free. (Well, provided at no extra charge to you. It is covered by your Medicare levy contribution.)

Conversely, if you are a private patient in a public or private hospital, you can have your choice of practitioner to treat you and Medicare will pay 75% of the scheduled fee for those services. For out-of-hospital services (e.g., doctor or specialist consulting fees, pathology tests or X-rays, some dental costs, other surgical or therapeutic procedures) you can again choose the doctor who treats you and Medicare will normally reimburse you for 85% of the scheduled fee for those services.

Now this is where you have to be careful. While Medicare covers you to some extent, it will only reimbuse you up to 75% of the scheduled fee if you are a private patient in a hospital and 85% of the scheduled fee for out-of-hospital fees. How many specialists do you know who charge anything close to the scheduled fee? It is not uncommon for specialists to charge twice the scheduled fee. Which means that if you don't carry private health cover you will have to make up the difference yourself.

Also, as you will have often seen in the media, if you go without private health insurance and are in need of 'non-urgent' hospital treatment ('elective' surgery), it is common to find yourself on an uncomfortably long and slow waiting list. It can be well over a year before you receive direct treatment for the problem. And from what I hear, what you may describe as 'urgent' may translate in Medicare-speak as 'elective'. You may not even necessarily wind up with your choice of doctor.

There are also many items not actually covered by Medicare, such as:

- private patient hospital logistics costs (for example, theatre costs or accommodation);
- dental examination and treatment;
- ambulance services (although provided free in some states);
- home nursing;
- some additional therapies such as physiotherapy, speech or occupational therapy;
- medicines;
- hearing aids, glasses and contact lenses;
- medical and hospital costs incurred overseas.

Related to Medicare is the Commonwealth Pharmaceutical Benefits Scheme (PBS) which ensures Australian residents have access to necessary and lifesaving medicines at an affordable price. Generic brands of prescription medicines are subsidised. You pay a maximum of between $20 and $60 per prescription medicine or $3.30 with a concession card. There can be a surcharge if you select a non-generic brand of medicine where an 'equivalent' generic brand is available. Concession cards are available for those who hold a Centrelink card or are covered under concessions from the Department of Veteran Affairs.

There is also a PBS safety net. If you spend more than a set threshold on prescriptions, then your medicines will be cheaper or free for the rest of the calendar year. In 2000 the threshold is $631.20 for you or your family in any calendar year and $171.60 if you are a concession card holder.

## PRIVATE HEALTH FUNDS

Currently about 40% of the Australian population is covered by private health insurance (this number rose from 30% following the Federal Government's Lifetime Health Cover initiative in July 2000). Traditionally the majority of people who carry private health insurance are on average wealthier and older (and also apparently in better health). There are currently 48 health benefit organisations of which most are mutuals (not-for-profit) and by far the largest, Medibank Private, is a Commonwealth non-profit body. Very few organisations operate for profit, which reveals just how difficult it is to run healthcare services provision efficiently (i.e., difficult to exploit commercially on a large scale).

Since regulatory changes in 1995, however, things are changing as health funds are being allowed to operate in a more competitive manner by offering wider choices of policies, services and benefits. (Rest assured that in the future many funds will become driven by 'healthy' profits along the lines of the US model as larger insurance conglomerates move into the health insurance area, whether directly or via underwriting.)

When you join a private health fund you effectively insure against some or all of the health service costs Medicare does not cover. Private funds are now developing new types of policies, which include:

- 100% cover (no 'gap');
- 100% hospital cover with partial medical cover;
- exclusionary cover;
- specified co-payment cover;
- unspecified co-payment cover – fixed benefits a day;
- ancillary cover.


On top of these options there are four types of **membership**: single; family; couple or single-parent family.

All types of membership allow you to elect to carry a certain level of **excess**. This means that you pay for a minimum level of medical costs, either annually or for each hospital visit. The higher the level of excess you agree to, the lower your premium should be (this is a form of self-insurance and for a healthy or 'low-risk' individual can save a lot of money over the long term). Be careful with the level of excess though because under the new government health insurance reforms there are maximum excess levels ($500 for single and $1,000 for family) above which you will attract the 1% Medicare surcharge levy just as if you did not have private health insurance at all. This penalty seems to discourage self-insurance and thus appears to contradict the government's policy but it is nonetheless the current situation.

Here are the various policy options in more detail:

1. **100% cover.** This pays for all in-hospital services except PBS medicines. It covers the costs of all hospital and medical services you receive from hospitals and doctors who are party to 100% agreements with your health fund. This type of cover is currently being developed by funds and they are putting relevant agreements into place.

2. **100% hospital cover with partial medical cover.** This offers the same cover as above, except out-of-hospital services are only partially paid. This means insured patients have to pay for any specialists' charges that exceed the scheduled fees.

3. **Exclusionary cover.** This is where certain benefits are excluded in return for a lower premium. Such exclusions might be for obstetrics, joint-replacement or heart surgery. Remember, if something is excluded, then Medicare can be claimed for up to 75% of the scheduled fee, but the gap cannot then be claimed from your private health insurer.

4. **Specified co-payment cover.** You can opt to bear some of the costs incurred in-hospital or out-of-hospital in return for lower premiums. This is like the excess on your car insurance. The excess can be on either the hospital, doctor or both. Specified co-payment cover can also be adjusted for 100% cover or exclusionary cover as well.

5. **Unspecified co-payment cover – fixed benefits a day.** This covers all hospital charges you incur as a private patient in shared ward accommodation in a public hospital. It may also cover some or all of accommodation charges in a private hospital. This insurance will also pay the 25% gap that Medicare does not pay in the case of in-hospital medical services.

6. **Ancillary cover.** This is for non-hospital services such as dental or optical treatment, or physiotherapy. It can be charged separately or added to one of the above. Some policies offer cover for treatments and services as diverse as acupuncture, iridology, therapeutic massage, gym membership fees and sporting footwear costs.

The concept behind the different types of cover is that benefit payments will be based on the condition being treated rather than on average daily fees. Health funds are trying to organise agreements with hospitals and doctors so that you are aware of the costs (if any) you have to pay for treatments, before they begin. Australia is thus moving towards a tighter *user pays* model of health insurance, reflected in lower tailored premiums for those who do not require many services offered or who are prepared to adopt a higher level of self-insurance. Conversely those who require or choose complete coverage, or avoid private coverage under the public system, will pay more in one way or another for their health coverage.

Before I give you some tips on getting the right health cover, let's now look more closely at the so called 'incentives' the Federal Government has introduced, trying to get people to join private health funds (or repel us from the public system).

1. **30% rebate on private health insurance.** From 1 January 1999, anyone eligible for Medicare who is also a member of a registered private health fund is eligible for the rebate. It is available irrespective of family type or income and is available on premiums for hospital cover, ancillary cover or combined cover.

   The rebate means that if your premium is say $1,000, then you will receive $300 back from the Federal Government. There are three ways to receive the rebate:
   • Ask your health fund to adjust your premium for the rebate so you only pay the (reduced) net amount;
   • Pay the full premium then claim the rebate in your next tax return;
   • Pay the full premium then apply to Medicare for a cash or cheque reimbursement of the amount of the rebate.
   **Hot Tip:** Note that even if your employer has paid your premium on your behalf, you can still claim the 30% rebate.

2. **Lifetime Health Cover Scheme.** This scheme became effective from 1 July 2000. It is designed to slow down the rate of premium increases and make private health insurance more affordable. Lifetime Health Cover rewards, through lower premiums, those who remain in health funds for

longer periods of time. It encourages people to join a fund at a younger age and maintain their membership over their lifetime. The Federal Government hopes this initiative translates to improvements in the overall health profile of private health fund members (through encouraging more proactive use of insured services and thus better disease prevention for members). Hence it is hoped that premiums will become more affordable to all members. From early indications, based upon the high take-up of the scheme (some 2 million extra people took out private cover before the July 2000 deadline), the initiative is off to a strong start.

If you delayed taking out hospital cover past the age of 30, (and past the July 15, 2000 commencement of the scheme) your premiums will increase 2% above the base 30-year-old rate for each year you are aged above 30 when you join. For example, if you joined a fund in December 2000 and you are 45 you will pay 30% more than the 30-year-old rate for as long as you retain membership (15 yrs x 2% = 30%).

3. **Medicare surcharge levy.** Since 1 July 1997 there has been an additional tax of 1% (a surcharge on top of the base 1.5% Medicare levy) payable on taxable income for certain people who do not carry private health insurance. You must pay the surcharge if you do not have private health insurance cover and you are:

- a single person with a taxable income greater than $50,000; or
- a family with a combined taxable income greater than $100,000 (this threshold increases $1,500 for each dependent child).

The surcharge is applied by the tax office when you lodge your tax return. There are exceptions to this but the exceptions apply to very few people.

## THE BIG QUESTION: SHOULD YOU CARRY PRIVATE HEALTH INSURANCE?

As you can see, there is quite a lot to consider on the subject of health insurance. I have experienced all this and more in the US where health insurance premiums can be extremely expensive, with policies all but impossible to understand and where a litany of insurance companies compete for the consumer dollar in ways that would make the unitiatiated giddy. In my home city of Phoenix, Arizona, for example (about the same population as Sydney), the advertisements in the Yellow Pages for health insurance companies alone cover more than 40 full pages!

In Australia, you have begun heading down the same road. In the early stages of these 'reforms' the choices will seem relatively uncomplicated (don't laugh!) with funds able to offer a greater range of services coupled with the Federal Government offering 'incentives' to become a member. Down the line however these reforms open windows of opportunity for the larger insurance companies (read: profit-pumping behemoths) to enter the market and offer a myriad of interconnected and multi-layered new products which are difficult to unravel and designed solely to increase company profits.

Enough of the doom and gloom. What can you do now to take advantage of the Federal Government initiatives? Due to the rapidly changing Australian health insurance market, it is hard to direct you at this stage to particular funds which I consider better than others. From my experience, you should consider the following questions when making your own decision as to which (if any) funds to join.

## FIVE PRIVATE HEALTH INSURANCE QUESTIONS TO CONSIDER

1. **Do the Federal Government incentives help me?** If I am a family man or woman paying an annual insurance premium of $2,500, my premium reduces to $1,750 after the 30% rebate. If I did not have the insurance and had to pay the Medicare surcharge levy instead, then I would be up for an extra $1,000 tax on a combined taxable income over $100,000. Net saving by not having the insurance is $750. That's not taking into account the likelihood of extra premiums to be charged later because of Lifetime Health Cover initiatives, nor any judgments as to quality of care under public versus private services.

2. **Do I need 100% cover?** If you are young and healthy you may not think this is necessary. You may opt for some exclusions such as obstetrics or joint-replacement and look to get extra cover when necessary. You may only require hospital cover for emergencies. If your income is not high (i.e. less than $50,000) then the Medicare levy may not affect you too severely and you may wish to adopt a higher level of self-insurance. This will reduce your premiums. Alternately, if you are thinking about starting a family or have a young family, 100% cover may be more suitable.

3. **Should I have an 'excess' (or co-payment)?** If you have the capacity to pay the first, say $500 of hospital treatment, this will significantly reduce your premiums and for a healthy low-risk individual (as a form of self-insurance) this is usually a much more financially beneficial arrangement over the mid to long term. As we said before though, watch out for the extra 1% Medicare surcharge levy which kicks in on policies with $500 excess for individuals and $1,000 for families.

4. **Am I covered by my parent's plan?** Unmarried dependent children, step-children and foster children who are under 21 years of age, or under 25 if the dependent child is a full-time student, are usually included as part of the family membership (this varies from fund to fund).

5. **Should I consider a group plan?** Groups have greater buying power and thus usually pay lower rates than individuals. Enquire if there is a professional, trade, sporting or other organisation through which you can gain coverage. Ask other people in your industry what coverage they have. Sometimes policies offered by member organisations are better than retail deals.

If you do opt for private health insurance, which I certainly recommend on some level for most people, then you need to search for the most affordable health insurance to satisfy you particular needs. To determine your particular needs there are a few more questions you should consider and ask the health funds:

• How much will a satisfactory policy cost?
• Which hospitals are under agreement with the fund?

- Which doctors are under agreement with the fund?
- Is there a waiting period (and how long) before benefits are paid?
- Does the level of cover mean I qualify for the Federal Government rebate?
- Can I choose my own doctor?
- What happens to pre-existing medical conditions?
- What hospital treatments are not covered?
- Are there any other exclusions?
- What is the level of dental cover?
- Will my premiums be reduced if:
  - I opt for an excess?
  - I pay in advance?
  - I pay by credit card or direct debit?
- Although they are not available in Australia yet, it is always worth enquiring if your insurer offers 'good health' discounts. These discounts are commonplace in the US (along with good student discounts for teenagers), where funds offer special discounts for people in 'good health' or incentives for those who take proactive lifestyle care of their health. In the US smokers pay almost twice as much for health insurance as non-smokers and will sometimes not even qualify for insurance to cover certain medical procedures to correct serious problems caused by their smoking habit (sometimes the procedure itself will not even be available, insured or not).

Once you know what you want, shop around. Get the most benefits for the least price. Ask your friends what cover they have (a lot of them won't know) and with whom. There are various health funds which may be linked to your credit union, employment or profession so don't just look at the larger (more prominent) health funds. Grand United, for example, has a long history as a non-profit and very efficiently run and flexible organisation which focuses on providing high levels of member satisfaction and ancillary benefits tailored to the individual, but they don't advertise much at all.

Some of the best sources of information to 'shop for a policy' are available on the Internet (or by telephone). Start with:

- Doctors Reference Site at www.drsref.com.au lists 20 health insurers and has general information on private health insurance;
- Health Insurance Advisers Australia at www.hiaa.com.au (1300 366 603) is an independent organisation which assists consumers to manage, understand and find the best value-for-money private health cover;
- iSelect Pty Ltd at www.iselect.com.au (1800 10 2000) offers a free support service that helps you choose the health policy that best suits your individual needs;
- Australian Consumers' Association CHOICEOnline website which provides articles/reports on insurance products at www.choice.com.au.

Other websites which have price calculators or online applications include:

- HCF at www.hcf.com.au; (13 14 39);
- MBF at www.healthsmart.com.au; (132 623);
- Health Partners at www.healthpartners.com.au;
- Medibank Private at www.medibank.com.au; (1800 188 188).

I won't apologise too much if the preceding pages have sent you into a state of brain meltdown, because the content provided here really is about as simple as it gets in the insurance industry. We cannot simpy put our heads in the sand. As *Financially Competent (Intelligent and Responsible)* **Level Four Automatic Investors** we must apply due diligence to all decisions involving the enhancement or reduction of our wealth. Take the time to understand what you need to in order to be able to make an informed decision.

## INCOME PROTECTION INSURANCE

What would happen if you were in a terrible car accident and you couldn't work for 18 months? Could you live off your savings or assets? If not, do you have income protection insurance?

Your employee entitlements such as annual leave and sick leave may only pay you for a few weeks, or at most a couple of months. If your income stream is vital to your current life commitments do not rely on these entitlements! Also, don't expect workers' compensation to look after you. It is designed for accidents specifically connected to the workplace and typically the benefits are closely defined and limited.

Income protection insurance provides you with a regular income if you are unable to work in your normal employment due to accident or sickness. Benefits are paid monthly as income, not by lump sum. Usually the income paid is 75% of your 'personal exertion' income after any business expenses. Premiums are tax-deductible. This insurance is sometimes called *sickness and accident, income replacement, disability income* or *salary continuance* insurance.

Remember the primary purpose of income protection is to replace your income if an unforeseen event interrupts it for a financially significant period of time. **It is not designed to cover the associated costs of the event**. Your health insurance should do that.

For most people, some degree of income protection insurance will be necessary where they *need* a regular income to support their family and lifestyle.

## SIX INCOME PROTECTION INSURANCE POINTS TO CONSIDER

Insurance companies offer all kinds of confusing extras attached to their policies. In most cases these options should be avoided. Here are some of the points to consider:

1. **Waiting (qualifying) period.** Consider how long you can wait before receiving benefits (typically 14, 30, 60 or 90 days – some waiting periods may be as long as two years). Consider your financial commitments before deciding. Lower premiums can be achieved by accepting a longer waiting period.
2. **Definitions and coverage.** Look for exclusions. Usually there are few and most refer to both *illness* and *accident*. Some policies differ in the definition of 'total disability'. The types of duties or employment you must be unable to perform will govern whether you are considered 'totally disabled' or not. Some policies refer to employment as 'any employment',

206 MONEY SECRETS OF THE RICH

including lower-paid unskilled work unrelated to your previous career. So look for a policy which covers you when you cannot perform your current *regular* work.

3. **Guaranteed renewable.** This guarantees you can renew your policy each year without undergoing a medical examination. The insurance company cannot single you out for a rate increase just because you made (a lot of) claims. Your premiums can only be increased in accordance with normal rate increases.

4. **Residual benefit protection.** If you are partially disabled, some policies will pay you a portion of your disability benefits. This is known as **residual benefits**. This coverage is important in the event that you become partially disabled and can work only part-time or in a lower paying line of work. Once again however, it will be expensive if you really do not need it. Consider the real risks you are protecting against.

5. **Non-cancellable.** This means the insurer cannot cancel your current policy or raise your premium for any reason. This can be an extremely attractive feature but may come at the cost of a higher base premium.

6. **Shop around and compare quotes.** There are currently over a dozen insurance companies in Australia which offer income protection insurance so there is plenty of competition.

   The Australian Services Directory at www.afsd.com.au provides a list of insurance brokers, agents and underwriters on a state-by-state basis. There are many online applications and telephone quote services available:

   • The Money Shop at www.themoneyshop.com.au/insurance; (02) 9957 1962;
   • MyFinance at www.myfinance.com.au;
   • Insurance Watch at www.insurancewatch.com.au;
   • Financial Choice at www.financialchoice.com.au; 1800 644 479;
   • DirectChoice at www.directchoiceinsurance.com.au; 1800 245 123.
   • Les McIntosh Insurance Agencies at www.lesmac.com.au.

## TRAUMA INSURANCE

Trauma insurance pays you a lump-sum benefit in the event of trauma or a specified disease. It differs to life insurance in that the benefit is paid when the diagnosis is confirmed, not after death from the condition. This can enable people to pay additional medical care, relieve financial pressures and be given greater opportunity for recovery.

In the case of accidental trauma, most insurers pay immediately whereas a waiting period of 90 days is usually imposed for particular illnesses. As with other insurances, beware of the exclusions and other conditions associated with the policies.

## FIVE TIPS FOR SELECTING TRAUMA INSURANCE

1. **Duplicate coverage.** If you already have private health insurance, income protection insurance and life insurance, consider how much (if any) trauma insurance you really need. For example, if you had a heart attack and had all other types of insurance, do you need trauma insurance as well?
2. **Review conditions.** Review what illnesses are covered. To do this properly you will need to compare policies to shed light on some of the medical terms used which may be otherwise quite meaningless (to non–medically trained people). Claims experience suggests the cause of claims to be about two–thirds from cancer and one–quarter from heart attack, stroke or coronary bypass.
3. **Be careful of additional benefits.** Many policies charge additional premiums for waiver of premium, buy-back options, additional death benefits and childrens' benefits. Don't buy these! Work out what you *really* need and stick to this. Analyse the risk without emotion.
4. **Waiting period.** Review your financial commitments and determine the length of time before payment is made from the insurer. Increasing this period will reduce your premium.
5. **Shop around for the best deal.** For all the reasons we have already discussed, shop around for your policy. Refer to the sources listed for income protection insurance quotes and information.

If you have any concerns about various insurance policies, companies or funds, a useful reference source is the Insurance Council of Australia on 1300 728 228 (or visit www.ica.com.au and view the Code of Practice and other useful insurance industry and policy information).

## CHAPTER 17 ACTION STEPS REVIEW

1. Practice **Money Step #6 – *Financial Competence (Intelligence and Responsibility)*** by determining your requirements for private health insurance and, if you need it and you haven't got it, get it. To find affordable coverage check a variety of insurers, particularly funds that are targeted towards your occupation or profession. Follow the guidelines in this chapter to find a suitable fund. Review the **Five Private Health Insurance Questions to Consider**.
2. Consider the true need for income protection insurance and review the **Six Income Protection Insurance Points to Consider**.
3. Consider the true need for trauma insurance and review the **Five Tips for Selecting Trauma Insurance**.

## CHAPTER 18

# Getting the right home and home contents insurance for less

'The distance is nothing; it is only the first step that is difficult.'

MARIE DE VICHY-CHAMROND (1697-1780)

In this chapter we are going to cover home and home contents insurance. Most people are able to save several hundred dollars (if not over a thousand) each year by becoming *Financially Competent (Intelligent and Responsible)* in the handling of these critical areas of protection. Do not just blindly buy these policies. *Know what your money is doing.*

## HOME INSURANCE

If you own a home, you probably already have home insurance. If, however, you are like many homeowners, you do not carry enough coverage or you are paying *too much* for the coverage you have (the Insurance Council of Australia suggests up to 60% of homes are inadequately insured based upon current replacement costs).

## YOUR INSURANCE RISKS (PERILS)

In a nutshell, home insurance covers the replacement or repair of your home as a result of unexpected damage.

Most home insurance policies specify the events that they cover. Typical specified events are:

- fire;
- explosion;
- theft or attempted theft;
- lightning;
- earthquake;
- storm;
- bursting, leaking, overflowing or discharging liquid from pipes, tanks and waterbeds;
- malicious damage or vandalism;
- riot or civil commotion;
- impact of vehicles, space or aerial debris, falling trees or aerials;
- damage by vehicles.

Policies do not always mention what is *not* covered. Check for exclusions which may not be suitable for you, such as flood, which in many cases is excluded but can be added as extra.

Home insurance usually covers:

- the main residence;
- garages and other buildings, usually if they are specified in council plans;
- driveways;
- walls, gates and fences;
- verandahs;
- in-ground swimming pools;
- landlord's fixtures and fittings;
- hot water services, air-conditioners, exterior blinds and awnings.

Some insurers include (and others will add on) such items as:

- accidental damage to glass in windows, skylights and cooktops;
- the cost of temporary accommodation if the damage is so

bad you cannot live in the house;
- cost of removing debris, employing architects and engineers to repair the damage;
- liability cover for when you are legally liable for someone's injury or for damage to their property.

You need to buy enough insurance to cover the full cost of rebuilding your home (insurance companies call it 'reinstatement'). Insurance companies use 'rebuilding guides' to help calculate the cost of rebuilding your home. If you believe the insurance company's assessment is inappropriate (likely to be too high) you can contest the amount of required coverage. If necessary, a building contractor (for a fee) can provide evidence as to the true cover required.

Be careful though. If you are underinsured, some insurance companies may disqualify part of your claim even if the claim is for less than the full sum insured. That is, if you underinsure by say 30% of the building replacement cost, they may only pay you 30% less of the *overall* claim. This is known as 'averaging' and should be avoided wherever possible.

## HOME CONTENTS INSURANCE

Standard home contents insurance covers the replacement of your contents in the case of unexpected damage or loss. As with home insurance, the insurance company specifies the events for which they will cover you. It is usually up to you to specify the amount of contents cover you require. Home contents insurance usually covers:
- personal items;
- furniture and furnishings;
- household goods;
- carpet;
- clothing.

Always make sure that your contents insurance covers the replacement cost, not *actual cash value* of your home's contents ('new-for-old'). **Replacement cost** gives you enough to buy new comparable items to replace your belongings. **Actual cash value** pays the cost to replace your possessions with similar used items (depreciated value) or the repair cost, *whichever is less.* There is a vast difference. Note that some insurance companies provide 'new-for-old' cover only if the contents are less than 10 years old.

Do you have expensive computer equipment? If so, the maximum coverage is usually around $10,000 and in some cases you may have to specify the equipment on your policy. Depending upon what you own, you may need to specify unusual or expensive items on your policy, such as jewellery, works of art or antiques.

If you work at home, your office equipment may or may not be covered by your home contents insurance policy. So check your policy carefully – you may need an endorsement for any additional required coverage or for specific items.

It is a good idea to video-tape your valuables for insurance records. After all, you can only collect for what you can *prove* you lost. This is why a video record of all the valuables in your house is the best way to document a loss. Walk through your home room by room and record (with narration) what everything is and its current replacement cost. Be sure to list the make, model and serial number of valuables. An up-to-date list of your CDs may also be required. Keep a copy of the video tape and list for yourself and another copy off-premises with a trusted friend or relative. (There are also companies available who will document your valuables for you if you are unable to and will store digital images at their premises that you can access via the Internet. If such services represent good value and peace of mind you might consider them: such as Prometheus service from www.insuru.com.au).

The Insurance Council of Australia has a handy brochure entitled *Do you Have the Home and Contents Cover You Need?*, which is a step-by-step guide to determining the insurance you realistically require. It also has advice on how to make a claim (1300 728 228 or www.ica.com.au).

There are two main extras to your contents insurance which are usually provided as part of your standard contents insurance, but in some cases you need to pay an additional premium. These are:

1. **Personal valuables cover.** You can extend cover to include

items you frequently take outside the home as long as they are in Australia (sometimes New Zealand as well). These effects must be nominated with a limit of value placed on them. Items may include:

- camera equipment;
- rings or other jewellery;
- laptop computers or electronic organisers etc;
- golf clubs.

Sometimes you can select a limit for your unspecified valuables. This type of cover may be necessary if valuable items are taken outside the home regularly and can take the place of other insurance which might be expensive (e.g., domestic travel insurance).

2. **Personal liability insurance.** This usually is a part of contents insurance and covers you if you negligently injure other people or damage their property and they make a claim against you. Look for a policy which has this, particularly if it includes your children residing with you or applies to you and your family when away from home within Australia. Such cover usually offers in the range of $10 million to $20 million protection. It is also a good idea to make sure that your policy covers injury to tradespeople (including cleaners, babysitters and gardeners) while they are on your premises. These people may not carry their own insurance despite what they may claim when asked.

## ADDITIONAL COVERAGES TO BE AVOIDED

In addition to items specified on your contents insurance, there are several other additional coverages available on the contents policy. I would not generally opt for any of these coverages unless they are

'When you distinguish between reasonable financial concerns and decisions based solely on fear, you can free up a great deal of financial as well as emotional power. The trick is to be courageous enough to admit that your fear is not working to your advantage and to be truthful about where your decision is coming from. Remember, fear keeps you focused on little details and unlikely events. It's far wiser to assume the best – know that most of the time your fears will not manifest.'
**RICHARD CARLSON**

'free' inclusions. As options they are not usually good value in relation to the premium charged. Typically they include:
- fusion cover for electronic motors;
- cover for spoilage of frozen food up to $500;
- cover for such items as boats and trailers;
- cover for stolen credit cards up to $500;
- accidental breakage of glass;
- pet cover up to $500.

## IF YOU ARE RENTING

If you rent a home unit or house, you should also consider purchasing home contents insurance. This is because it not only covers your possessions, but offers public liability insurance for inside and outside your home. Did you know that, as a renter, you can be held liable for damages to the property and that if someone slips and falls inside your home, you can be held liable? Contents insurance will provide you with protection.

## SIX WAYS TO REDUCE THE COST OF HOME AND HOME CONTENTS INSURANCE

1. **High excess.** Opt for a high excess so you can keep your annual premium low. Make sure you have the money to cover the high excess.
2. **Limit your claims.** Many insurance companies offer 'no claims' discounts to the annual premium of 25–45%.
3. **Ask if you are eligible for any discounts.** Ask for the following common discounts:
   - Over 55 years of age (Australian Pensioners Insurance Agency (APIA) or Over 50's Friendly Society, for example);
   - Burglar alarms;
   - In residence during weekdays (home office);
   - Dead-locks and keyed window-locks;
   - Fire extinguishers and smoke-detectors.
4. **Place your home contents and home insurance with the same insurance company**. By placing all your home insurance policies with the one company you can usually receive at least a 10% discount. Even greater discounts may apply where

you also have car or boat insurance with the one insurer. I have seen discounts of up to 40% for bundling three or more policies with the one company (AAMI as a recent example).

5. **Consider 'pay-by-the-month' premium options via direct debit from your bank account.** Provided there is no premium loading for this feature, consider pay-by-the-month premiums. If you pay your premiums over 12 equal monthly payments instead of yearly you are then able to invest (or budget) your cash flows to better advantage. Direct debit of premiums may also attract slight premium discounts (2–3%) for the efficiencies that it offers the insurance companies. With proper planning you will be better off.

6. **Call or surf for quotes.** Start with the Yellow Pages directory. There are many well-known insurers from which to choose. On the Internet there are also some helpful sites:

   • Australian Financial Services Directory – this is a listing by state of insurance brokers, agents and underwriters just so you can see what is available at www.afsd.com.au.

   • Insurance Bids – an exciting site which guarantees to reduce your current home and contents renewal by at least 7.5%. It is a type of auction house where various insurers bid for your coverage. Check them out at the end of your search for rock-bottom rates at www.insurancebids.com.au.

   • Quicken Insurance Mart – offers a five-minute quote form on home and contents insurance. Fill in your quote details and you receive an email reply from www.quicken.com.au; 1800 674 888.

   • A few other sites which may be of interest:
     – Insurance Watch at www.insurancewatch.com.au;
     – Commonwealth Bank at www.commbank.com.au (has a calculator to estimate the value of your home);
     – WWW Insurance Agencies at www.insuru.com.au;
     – Colonial Insurance at www.colonial.com.au; 13 27 90;
     – NRMA Insurance at www.nrma.com.au; 132 132;
     – Summerland Credit Union at www.summerlandcu.org.au; 1300 361 561;

- CGU Insurance Australia at www.commercial-union.com.au; 1300 362 893;
- Australian Consumers' Association CHOICEOnline website which provides articles/reports on insurance products and downloadable contents insurance calculator at www.choice.com.au;
- Greater National Group at www.gng.com.au; (03) 9572 5755;
- MyFinance at www.myfinance.com.au;
- The Money Shop at www.themoneyshop.com.au/insurance; (02) 9957 1962;
- Financial Choice at www.i-choice.com.au; 1800 644 479.

---

## CHAPTER 18 ACTION STEPS REVIEW

1. Practice **Money Step #6 – *Financial Competence (Intelligence and Responsibility)*** by determining what type of home and home contents insurance you now have.
2. Determine if your home is insured for the proper value. If in doubt get some advice.
3. Make sure you have replacement cost coverage for your home contents insurance. Do you need to specify high-value personal property on your policy?
4. Video-tape your valuables. Keep a copy of the tape for yourself and a copy off-premises with a trusted friend or relative.
5. Remove unwanted additional coverages.
6. Implement the **Six Ways to Reduce the Cost of Home and Home Contents Insurance**: high excess; limit your claims; ask for discounts; combine home and contents insurance and car and boat insurance with the same insurer; consider pay-by-the-month premiums; and call or surf for quotes.

## CHAPTER 19

# Slashing your car and miscellaneous insurance costs

*'Some terrible things happened in my lifetime –
a few of which actually happened.'*

BENJAMIN FRANKLIN

Car insurance. Car rental insurance. Domestic travel insurance. Loan insurance. Service contracts. Mortgage life insurance. Flight insurance. So many different types of insurance! ***Only one of these is truly necessary: car insurance!***

All the others (in most cases) are of marginal value (at best) and often a complete rip-off designed to provide great profits for the insurance companies. On most of these policies the agent will make very large commissions, often as high as 60%. These types of insurance overcharge you between 200 and 800% in comparison to equitable coverage (without a fancy name). **Remember, if an insurance company has a great new idea, you can be sure it is great for them, not you**.

## CAR INSURANCE

Every state has enacted laws to ensure cars have compulsory insurance to protect innocent victims of accidents from serious financial loss (e.g., people who are hurt by an illegally uninsured motorist or unregistered vehicle). In addition it is usually advisable to top up this compulsory insurance with a policy designed to cover damage to other vehicles or property, or to your own vehicle. Car insurance is one of your bigger insurance costs. In this chapter we will show you how to reduce your premiums 20–50%. There are four different types of coverage:

1.  **Third party injury.** This is the compulsory insurance you need before you can register your car. In some states you pay this insurance to the government and they administer the scheme. In other states (such as New South Wales and Queensland), the compulsory insurance is privately administered and therefore you can shop around for the best prices. Third party insurance cover insures the owner of the car and any other person who drives the car against liability in respect of death or injury to a person caused by the fault of the car owner or driver within Australia. Typically this insurance does not cover damage to your car, other cars or property.

2.  **Third party property damage.** If your car damages another person's property and you are at fault, third party property damage will cover these costs as well as your legal bills. The policy is usually for cover up to $20 million. Some policies also include cover of $3,000 for your car if you are not at fault in an accident, the other driver can be identified and the other driver has no property damage insurance.

    This type of cover is recommended if your car is not worth replacing or repairing. If you have any assets or the hope of developing assets then this insurance is absolutely necessary. Failure to have at least this cover can leave you highly exposed to a large claim possibly resulting in financial disaster.

3.  **Third Party, Fire and Theft.** As the name suggests, this type of insurance covers your car against fire damage or if it is stolen. It is usually an add-on to a third party property damage policy. It does not cover your car in the event of a collision. I usually feel this is an unnecessary extra as it is only of benefit if your car is a total loss, but not as a result of an accident. In most cases, your comprehensive insurance would better meet this need.

4. **Comprehensive insurance.** This is the most common type
   of car insurance, covering all third party property damage and
   liability along with insuring for the repair or replacement of
   your car if it is damaged or stolen. If your car is financed, it is
   likely the financier will insist that you take out comprehensive
   insurance.

   Some insurers include policy benefits such as:
   • car rental following an accident, usually up to 14 days;
   • replacing your car with a new one if it is written-off and
     less than 12 months old;
   • insurance of personal items which are stolen from your
     car or damaged;
   • emergency repairs and emergency travel costs.

One of the biggest considerations when shopping for
comprehensive vehicle insurance is the difference between
the concept of *agreed value* and *market value*.

**Agreed value** is where the insurer guarantees to pay the
amount nominated on your policy as the insured value of
the vehicle, in the event of total loss. **Market value** means
that the amount nominated on your policy is the *maximum*
paid in the case of total loss. It is very unlikely that this
amount *will* be paid to you by the insurer as this amount is
regularly adjusted for car depreciation and will reflect the
market value (replacement cost) of a similar condition make
and model car.

*Agreed value* may be the best option if you own an unusual
car (e.g., a vintage, classic or pristine-condition car) and it is
certainly my preference. However, with a normal vehicle this
type of policy is usually more expensive so you will need to
weigh up the true value of the extra expense when making
a decision.

Also, don't forget that the agreed value will also depreciate
each year and you should keep an eye on this. If you have
cause to dispute the agreed value of your car (i.e., it is too
low, given that your car is 'special' and could not be replaced
for the lower value) then you can arrange for an inspector
from the insurance company to make a special inspection of

your car to 'agree' on a higher value. You must remain vigilant with these higher agreed values as to whether they are realistic or not each year.

## TEN WAYS TO LOWER YOUR CAR INSURANCE PREMIUMS

1. **Consider the type of cover.** Most people have comprehensive insurance without considering whether it is really necessary. Don't be emotional about your car. If the difference between your premium and the true (impersonal) value of your car is not too much, consider third party property damage insurance and self-insure the additional exposure.

2. **Excess on policy.** Opt for a high excess to keep your annual premiums low (making sure you have money available to cover the higher excess). I realise that a low excess can make you feel warm and fuzzy. However, the facts are that fewer than 10% of all cars will be involved in a claim (annually) and only half of these policyholders will have to pay any excess. The aim is to pay less in premiums than you are likely to claim in damages over the medium to long term.

   Low excesses cost the insurance company more than high excesses because of the administrative cost of each and every claim (over $400). The company knows that if you have a low excess you are more likely to file a claim, so they factor that into the premium. Do yourself a favour, consider a $500 to $1,000 excess. This can reduce your comprehensive insurance premium by up to 30%.

   Also remember there can be different excess levels for the one policy, such as for inexperienced or young drivers. The same principles apply but better still, keep young or inexperienced drivers away from your car.

3. **Never lodge an insurance claim for under $1,000 unless you are guaranteed that it will not effect your no-claim bonus or your future premium and excess level.** Insurance companies will often increase premiums or cancel insurance for policyholders who lodge claims on a repetitive basis. You may lose your no-claim bonus or if you

don't have one, it will be unlikely you will ever qualify for one. Raise your excess and self-insure the little stuff. It will keep your premium low and prevent your insurance from being cancelled.

Some companies do offer one minor claim a year for incidents such as windscreen damage while the car is moving without affecting your insurance arrangements. Shop around for this.

4. **Use a low (or no) annual fee credit card for any excess.** Save one VISA card or MasterCard just for emergencies. Keep it in a safe place (other than your pocket, wallet or purse) and use it only for emergencies. It will provide you peace of mind and save you those wasted premiums.

5. **Do not take extra coverages.** Premiums for extras on a car policy make absolutely no financial sense. The odds of collecting versus the premiums charged are astronomical. Emergency travel costs, repairs and car rentals coverage can cost more than $100 a year. How often will you use them? This is insurance overcharging at its best.

6. **Ask if you are eligible for discounts.** Discounts are commonly available in these particular circumstances:
   - Multi-car policies – more than one car insured by the same company.
   - Car not driven to work – some companies offer substantial discounts if your car is not driven to work (the risk of collision is dramatically reduced). It is assumed that the car is garaged during the week, or out of danger.
   - Driver training – take an advanced driver course.
   - Garage – if the car is always garaged securely to deter theft.
   - Anti-theft equipment – car alarm or tracking device.
   - Airbags – driver and passenger airbags can make a difference.
   - Country driver – premiums are lower for country drivers. Some insurers charge different premiums depending on in which suburb the car is garaged.
   - Pensioner, retired or people over 55.
   - Direct debit for premium discount – may be as high as 4% because it reduces insurance company overheads.
   - Annual lump sum payment of premium discounts – if you

pay for 12 months in advance in one hit you may get 12 months for the price of 11 (NRMA, for example, offers such discounts on some insurance products. Call for quotes on 132 976 or visit www.nrma.com.au).

7. **Drive carefully.** No-claim bonuses of up to 60% are given for drivers who have minimal claims and a good driving record. Conversely, consistent speeding and other traffic expenses (especially drink driving) will cost you a lot extra in premiums.

8. **Consider the type of car you drive.** Conservative family types of cars will cost you less to insure compared to those styled as sports cars or fitted with turbos. Modifications to your car such as window tinting, wider tyres, engine changes and accessories will also cost you higher premiums. Check the insurance company ratings for each car as part of your due diligence buying decision.

9. **Place your car insurance and home insurance with the same company.** As stated before, many insurers will offer multi-policy discounts of between 10 and 40%!

10. **Call or surf for quotes.** Car insurance companies set premiums based on the amount of claims paid in each area. Rates can vary greatly from company to company:

    • eChoice at www.echoice.com.au specialises in finding the best car insurance deal for you based on your selected criteria. It also provides insurance information and finance calculators.

    • WWW Insurance Agencies has a website which provides information on car insurance and allows you to complete an online form. It can also provide comparison quotes, available at www.insuru.com.au; (08) 8267 2027.

    • Union Shopper Insurance Brokers provide an independent service for members at www.unionshop.org.au; 1300 368 117.

    • Insurance Watch at www.insurancewatch.com.au has a range of 11 different insurance underwriters which it uses to obtain the best quote. It also has an online request form to assist you.

    • Greater National Group at www.gng.com.au operates a quote service; (03) 9572 5755.

- MyFinance at www.myfinance.com.au operates a quote service.
- Insurance Mart at www.quicken.com.au/insurance; 1800 674 888.
- Financial Choice at www.i-choice.com.au; 1800 644 479;
- If you have a 'unique' car and find insurance difficult to obtain, you may like to try Unique Car Insurance at www.uniquecar.com.au; (03) 9878 2600.
- In New South Wales the Motor Accidents Authority provides a list of Green Slip insurers, available at www.maa.nsw.gov.au.
- Car insurance can also be originated through the motoring organisations which were listed in Chapter 14.
- Other insurers which have a presence on the Internet are:
  - www.aami.com.au; 13 22 44;
  - www.carnet.com.au; 136 134;
  - www.mmicentre.com.au; 132 664;
  - www.amp.com.au; 133 888;
  - www.carsearch.com.au; (02) 9456 5500;
  - www.quoteseek.com.au;
  - www.netquote.com.au; (07) 3229 8671.

If you make a car insurance claim and have a dispute with the insurance company, the General Insurance Enquiries and Complaints Scheme can help you. The scheme also provides free advice and information about any general insurance matter. Contact them on 1300 363 683 or www.ica.com.au. You can also check out the Insurance Council of Australia website at www.ica.com.au (1300 728 228) for useful information on motor vehicle insurance policies.

## THE BOTTOMLINE ON CAR INSURANCE IS FOUR-FOLD

1. Consider eliminating all duplicate or worthless coverage.
2. Consider raising your excess, to lower the premiums.
3. Aggressively shop (every year) for the best rates in your area.
4. Be proactive by requesting all available discounts.

By following through on these suggestions you can save a tremendous amount of money on your car insurance. Take it seriously and make the *Financially Competent (Intelligent and Responsible)* changes required.

## MISCELLANEOUS INSURANCE

Miscellaneous insurance is almost always overpriced. In virtually every case, it is unnecessary, duplicate or worthless coverage. These types of insurances provide billions of dollars in profits worldwide for the companies that aggressively market the policies. Beware, rarely are these policies to your benefit. The ratio of premiums paid in by customers compared to the benefits paid out make miscellaneous insurance policies easily the most profitable an insurance company can sell. Don't ever buy these policies unless you receive 'true' financial value, again, something you will rarely receive with this type of insurance. Read on and discover the cost of *Financial Incompetence (Ignorance and Irresponsibility)*.

### CAR RENTAL INSURANCE

Car rental insurance is *completely optional*. You are not required to take out the insurance to rent the car. The coverage offered is nothing more than a huge profit generator for the rental car company. **The insurance is often totally unnecessary because you may already have the coverage on your existing car insurance policy** (assuming you already have car insurance). The policies are also incredibly overpriced. The three different types of coverage are outlined below to help you understand why (if you have existing car insurance) you should always decline car rental insurance.

1. **Collision Damage Waiver (CDW)** – The excess on damage to a rental car is usually a maximum of $2,500. The rental car company usually charges about $16 a day to cover the excess (although some discount car rental companies such as Bayswater car rental in Perth and Sydney may charge as low as $4 a day to reduce the excess to around $200).

    Even without this insurance, you are usually covered by the rental car company for fire and theft. Under the 'occasional driver' clause in your personal car insurance policy you are probably covered for collision damage (check this out). Any damage excess you would have to pay could be reimbursed to you by your insurance company based on the limits in your personal car insurance policy. Check your policy first.

In addition, you may find that some major credit cards offer automatic coverage of the excess when you charge the rental to their credit card. This is standard practice in the US (especially for Gold and Platinium cards) and you may find with a little research that it is now offered in Australia by your credit card provider.

2. **Personal Accident Insurance (PAI)** – This is an expensive life insurance policy with medical payments, typically for a maximum $75,000 cover. The policy states: 'This coverage pays for death directly caused by a car accident independent of all other causes.' This is so expensive, it would be like paying $500 a year for a $75,000 life insurance policy that only covered you while driving a car. What a joke! Never take this insurance. This is the same old product in different wrapping. You should already have adequate health and life insurance.

3. **Personal Effects Coverage (PEC)** – This policy covers loss or damage to your personal property in the rental car while you are renting the car. The coverage is limited (usually to around $2,500) and only covers you and your immediate family. Depending on the policy, there can be many exclusions that they will not pay for such as false teeth; contact lenses; furniture; currency; coins; credit cards; tickets; documents; and perishables or mysterious disappearances. Not a whole lot left to cover, is there? Your home contents policy will usually automatically cover all these items (without the exclusions). **Never take this worthless coverage**.

---

**Bottomline:** Consider declining all coverages offered by the car rental company that your existing insurance policies already cover. These miscellaneous policies are expensive, duplicate and worthless.

**Warning:** if your credit card offers no excess protection and you do not have car insurance (i.e., you do not own a car or do not carry comprehensive insurance on your car) or home and contents insurance which covers you for driving a rental car, then you *must* ensure that the car rental company has provided you with suitable automatic rental liability insurance. If they have not then you *should* purchase it.

## DOMESTIC TRAVEL INSURANCE

Domestic travel insurance is a total rip-off. The premiums are 500–800% higher than necessary. The restrictions are often impossible to meet. These policies cover you for accidental injury, death, medical and dental costs, luggage replacement (usually up to $3,000), travel and accommodation in the case of emergency and cancellation and lost deposit insurance (usually up to $10,000). Other than cancellation and lost deposit insurance, the other risks are covered by your life, home contents or health insurances.

Lost or stolen luggage might also be claimed against the hotel, airline or other carrier. Qantas, for example, provides for a maximum daily allowance to expend on necessities (around $100) should your baggage be lost or delayed. They will usually only tell you this if you ask (insist) and may still expect you to carry (claim on) travel insurance even if the loss/delay is their fault. Why should you or your insurance company pay for these costs? Know your rights and stick to your guns. And remember, the risks of travelling domestically are really not much different to travelling around your own suburb.

## INTERNATIONAL TRAVEL INSURANCE

If you are travelling overseas, and the coverage does not duplicate your life, health, homeowner's insurance or credit card benefits, you *should* consider the value of obtaining travel insurance for emergency medical treatment and evacuation and/or trip cancellation/interruption. Emergency medical treatment and evacuation (EME) coverage is a good idea when travelling overseas, particularly if you have pre-existing health concerns, because usually such emergency treatments are not included in your personal health insurance policy. Before obtaining coverage, check your health policy to avoid duplicate coverage.

Trip cancellation/interruption (TCI) can be worthwhile if the trip being taken is expensive and involves a large non-refundable prepayment. You will typically pay between 5 and 8% of the cost of the trip for this insurance, though policy rates will vary significantly from company to company. It is often best to buy this type of insurance directly from the insurance company, rather than from a travel agent, and thus reduce the commission.

Exceptions to this general rule may occur in the case of organisations with substantial buying power which can offer good deals to members. An example would be Qantas executive travel insurance offered to frequent flyers for periods of up to one year for unlimited overseas trips of up to three months each trip. If you travel a lot in a given year this type of policy may be better value rather than buying individual policies each time you travel.

Some credit cards offer free or discounted travel insurance, particularly gold cards offered by Westpac, Citibank, Commonwealth Bank and ANZ.

Check the Internet for travel insurance providers. For example:

- Toursafe Travel Insurance at www.compusure.com.au;
- Travel Insurance on the Net at www.travelinsurance.com.au;
- The Money Shop at www.themoneyshop.com.au/insurance.

## LOAN INSURANCE

You can save a few hundred dollars (or more) every time you borrow money by declining loan insurance. How? Imagine you are buying a $20,000 car and financing it at the bank. The last question the loans officer will ask, just before he or she approves your application is: 'By the way, you do want loan insurance protection, don't you?' You look up (still worried about whether or not the loan will be approved) and ask 'What's that?' The loan officer smiles warmly and tells you that 'Loan insurance pays off the loan if you die, or makes the loan payments if you can't work.' It sounds like a good idea, doesn't it? The problem? This insurance is overpriced by up to 800%, and in some cases up to 60% of that goes to the loan officer as a commission.

**The fine print:** the insurance (if you die) only pays the *balance* of the loan, or the remaining payments (while disabled). If you die owing $1,000 on the car, this is the amount paid. Your family gets the car paid off with the $1,000 going to the bank, but the remaining $19,000 of the insurance is not paid to you or your family. The bank keeps it!

**Bottomline: Never purchase loan insurance.** If you require coverage, handle it with an inexpensive life insurance or income protection policy.

## SERVICE CONTRACTS

These are the contracts that people try to sell you when you buy something such as a TV, stereo or refrigerator. In many cases these contracts carry a 50–60% commission for the salesperson. This type of insurance is a huge money maker for large electronic and appliance stores. It is overpriced coverage from which most people rarely benefit and would be better off not buying.

## MORTGAGE LIFE INSURANCE

Mortgage life insurance is designed to pay off your home if you meet with an untimely demise. Nice idea. If something happened to the family breadwinner, it would be a comfort to know that the mortgage was covered. The first problem: the high cost of mortgage life insurance. Did you know that in most cases mortgage life insurance, which is nothing more than term life insurance with a fancy name, costs 200–500% more than term life insurance? The second problem: the payout sum goes directly to the lender! Wouldn't your family rather have the option of making the mortgage payments from the earnings the insurance pay-out could create?

**Bottomline: For pure protection, only buy term life insurance.** Never buy insurance with a fancy name.

## FLIGHT INSURANCE

If you need life insurance, a vending machine at the airport is not the place to purchase it. This is another insurance rip-off. The idea is to prey on your fear of flying and charge you a month's (or more) premium for a few hours in the air. Your chances of slipping on the escalator and dying on the way to the departure gate are much greater than dying in a plane crash (and did you know that many policies do not cover acts of terrorism?). Besides, you are probably already covered. Many credit card companies provide automatic flight insurance when you purchase your tickets with their card.

**Make sure not fall for TV ads, slick marketing pieces, mailers or smooth salespeople!**

I believe you now understand why I state: 'Miscellaneous insurance is almost always a complete waste of money.' Do not be sucked into the insurance company's games. Be *Financially Competent (Intelligent, and Responsible)*. Only purchase insurance that offers you *true* financial value covering real risks.

---

## CHAPTER 19 ACTION STEPS REVIEW

1. Practice **Money Step #6 – *Financial Competence (Intelligence and Responsibility)*** by reviewing your car insurance policy. Ensure you have compulsory personal injury and enough third party property damage liability coverage.
2. Consider dropping comprehensive insurance coverage if your car is not worth repairing or replacing.
3. If you already have private health insurance, consider dropping duplicate types of insurance.
4. Implement the **Ten Ways to Lower Your Car Insurance Premiums**: type of cover; high policy excess; never lodge small claims; use a low (or no) fee credit card for potential excess liability; decline extra coverages; ask for the seven basic car insurance discounts; drive carefully; consider the type of car you drive; combine car and home insurances with the same company; and call or surf for quotes.

5.  Miscellaneous insurance is almost always a total rip-off.
    Never purchase insurance that does not offer true
    financial value.

## CHAPTER 20

# The truth about life insurance and how to save big bucks

'There are three kinds of lies – lies, damned lies and statistics.'

BENJAMIN DISRAELI

Over the years a lot has been said about life insurance. And like many other people, I have my own opinion as well. Starting out let me say this, as a financial planner for several years I placed millions and millions of dollars worth of policies. In all my years I never delivered a settlement (money) to a beneficiary (usually a widow or widower) that was too large. However, I did witness several instances where people received a cheque that was all too small.

The fact is that many people are vastly underinsured. As a rule of thumb, if you support a family (or have dependants) you need somewhere between five to 10 times your annual income for your family to maintain their standard of living. Most people don't have anywhere near this much insurance.

In the early years of raising a family (when your expenses are generally fairly high and your assets are usually fairly low), you may need a lot of coverage, depending on the needs of your family. In the later years (when children have grown beyond school age and even moved out of home!) you will probably require less (if any) coverage, because your assets have increased and your expenses have hopefully decreased. (No doubt parents of teenage or university-age children will be laughing at this notion!)

## THE TWO BASIC TYPES OF LIFE INSURANCE POLICIES

Let's discuss the fundamentals of life insurance. There are two basic types of life insurance policies: life insurance *with* a savings plan and life insurance *without* a savings plan. In Australia, life insurance with a savings plan is commonly known as *whole-of-life* or *endowment*. (In the US it is also offered as *variable*, *adjustable*, or *universal life*.) Life insurance without a savings plan is known simply as *term* insurance, in both Australia and the US.

For almost everyone, life insurance without a savings plan – term insurance – is the best answer. The reason: it is far more reasonably priced because you only pay for what you need – a payout for your family when you die. Nothing else. No fancy gimmicks, no add-ons, no savings/investment plan added. Just insurance for your family and dependants when you die. This is the type of life insurance most people need.

## THE INSIDE STORY OF LIFE INSURANCE

Life insurance with a savings plan is the one type of insurance for which more people overpay than any other. Insurance companies train their agents to pull out all stops to market this product. Taking advantage of every opportunity and using every possible statistical and emotional influence, agents are trained to use our fears of dying prematurely and leaving dependants without adequate financial provisions.

The life insurance agent can make a tremendous income when selling life insurance products if he or she can learn the 'tricks of the trade'. As I mentioned before, I was a successful agent for one of the top 10 insurance (financial) companies in the world. I received several awards for sales excellence and made a very good income. Here are the trade secrets of the life insurance industry.

> **Review this section closely. Over your lifetime it could save you tens of thousands of dollars!**

You need to understand that the average person has very little idea of how life insurance works. Life insurance is not what most people think it is. Let me explain what I mean.

Most insurance companies train their salespeople to 'push' life insurance *with* a savings plan. The salespeople make much larger commissions on this type of insurance than they do on term insurance and the insurance company gets to own more of your money for a long time. Great policy for them. It could not be a worse policy for you! You make them a ton of money while making almost none yourself on your 'investment'.

'He uses statistics as a drunken man uses lamp-posts – for support rather than illumination.'
**ANDREW LANG**

Because of the *huge* profits, insurance agents have been well trained to creatively package life insurance with a savings plan so it appears to be a good deal (to the financially *illiterate*). Do not believe the presentations. In recent years (in the US) several major insurance companies have been sued and have paid billions of dollars to policyholders because of misrepresentations and non-disclosure by their agents. You need to be aware of techniques the agents use to separate you from your money. Here is the truth.

## SINGLE WITH NO DEPENDENTS

What group of people really need life insurance? Individual life insurance is only important for those people who have family responsibilities. If you are single with no dependents you probably do not need, and therefore should not spend your money buying, life insurance.

With that said, about 30% of all active life insurance policies today are held on the lives of single people with no family responsibilities. Life insurance should be used only to prevent a financial hardship that would be created if the insured person dies. If you are single, invest your money for use while you are living. Not for use by non-dependants after you are gone.

Fact: in excess of $1 trillion dollars of life insurance is currently in force in the US alone and around $300 billion of that is held on the lives of single people with no dependants. This is a perfect example of how well life insurance salespeople are trained and how little most people know about money and insurance. The chances of you dying when you are single (usually in your 20s) are **15 out of 1,000**. That's a 1.5% chance that you could win (by dying) on a life insurance policy when you are single. No one but you is relying on you for financial support. Keep your money. Invest in something producing a proper return during, not after, your lifetime.

## CHILDREN'S LIFE INSURANCE OR 'KIDDIE' POLICIES

The purpose of insurance is to protect against the loss of your financial asset (your ability to earn income). Children are the greatest *emotional* asset we as parents will ever have. However, children are not normally a *financial* asset. You do not need to insure their lives.

Some life insurance agents view children as a great way to tack on a couple of hundred dollars in extra commission. They will lay it on thick. They will tell the parents (and grandparents) to buy life insurance for their children because it is the loving, responsible thing to do. They will tell you what a great gift it would be and how you can be there to help not only with money for university, but a first home for them as well. They will say: 'It's only $50 a month per child, aren't little John and Danielle worth that?' 'Well, of course they are', you nod with a tear in your eye as you sign the cheque. *Stop*! Do not buy that insurance! Put that $50 a month into their **AIP**!

**Note**: In most child policies if the child dies before age 10 then the life cover is limited to premiums paid plus compound interest of 5% or so. So policies on children younger than this are completely useless.

Another ridiculous pitch you will hear is that if you buy insurance on the children *now* you can guarantee their future insurability. Factually, at age 18, *99% of adults will easily qualify for life insurance on their initial application.*

Whole-of-life insurance is often sold as a method of building cash value to pay for a college education for the insured child. Parents are told it is a great investment.

> **A \$50,000 whole-of-life insurance policy on a one-year-old child costs about \$250 a year. It would provide a \$4,500 cash value at age 18. That same \$250 a year invested in a term deposit at (a horrible) 6% would create \$6,907.50. Invested in an average managed fund (12% annual return) it would produce \$15,786.24. Invested, at say 16%, it would produce \$25,743.47. That great life insurance policy the insurance salesperson sold you just cost your child \$10,000–\$20,000! Do *not* buy it.**

If you don't believe me, calculate it yourself or check out the compounding interest calculator at Enterprise on the following website: www.afr.com.au.

Another gimmick is to tell you that you should buy life insurance on children because you are 'locking in' low rates. The truth is that the only reason the rates are lower is because the chance of death is lower and because you will be paying the premiums for much longer, beginning decades earlier than necessary at the lower premium with no worthwhile benefit accruing during that time.

**Please Note:** There is a rare exception where child life insurance is appropriate. If your child becomes a TV or movie star or a professional athlete then there is a good chance that the child could become the family's primary breadwinner. In this case definitely consider term life insurance for the child.

## INSURANCE FOR YOUR SPOUSE
If your spouse is responsible for a significant amount of family income, he or she is a *financial* asset. An appropriate amount of inexpensive term life insurance should be purchased to protect

against the loss of this *financial* asset. If your spouse does not work and you have no children then there is no real need for life insurance on your spouse. If your spouse does not work, but you have children then you should acquire inexpensive term life insurance to handle the *extra* real costs of household and child care until the kids are fully grown.

If you are a two-income family with no dependants then the main consideration would be that the surviving spouse has *enough* money (from assets and life insurance) to maintain the current standard of living (i.e. mortgage, car, etc.). Other than that, in the long run you would be much better off investing your money over time than paying inflated life insurance premiums.

## HOW MUCH LIFE INSURANCE DO YOU NEED?

The purpose of life insurance is to **replace lost income** in the event of the death of one or both spouses or parents. There are many theories and formulas for determining how much life insurance is enough. A good rule of thumb is to multiply the amount of potential lost annual income by a factor of five to 10 (depending on the level of your acquired assets). This should provide sufficient principal to earn enough income when invested to maintain the needs of the dependants over time without reducing the principal.

For example, if you were earning $50,000 a year and had little in the way of assets, a $500,000 term life insurance policy should be more than adequate to provide for the needs of your family. Your family could then invest the $500,000 at 10% to produce $50,000 a year.

If your children are fully grown, or you have other assets that provide passive income, you can reduce the amount of term life insurance you carry. Just make sure you have enough assets and insurance to meet the 10 times rule. Keep in mind that the less financial responsibility you have to others, the less life insurance you require.

As we grow older, our responsibilities (to support a spouse and/or family) usually decrease at the same time as our assets are increasing. The objective for most of us as we approach retirement age should thus be to become *self-insured*. That is, to have accumulated sufficient assets so there is no longer a financial need for life insurance.

## WHICH LIFE INSURANCE COMPANY SHOULD YOU USE?

There are many life insurance companies in Australia but only a limited number of different *types* of insurance policies. Once you know what type of insurance you require the only two considerations are: the rates and the ratings. Insurance companies are rated by rating agencies from time to time.

When rating an insurance company the prime concern is the financial strength of the company. Because of this, I recommend that you only do business with a company that is given a high rating.

At 30 June 1999, the rating agency Standard & Poor's Comstock rated the financial strength of insurance companies. Some of the results are as follows:

| Company | Rating |
|---|---|
| Australian Casualty and Life | AA– |
| AMP Adviser Services | AAA |
| Bankers Trust | A |
| Citicorp | A |
| Legal & General | A |
| Mercantile Mutual Life | A |
| MLC | AA |
| AXA Australia (was National Mutual Life) | AA– |
| Norwich Union Life | BBB |
| Royal & Sun Alliance Life | AA– |
| Zurich Life | AA |

To contact Standard & Poor's Comstock, telephone 1300 365 787 or visit the Internet at www.spcomstock.com.au.

Do not buy a life insurance policy simply because you recognise the company name. Insurance premiums can vary substantially from company to company. Large companies may charge more than necessary to cover the high cost of their advertising and overheads. Choose insurance based on the lowest rates from a company with an 'A' rating or better, not on name recognition.

**It definitely pays to shop around. In the last few years the cost of term life insurance, for example, has reduced by an average of between 30 and 50%.**

---

**Bottomline: Agressively shop around for your policy!**

**Warning:** *Never* cancel a *needed* existing policy until new coverage is approved. If you do, you may become uninsurable.

---

## WHOLE-OF-LIFE INSURANCE

In my opinion, whole-of-life insurance is not an investment in any sense of the word for the average person. Unless specifically set up otherwise, your **cash value** is actually *owned* by the insurance company which means that for the return you get, the insurance you are buying is overpriced by 300–600%. Should you wish to retain *your* cash value, the insurance company will require you to buy *additional* insurance to reimburse them.

Whole-of-life policies usually have level premiums (equal monthly, quarterly, semi-annual or annual instalments), and claim to build *tax-paid* cash value. On most policies that claim is very misleading because your beneficiary will receive the **face value** of the policy *or* the cash value, whichever is greater, but not both (unless specific additional premiums were paid to ensure this outcome).

## COMMISSIONS

Whole-of-life insurance provides the insurance agent with the highest possible commission. In talking with top Australian agents I have confirmed that, in the first year, it is common for a tied agent to receive a commission rate of 70–130%! That's right, the agent can often receive more than 100% of *your* money in the first year. In the second and third years the agent will receive up to 25% of every dollar you contribute. Every year after that the agent will receive 5% of every dollar you contribute.

Let me ask you a fair question: If you were working for a life insurance company (on commission only), what would you recommend to a family who wanted to invest $200 a month ($2,400 a year)? That they pay $400 a year for a $500,000 term life policy and invest the balance of $2,000 into a managed fund or that they pay $200 a month into a $200,000 whole-of-life policy? Before you answer, we will review the commission structure.

In the first scenario, the agent would receive approximately $140 commission for the term life insurance policy and a $40 commission for the managed fund, that is a total commission of $180. In the second scenario, the agent would receive a commission of $1,500–$2,400+ for the whole-of-life policy. In today's financially competitive world it would be very difficult for an agent to sell the term life insurance and a managed fund and still earn enough money to make a decent living.

It is not surprising then that many agents are trained that the non-term insurance is the best to sell. Starting to get the picture? These people are simply showing you what the company has shown them. And let's be realistic, life insurance companies are in business to make a profit (just like all other companies). They are not benevolent non-profit organisations. They want to make the largest profit possible. And the best way for them to do this is to market life insurance *with* a savings plan.

To this end they arm their agents with information and persuasive presentations and then send them out to the general public to sell, sell, sell. And if you have ever seen an investment life insurance presentation, you will know that they can be *very* persuasive. The agent has flip charts and illustrations, all of which 'clearly demonstrate' (what appears to be) a very sound investment. Let me show you what is really happening with these numbers.

## THE DISAPPEARING CASH VALUE
Here is what happens to the **cash value** of a standard whole-of-life insurance policy.

Male age 35 buys a whole-of-life insurance policy:

| $100,000 | Death benefit (face value) |
|----------|----------------------------|
| $1,300   | Annual premium             |
| $35,400  | Cash value after 20 years  |

At age 55 he dies. How much do you think the family would receive? If you thought they would receive their cash value of $35,400 plus the $100,000 death benefit for a total of $135,400 you are sadly mistaken. On a *standard* issue whole-of-life policy the cash value becomes the *property* of the insurance company. All the family receives is $100,000.

## THE DISAPPEARING INSURANCE VALUE

Let's examine the disappearing **insurance value**.

Since the insurance company is only responsible for paying the death benefit (**face value**) of the policy regardless of cash value upon the death of the insured, the more cash value you build, the less money the insurance company will have to pay out of its own pocket. The result, as the *cash value* grows, the insurance company's *liability* shrinks.

Thus, in the previous example, if the cash value was $35,400, the insurance death benefit (face value) would only be $64,600, giving a total death benefit of $100,000.

What you really have is a *decreasing term life insurance policy*: a policy where the premiums remain constant, but the amount of life insurance decreases as the insured person grows older. The reality: these savings/investment life insurance policies are nothing more than cleverly disguised, overpriced decreasing term life policies. The insurance company is giving you nothing but simple insurance. In return you are providing them with free use of thousands of dollars of your cash value each year.

Both the *disappearing cash value* and the *disappearing insurance value* examples are the reality for a *standard* issue whole-of-life policy. Some insurance agents will fight this objection by offering a 'paid-up additions' option. This is an option where your dividend (the return your policy makes) is used to buy more life insurance.

By taking this option you are paying much more for your insurance. It is like buying mini-policies *with* your cash value to offset what the company *keeps* of your cash value. As your cash value grows your total coverage grows. However, even though you are significantly reducing the cash value, the *insurance value* does not disappear. The end result, you pay even more for insurance while receiving less cash value.

## THE WHOLE-OF-LIFE INSURANCE SURRENDER CHARGE PROBLEM

Some of the worst features of savings/investment life insurance (whole-of-life) are the exorbitant **surrender charges**. If at any time during the first two years (with a standard policy) you decide to cancel the policy, you will receive *no money back.* That's right, no money. Why? Because the insurance industry has built in a high surrender charge penalty. They do this for two reasons:

1.  The first reason (if you are financially solvent) is to make it so painful to quit that you will continue paying into this lousy investment forever, to avoid losing what you have already invested.

2.  The second reason is that they know that many people are incapable of continuing a disciplined payment program (with no flexibility whatsoever) over a long period of time. The result: a lot of people pay for a few years and then lose their entire contribution for defaulting on the premiums. Often the insurance company will even make you feel like it is your fault because you were not disciplined with your money and properly committed.

**Cancel at any time during the first seven years and you will usually always pay an exorbitant penalty.** (There are ways to avoid the surrender penalties which we will discuss later in the chapter).

## THE WHOLE-OF-LIFE UNDERINSURED PROBLEM

My biggest problem with the marketing of whole-of-life (and other *investment* insurance) as the best form of life insurance is that after buying whole-of-life insurance many people are still left *underinsured*. Most people have a limited amount of money to spend on life insurance. A term life insurance policy will provide five to 20 times more coverage than a top-of-the-line whole-of-life insurance policy. The main purpose of insurance is to *adequately protect against risk*. Thus, a sufficient amount of coverage should be the most important consideration for both the seller and the buyer of a life insurance policy.

Yet time and time again agents 'sell' people a whole-of-life policy that leaves the insured with insufficient death benefits. Why? The answer is very simple. The company trained them to. And why did the company train them in this way? Profit, and more profit! The agent and the company both make far more profit on a whole-of-life or other savings/investment policy than on a term life policy. Often 2–300% more! (Read or watch John Grisham's *The Rainmaker* for a *dramatic* taste of the industry practices followed by the mythical 'Great Benefit' life insurance company.)

## THE WHOLE OF LIFE INSURANCE 'LINES'

The following are some of the more frequent 'lines' used by insurance salespeople to convince you to purchase whole-of-life (or other savings/investment) insurance:

### ✗ 'You can borrow the cash value at a low interest rate [5–8%].'

Oh, now this is exciting. The insurance company is offering you the incredible opportunity to borrow your own money and pay them interest for the privilege. Keep in mind that the money you borrow is what you overpaid in premiums and that whatever you borrow reduces your death benefit by that amount. And in any case, you can go to any bank and borrow against any *real* investment assets that you own.

### ✗ 'Your policy will eventually be paid up.'

What they are really saying is that because we overcharge you so much at some point we will have taken enough of your money to cover the future premiums. A paid-up policy is nothing more than a policy that has been prepaid. There is no free lunch, you just overpaid. Why would you ever want to over-pay in advance just so you don't have to pay later? That would be like offering to pay all your income taxes for the next 40 years, in advance over the next 10 years! What *Financially Competent (Intelligent and Responsible)* person would do that?

### ✗ 'You will be earning interest.'

Whole-of-life policies pay an 'effective' average rate of return of less than 3% interest per annum. Worse yet, in most cases you will never receive that interest. The interest earned is added to your cash value, which in reality remains the property of the insurance company unless you pay added premiums for the privilege of owning it yourself.

### ✗ 'Your insurance policy is a tax shelter.'

This is one of their biggies. Insurance agents love to brag about how life insurance enjoys some 'special tax status'. They will tell you that you can borrow money from your insurance policy *tax-free*. Big deal! You can borrow money from *anywhere* tax-free. No loan is considered income. Never has been.

### ✗ 'All your earnings will be tax-paid which would be much better than investing in a managed fund where you'd have to pay taxes.'

This is true. The earnings are tax-paid. So what? What they conveniently forget to tell you is that so much of your money is being removed for commissions and expenses that the tax-paid treatment will never compensate for the investment capital that can never be recovered.

### ✗ 'If you buy life insurance when you are young, it will cost less.'

This is a fallacy. It is true that when you are young the yearly premiums are lower. This is only because the odds of you dying are less, and you are thus a better insurance risk. But you will now pay over a much longer period of time and thus, in the long run, you will end up paying much more money for the same benefit, not less.

> The only reason to buy life insurance when you are young is financial protection for your dependant family, not as a means of saving money.

### ✗ 'It provides you with an Automatic Investment Plan.'

True. However, the insurance companies often make it sound like they are the *only* people who will help you set up a plan to invest a small amount of money on a regular basis. Twenty years ago this may have been generally true, with very few companies offering 'investments' linked to an **Automatic Investment Plan** (or *regular contributions plan*). Today virtually every managed fund company will set you up with an AIP. **The big difference is that with the managed fund company you can get a fair rate of return with low or no commissions.**

### ✗ 'It's a good investment. Just look at the illustrations. Numbers do not lie!'

The agents present computer-generated illustrations that 'prove' how good an investment whole-of-life insurance is. These illustrations can be very persuasive. They *project* huge amounts of money after 20, 30, or 40 years.

'Torture numbers, and they'll confess to anything.'
**GREG EASTERBROOK**

The reason these numbers look so appealing to most people is simply because most people have little understanding of the true power of **compound interest**. The agent is correct. Numbers do not lie. If you want to see a really good investment run the same numbers (same amount a month for the same length of time) invested in a managed fund at 12–14%. Subtract the cost of a term life insurance policy. You will be way ahead without the whole-of-life insurance policy. How far ahead?

A 25-year-old buying term life insurance and investing the difference between that premium and the whole-of-life premium, until age 65 (assuming historical returns), will earn more than **$1,000,000** more than the 25-year-old who buys whole-of-life insurance over the same period.

### ✗ 'You should buy now because you may not be insurable in the future.'

Because a life insurance policy can be cancelled by the company only for non-payment of premiums, agents will often use the threat of future uninsurability to induce you to buy now.

> The truth is that more than 95% of people who apply for life insurance are accepted (99% at age 18). Fewer than 10% are charged extra premiums because of pre-existing conditions.

There, I trust that gives you insight into why whole-of-life insurance is not what it's cracked up to be. In Australia you have several fewer types of life insurance product than are thrust upon people in the US. I think that this is a good thing for Australia because most of the US variations centre on life insurance with savings or investment plans of one sort or another. *Variable life insurance* (insurance linked to a mutual fund) is one such example that you thankfully do not have in Australia… yet. It became extremely popular in the 1990s in the US, reflecting the explosion in mutual fund investment activity. Many agents enjoy marketing this product because it sounds so 'sexy'.

I believe that it is now worth sharing with you what I would call a 'typical' life insurance with an investment *sales presentation* that I encountered a couple of years ago, so that you get the idea of the type of life insurance product to steer clear of in Australia, both now and in the future…

### INVESTMENT LIFE INSURANCE SALES PRESENTATION

Tiffany, the 18-year-old who used to work in my office (the one you read about in Chapter 3 who will be a millionaire at age 50), was approached by a friend of her family, who wanted to help her 'invest' her money. Before she met with him I explained to Tiffany exactly what his motives would be. I told her that the only way he could afford to drive out to meet her (she only has

$100 a month to invest) was if he was selling *investment* life insurance. After all, there is no way he could afford to drive out for $2 a month (2% is a normal tied agent's share of the commission on a $100 a month managed fund policy premium). I told her all the 'lines' he would use.

He followed the script to the letter. The statements this man made (a top agent) were, in my opinion, scandalous, bordering on fraudulent. However, they truly are representative of the training which many agents in the industry receive.

The following is a summary of his statements. My responses and comments are italicised:

☒ The agent told her that this was a 'special' investment. *No reason why, it was just 'special'.*

☒ He told her that investing in a mutual fund (even if it was in an individual retirement account (IRA)) was not as good as his 'special' investment. (Translation: like putting superannuation money into a managed fund). *Again, no supporting evidence was given, just a brazen statement.*

☒ He told her that the 'investment' enjoyed 'special tax status'. *There is tax status available, however he never explained what it was nor how Tiffany would benefit. The reality (as discussed before): the tax deferred build-up will never compensate for the horrible return (because of the cost of insurance, the commissions and the up-front load).*

☒ He showed her an illustration depicting a 16% annual rate of return. He ran the return out to ages 65, 75, 85. *This is a ploy agents often use. They run the returns for very long periods of time. They do this because their product is so lousy for the first 10 or more years and because they assume you don't understand how compound interest works. They believe that if you see a big number in the cash value account ($100,000 to $1,000,000+) you will not bother to ask how large it would grow at the same rate in a mutual fund. For Tiffany, based on the projected rate of return, the difference between investment life insurance and a good mutual fund, by age 85, was more than 250 million dollars ($250,000,000)!!!*

☒ The agent never mentioned that this was a hypothetical illustration with no substantiating history or guarantees whatsoever. *Blatant misrepresentation.*

☒ The agent never disclosed that, historically, the fund he was recommending had never performed (for three or more years in succession) at the 16% rate he was claiming (in writing) as Tiffany's rate of return for the next 67 years. *In my opinion, this type of flagrant misrepresentation constitutes a criminal act. To represent that a loaded mutual fund, with insurance charges and commission could return an average of 16% a year for 67 years is outrageous and insane!*
**Note:** If you are involved with a whole-of-life policy, check the factual returns (historically) versus the projected rates of return. In the 1990s many insurance companies greatly under-performed the (hypothetical) illustrated performance tables – some by as much as 50%!

☒ The agent told her that with his 'special' investment she could borrow her own money at any time. *Big deal, see earlier point.*

☒ He never discussed the actual cost of the insurance. *Non-disclosure.*

☒ The agent never told her that if something happened and she could not make the payments for just a few months that she could lose *all* her money. *For a young person like Tiffany it is very risky to plan investments in this way. She is only 18. A lot will change in her life in the next 10 years. The chances of her being able to commit to an insurance investment premium, every month, without exception, throughout that time are not that high. If she cannot pay into a mutual fund she loses nothing. If she cannot pay into a life insurance policy she could lose everything. Not fair, but true.*

☒ The agent never discussed the fact that well over half of her money (in the first year) would go directly into his pocket. *Somebody has to pay for that Mercedes. After all, you know the return on **his** life insurance policy isn't paying for it. Seriously, I have no problem whatsoever with a salesperson making a 'fair' commission, but does this rate of commission seem fair?*

☒ And finally, the agent never explained to Tiffany that even at his totally unrealistic, projected return of 16%, she would not break even until well into the fifth year of the policy. *This is an all too common operating procedure for insurance agents. Gloss over the short term and go to the next page of the illustration.*

I guess the agent forgot a couple of insignificant little details. After all, he was a *good friend* of her family. He had driven all the way out there just to *help* Tiffany. She should do the paperwork *today*!

Fortunately, Tiffany did not do the paperwork. Instead, she did what she promised me she would do. She met with me and told me exactly what had happened. Even though I had briefed her on everything that would happen she still thought it all sounded like it might be a good deal. She said, 'He made it sound so good,' and that 'he was very persuasive.'

Her dad could not understand why I thought it was such a terrible investment (he had just committed a very large amount of money to this plan). He wanted to talk to me. I welcomed the opportunity. I explained to her father everything that I had explained to Tiffany. I told him that I cared very much for Tiffany. That she was more than an employee, she was a friend of my family (and had often watched our children, and shared meals with us).

I reminded him that I was only looking out for *her* best interests. I also reminded him that whatever she did I would make *no commission*. I asked him to telephone the agent to tell him: who I was, and my background in the insurance industry (I had been much more successful than him); that I thought it sounded like one heck of a product; and that I would love to sit down with him, Tiffany and her father to review the investment point by point. If it was as he said, I would give my 'blessing', as it were, for Tiffany and her dad to proceed with the plan.

Funny thing happened. Once he discovered who I was he did not want to meet. On this rare occasion, the story had a happy ending because one more family was saved from committing to an inappropriate insurance policy.

**What is *your* life insurance story?** Do you need to be saved? Are you currently putting money into an investment life insurance plan? If so, what are you really earning? How much money do you have to show for all the premiums you have paid? Based on what you have learned in this chapter, do you feel good about the investment? Should you consider repositioning your money into something that makes better financial sense?

I am not saying that life insurance is bad per se. Far from it. I believe that most people need more of it. The question is *what kind?* For most people, the best *personal life* insurance solution is **term life insurance**.

## TERM LIFE INSURANCE

Term life insurance is pure protection. No fancy packaging, no investments. No extra costs. Just insurance. Insurance at the lowest possible cost. Term life insurance is the least expensive life insurance available, usually costing just 20–35% of what investment life insurance costs.

Term life insurance is exactly what life insurance is supposed to be. If you die, your beneficiaries collect the *full* amount of the policy. If you live, the insurance company keeps the small premium and you receive nothing. Obviously life insurance is one bet you would always hope to lose.

Term life insurance becomes more expensive each year of your life. This is obviously because the older you are the more likely you are to die. Many people have been led to believe that you cannot buy term life insurance when you are older. Many companies guarantee your insurability to age 90, some companies go all the way to age 100! You can be assured however, that the insurance premium for a 90- or 100-year-old is rather high.

## MAILBOX OFFERS

Be very wary of insurance offers received in the mail. They often promise automatic insurability regardless of current health. Normally they are very expensive. Read the fine print carefully and if you have any problems with the company backing out on advertised promises, which it is bound by law not to do, then contact the Claims Review Panel operated by Insurance Enquiries and Complaints Limited on 1300 363 683 or the Life Insurance Complaints Service on 1800 335 405. They will first expect you to have already attempted mediation through the insurer's internal dispute resolution process.

## OPTIONAL COVERAGES

There are two basic life insurance optional coverages available:

1. **Total and permanent disability.** This provides a full lump sum payment if a permanent disability prevents you from working in your chosen occupation. The lump-sum payment is limited to the amount of the life cover purchased. Sometimes the permanent disability is defined as the total and permanent loss of the use of two limbs, or the permanent loss of the sight of both eyes or a combination of the two.

   The concern I have with this is that the definition of 'totally and permanently disabled' is often very restrictive. For the additional premium it is probably more realistic and economical to look at trauma insurance instead which we discussed in Chapter 17.

2. **Double total and permanent disability.** In the event you are covered for total and permanent disability, usually the payout reduces the term life insurance benefit. With double total and permanent disability, the amount of benefit paid will not reduce the amount of your term life insurance.

   **Hot Tip**: If you want this coverage, simply buy more life insurance instead. That way your beneficiaries will definitely receive the money. The reality is that the chances of you dying accidentally throughout your entire lifetime are about 6%. This type of statistic is how the insurance companies convince you to spend more money on *optional coverages*.

## SIX WAYS TO LOWER YOUR LIFE INSURANCE PREMIUM

1. **Buy term life insurance.** For personal life insurance needs this will give you the best value.
2. **Don't add the single or double total and permanent disability insurance options.** They are extremely over-priced and these needs are best met through trauma insurance and/or more term life insurance.
3. **Don't take up offers of small amounts of life insurance that arrive in the mail.** The coverage offered is totally inadequate and expensive in comparison with other term life insurance.

4. **Quit smoking.** Non-smokers pay up to half as much for life insurance as smokers do. The insurance companies are not discriminating. Rates are based on genuine actuarial data. Smokers live shorter lives and are on average certain to die of smoking-related diseases 50% of the time and even non-smoking related diseases at least 50% more often than non-smokers.

5. **Examine the possibility of your superannuation fund insuring you.** Payments by superannuation funds for life insurance are tax-deductible. Again, look at term insurance, not savings/investment insurance policies.

6. **Call or surf for quotes.** Life insurance premiums vary dramatically from company to company. Bearing in mind what I said earlier about the importance of considering the rating of an insurance company, try companies that sell low-commission term policies. Search the Internet and try different agents until you get the best quote.

   To get you started, the Australian Financial Services Directory has listings by state of insurance brokers, agents and underwriters. The directory also provides a financial calculator to determine how much insurance is enough. The directory is at www.afsd.com.au. Of course, check the Yellow Pages directory which also has long lists of life insurance providers.

   There are also many Internet and telephone quote services available for the conscientious shopper of insurance:

   - Insurance Watch at www.insurancewatch.com.au;
   - Lifequotes at www.lifequotes.com.au (also has 'How Much Cover?' online calculators); 1800 778 000;
   - Greater National Group at www.gng.com.au; (03) 9572 5755
   - Insurance Mart at www.quicken.com.au/insurance (also has 'How Much Cover?' online calculators); 1800 674 888;
   - Financial Choice at www.i-choice.com.au (also has online calculators); 1800 644 479;
   - Les McIntosh Insurance Agencies at www.lesmac.com.au; (02) 6762 3401;
   - DirectChoice at www.directchoiceinsurance.com.au; (1800 245 123).

## HOW TO REPLACE YOUR EXISTING INVESTMENT LIFE INSURANCE POLICY

When it comes to investing, most people have it all wrong: they want to 'sell their winners and ride their losers'. In other words, most people sell an investment (like a parcel of shares) when it goes up a little. Then, when the share goes down they hold onto it forever, hoping it will come back. Pretty silly, huh?

Well, if you have an investment life insurance policy, how is it doing? Is it a winner or a loser? Remember, I am not trying to sell you anything. In fact, I even allowed my insurance and securities licences to lapse long ago so that no one could ever accuse me of having a conflict of interest by offering the following advice (i.e. be accused of trying to sell you something). The fact is that pouring more money into a bad investment is *Financially Incompetent (Unintelligent and Irresponsible)*. You are throwing more good money after bad. If you made a bad investment and have realised that there is no possible way for it to become a good investment, isn't it time to get rid of it?

If you bought 1,000 shares of stock for $10 a share and the stock fell to $5 a share what would you do? If you were *Financially Competent (Intelligent and Responsible)* you would determine if the company was still a good investment or not. If it was a good investment you would probably buy more (at the *discount*) or hold on and wait for the share price to rebound. If it was a bad investment and had no realistic future you would sell the shares ASAP and get out, then invest in a company with greater potential to make your money back.

**For most people, personal investment life insurance is a bad investment.** Therefore, if you have investment life insurance I recommend you consider replacing your existing insurance with term life insurance.

## EIGHT STEPS TO ACCESS YOUR EXISTING CASH VALUE

1. *Never cancel* **an existing life insurance policy until you have first obtained a replacement policy.** You do not want to risk being uninsurable and uninsured.

2. **Do not call your agent.** They will try to talk you out of your decision, to protect their commission. Do what is in your best interests, not the best interests of your insurance agent. Do not be intimidated. Do not be bullied. Simply bypass the agent. The agent will not know what happened to *your money* until it is too late.

3. **Examine your policy documents.** Photocopy the declaration sheet, cash value tables and surrender values, and the application. Store the copies in a safe place.

4. **Cancel the life insurance policy by stopping the payment of premiums.** If you have automatic premium deduction you should contact your bank and the insurance company notifying them to cease premium payment.

5. **Next, remove your cash value during the 30-day grace period to stop its automatic conversion into a paid-up policy.** If you don't do this, they will use the cash value to pay for the insurance until no cash value is left. Do this by:
   ✓ **writing a letter to the insurance company requesting the** *total cash surrender value* **be mailed to you immediately** (be sure to include your name, mailing address, and policy number);
   ✓ **signing the letter exactly as it is on the policy application** (if the beneficiaries are adults, have them (if available) also sign the letter; photocopy the letter and store it with the other copied documents);
   ✓ **enclosing your original policy with your letter** (direct the letter: Attention Policyholders Service Department; mail the letter 'return receipt requested'; keep the receipt with the copies).

6. **You should have your cheque within seven to 10 working days after the signed receipt is returned to you.** If there is a discrepancy between the amount you receive and the amount of your surrender value, contact the

company immediately. In almost every case no one will contact you. The people in this department just process paperwork. They are rarely concerned why the company is losing a client. They work for a salary, not on commission.

7. **If you need to call the insurance company make sure you use their toll-free number.** Write down the name of every person you talk to. Start out by asking for the manager.

8. **If by chance you are unable to get satisfaction via your insurer's internal dispute resolution process, contact the Claims Review Panel on 1300 363 683 or Life Insurance Complaints Service on 1800 335 405.**

## TRADING YOUR POLICY INSTEAD OF SURRENDERING

There are alternatives to actually surrendering your whole-of-life or long-term endowment policy which can offer better returns. You could take advantage of the growing market in traded life policies in Australia which is expected to top A$250 million worth of policies this year. Specialist traded policy brokers will usually offer you between 6 and 10% more than the policy surrender value offered by your insurance company.

The reason these brokers can do this is that after buying eligible policies they organise the restructuring of the policies by converting them into medium- or long-term investments which they onsell to other investors. A whole-of-life policy might be converted into a shorter-term and more investment-attractive endowment policy which might appeal to people with self-managed superannuation funds. Restructuring the policies can allow the continued entitlement to the **terminal bonus** (only paid when the policy matures) which would otherwise be lost if the policy was simply surrendered. By bringing forward the maturity date and factoring in the terminal and various reversionary and annual bonuses, the yield of the 'investment-linked' life insurance policy can actually improve to a point where it *does* represent a worthwhile investment for some investors.

Not all whole-of-life policies are suitable for such restructuring but the brokers are experts at working out which ones are (they seem to prefer policies from companies such as AMP, MLC and National Mutual). You can even buy into managed funds which trade in restructured life policies if you are wanting a medium-term capital-secure form of investment. This type of investment can suit a self-managed superfund because the lower tax rate on super-funds can boost the net yields of these tradeable policies to over 7%. As an alternative to investment in tradeable fixed interest bonds or debentures this type of investment can be more secure and offer windfall gains when policies mature *but* it is certainly not the type of yield we are looking for as a **Level Four Automatic Investor**, as discussed in Chapter 5.

If you want more information on improving the return on a whole-of-life or endowment policy via trading rather than surrendering, contact one of these brokers after you have ascertained your policy's surrender value to see if you can get a better deal:

- PolicyLink Limited www.policylink.com.au or 1800 803 656 (offices in Sydney and Melbourne);
- The Life Insurance Policy Exchange at www.lipe.com.au or 1800 678 466 (Perth based);
- www.moneyinpractice.com.au (for information on this subject).

## LIFE INSURANCE SUMMARY

Congratulations, you are now an insurance expert. You now know more about insurance than most agents do. You have now learned how to save many thousands of dollars. I know that it requires a little effort, but do not let this knowledge go to waste. If you apply what you have learned on this subject you will be able to significantly improve your financial situation. Be *Financially Competent (Intelligent and Responsible)*. Get busy, and enjoy all your extra money. After all, you deserve it.

## CHAPTER 20 ACTION STEPS REVIEW

1. Practice **Money Step #6 – *Financial Competence (Intelligence and Responsibility)*** by only carrying insurance on people who have dependants relying on them for financial support.
2. Make sure you have adequate life insurance coverage. Many people are woefully underinsured. To start, a 'safe' rule of thumb is to carry 10 times your annual earnings in coverage. Modify this number based on your personal situation and net worth.
3. Research the insurance company you decide to use. Contact the major rating agencies. Make sure you understand their ratings systems. It is best to work with an insurance company that receives the highest rating.
4. Understand *whole-of-life* insurance products. Review the disadvantages and the 'lines' used to market these policies. Read the sales presentation. For *individual* life insurance, *investment* insurance is almost always inappropriate.
5. Own *term* life insurance.
6. Do not opt for total and permanent disability or double total and permanent disability options. They cost too much money. Purchase trauma insurance and/or additional term life insurance instead.
7. Follow the **Six Ways to Lower Your Life Insurance Premium**. Consider life insurance within your superannuation fund.
8. Consider replacing your existing investment insurance. Follow the **Eight Steps to Access Your Existing Cash Value**. Remember to 'ride your winners and cut your losers'. Not the other way around. *Never* cancel an existing policy before you have replacement coverage.
9. Consider trading your investment life insurance policy as a more lucrative alternative to simply surrendering it.

## CHAPTER 21

# Review II – The walls are built

'Be rather bountiful than expensive; do good with
what thou hast, or it will do thee no good.'

WILLIAM PENN

'A man there was, tho' some did count him mad,
The more he cast away, the more he had.'

JOHN BUNYAN

Congratulations! You have now made it two-thirds of the
way through the program! At this point you have learned
most of the (Level Four) *Money Secrets of the Rich*. Much of the
focus of the middle third of the book was on ways to
dramatically decrease your expenses without lowering your
*standard* of living. Although some of the information is tedious it
is *critical* to your becoming rich. Understanding how to control
expenses and eliminate waste is one of the key components to
any financially successful business: so should it be for your family.

Use the information from the last section. Reduce your
expenses, maximise your after-tax income, and obtain the
protection (insurance) that you need. I strongly urge you to now
complete any outstanding assignments.

As you reflect on the last 20 chapters take notice of changes in your outlook, your optimism towards your future, and your own sense of generosity. Feel good about that increased confidence in regard to money matters.

I want to stress how important I believe it is that you proceed through life, particularly your financial life, with the expectations of *abundance* and *prosperity*. In Chapter 22 I will approach in greater detail the power of your mindset in assisting you in achieving a successful financial future. For now I encourage you to rest with your thoughts and begin to consider the possibilities of giving to others (financially and of your time) in at least the same degree as you are now learning to give to yourself via the **Seven Money Steps** and your new-found financial competence.

> 'We enjoy thoroughly only the pleasure that we give.'
> **ALEXANDRE DUMAS**

> 'Plenty and indigence depend upon the opinion every one has of them; and riches, like glory or health, have no more beauty or pleasure than their possessor is pleased to lend to them.'
> **MICHEL DE MONTAIGNE**

> 'Money may be the husk of many things but not the kernel.'
> **HENRIK IBSEN**

In my experience I have found that generosity of spirit, time and money are three key elements which characterise the typical wealthy individual. Over the years I have come to know a few hundred people who are millionaires and with the exception of only one person they all are spiritual and generous of their time and money in helping others. And their generosity and helping of others did not happen *after* they became rich. It happened *before* and *while* they were becoming rich. For me, being prosperous and benevolent (giving) go hand-in-hand.

I'd like to briefly share with you the story of a very wealthy man who for many years of his life did not follow these three key elements: generosity of spirit, of time and of money.

This is the story of the life of John D. Rockefeller, before and beyond the age of 53. I think this story graphically explains what happens when one attempts to break the universal principles of giving.

John D. Rockefeller, before almost killing himself with worry and stress centered in his beliefs of scarcity (even though he was at the time the world's richest man), lived the tyrant's life for most of his business career. It is written (in the book *Titan*) that he was a despised and feared individual whose only joy seemed to come from 'news of a good bargain'.

Rockefeller worried himself to the point where he developed a myriad of stress-related maladies, including complete hair loss and intestinal dysfunction of such severity that he was only able to stomach acidulated milk and crackers. He was earning more than $1,000,000 a week at the turn of the 20th century and spending less than $2 a day on food! John T. Flynn described Rockefeller at 53 in a biography: 'When he looked in a glass, he saw an old man. The ceaseless work, the endless worry, the streams of abuse, the sleepless nights, and the lack of exercise and rest had wrecked the man.'

Up until the age of 53 Rockefeller had approached wealth from the rather paranoid perspective of scarcity, suspicion and fearfulness of loss. He behaved accordingly, with ruthless determination. He once remarked of his first 53 years that 'I never placed my head upon the pillow at night without reminding myself that my success might be only temporary.' These were not the thoughts of a confident man who trusted in the accessibility of prosperity. And his attitude almost killed him from the inside out.

Andrew Carnegie relates Rockefeller's story in his 1953 book *How to Stop Worrying and Start Living*, which I thoroughly recommend, and tells that Rockefeller was given three rules by his doctors as they forced him to retire at 53:

1. *Avoid worry. Never worry about anything, under any kind of circumstances.*
2. *Relax, and take plenty of mild exercise in the open air.*
3. *Watch your diet. Always stop eating while you're still a little hungry.*

An unexpected by-product of his new doctor-imposed regime was time for reflection and Rockefeller soon found himself considering the plight of others and the effects his wealth could

> 'The penalty of a selfish attempt to make the world confer a living without contributing to the progress or happiness of mankind is generally a failure to the individual. The pity is that when he goes down he inflicts heartache and misery also on others who are in no way responsible.'
> **JOHN D. ROCKEFELLER**

> 'Prosperity cannot be divorced from humanity.'
> **CALVIN COOLIDGE**

have if generously given to charitable causes, rather than stockpiled to support his own scarcity concerns. The Rockefeller Foundation was thus born and quickly became the most philanthropic foundation ever to exist. John D. Rockefeller lived another 45 years until the ripe old age of 98 as a happy and worry-free man.

'I would have a man generous to his country, his neighbours, his kindred, his friends, and most of all his poor friends. Not like some who are most lavish with those who are able to give most to them.'

**PLINY**

'It's critical to realize that you won't stop worrying simply because your income rises… The trick is to trust, without any doubt whatsoever, that the magic works in the other direction. You need to stop worrying first, and then you'll do what it takes to create the abundance you deserve.'

**RICHARD CARLSON**

So, avoid worry. Begin to trust more fully in your financial future. Let each small step you take empower and encourage you. Take time to feel good about the victories (no matter how small) and let them build up your confidence. Success builds upon success. As you review the progress you have made by implementing the Seven Money Steps, congratulate yourself. And always hold steady to your financial goals and objectives.

Whenever I teach a seminar I always ask this question: 'Does anybody know anybody who became rich on one deal and kept the money?' And you know what, in asking this question to tens of thousands of people throughout the world no-one has ever answered 'Yes!' Oh sure, a few people have been lucky and pulled off a big deal, but inevitably, because they did not have a **Level Four Automatic Investor** foundation, they were soon back to being broke.

The reason: becoming rich is not an instantaneous event. Becoming rich is a natural progression. It comes by taking (many) small steps forward. Slowly, a little at a time, you become richer. You set up an **AIP**, you pay off some debt, you reduce some expenses, you put more money into your AIP, you restructure and lower your taxes, you pay off some more debt, you buy a house, you buy some shares… and then over a period of time you naturally and progressively (one step at a time) become rich.

Stick with the plan. Follow the *Money Secrets* program and you will become rich (little by little). Have confidence in your ability to take this journey to riches one step at a time.

Practise looking at the world as a place of abundance and prosperity. Know that money is not your end, it is your means, and you should not approach money as something that should be hoarded or insulated from others. Abundance and prosperity come to those who are open to receiving them, and stay with those who are respectful, and generous with them.

So remember to give of yourself and your resources. It has been my personal experience that this belief and expectation of success dramatically affects the results you obtain. Start looking at how you want your world to be and then begin taking one small step at a time in that direction. All the while remembering the need to share the benefits of the abundance that you are now beginning to receive.

In the final section of *Money Secrets of the Rich* we will be covering material that will dramatically accelerate your path to riches:

- The belief systems of the rich and how *you* can adopt them;
- **Money Step #7 – *Avoiding Debt and Living Debt-Free*** – (featuring: *The Debt Terminator)*
- The **Nine Generalised Principles of Active (Level Five) Investing**;
- My **17 Personal Rules of Active (Level Five) Investing for 20–100%+ Returns**;
- Advanced (Level Five) investing techniques (including real estate);
- Business and investment structures and tax reduction strategies; and
- Building a financial library.

> 'Many people think that by hoarding money they are gaining safety for themselves. If money is your only hope for independence, you will never have it. The only real security that a man can have in this world is a reserve of knowledge, experience and ability.'
> **HENRY FORD**

> 'He that is proud of riches is a fool. For if he be exalted above his neighbors because he hath more gold, how much inferior is he to gold mine.'
> **JEREMY TAYLOR**

In short, we will be moving from the Level Four *Money Secrets of the Rich* to some of the Level Five and Level Six *Money Secrets of the Rich*.

Read on.

---

## CHAPTER 21 ACTION STEPS REVIEW

1. Review the first 20 chapters of the program.
2. Take a look at changes in how you now think about money.
3. Make sure you understand the key elements and requirements for adopting the first six *Money Steps*.
4. Catch up on any assignments missed.
5. Rest and reflect, without worry, on the abundance in your life and how you might best share it with those around you.

## PART THREE

# The Magic of Financial Freedom

'Beware of the thief on the street who is after your purse. And beware of the thief in your mind who is after your promise.'

JIM ROHN

'A person is more likely to be successful managing money if he uses spiritual principles, and the more you practice spirituality, the more you learn.'

SIR JOHN TEMPLETON

## CHAPTER 22

# Financial Beliefs

'You create your own universe as you go along. The stronger your imagination, the more variegated your universe. When you leave off dreaming, the universe ceases to exist.'

WINSTON CHURCHILL

'Imagination grows by exercise and contrary to common belief is more powerful in the mature than in the young.'

W. SOMERSET MAUGHAM

'You can't depend on your judgement when your imagination is out of focus.'

MARK TWAIN

In this chapter, I want you to spend more detailed time examining your **Financial Beliefs**. Your belief system has a tremendous effect on your wealth. Your belief system is actually the single biggest factor (the vital prerequisite) to your wealth creation capabilities.

Do you know somebody who makes money no matter what they do? It just seems as if they have the Midas touch, doesn't it?

'If you think about disaster, you will get it. Brood about death and you hasten your demise. Think positively and masterfully, with confidence and faith, and life becomes more secure, more fraught with action, richer in achievement and experience.'

**EDWARD RICKENBACKER**

And on the other hand, I am sure you know people who always lose money. It does not matter where they invest, or what they do, they always lose. It is almost as if you could make great investment decisions (every time), just by doing the exact opposite of what they do (known these days as the Costanza!).

The first person described is what I call '**Money Attractant**'. The second person '**Money Repellent**'. Which of the following would you say best describes you?

## I AM MONEY ATTRACTANT
## I AM MONEY NEUTRAL
## I AM MONEY REPELLENT

I have learned that most people (essentially almost all people who are Level Zero, One, Two, or Three Investors) are Money Repellent. Most people, because of their conscious (and sub-conscious) belief systems, have actually programmed themselves to be poor (or middle class, which today, really means poor, doesn't it?).

Take a minute right now to write down the things you were taught at home about money and 'rich people' when you were growing up. What did you learn from your family, friends, school, and church?

'Every man, wherever he goes, is encompassed by a cloud of comforting convictions, which move with him like flies on a summer day.'

**BERTRAND RUSSELL**

Were the associations to money and rich people good or bad? Were they associated with scarcity or abundance? For most people the associations to money and rich people were and continue to be disempowering and based upon the scarcity mentality. Do you resent rich people and their success? Do you believe that there is a limited supply of money and opportunity to go around?

Growing up, were you told, taught or led to believe any of the following?

- Money is the 'root of all evil.'
- Rich people are evil.
- Money doesn't grow on trees.
- Rich people are greedy and selfish.
- Rich people are misers and hoard money.
- Rich people never give money to charities
  or to the church.
- To get rich you have to be a crook, a liar, a thief,
  or get lucky.
- Rich people are like J.R. Ewing (from the TV show
  *Dallas*) or Alexis Colby (from the TV show *Dynasty*).
- Money won't make you happy.
- Money isn't that important anyway.
- There are more important things in life than money.
- We don't have a lot of money because we love our
  children.
- If God wanted us to have money, he would give it to us.
- You have to work hard to make money.
- Having a lot of money could (would) make you a
  bad person.
- If you had a lot of money, you would lose it.
- If you had a lot of money, you would get sued or audited.
- If you had a lot of money, your friends and family
  wouldn't like you any more.
- Having a lot of money would be complicated or a hassle.
- Having a lot of money would mean that you would have
  to spend a lot of time watching and protecting it.
- The rich keep getting richer and the poor keep getting
  poorer.
- You better save your pennies for a rainy day.
- A good job is the way to become rich.
- When you grow up you'll learn the value of money.
- If you went through the Depression like we did...
- A fool and his money are soon parted.
- Clean your plate, children are starving in India.

Do any of these cliches sound familiar? I bet you have more of your own, don't you? In reality, most people are Money Repellent because their brains are full of negative attitudes towards money and wealth. These Money Repellent attitudes (cliches) serve to bolster people's capacity to justify their own poor financial predicament. If they do not have money it is because of any one of the cliches and certainly not their own fault. They live in denial and with false belief systems in relation to money.

'To be ambitious for wealth, and yet always expecting to be poor; to be always doubting your ability to get what you long for, is like trying to reach east by traveling west. There is no philosophy which will help man to succeed when he is always doubting his ability to do so, and thus attracting failure.'
**CHARLES BANDOUIN**

'To your subconscious mind the solution to your problems of poverty is to become rich, but it is logically invalid for it to pursue this course of action if it has been told that it will make you a bad person.'
**SIMON HALL**

If your experiences were like mine, the people you most loved and respected (your financial mentors as it were: parents, grandparents, teachers, friends and clergy, etc.) meant well and certainly wanted you to succeed (financially). Unfortunately, since they had never been taught how money really works, all they could pass on to you was their system (which probably didn't work). In most cases, they grew up from a place of scarcity thinking not prosperity thinking. The end results were usually financial failure (insecurity) and negative views on money, money-making and people with money.

Living by those old negative thought patterns was of little real consequence in a by-gone era of stable work, low inflation, nationally run industry and liberal welfare systems. The world has changed radically though since our grandparents' (or parents') day and the pace of change is accelerating. These changes require us to adopt different beliefs, to rethink our views and attitudes in regard to money.

**Question**: If you hate (dislike, resent) rich people, how can you ever become one yourself? You can not! If you think that all rich people are bad, then automatically your subconscious mind will never let you become rich, because if you did, then you would be a bad person. Do you see the dilemma? It is a real 'Catch 22'.

Many people live their entire lives pretending that money is not important to them. They believe wealthy people worship their money for its own sake and would do anything to get it and to keep it. The reality is that the people without money are usually the people who actually worship money. They live their lives for it.

After all, who is working all day long, year after year after year, at a job they hate, just for the money? Who is always wishing they could have just a little more money? Who is always worried about money? Who is always talking about money? Who is always sacrificing time with their families for more money? The people with the money or the people without it? We all know the answer!

I know many more than 100 people who are millionaires and one who is a billionaire. Without exception, they do what they love to do. To them, what they do (to earn money) is not even work. In fact, most of them are semi-retired (like myself). Why? Because the money itself is not what drives them. They would rather spend 'quality' time with their families. They only work because they enjoy what they do. They don't work for money. Their money works for them.

> 'I have nothing but contempt for the people who despise money. They are hypocrites or fools. Money is like a sixth sense without which you cannot make a complete use of the other five. Without an adequate income half the possibilities of life are shut off.'
> **W. SOMERSET MAUGHAM**

> 'Money is a by-product of something I like to do very much. Every day, when I get to the office, so to speak, I do a little tap dance.'
> **WARREN BUFFETT**

---

**Bottomline:** most people are poor (middle class) because they are **Money Repellent**. At some level, they believe rich people and/or money are evil, or that wealth is out of their reach or that they themselves do not deserve to be wealthy. They may justify that they do not have money because they are either a 'good person' or an undeserving person, or an uneducated or unintelligent person (or any other series of disempowering beliefs). This is their mindset and hence their reality. To quote the timeless verse of Milton: 'The mind is its own place, and in itself can make a heaven of hell, a hell of heaven.'

'Work is love made visible. And if you cannot work with love but only with distaste, it is better that you should leave your work and sit at the gate of the temple and take alms of those who work with joy.'
**KAHLIL GIBRAN**

'The good news is that, the moment you decide that what you know is more important than what you have been taught to believe, you will have shifted gears in your quest for abundance. Success comes from within, not from without. It begins by listening to your inner calling and wisdom.'
**RICHARD CARLSON**

'No one can cheat you out of ultimate success but yourselves.'
**RALPH WALDO EMERSON**

Think about it. I am sure you have seen an interview where a wealthy person said they would do what they were doing whether they got paid or not? I have, many times. Why do they say this? Because they love what they do, not the money they make for doing it. I have several friends who make tens of thousands of dollars a day public speaking. The money is great (and they deserve it for all the good they do), but guess what? They would speak for free if they had to.

With all that said, let me ask you a question: would you like to have more money *and* feel good about it? Would you like to be able to provide for your family all the good things in this bountiful world? Would you like to have more time to do the things that are really important to you, rather than work all day at a job, as a slave to money?

Of course you would! That is why you committed to this program! It is actually quite easy to unlock the door to the world's bounty. The door has three keys:

## FIRST KEY: AWARENESS

The first key is **awareness** that many of your current financial beliefs are not working. The reason, as stated, is that the world has changed dramatically from the world our parents and grandparents grew up in. The lessons of money that were handed down from generation to generation, often were not updated to suit current times. Consequently, many of us were taught inaccurate, out-of-date information.

By maintaining your awareness you will be able to review your financial position and money habits (money steps) on a regular basis. This will prevent the damaging effects of complacency or ignorance. Awareness is a 'key' that if well-polished (from constant use) will 'unlock' unlimited riches for you and your family.

## SECOND KEY: NEW BELIEF SYSTEMS

The second key is to adopt the **belief systems** of today that do work. Belief systems such as 'Be, Do, Have.' Simply stated, such techniques generally involve adopting the attitudes (in relation to money), of the type of person you want to be (financially). This is the fastest and most effective way of training yourself to become that financially successful person. By adopting the *attitudes* of the financially successful your conscious brain will become the trainer of your mighty subconscious mind.

By definition you become the person you want to be as soon as you start acting like that person, thinking like him or her. If you want to be rich, be rich in your mind first, act rich. This does not mean running around spending money being extravagant. We have seen that this is not how the rich act. They live well within their means. It means adopting the mindset, the thought patterns of abundance, prosperity and success that the wealthy practice. Follow the **Money Steps of the Rich**, their rules, their principles and you are already becoming rich. It is a foregone conclusion.

And if it is a foregone conclusion then on some level your financial success has already begun and the best way to handle it is to accept it with trust. Bring the outcome, your money goals, forward from the future into the present and make it your reality. No more distant dreams and hopes for some far off and disconnected future. Only the reality of your new financial future firmly grounded in your present thoughts and actions. This is adopting **new belief systems**.

'If we can only get it firmly into our heads, and will eternally keep it at the forefront of our mind, that thinking is the material of which success is made, will it not influence us so to plan our days and our weeks that we shall set aside more time for calm, sustained thinking?'
**B.C. FORBES**

'My stated objective is my foreseen outcome.'
**SIMON HALL**

'There is no success without hardship.'
**SOPHOCLES**

## THIRD KEY: POSITIVE ACTION

The third key is to act on those beliefs, and pay as little attention as possible to old self-limiting beliefs that held you back from becoming rich in the past.

> It is important that you understand that **you are fully responsible for your own financial situation**. You must be aware that *you* (fortified with outdated beliefs) have engineered *your* financial results. That right now, today, based on your beliefs and actions you are exactly where you deserve to be financially.
>
> If this upsets you, don't be upset at me. Be upset at what is now your past and vow to make the changes necessary to change your future situation forever. Use your emotion to motivate you to change.

I repeat: **We are all exactly where we deserve to be financially!** No one did it to you, but you. In case you hadn't noticed, no matter how many times you have moved, changed jobs, changed partners, etc., there has always been one common element. YOU! You were always there in the driver's seat.

If things are not working the way you want them to, stop taking the easy way out and blaming others (spouse, parents, government, teachers, God, etc.) for your financial failure(s). Stop justifying why you are not as financially successful as you should be (bad economy, taxes, lack of intelligence, too old, living in a bad area, everybody is a crook, etc.).

> 'Money, after all, is extremely simple. It is a part of our transportation system. It is a simple and direct method of conveying goods from one person to another. Money is in itself most admirable. It is essential. It is not intrinsically evil. It is one of the most useful devices in social life. And when it does what it was intended to do, it is all help and no hindrance.'
> **HENRY FORD**

## TAKE RESPONSIBILITY FOR YOUR LIFE AND ALL THAT YOU HAVE AND ALL THAT YOU DO NOT HAVE!

Great! With that said, let me ask you another question, 'Do you want things to change financially in your life?' If so, then *you* must change first. Absorb a wise old saying popularised by Tony Robbins:

## FOR THINGS TO CHANGE, FIRST, I MUST CHANGE!

By following the first 21 chapters of this program you have already created phenomenal change in your financial life. In fact, I want to take a moment to again congratulate you on your many successes. I realise that many of the assignments have caused you to 'stretch' and to do things that you have never done before. I commend you for your efforts and your willingness and ability to change. Keep up the good work and your momentum.

> 'You can't rise unless you set goals that make you stretch.'
> **TOM HOPKINS**

> 'Most folks are about as happy as they make up their minds to be.'
> **ABRAHAM LINCOLN**

This program has been instructing you how to change the way you handle money. Would you like to now learn to change what you believe about money?

## HOW TO CHANGE YOUR BELIEFS ABOUT MONEY

Changing your beliefs about money can be quite simple. It is a two-stage process: **Awareness**; then a **Program for Change**. Once you are aware of the thoughts and beliefs you would like to change you can then train your mind with new thoughts and beliefs.

Think of this process as similar to reprogramming or reconfiguring a computer. If your computer operated on an old software program that wasn't working for you any more, what would you do? That's right, you would simply delete the old program and then install a new program (one that met your needs today). You would not think twice about doing this. The old program was outdated and simply not performing. The obvious answer is to install a better program.

When human beings malfunction or underperform financially (or otherwise), we too need to be able to review our operating software and if necessary install a new program. A program that is Money Attractant, not Money Repellent.

So how do we go about reprogramming Money Repellent beliefs? I have found three methods that work exceptionally well. You can use them in any combination you want. Although they are all similar techniques, I prefer to combine all three for the best results: **Prayer**; **Affirmations**; and **Imagination**.

## PRAYER

My family and I firmly believe in God and live with Christian beliefs as a major part of our lives. This is what we believe and this is our faith. However, if you would be more comfortable with a term other than 'God' to represent your beliefs, such as 'The Great Spirit' or 'The Universe' or 'Universal Energy', then please substitute that term when I speak of 'God'.

> I strongly believe that God wants us to experience a full abundant life. It is my ardent belief that the very act of reading (aloud) empowering spiritual passages (ideally on a daily basis), opens your mind up to the vast riches and blessings that are available to all of us.

The following are the three steps that Dr Joseph Murphy outlines in his excellent book *Your Infinite Power to Be Rich* (a book I highly recommend) to change negative money beliefs into positive money beliefs:

**First Step: Always make positive statements about finances.** Never say, 'I can't make ends meet', 'I don't have enough money', etc. Instead say: 'I am one with the infinite storehouse within me, and all my needs are met instantaneously.' In the beginning, it may be necessary to do this 50 times in one hour, but persist and the negative thoughts will cease to trouble you. They will be smothered by the positive ones.

**Second Step: Make it a habit during the course of the day to condition your mind to the riches of the infinite** by affirming: 'God is an ever present help in time of trouble', and 'God is the instant and immediate source of my supply, presenting me with all the ideas necessary at every moment of time and point of space.'

**Third Step: Lull yourself to sleep every night by reiterating this great truth: 'I am ever grateful for God's riches that are ever active, ever present, unchanging, and eternal.'**

I began faithfully following these three steps several years ago. The results were amazing. Try it for yourself. I also recommend Richard Carlson's book *Don't Worry, Make Money* for 'Spiritual and Practical Ways to Create Abundance and More Fun in Your Life'.

'I bargained with Life
for a penny,
And Life would pay no more,
However I begged at evening
When I counted my scanty store.

For Life is a just employer,
He gives you what you ask,
But once you have set the wages,
Why, you must bear the task.

I worked for a menial's hire,
Only to learn, dismayed,
That any wage I had asked of Life,
Life would have willingly paid.'

## THE POWER OF FAITH

As I stated, I have deeply held spiritual convictions seated in my Christian faith. And whether or not you are a Christian, I have found that there is *great power in the belief.* By having 'faith' that a power other than myself is there to help me in times of need and to achieve my goals, I enlist a most powerful ally.

I do not know of anyone who went forward and completed a mighty task without faith. The world is full of example after example of people who forged forward, committed faithfully to their cause, to become successful. Whether this is in the world of business, sport, politics, spirituality or investing is irrelevant. The key is having faith that you can successfully complete the task. Call it *faith*, call it *positive thinking*, call it a *belief in one's self* and *plan*, call it *self-fulfilling prophecy*. It doesn't really matter what you call it as long as you have it. The power is in the *believing* and *having faith*.

**My advice:** Believe that you can become rich. Believe that financial abundance is available to you. Believe, have faith and move forward!

## QUIETING DOWN, TUNING IN, AND GETTING OUT OF YOUR OWN WAY

Arriving at and 'maintaining the faith' necessary to triumph comes with time and patience. Like everything else worthwhile it also takes commitment and practice. One spends time to learn a language, a trade or a vocation, a sport or a hobby. Many people spend time getting in touch with their feelings on occasion. Often these skills are not intuitive for adults. They can take time and effort to learn.

'The whole course of things goes to teach us faith. We need only obey. There is guidance for each of us, and by lowly listening, we shall hear the right word.'
**RALPH WALDO EMERSON**

'The point is to firmly imprint your expectation on the source of abundance through reprogramming your brain. You will enable your brain to access its own born potential (true and unstoppable spirit) and thereby determine your own outcome (any outcome). Abundance is there if you have the courage to ask for it, the ambition and confidence to expect it and the trust and commitment to receive it without sabotaging yourself with negative thoughts and shackled expectations.'
**SIMON HALL**

So, you must also spend time connecting with your faith and the greater forces that enable you to succeed without restriction. For children such connectedness is usually intuitive. Too often though, as we 'grow up' the 'real world' erodes our intuitive access to our own spiritual momentum. We are bombarded so often with negative, restrictive, conditional and judgmental information: grounded in concepts of scarcity; assumptions of failure; motivations of fear; and shallow interpretations and definitions of self-worth, success, value and obligation. We need to reconnect to our childhood intuitive ways. It helps to quiet down, tune in and get out of our own way. Relax and enjoy the process.

How do *I* do it? I carry a planner with me. In that planner I have written several passages and inspirational affirmations to keep myself on track. The passages I employ are mainly from the powerful text of the Bible (New International Version). The Bible is filled with affirmations that you were born to be rich, that God wants only the best for his children. You are to expect and actively seek out the best for yourselves. The Bible contains passages that will empower you in a positive way. The inspirational quotes are from many great authors. Here are some of my favourites.

## Empowering Biblical Scriptures

- *What things soever you desire, when you pray, believe that you receive them, and you shall have them.* (Mark 11:24)
- *Whatever you ask in prayer, believe that you receive it, and you will.* (Mark 11:24)

- *If thou canst believe, all things are possible to him who believeth.* (Mark 9:23)
- *According to your faith be it unto you.* (Matthew 9:29)
- *If ye have faith as a grain of mustard seed… nothing shall be impossible unto you.* (Matthew 17:20)
- *Have faith in God. For verily I say unto you, that whosoever shall say unto this mountain, be thou removed, and be thou cast into the sea; and shall not doubt in his heart but shall believe that those things which he saith shall come to pass; he shall have whatsoever he saith.* (Mark 11:22–23)
- *If God be for us, who can be against us?* (Romans 8:31)
- *I can do all things through Christ which strengtheneth me.* (Phil. 4:13)
- *The Kingdom of God is within you.* (Luke 17:21)
- *And all things, whatsoever you shall ask in prayer, believing, you shall receive them.* (Matthew 21:22)
- *Ask, and you shall receive, seek, and you shall find; knock and the door shall be opened unto you. For everyone who asks receives, and he who seeks finds, and to him who knocks it will be opened.* (Matthew 7:7–8)
- *Go; be it done for you as you have believed.* (Matthew 8:13)
- *The good man out of his good treasure brings forth good.* (Matthew 12:35)
- *For to him who has will more be given, and he will have abundance; but from him who has not, even what he has will be taken away.* (Matthew 13:12)
- *Great is your faith! Be it done for you as you desire.* (Matthew 16:28)
- *If two of you agree on earth about anything they ask, it will be done for them by my Father in heaven. For where two or three are gathered in my name, there am I in the midst of them.* (Matthew 18:19–20)
- *With God all things are possible.* (Matthew 19:26)
- *For to every one who has will more be given, and he will have abundance; but from him who has not, even what he has will be taken away.* (Matthew 25:29)
- *Take heed what you hear; the measure you give will be the measure you get, and still more will be given to you. For to him who has will more be given; and to him who has not, even what he has will be taken away.* (Mark 4:24–25)
- *Do not fear, only believe.* (Mark 5:36)

- *I believe; help my unbelief.* (Mark 10:27)
- *I am come that they might have life, and that they might have it more abundantly.* (John 10:10)
- *The earth is full of the goodness of the Lord.* (Psalms 33:5)
- *You will eat the fruit of your labour; blessings and prosperity will be yours.* (Psalm128:2)
- *The blessing of the Lord brings wealth, and he adds no trouble to it.* (Proverbs 10:22)
- *The Lord is my strength and my song; he has become my salvation.* (Psalm 118:14)
- *But my God shall supply all your needs according to his riches in glory…* (Phil. 4:19)

'When you affirm big, believe big, and pray big, big things happen.'
**NORMAN VINCENT PEALE**

Obviously, the Bible and other great spiritually empowering texts contain many more powerful passages, but I am sure that you get the intended message.

**Acknowledgment:** I would like to thank my good friend and pastor Bryan Fergus for his input and assistance in this chapter.

## AFFIRMATIONS

Here are some great life-empowering affirmations that I have heard or developed.

- This is going to be a Glorious Day.
- Enthusiasm! Enthusiasm! Is my best friend!
- Each and every day, in every way, through the grace of God I am better and better through PMA [Positive Mental Attitude].
- Do it Now!!!
- Every adversity has the seed of an equivalent or greater benefit for those who have a positive mental attitude.
- You can do it if you believe you can.
- Have the courage to face the truth.
- To be enthusiastic, act enthusiastically.
- Anything in life worth working for is worth praying for.
- Apply faith. Do it now.
- Now is the time to act.

- Open your mind and learn to see.
- Change the adversity into seeds of greater benefit.
- You've got a problem? That's good. For it is the seeds of greater benefits for those who have a Positive Mental Attitude.
- You must face fear, not run from it, or it will haunt you forever.
- Feel the fear and do it anyway. (Susan Jeffers).
- To the degree you give others what they need, they will give you what you need.
- Listen, really listen, to what others are saying. Listening is Loving.
- You can get everything in life you want if you just help enough other people get what they want.
- Where there is nothing to lose by trying and everything to gain if successful, by all means try. Do it now!
- Belief at the beginning of a doubtful undertaking is the one thing that will guarantee the success of any venture.
- If you think you can, you can. So think you can!
- I'm going to win today. Why? I'll tell you why, because I've got Faith, Courage and Enthusiasm!
- Never Give Up. Never, Never, Never Give Up.
- I am whole, perfect, strong, powerful, loving, harmonious and happy.
- I Believe, I Believe, I Believe I am in God's hands. I Believe I am now receiving his power. I feel it flowing into me.
- I place this day, my life, my loved ones, my work in the Lord's hands. There is no harm in the Lord's hands, only good. Whatever happens, whatever results, if I am in the Lord's hands it is the Lord's will and it is good.
- There is only one way with the Lord and that is straight ahead.
- God is always a good God.
- God is with me now. He is by my side always. God is my partner. With him as my partner all good shall come to me.
- I believe I am always divinely guided. I believe I will always take the right turn of the road. I believe God will always make a way where there is no way.

## MONEY ATTRACTANT AFFIRMATIONS

If your belief system with regard to money needs positive reinforcement then I recommend that you repeat prosperity (Money Attractant) affirmations throughout your day. Write them on flash cards and tape them up around your house and car. Make a recording of your own voice and listen to *your* positive affirmations. Always state affirmations in positive grammar: the mind cannot concentrate on the reverse of a negative affirmation (i.e. 'I will become rich' is better than 'I don't want to be poor'). Over the years I have come across and developed many **Money Attractant affirmations**. My thanks to my many mentors who are too numerous to list. Here are some of my favourites, but feel free to customise them for your own use:

> 'A particular train of thought persisted in, be it good or bad, cannot fail to produce its results on the character and circumstances. A man cannot directly choose his circumstances, but he can choose his thoughts, and so indirectly, yet surely, shape his circumstances.'
>
> **JAMES ALLEN**

- Day and night I attract money and prosperity.
- I am open to receive riches and abundance.
- I am a success in life.
- I am open to receive more money and success.
- Creative ideas for money and success flow from me.
- Prosperity is mine. I deserve it. I expect it.
- I reap an abundant harvest of money.
- My life is filled with harmony and happiness.
- There is always a surplus in my life.
- I am filled with confidence and success.
- Success is mine. I think BIG.
- Money and success flow to me in avalanches of abundance.
- I attract my share of abundance and possessions.
- I deserve to be rich and successful.
- Like a powerful magnet, I attract success and riches.
- Like a magnet attracts iron filings, I attract success and riches.
- I have tremendously good luck.
- Rivers of prosperity and abundance flow to me.
- It's OK to make more money than Dad.
- It's OK to be rich. I am wealthy. I deserve riches.

- I am lucky.
- I am a self-starter. I enjoy getting things done. I have high energy to accomplish.
- I feel great satisfaction in accomplishment.
- I am an energetic person.
- I am energised to start and complete tasks.
- I am a motivated and energetic person.
- I feel good about my life. I can do it.
- Each day I do what needs to be done. I am a doer!
- I am a happy person. I enjoy life. Life is good to me.
- I am a high-achiever. I am energised for success.
- Each and every day brings fresh new opportunities.
- I excel at whatever I do. I have a positive expectancy.
- I am at peace with the world around me.
- I achieve my objectives.
- I am a positive and successful achiever.
- Automatic Wealth is mine.
- My success is assured.
- Every day I achieve more and more.
- I have inner strength and confidence to win.
- I am charged with energy and alert of mind as I start each new day.
- I enjoy being a top producer.
- I am optimistic and filled with enthusiasm.
- My life is a reflection of success.
- Life is filled with many wonderful opportunities.
- I am motivated and energised to accomplish my objectives. I have clear goals in mind for life.
- I feel great about my life. I know that I am a winner.
- I feel good about my achievements.
- I believe in myself. I am a winning achiever.

'Let a man radically alter his thoughts, and he will be astonished at the rapid transformation it will effect in the material conditions of his life.'
**JAMES ALLEN**

'In adversity assume the countenance of prosperity, and in prosperity moderate the temper and desires.'
**LIVY**

'The man who doesn't make up his mind to cultivate the habit of thinking misses the greatest pleasure in life. He not only misses the greatest pleasure, but he cannot make the most of himself. All progress, all success, springs from thinking.'
**THOMAS ALVA EDISON**

- I deserve to succeed. I am a success.
- I am confident of my ability to succeed.
- I derive great satisfaction and reward in accomplishment.
- I am motivated and energised to achieve my goals.
- I accomplish more in less time than ever before.
- I have high energy and stamina to achieve.
- I am successful in everything I do.

How did you feel as you read these Money Attractant affirmations? If you are like me, you probably started to feel a little self-conscious or hypocritical the first time through. Don't worry, that will change. As you read (aloud) these affirmations more and more they will become a part of you. They will become your reality, your mindset, your new program. Your mind is the most powerful computer in the world. Your imagination does not know the difference between reality and fantasy.

Not happy with your financial reality? No problem, let your mind create a new reality (through the use of affirmations). Soon it will be your new reality. This technique is not new. I didn't invent it. However, the technique did work for me. It has worked for millions of others. Have fun and enjoy your new future.

> 'I suggest that if you *firmly* imprint your expectations onto the Universe your yellow brick road will appear in front of you, as if by magic.'
> **SIMON HALL**

> 'I keep the telephone of my mind open to peace, harmony, health, love and abundance. Then, whenever doubt, anxiety, or fear try to call me, they keep getting a busy signal – and they'll soon forget my number.'
> **EDITH ARMSTRONG**

## IMAGINATION

Imagining is a technique where you 'see' in your mind how you desire your (financial) life to be, rather than how it is. I am sure you all remember your **Imagination**. Remember when you were a child? Anything was possible. One minute you were a cowboy, the next minute a dinosaur, a few minutes later an astronaut. Anything was possible as long as you had your good friend your imagination.

Unfortunately, adults are too often coerced to forget about their imagination. However, their imagination has not forgotten about them.

Your brain is similar to a garden. If good seeds are not

planted, and then fertilised, weeds will grow. The same thing applies to money. If you do not introduce positive images about money, negative ones will sprout. Before you know it, your image of money has become one of lack and scarcity, rather than of plenty and abundance. This technique will allow you to fully utilise your imagination.

> Do not underestimate the power of your *Imagination*, for, when the *Will* and the *Imagination* are in conflict, the *Imagination* always wins. It is infinitely more powerful.

## How to Imagine

First of all remember that there is no right or wrong way to imagine. However you like to do it is just fine. If you find it difficult to get started you may want to try what I often do. Sit or lay down in a quiet place. Take a few deep breaths to clear yourself out: to clear away the brain cobwebs. Slowly start to imagine your financial life the way you want it to be. Envision yourself as a successful person. Picture your investment statements. See your debt dwindle and your assets increase.

When you imagine, try to recognise if it is a still picture or a movie that you see? Is it in colour or black and white? Is it bright or dim? Is it large or small? Are there voices? Are you an observer or are you in the picture? There is no right or wrong way to do this exercise provided you are aware of what you see. However it works for you is the right way.

Practise making the picture in your mind. Is the image more positive when the picture is bright or dark? Moving or still? Close or far away? With just a little practice you will find that you can imagine a very positive, abundant life 'up close and personal' in full 64–bit digital colour with THX Theatre surround sound.

'The problem is, many of us don't use our present-moment energy to its fullest because we are constantly trying to use our "wake", that which is behind us, our past, to move us forward. But like the wake in the ocean, our past has no power. It is nothingness.'
**RICHARD CARLSON**

'Employing your imagination as engineer, construct an impenetrably positive fortress of visualised images of how you want your life to be. Reconstruct the power of your childhood: rebuild your own dream terrain, your wishville, your "image-nation!"'
**SIMON HALL**

**Tips:** For many people making the picture bigger, brighter, and more colourful enhances the image. Try it. Now try the opposite, make the picture smaller, dimmer, and in black and white. What happened?

Negative experiences can often be diminished by moving them further away or making them smaller, in effect shrinking them by distancing perspective on them. The opposite effect is usually true for positive experiences. Learn how to enhance the images, thoughts and feelings for that which you want and to lessen the images, thoughts and feelings for that which you do not want. Strive to clean out the stale images that may be in your mind and replace them with fresh, healthy ones.

---

For further information see the recommended reading list (for self-improvement) and in particular, works by Dale Carnegie, Richard Carlson, Ph.D., Dr. Wayne Dyer, Dr. Jonathon Parker, Napoleon Hill, Dr. Joseph Murphy, Donald M. Wolfe and Anthony Robbins.

---

The use of these techniques will align the power of your subconscious mind and your imagination on your side, to work for you, instead of in conflict against you. Bring your Will into the picture by taking positive Action and you will be unstoppable. Your life will be greatly enhanced in happy, positive, prosperous ways.

---

## CHAPTER 22 ACTION STEPS REVIEW

1. Determine whether you are **Money Attractant**, **Money Neutral**, or **Money Repellent**.
2. Determine what your childhood **Beliefs** are about money and rich people.
3. Commit to accepting full (financial) responsibility for your life. No longer blame others or justify your lack of financial success.
4. Become a person of **Change**.
5. Set up your own daily **Prayer**, **Affirmation**, and **Imagination** program to dramatically assist you in your financial success.

## CHAPTER 23

# Money Step #7 – *Avoiding debt and living debt-free*

## (featuring: *The Debt Terminator*)

'Debt robs a man of his self-respect, and makes him almost despise himself. Grunting and groaning and working for what he has eaten up or worn out, and now when he is called upon to pay up, he has nothing to show for his money: this is properly termed "working for a dead horse."'

P.T. BARNUM

Now we are going to tackle, what for many people, has become one of their biggest and most relentless problems: **debt**. And we are going to introduce you to *The Debt Terminator*! At no other time in history has there been such a tremendous financial burden placed on the average family. I know this from personal experience as well as from extensive study of the subject. But with *The Debt Terminator* by your side, you will be armed with enough financial firepower to annihilate your debt forever!

According to recent news reports (December 2000), Australians are currently the proud owners of 9.3 million credit cards, with a total of $15.1 billion in outstanding debt (up 18% from last year).

Monthly interest paid on these credit card debts tops a whopping $130 million. Over the past decade total household debt in Australia has almost doubled. The average family now owes over one year's after-tax income in consumer debt and since the June quarter of 2000, pays out 103% of disposable income to service total household debt (using savings to make up the shortfall). The Department of Fair Trading states that the average individual over 18 owes $5,445 on consumer credit, up 18% on the previous year. The Reserve bank estimates that an average outstanding balance of $1,706 is held on each credit card, up from $1,464 the previous year (and up 60% over the last three years). And about 70% of this credit card debt is generating monthly interest income for the banks and other card issuers, meaning that the credit card game is truly a big loser for the average consumer.

> 'So rather go to bed supperless than rise in debt.'
> **BENJAMIN FRANKLIN**

I can relate to this. Just a few short years ago I was deeply in debt. I owed more than $20,000 on credit cards. My monthly car lease was $625, my sports utility vehicle (SUV) payment was almost $500. I owed more than $215,000 on my home. I made good money but I was nonetheless deeply in debt. I didn't think I would ever get out of debt. Just as I started to make a dent in the credit card balance another expense would come up. It was very frustrating and certainly depressing. I felt like the only way I would ever be able to pay off all my debt was if I won the lottery or inherited money from some rich relative (I didn't have).

---

The monthly payments just keep rising and rising. Bringing with them ever mounting pressure and stress. To most it does not seem like this rising tide of debt will ever recede. And for many people that is the hard truth. They will ultimately drown in this choking sea of debts and liabilities, of endless bills, payments and anxiety. The average family will continue to make monthly payments until the day they die or until they are forced into bankruptcy by their negative cash flow. ***This all stops now!!***

I was living my life like many people do: heavily in debt with no light at the end of the tunnel. I truly believed I would probably be in debt for my entire life. I certainly believed that I would *always* have a mortgage. My family was like most families who are weighed down by thousands, if not tens or hundreds of thousands of dollars in consumer debt.

Luckily for me, I *did* realise that things had to change. I sat down with my wife Shari and we set up a plan to systematically pay off all our debt. It took us a little over four years to be completely debt-free (the only debt we now have is intentional investment debt where someone else makes the payments for us). I cannot really describe just how good it feels to go to sleep at night without having to worry about bills and owing other people money. Our only monthly expenses now are utilities, food and insurance. The remainder of our income is ours to spend just as we want to.

> '... a ploughman on his legs is higher than a gentleman on his knees.'
> **BENJAMIN FRANKLIN**

> 'Advertising may be described as the science of arresting the human intelligence long enough to get money from it.'
> **STEPHEN LEACOCK**

> 'Though a taste of pleasure may quicken the relish of life, an unrestrained indulgence leads to inevitable destruction.'
> **DODSLEY**

The sense of freedom is wonderful. To have freed ourselves from the bondage of debt is exhilarating. Today, rather than struggling to stay ahead of a monthly payments burden, we now have the freedom to purchase what we want, when we want it, on a cash basis. You too will soon experience the exhilaration of being debt-free.

Before I show you my *The Debt Terminator* method for becoming *Completely Debt-Free in 3–7 Years (Including Your House and Cars)* – let's examine why it is that people become so deeply in debt in the first place? There are three major reasons:

| Advertisers and marketers | Banks and other lenders | Financial advisers |
|---|---|---|

You must understand that it is the mission of these three types of commercial groups to hold you in perpetual and escalating debt. I call it perpetual bondage and slavery. In reality, most people have become *slaves* to their debt and to their debt masters. So how do these groups create this control? How have they made so many people in the free world their debt slaves?

## THE ADVERTISERS

It is the job of the advertisers to entice you to want and convince you to need everything that was ever made. Think about it, in a matter of moments you can open a magazine or a newspaper, turn on the radio or the TV, and in an instant *desperately need* something that moments before you did not even know existed. The impact that advertising has had on the 'free' world is dramatic. We have been highly trained to become voracious consumers. To live and die by the motto: 'Charge it!' Buy it now and worry about paying for it later with 'small' monthly payments. New TV! New stereo! New bigger car! New boat! Great holiday! New house! And on the list goes.

---

**Consume! Consume! Consume! Spend! Spend! Spend! Want! Want! Want! And then want some More! Bigger and better! Newer and cleaner! Faster and leaner! Oh what a feeling!**

---

Now don't get me wrong. I too like buying and owning nice things. The difference between what I do and what the average person does is that I live debt-free and I only buy what I can pay for in cash. What I can truly afford. I do not fall for the easy monthly payment plans and spend beyond my means. An overwhelming majority of millionaires follow the same principles.

**Clarification:** I am not, nor do I believe you should be, a fanatical penny-pinching miser. I do not want you to *lower* your standard of living. Far from it. I actually want you to *increase* your standard of living. I advise you that the best way of doing this is to follow the techniques you learned earlier in the *Money Secrets* program for reducing your cost (not standard) of living by 20–50% and then follow **Money Secret #7 – *Avoiding Debt***

*and Living Debt-Free.* As you do this you will be able to own the nice things you want (and deserve) by paying for them on a cash basis, not via the perpetual debt basis.

## BANKS AND LENDERS

As I have stated many times, the major objective of the banks and other lenders of the world is to make as much profit as they legally can. They are not necessarily looking out for your best interests. Again, let me make this perfectly clear. I am not saying that your bank manager or the bank teller is a bad person. What I *am* saying is that the main objective of the lending industry is to separate you from as much of your hard-earned money

> 'But, ah, think what you do when you run in debt; you give another power over your liberty.'
> **BENJAMIN FRANKLIN**

as possible. And they best accomplish this by charging their customers plenty of interest and lots of little fees.

Banks and other lenders want you to be a debt slave to them for eternity. They want to take money from you (in small monthly payments) until the day you die and then beyond that time from your heirs. In essence, you become their slave. By definition, if you owe money to anybody for anything you are an indentured servant to your debtor.

> **Remember the golden rule: He who has the gold makes the rules!**

Do you know how credit cards really work? They are designed deliberately with a very small monthly payment. Do you know why? It is so you will *never* pay them off. The lenders want you to pay interest for as long as possible. With most cards, if you only paid the minimum monthly payment, you would spend close to four times more than what you actually paid for the original item.

> **The average credit card would take 15–20 years to pay off if you only made the minimum payment.**

Here is a concrete example: Say you purchase a new living-room set for $2,500. The minimum monthly payment is just $44.44 a month with an interest rate of 21% (quite normal for a furniture store). At $44.44 a month it would take you *20 years* to pay for that living-room furniture. What would the furniture be worth in 20 years? If you still had it, maybe $200. How much did you really pay for the furniture? No, not $2,500. You wound up paying the furniture company $10,665. This is how they get you, on all those small, silent, sneaky and seemingly harmless monthly payments. They know what they are doing.

And how about the car industry? Did you know that the president of General Motors recently stated that General Motors is not in the automobile business, but in the lending business? The only reason they build cars is so they have a 'vehicle' through which to lend (or lease) money. The same practices are prevalent in the home appliance and home furnishings business too.

Here is an example of just how expensive those low monthly car payments are: Our sample driver is a woman aged 25. She leases a new car for $400 a month. The car salesman was ever so helpful. He explained how with a lease program she could 'roll over' into a brand new car every two years. Have a guess at how much money you think the car company is going to make from this woman? Assuming she keeps driving to age 65, she will spend a whopping $417,867 on cars she will never own. You don't believe me? Let's do the maths: $400 a month for 40 years with a car inflation index rate of 3.5% per annum totals $417,867! Want to lease that fancy luxury sedan or sports car? That $1,000 a month lease will cost you more than $1 million!

Just try to imagine more than $400,000 in small monthly car payments! The lenders of the world are not here to help you, they are here to turn a profit. Do not believe their sales pitch, however it is disguised, whether as 3.9% first year credit card interest rate or easy lease payments on a shiny new sedan for only $399 a month over 36 months. All these great deals are *wolves in sheep's clothing*. The companies offering you the 'freedom to choose your lifestyle' are really offering you a ticket to perpetual bondage.

Most salespeople today are well trained by their companies to part you from your hard-earned income so painlessly that you slide into debt with a grateful smile on your face, thanking them for the ride, for their efforts and consideration, their flexibility and the opportunity to get caught in their trap. They have been highly trained to catch you. You have not been trained at all to escape or even recognise their traps. **UNTIL NOW!**

How about real estate? Residential real estate debt is an incredible burden placed on a family. You are usually told to take out a 25-year loan. The reason: smaller payments. The lenders advise this knowing full well that a typical family moves on average within seven years. The biggest profits for the lenders are in those first few years, when almost all the money paid by the borrower is applied to interest and not to reduction of the principal. The longer the loan term, the more the amortising schedule is skewed towards the lender in the early years of the loan.

Did you know that after seven years on a 25-year, $100,000 mortgage at 8% you would still owe $88,211! *Highway robbery!*

In those first seven years, on a $100,000 mortgage, you would have paid $64,833 and yet only reduced your debt by $11,789! (assuming an 8% interest rate on a 25-year principal and interest loan). What is even more startling, if you crunch the amortised numbers, is that in the first year you have only paid $1,309 off the *capital* yet paid out $7,953 in *interest*. In the second year you only pay an extra $109 towards the principal. Great deal… for the bank! You give them around $65,000 over the first seven years and they give you back less than $12,000, pocketing more than $53,000 in interest!

What's worse is that when people sell their house most go right out and buy a bigger one with a bigger 25-year mortgage. They start the whole small payments process again, from year one, heavily weighted in the bank's favour. Back to square one of the relentless cycle of *slavery to debt*. Plain and simple, slavery in perpetuity. This person is a slave to the lender for most, if not all, of the term of his or her natural life. Think about this for a moment.

Turning the amortising schedules in your favour is achieved by reducing the term of the loan and thus increasing the amount of the monthly payment that goes towards paying off principal rather than interest. For the $100,000 mortgage, if we elected to pay it off over 15 years instead of 25, we would actually be paying less interest from year one! ($7,870 instead of $7,953). Of course our monthly payment would be higher ($955.65 versus $771.82) but this would be entirely comprised of extra principal. The extra $183.83 a month may seem a burden for many but with the money-saving and financial management techniques you are learning in the *Money Secrets* program, it is certainly achievable for the average family. And certainly worth the saving of almost $60,000 in extra interest incurred over a 25-year loan. Of course, most banks are unlikely to volunteer this type of information to you.

> 'If money be not thy servant, it will be thy master.'
> **ENGLISH PROVERB**

> 'The greater our knowledge increases, the greater our ignorance unfolds.'
> **JOHN F. KENNEDY**

Please forgive the harshness of my words when I describe the pain and damage that debt has brought upon so many good people. I just want you to fully understand the awful trap that debt has become for so many. It may sound like I am talking about some terrible uncaring entities when I am describing lenders and their products. I am not. I am merely describing modern business practices wherein the almighty dollar, the profit margin in a company balance sheet, is the overwhelming determinant of company sales policy and advertising content. You are only a 'victim' if you play in the game of consumerism without knowing the rules, the ramifications and the structures of the game mechanisms: credit; leases; monthly payments, etc.

## FINANCIAL ADVISERS

We have touched on this topic before, but let me remind you that in many cases the 'average' financial adviser is not much more than a nice salesperson in a good–looking suit.

My experience, having worked in the industry for several years, is that a large number of financial advisers (but certainly not all) are in about the same financial situations as their clients (unfortunately). They too, go through life struggling to keep their heads above water, spending sleepless nights worrying about their bills and expenses (overcome by those tiny monthly payments). Giving financial advice does not automatically make someone a financial expert, nor does it mean necessarily that any of the advice given is right. Also, in many cases the advice being given is the same advice that the financial industry has been regurgitating for the last 100+ years. Advice that is just plain wrong for most people.

> 'It would be foolhardy as a fullback to simply gather the ball and then stand right in the path of a storming front-row forward if you did not know how to evade his tackle, where to run when you did and what to do with the ball. And yet this is what we, as consumers, do every day when we play the consumer debt game without knowing the rules nor the intentions of the opposing team. As amateurs we run blindly headlong into a crack team of professional players. Get educated and understand the rules by which the lenders play. Then you can consistently beat them at their own game.'
>
> **SIMON HALL**

I know that advisers make the argument that a home mortgage is a good thing. Sure, for your family home, it *usually* makes more sense to at least be building some equity for yourself (even at a mortgage premium of 8%) rather than endlessly flushing your rent money down the drain and contributing to someone else's equity. But do not be fooled into thinking that you have an investment, in the *true* sense of the word, on your hands. Do the numbers and be real about exactly how much that 'investment' is costing you over the entire term of the loan.

Also, be real about your intentions regarding the property. Are you ever going to cash out to realise your profit or will you simply upgrade to a more expensive house, thereby swallowing your cash again? Let's be honest, our homes are a 'lifestyle choice', no more, no less. Look at it that way when making decisions in relation to mortgages and other household debt.

For most people, I also strongly disagree with the concept of building up an emergency reserve fund in your bank account equivalent to three to six months of expenses, rather than first paying off debt with the money. I believe this is ridiculous advice for *most* people. By diverting what little money you have to invest (and pay off debt) into an interest bearing account paying 2–4% you are losing big time. Why? Because the interest on the debt is costing much more than the couple of per cent the banks pay on a positive account balance.

**The first thing most people should do when they have surplus cash is pay off their consumer debt.** Then and only then, should one start building up an emergency fund.

Think about it! Without any debt, how much of an emergency reserve fund will you need? I know some of you are saying: 'What if something happens and I *don't* have an emergency reserve fund?' The answer to remove your fears is simple. Keep one credit card for such emergencies (with low interest and no annual fee). Only use it in a true emergency (and no, a sale at your favourite department store does not constitute an emergency!).

> 'Let us keep a firm grip upon our money, for without it the whole assembly of virtues are but blades of grass.'
> **BHATRIHARI**

Remember, some advisers (particularly those on commission) will not always give you the advice that is in your best interest (refer to life insurance Chapter 20). Unfortunately some advisers have a tendency to lead their clients to the investments that carry the highest commissions. Be *Financially Competent (Intelligent and Responsible)* and decide what is best for your financial security, not the financial security of your advisers.

## MONEY STEP #7 – AVOIDING DEBT AND LIVING DEBT-FREE

Money Step #7 – *Avoiding Debt and Living Debt-Free* is extremely powerful and yet simple and easy to implement. It has three parts.

## PART 1

**Never use consumer credit on their terms.**

**Translation:** Never use credit cards if you cannot pay the full balance off each month when the statement arrives. If you cannot pay cash for it, you do not need it. If you think you still *need* stuff you cannot afford, I strongly suggest you re-evaluate what is important in your life: more stuff or financial freedom?

If you *are* serious about becoming rich but know that you are not yet able to discipline yourself to use credit cards the smart way by paying the full balance each month, then you need to **cut up your credit cards and throw them all away**! (As discussed, you may keep one no-fee credit card in a bottom drawer for *real* emergencies.)

**Please Note:** I am not recommending that you *literally* pay cash for everything and miss out on all those handy frequent flyer points. I rarely pay with actual *cash*. I use the 21st century equivalent. I use an American Express card which I pay off in full each month and a no-fee VISA card where American Express is not accepted. I always pay the VISA card off in full each month. I never carry over a balance. These cards give me frequent flyer points and an itemised record of spending for tax purposes. So while I rarely use actual cash, I am in essence using the modern version of cash.

> 'Swimming for his life,
> a man does not see much
> of the country through which
> the river winds.'
> **WILLIAM E. GLADSTONE**

---

The important point is that in my mind I am treating these cards as a beneficial and convenient method for spending cash and not as a source of credit for spending cash that I don't have. To me my cards are representative of the cash that I have, not the cash that I am borrowing from someone else.

---

If you are deeply in debt but still unwilling to destroy your credit cards then I am sorry to say that you are heading full-steam down the one-way track to a financial train wreck. You are following the path of a **Level Zero, Non-Existent**. You must end the cycle now! Go ahead and take your credit cards out and put them in front of you. Think about all the problems they have caused you. Ignore their glossy sheen. Think about the debt. The monthly payments. The pain. The slavery. The bondage.

## NOW CUT THEM UP!

Go on, do it *now*. Stop reading and cut those cards up *now*. I'm not kidding. I mean it. Get a pair of scissors and end the madness. Cut up those *!(#*(!#@!* credit cards and take the first step towards a **Debt-Free Life**.

## BECOME THE MASTER AND STOP BEING THE SLAVE!

Please listen. If you are constantly carrying credit card debt and have not cut up your cards by now (or determined to only use cards that require full balance payout each month and/or to keep only a no-fee card in a drawer for emergency use only) you are in a very precarious position. For the powerful information in this chapter to help you, you must be willing to help yourself. If you have a problem with debt, please, I urge you to get help. Contact one of the many non-profit agencies that are available for just such a situation (listed at the beginning of Chapter 10). My sincere apologies to those of you who have debt under control or are taking the necessary steps.

> 'All the money in the world is no use to a man or his country if he spends it as fast as he makes it. All he has left is his bills and the reputation for being a fool.'
> **RUDYARD KIPLING**

> 'Sixteen tons, what do you get? Another day older and deeper in debt. Say brother, don't you call me 'cause I can't go, I owe my soul to the company store.'
> **MERLE TRAVIS**

Shop around for the best no-fee credit card: to find a credit card that offers the best rates and fees (none) for your new *pay-as-you-go* philosophy.

*If and only if* you are determined to be well disciplined in the use of credit cards from now on (you will pay down the existing outstanding balances and then pay off each month's spending as it occurs), then consider transferring your outstanding balances to a new card, and cancelling the old ones, to take advantage of a low 'honeymoon' rate for the first year and a possible interest-free period at the beginning. You may slash your minimum monthly payments by as much as half and thus can devote more money to paying off the principal rather than the interest. Make sure that any balance transfers are not regarded as cash advances where interest accrues from the outset at a higher rate. Play the new credit card companies against your existing company who may match the switch offer if you remain with them.

Or consider a co-branded (or loyalty) credit card if the co-brand products suit your lifestyle enough to provide real savings from day-to-day use. There are well over a dozen such cards offering discounts or rebates for a wide range of products and services including accommodation, cars, banking, travel, sporting goods, utilities and car hire. Check out what is on offer for credit cards through the Internet:

- Banksmart at www.banksmart.com.au sets out the different types of credit cards including loyalty or co-brand types.
- Bankchoice at www.bankchoice.com.au lists all the credit cards available with comparisons of annual fees and interest rates, as well as providing tips regarding obtaining and using credit cards.
- eChoice at www.echoice.com.au finds you the best credit card for your needs according to a questionnaire completed online.
- BestBid at www.bestbid.com.au works like an auction site, where lenders bid for your home loan business.
- My Money at www.mymoney.com.au also has different comparisons for credit cards along with advice regarding their use and abuse.
- MyFinance at www.myfinance.com.au compares credit cards.
- http://moneyfinder.ninemsn.com.au has information on the most competitive credit card deals available.
- CANNEX *Pollfax* service provides up-to-date financial (rates) data via automatic fax (*PollFax* on 1902 935 667 for automatic Credit Cards two-page survey faxed at $0.83 a minute, costing about $1.90); www.cannex.com.au/surveys.

Make sure before you apply for a new credit card that the savings or benefits are real, and that you continue to pay all outstanding balances each month without incurring any interest.

**Warning:** Never order new credit cards without paying off the old ones (via the balance transfer) and then destroying the old cards and cancelling the accounts (in writing). If you don't take this step, you'll simply have more cards to get you into more trouble, further in debt!

## PART 2

### Follow the Debt Terminator Plan (DTP) – Step 2 of *The Automatic Money System*.

Follow the **Debt Terminator Plan (DTP)** and eliminate your debt by adding 10% of your (gross) income to your minimum monthly payments.

For example, if your (gross) income is $3,000 and your minimum monthly payments total $1,200, you would now pay $1,500 (the $1,200 minimum monthly payment plus the $300 representing the 10% of your gross income). Instead of just adding the 10% to the minimum payment for each debt we are going to strategically place the entire extra 10% ($300) on the debt we can eliminate the fastest. We do this so that we can develop momentum and see results more quickly. This strategy gives a great psychological advantage in the debt-reduction process. There is nothing like seeing quick results to encourage us to continue our efforts.

'More people should learn to tell their dollars where to go instead of asking them where they went.'
**ROGER BABSON**

This extra 10% is your own personal *Debt Terminator*. Like the character played by Arnold Schwarzenegger from the *Terminator* movies, you will now create a force to be reckoned with. A force that keeps on going, and doesn't stop until the mission is completed. Your *Debt Terminator* money, that small amount of money added to the minimum monthly payments, will quickly **terminate your debt forever**!

Again, ideally you should add 10% of your *gross* income to your debt reduction. However, if you are not currently able to devote 10% of your gross income then add at least 10% of the *total of minimum monthly payments*. The most important point is to start. You can always accelerate your debt pay-off with a larger amount in the future.

Let me now lead you step-by-step through the process of applying the Debt Terminator Plan (DTP). Please refer to the **Debt Terminator Plan (DTP) Form**. There are two copies at the back of this chapter. The first one is completed, showing an example of a starting situation for the DTP, for Stan and Barbara (who we will discuss shortly). The second is provided blank for you to complete with your own information. Let's get started.

## THE FOUR STEP DEBT TERMINATOR PLAN (DTP)

1. **Organise your debts** – The first thing you need to do
   is organise all your debts together in one pile. This would
   include all credit and charge cards, loans, mortgages, etc. You
   will need this information to complete the DTP Form (this
   was previously covered as part of the assignments completed
   in Chapters 6 and 7).

2. **Review the completed DTP Form** – The completed
   example will act as your guide for when you complete the
   form with your own information. Notice that each box has
   the critical information of one debt summarised.

3. **Fill in *your* DTP Form** – Designate one box for each debt
   and then fill in the lines. Each box has five line items to fill
   in. I'll walk you through them line by line:

   - **Line 1: debt name** – List to whom you owe the money.
   - **Line 2: total balance** – Fill in the current total balance
     owed.
   - **Line 3: monthly payment** – Fill in your current
     minimum monthly payment for that debt.
   - **Line 4: pay-off ratio** – Divide the current total balance
     owed (line 2) by the minimum monthly payment (line 3)
     and put the answer on (line 4) (this is your *payment to debt
     ratio* for each debt).
   - **Line 5: pay-off priority** – The DTP pay-off priority is
     determined by starting with the lowest ratio number from
     line 4 from all your completed boxes. These ratio numbers
     are used to determine in what order you should pay off
     your bills. The lower the ratio number the higher the pay-
     off priority.

     Number each one of your debts starting with 1, 2, 3, etc.
     until the DTP pay-off priority has been determined for all
     your debts. For example, with our sample DTP at the end
     of the chapter, the ninth debt ANZ (Car) had the lowest
     ratio number (10). Thus it is given the number one DTP
     pay-off priority. The ABC VISA debt is given the number
     two DTP pay-off priority (ratio 16.67), the David Jones
     debt the number three DTP pay-off priority (ratio 17.13),
     and so on.

4. **Pay-off your debt** – Start with the debt that was given the number one pay-off priority on your DTP Form. With your current minimum payment add *all* of your *Debt Terminator* money and make the new higher payment. Continue to make the minimum payments on all other debts (and refrain from creating any additional debt). Pay off all debts in this way until you are *Completely Debt-Free (Including Your House and Cars)*.

The best way to show you how the Debt Terminator Plan (DTP) works is to now introduce you to our DTP sample couple, Stan and Barbara. This is their situation. They are both 40 years old, married with two young children. And although they make a good living with a combined income of almost $70,000), they are deeply in debt, struggling just to pay their bills each month. They have no idea how they will ever be able to meet their long-term financial goals of paying for their children's education and funding their own retirement.

Their situation is so bleak that many financial advisers would recommend bankrupty as their best solution.

Like so many other people, they have taken a large portion of their income and given it away forever to their bill collectors. That money is no longer theirs. It is gone and will never come back. What's worse, should they pay a debt off, all they would probably do is go right back out and buy something else on 'affordable monthly payments'.

Currently, they carry consumer debt totalling $14,600 (personal credit debt in Australia has risen more than 50% in less than 10 years). Their minimum monthly payments for their consumer debt total $790. They owe $15,000 on two cars with monthly payments totalling $565. Their first and second mortgage total is $120,000 with combined monthly payments of $1,320. Their total monthly minimum payment for all debt is $2,675.

*Again, this is no longer their money.* Think about it for a second, $2,675 a month gone. *Gone forever* to pay for 'stuff'. And remember, most people who are in this trap will simply buy new 'stuff' if and when they ever pay off the old 'stuff'.

Truly, their financial situation is bleak. They have no

emergency reserve account to redirect towards paying off their debt and no savings. The drain of their (self-induced) minimum monthly payments has put them into a corner where they have virtually no money left for savings, investment, or paying off their debt. Often they pay for day-to-day expenses on credit while continuing to add to their debt with what is at times uncontrolled consumption.

> 'Success is precise and prompt obedience to the call of circumstance.'
> **LEON BLUM**

---

Review Stan and Barbara's situation on the completed **Debt Terminator Plan (DTP) Form** at the end of this chapter.

---

However, using many of the techniques that *you* learned in the earlier chapters, they have been able to reduce their expenses and have agreed to come up with an extra 10% to add each month to their minimum monthly payments. For the time being (because of their desperate situation), Stan and Barbara are *truly* unable to apply 10% of their [gross] income (the favoured solution) to their Debt Terminator Plan (DTP). They start by adding 10% to the minimum monthly payments and thus will put an extra $268 a month towards paying off that unwanted consumer debt.

## FINANCIAL SUMMARY FOR STAN AND BARBARA

| Consumer debt | Car loans | Mortgages |
|---|---|---|
| $14,600 balance | $15,000 balance | $120,000 balance |
| $790 monthly | $565 monthly | $1,320 monthly |

| Debt totals | Debt Terminator money |
|---|---|
| $149,600 balance | of extra 10% |
| $2,675 monthly minimum | = $268 a month |

Believe it or not, by following the Debt Terminator Plan (DTP) this family will be *Completely Debt-Free (Including Their House and Cars)* in just over five years! And at retirement (age 65), doing nothing from this entire book other than all three parts of **Money Step #7**, they will also be multi-millionaires! Let's take a look at how...

## STAN AND BARBARA DEBT TERMINATOR PLAN (DTP) IN ACTION

It is January 1, 1996. By looking at their DTP Form Stan and Barbara are able to determine that their first DTP pay-off priority is the ANZ (Car) payment of $300. Stan and Barbara add the entire *Debt Terminator* money of $268 to this bill. By paying $568 (original minimum monthly of $300 + *Debt Terminator* money of $268) they are able to completely terminate the payment on the second car by May (just five-and-a-half months later!)

Now they do it again. They take the entire amount. The original $300 ANZ (Car) payment and the $268 *Debt Terminator* money they add to the next highest priority debt.

It is important to understand that *all* of the money must be brought over until you are debt-free. I know in the old days I would have thought that I now had $300 a month to spend (from the ANZ (Car) debt payment). But under the Debt Terminator Plan (DTP) I do not. I understand that I have already given this money away forever. And that the only way I am going to get it back is to pay off *all* the debt. Otherwise I will just buy something else and continue the debt cycle.

By again looking at their DTP Form we find Stan and Barbara's next DTP pay-off priority is the ABC VISA. They take the entire $568 ($268 + $300 old car payment amount) and add it to the existing ABC VISA minimum payment of $300. This gives them $868 a month with which to terminate the VISA debt! Over the preceding five-and-a-half months they have been paying the normal $300 minimum payment to ABC VISA (and not charging any more). Thus the balance owed on the ABC VISA has been reduced to approximately $3,600. This means that the ABC VISA will now be completely paid off in just over four months!

Imagine their elation at paying off their second car and a credit card in just 10 months rather than over an entire lifetime.

Next, they focus on paying off the David Jones bill (DTP pay-off priority number three). At this point the balance is down to $675 (from making the minimum monthly payments). So, they are able to pay it off in one month! They then apply the surplus $263 ($868 + $70 − $675) to the Bank VISA (DTP pay-off priority number four) in the same month. And so it goes. I think you get the idea.

---

All consumer debt and car debt is paid in full in just under 21 months! **Their house is paid off less than four years later!**

---

That means that this family (previously in debt up to their eyeballs) is *Completely Debt-Free (Including Their House and Cars)* in five-and-a-half years! Their debt is terminated!

## PART 3
### Invest your 'debt-money' and get Automatic Investor rates of return.

Invest the money you now have that is not going towards paying off debt. Add this extra money to your **AIP** or other Level Four investment and watch your riches grow. This step is critical to maintaining your journey towards *Automatic* Financial Freedom. The debt money you have released from making all those minimum monthly payments will now be used for *your* benefit, not the lenders'. Remember, this money must not be used to repeat the debt cycle all over again by servicing new (non-investment) debts. Put this money to work *for* you!

Stan and Barbara now have **$2,943 a month to invest** (the $2,675 original total of minimum payments plus the $268 *Debt Terminator* money).

This is money that they had previously given away (to their debtors for the rest of their lives) that they now have back. And obviously, rather than spending it, they are going to follow *Step Three* and invest it!

That's $2,943 a month to invest into an AIP for the next 20 years (retirement at age 65).

At 10% compounding (easily obtainable in a managed fund such as Vanguard or one of many others available) they would have **$2,234,822** by age 65!

**They will be Multi-Millionaires!** Imagine that. This one-time-on-the-verge-of-bankruptcy couple are now multi-millionaires. Isn't it amazing just how simple becoming rich can really be?

And… at a return of 16% they would have **$5,080,917**!

At 25% (easily obtainable for a Level Five Investor) they would have **$19,774,351**!

All of that from a couple whose financial life lay in ruins. With no hope of getting back on the right track.

## *YOUR* FINANCIAL FREEDOM DATE

To determine how long it will take *you* to become *Completely Debt-Free*, simply examine the **Financial Freedom Planner** at the end of this chapter. Find your total amount of debt and the new +10% *Debt Terminator* money total monthly payment you are going to make. Then determine how many years it will take for you to become *Completely Debt-Free*. Using this strategy most families are able to become *Completely Debt-Free (Including the House and Cars) in 3–7 years*.

Next, look at the **Wealth Creation Calculator**. Compare the amount of money you are going to be able to invest each month (this would include the old debt money you have learned to reclaim, your AIP, super contributions and any other investments you make on a periodic basis), with the rate of return you anticipate, plus the length of time. This will allow you to calculate when you will have enough wealth to live on for the rest of your life without having to work.

The **Debt Terminator Plan (DTP)** is a very simple, realistic plan. It has worked for tens of thousands of people throughout the world. Put it to work for you.

**Please Note:** I recommend you do not overly concern yourself with which account has the highest interest rate. The DTP so quickly accelerates bill pay-off that you will not be paying enough months of the higher interest for it to make a significant difference to you. For most, it is better to stick with the DTP as described. This eliminates confusion and becoming sidetracked. Stick to what really matters. Starting the system and paying off the debt. You will get further faster.

---

*The key to this process is momentum!* By being able to see the bills completely eliminated (forever) it becomes so much easier to keep going. You gain enthusiasm and a real sense of achievement by being able to pay off your debts so quickly.

---

In many cases people with high debt will not be in a position to qualify for lower interest rates because they are over-extended and/or have poor credit. However, if you can qualify for credit cards that offer significantly lower rates you should apply for them and transfer your higher interest balances. Or you may be able to refinance all the smaller consumer debts with a low-interest personal loan. *Remember though, this is not to establish more credit, but rather to lower the interest paid.*

If you do get new lower rate cards make sure to heed the warning I gave earlier to cancel your old cards (and cut them up) once the balances are paid off. Do not leave yourself open to future temptation. Remember, people become deeply in debt for a reason. A lack of control! So the last thing you would want is a pile of paid-off old cards laying around tempting you to go back into spending action. The results would likely be much worse the second time around.

'Nothing in the world can take the place of persistence.

Talent will not; nothing is more common than unsuccessful men with talent.

Genius will not; unrewarded genius is almost a proverb.

Education will not; the world is full of educated derelicts.

Persistence and determination alone are omnipotent.

The slogan "press on" has solved and always will solve the problems of the human race.'
**CALVIN COOLIDGE**

If you do refinance or lower the interest rate on existing debt, never fall into the trap of making the new lower payment. Often people do this. They take out a new loan with a lower interest rate (and often a longer term), thus lowering their monthly payments. This is falling into the lender's trap. By doing this you will simply be in debt longer, pay more in interest (over the long term) and be tempted to get new debt to occupy the 'surplus' monthly money you now have to spend. Please remember, if you refinance debt, always maintain the higher old payment to ensure the debt is paid off as soon as possible (the original reason for getting the new loan in the first place).

> 'Happy is the man who, far away from business, like the race of men of old, tills his ancestral fields with his own oxen, unbound by any interest to pay.'
>
> **HORACE**

## DEBT SURFING

The Internet offers many great software programs for free trial periods. Debt Analyzer and Debt Relief, for example, from Insight Software Solutions (available at www.debtanalyzer.com). Based upon information you enter, this site offers advice and reports generated from three built-in approaches to eliminating debts: Timed Debt Elimination; Debt Reduction Schedule; and Loan Consolidation.

---

**In summary:** The freedom that this **Debt Terminator Plan (DTP)** has brought to so many people throughout the world is incredible. Many people teach this or similar information in regard to debt reduction. I urge you to please share my Debt Terminator Plan (DTP) with all your friends and family. Without the burden of consumer debt the world would be such a happier and more enjoyable place. So please show friends and family how to become debt-free using this Debt Terminator Plan (DTP).

Over the years we have heard from so many students who have made dramatic progress in paying off debt. Please feel free to contact us with your success story at www.johnburley.com.

---

## CHAPTER 23 ACTION STEPS REVIEW

1. Commit to **Money Step #7 – *Avoiding Debt and Living Debt-Free*.**
2. Get rid of unnecessary credit cards immediately. Most people only need one or two credit cards for emergencies. For non-emergencies, I recommend a card such as American Express/Diners Club or a debit card that requires you to pay the outstanding balance in full each month.
3. Vow to only pay cash (or the modern equivalent) and never charge unnecessary consumer items again.
4. Complete the **Debt Terminator Plan (DTP) Form.**
5. Use the **Financial Freeedom Planner** to determine when you will be debt-free.
6. Use the **Wealth Creation Calculator** to determine when you will have enough wealth to be able to live for the rest of your life without having to work.
7. Implement and stick to the **Debt Terminator Plan (DTP)** and become *Completely Debt-Free (Including Your House and Cars) in 3–7 Years!*

## DEBT TERMINATOR PLAN FOR  _Stan and Barbara_

| Debt name | ABC VISA |
|---|---|
| Total balance | $5,000 |
| Monthly payment | $300 |
| Pay-off ratio | 16.67 |
| Pay-off priority | # 2 |

| Debt name | BANK VISA |
|---|---|
| Total balance | $3,000 |
| Monthly payment | $150 |
| Pay-off ratio | 20 |
| Pay-off priority | # 4 |

| Debt name | MASTERCARD |
|---|---|
| Total balance | $2,000 |
| Monthly payment | $100 |
| Pay-off ratio | 20 |
| Pay-off priority | # 5 |

| Debt name | DAVID JONES |
|---|---|
| Total balance | $1,200 |
| Monthly payment | $70 |
| Pay-off ratio | 17.43 |
| Pay-off priority | # 3 |

| Debt name | Q & DEPT STORE |
|---|---|
| Total balance | $1,000 |
| Monthly payment | $50 |
| Pay-off ratio | 20 |
| Pay-off priority | # 6 |

| Debt name | FURNITURE ONE |
|---|---|
| Total balance | $1,000 |
| Monthly payment | $50 |
| Pay-off ratio | 20 |
| Pay-off priority | # 7 |

| Debt name | JACQUES DEPT |
|---|---|
| Total balance | $8000 |
| Monthly payment | $40 |
| Pay-off ratio | 20 |
| Pay-off priority | # 8 |

| Debt name | EZ HARDWARE |
|---|---|
| Total balance | $600 |
| Monthly payment | $30 |
| Pay-off ratio | 20 |
| Pay-off priority | # 9 |

| Debt name | ANZ (CAR) |
|---|---|
| Total balance | $3,000 |
| Monthly payment | $300 |
| Pay-off ratio | 10 |
| Pay-off priority | # 1 |

| Debt Name | BANK (CAR) |
|---|---|
| Total balance | $12,000 |
| Monthly payment | $265 |
| Pay-off ratio | 44.78 |
| Pay-off priority | # 10 |

| Debt Name | CENTENNIAL (HOUSE) |
|---|---|
| Total balance | $100,000 |
| Monthly payment | $1,000 |
| Pay-off ratio | 100 |
| Pay-off priority | # 12 |

| Debt Name | FINANCE ONE (HOUSE) |
|---|---|
| Total balance | $20,000 |
| Monthly payment | $320 |
| Pay-off ratio | 62.5 |
| Pay-off priority | # 11 |

## DEBT TERMINATOR PLAN FOR _____

| Debt name _____ | Debt name _____ | Debt name _____ |
|---|---|---|
| Total balance _____ | Total balance _____ | Total balance _____ |
| Monthly payment _____ | Monthly payment _____ | Monthly payment _____ |
| Pay-off ratio _____ | Pay-off ratio _____ | Pay-off ratio _____ |
| Pay-off priority_____ | Pay-off priority_____ | Pay-off priority_____ |
| Debt name _____ | Debt name _____ | Debt name _____ |
| Total balance _____ | Total balance _____ | Total balance _____ |
| Monthly payment _____ | Monthly payment _____ | Monthly payment _____ |
| Pay-off ratio _____ | Pay-off ratio _____ | Pay-off ratio _____ |
| Pay-off priority_____ | Pay-off priority_____ | Pay-off priority_____ |
| Debt name _____ | Debt name _____ | Debt name _____ |
| Total balance _____ | Total balance _____ | Total balance _____ |
| Monthly payment _____ | Monthly payment _____ | Monthly payment _____ |
| Pay-off ratio _____ | Pay-off ratio _____ | Pay-off ratio _____ |
| Pay-off priority_____ | Pay-off priority_____ | Pay-off priority_____ |
| Debt name _____ | Debt name _____ | Debt name _____ |
| Total balance _____ | Total balance _____ | Total balance _____ |
| Monthly payment _____ | Monthly payment _____ | Monthly payment _____ |
| Pay-off ratio _____ | Pay-off ratio _____ | Pay-off ratio _____ |
| Pay-off priority_____ | Pay-off priority_____ | Pay-off priority_____ |

Write down each debt on line 1, total balance on line 2, the monthly payment on line 3. Then divide the total balance by the monthly payment, putting the answer (ratio) on line 4. Prioritise pay-off starting with the lowest ratio as the first bill to pay off, and so on.

# FINANCIAL FREEDOM PLANNER

| Total debt amount ($) | Total monthly payment amount over time | | | | | | |
|---|---|---|---|---|---|---|---|
| | 1 yr | 2 yrs | 3 yrs | 4 yrs | 5 yrs | 6 yrs | 7 yrs |
| 1,000.00 | 88 | 46 | 32 | 25 | 21 | 19 | 17 |
| 3,000.00 | 264 | 138 | 97 | 76 | 64 | 56 | 50 |
| 5,000.00 | 440 | 231 | 161 | 127 | 106 | 93 | 83 |
| 7,000.00 | 615 | 323 | 226 | 178 | 149 | 130 | 116 |
| 10,000.00 | 879 | 461 | 323 | 254 | 212 | 185 | 166 |
| 15,000.00 | 1,319 | 692 | 484 | 380 | 319 | 278 | 249 |
| 20,000.00 | 1,758 | 923 | 645 | 507 | 425 | 371 | 332 |
| 30,000.00 | 2,637 | 1,384 | 968 | 761 | 637 | 556 | 498 |
| 40,000.00 | 3,517 | 1,846 | 1,291 | 1,015 | 850 | 741 | 664 |
| 50,000.00 | 4,395 | 2,307 | 1,603 | 1,268 | 1,062 | 926 | 830 |
| 75,000.00 | 6,591 | 3,461 | 2,470 | 1,902 | 1,594 | 1,389 | 1,245 |
| 100,000.00 | 8,792 | 4,614 | 3,267 | 2,536 | 2,125 | 1,853 | 1,660 |
| 125,000.00 | 10,989 | 5,768 | 4,023 | 3,170 | 2,656 | 2,316 | 2,075 |
| 150,000.00 | 13,187 | 6,922 | 4,830 | 3,804 | 3,187 | 2,779 | 2,490 |
| 200,000.00 | 17,583 | 9,229 | 6,453 | 5,073 | 4,249 | 3,705 | 3,320 |
| 250,000.00 | 21,979 | 11,536 | 8,067 | 6,341 | 5,312 | 4,631 | 4,150 |
| 300,000.00 | 26,375 | 13,843 | 9,680 | 7,609 | 6,374 | 5,558 | 4,980 |
| 400,000.00 | 35,166 | 18,458 | 12,906 | 10,146 | 8,498 | 7,410 | 6,640 |
| 500,000.00 | 43,958 | 23,072 | 16,134 | 12,682 | 10,624 | 9,262 | 8,300 |

## WEALTH CREATION CALCULATOR

| Number of years | 1 yr | 2 yrs | 3 yrs | 4 yrs | Monthly investment amount per cent of return 5 yrs | 6 yrs | 7 yrs |
|---|---|---|---|---|---|---|---|
| | 500.00 | 1,000.00 | 2,000.00 | 3,000.00 | 5,000.00 | 7,500.00 | 10,000.00 |
| | 10% | 10% | 10% | 10% | 10% | 10% | 10% |
| 1 year | 6,282 | 12,566 | 25,131 | 37,697 | 62,828 | 94,242 | 125,656 |
| 5 years | 38,719 | 77,437 | 154,874 | 232,311 | 387,185 | 580,778 | 774,370 |
| 10 years | 102,422 | 204,845 | 409,690 | 614,535 | 1,024,225 | 1,536,337 | 2,048,450 |
| 20 years | 379,684 | 759,369 | 1,518,738 | 2,278,107 | 3,796,844 | 5,695,266 | 7,593,688 |
| 40 years | 3,162,040 | 6,324,080 | 12,648,159 | 18,972,239 | 31,620,398 | 47,430,597 | 63,240,796 |
| | 15% | 15% | 15% | 15% | 15% | 15% | 15% |
| 1 year | 6,430 | 12,860 | 25,721 | 38,581 | 64,302 | 96,453 | 128,604 |
| 5 years | 44,287 | 88,575 | 177,149 | 265,724 | 442,873 | 664,309 | 885,745 |
| 10 years | 137,608 | 275,217 | 550,434 | 825,651 | 1,376,085 | 2,064,128 | 2,752,171 |
| 20 years | 748,619 | 1,497,240 | 2,994,479 | 4,491,718 | 7,486,197 | 11,229,296 | 14,972,395 |
| 40 years | 1,550,8027 | 31,016,055 | 62,032,109 | 93,048,164 | 155,080,274 | 232,620,411 | 310,160,548 |
| | 25% | 25% | 25% | 25% | 25% | 25% | 25% |
| 1 year | 6,738 | 13,475 | 26,950 | 40,425 | 67,376 | 101,063 | 134,751 |
| 5 years | 58,699 | 117,399 | 234,797 | 352,196 | 586,993 | 880,489 | 1,173,986 |
| 10 years | 260,966 | 521,931 | 1,043,862 | 1,565,793 | 2,609,656 | 3,914,483 | 5,219,311 |
| 20 years | 3,359,557 | 6,719,113 | 13,438,227 | 20,157,341 | 33,595,569 | 50,393,353 | 67,191,137 |
| 40 years | 476,995,040 | 953,990,081 | 1,907,980,165 | 2,861,970,247 | 4,769,950,411 | 7,154,925,617 | 9,539,900,823 |

# The nine generalised principles of active (level five) investing

'Those who dream by night in the dusty recesses of their minds
awake to find that all was vanity;
But the dreamers of day are dangerous men, That they may act
their dreams with open eyes to make it possible.'

T.E. LAWRENCE (OF ARABIA)

'It is far more important to learn what not to do than what to do.
You can learn this invaluable lesson in two ways, the first
of which and most inspired is by your own mistakes. The
second is by observing the mistakes of others. Any man that
learns all the things that he ought not to do cannot help doing
the things he ought to do.'

E.W. SCRIPPS

As you learned in Chapter 1, the final two levels of investor
(Level Five and Level Six) are reached by only a very small
percentage of the people on planet earth. Keep in mind that
contrary to what most people think (people who don't have

money), you do not have to become a **Level Five Active Investor** or **Level Six Capitalist Investor** in order to become rich.

Under no circumstances should you forego upgrading yourself to a **Level Four Automatic Investor** just because you are sure you can become a 'big-time investor'. I have personally seen several friends take this approach and the results have been disastrous. Remember, *if you skip you will trip!* If you want to become a Level Five or Level Six Investor that's great, I am going to teach you the **Principles** and **Rules** involved. Be sure however, to become a Level Four Automatic Investor *first*.

> 'If a man looks sharply and attentively, he shall see Fortune; for though she is blind, she is not invisible.'
> **FRANCIS BACON**

> 'Be like a postage stamp – Stick to one thing until you get there!'
> **JOSH BILLINGS**

With that said, the Level Five Active Investor is the level where thousands of my students from around the world have gone. These people, on either a part-time or full-time basis, have become highly successful private investors.

These investors understand that to graduate to Level Five they must first become very clear on **The Nine Generalised Principles of Active (Level Five) Investing** and their own *Rules* of investing. Their Level Five investment vehicle might be real estate, debt instruments, businesses or shares.

Level Five Active Investors actively participate in the management of their investments. They strive to *maximise performance* while *minimising risk*. It is normal for this type of investor to have long-term annual rates of return of 20–100%+. They understand money and how it works. They understand how to play **The Game**, The *Money* Game.

I call it The Game because to Level Five and Six Investors that is exactly what *money* and *investing* are: a game. A game played according to general Principles and particular Rules. A game that Level Five and Six Investors all love to play to win!

A major distinction that Level Five and Six Investors have made is that:

### Rich people work hard to have their money work harder while poor and middle-class people work hard for their money

These people become very wealthy. Their primary focus in relation to money is on *increasing their asset base with assets that create cash flow*.

To provide you with better insight into the habits and methods of the Level Five Active Investor I will fully outline The Nine Generalised Principles of Active (Level Five) Investing. And in the next chapter I will share with you my **17 Personal Rules of Active (Level Five) Investing for 20–100%+ Returns**.

---

### Clarification – the difference between Generalised Principles and Rules

**Generalised Principles** *always* apply. I have spent over 20 years studying money and how it works. Without exception, every millionaire I have interviewed has agreed with the concept that there are Generalised (or Universal) Principles of investing that when applied would allow *anyone* to become wealthy.

**Rules** on the other hand, will be customised and modified by each investor to suit the investment situation and the investor's personal investment experiences, preferences, and objectives.

**Principles** are the unwavering foundations upon which Rules can be built by the successful Level Five and Six Investor.

---

As you review these Principles, keep in mind that they are a *highly* upgraded version of the Principles and Rules of investing used by a Level Four Automatic Investor. These are the strict practices of the world's *top* investors.

8 MONEY SECRETS OF THE RICH

Failure to become a Level Four Automatic Investor and attempting instead to take the 'short-cut' to becoming a Level Five Active Investor will generally lead to financial disaster. The reason? You are not really a Level Five Active Investor. You are a **Level Three Passive Investor** who is just fooling him or herself. Want to see a Level Three Passive Investor in action? All you have to do is look to the stock market adjustment of October 1997, the Asian $1 trillion meltdown that began in December of 1997, or the NASDAQ correction of April 2000. The Level Three Passive Investors (*'Gone into a shell'*, *'You can't do it'* and *'Victim'*), or 'PIGS', as they are referred to by professional traders, got slaughtered. Many having option or margin accounts were wiped out (or saw a few years' worth of profits go down the drain) in just a few short hours.

> 'The first man gets the oyster, the second man gets the shell.'
> **ANDREW CARNEGIE**

> 'Lampis the shipowner, on being asked how he acquired his great wealth, replied, "My great wealth was acquired with no difficulty, but my small wealth, my first gains with much labour."'
> **EPICTETUS**

Level Five Active Investors, however, look forward to these situations because they are in positions to take advantage of buying opportunities and make money. Active Investors will *always* arrange their investments in such a way that they have **very little or no risk**. Thus, they can never be wiped out, or even severely hurt by a minor or major market adjustment or economic downturn. In addition, they have developed access to capital to allow them to quickly take advantage of market opportunities.

My serious advice is that you must first adopt the habits of the Level Four Automatic Investor prior to any attempt to play the Level Five Active Investor game. With that restated, here are **The Nine Generalised Principles of Active (Level Five) Investing**.

## THE NINE GENERALISED PRINCIPLES OF ACTIVE (LEVEL FIVE) INVESTING

### ONE: *DO WHAT YOU LOVE/LOVE WHAT YOU DO*
Find an area of investing that interests you. Ask yourself what you like to do. What type of investor are you? Do you love cash

or cash flow? Shares, futures, options or real estate? In other words, what excites you? What area of investing appeals to you in a way that really grabs and keeps your attention, above other types of investments? Does one area of investment stand out for you and your particular talents?

With very few exceptions, successful business owners and investors are very passionate about their work. They thoroughly enjoy their working hours and often treat their business and investments with the care they would treat a child: a child needing nurturing and care to grow and prosper.

> 'Passion for life and for our work is a critical element of success and abundance. Passion is a virtually unstoppable, attitudinal force that generates energy, creativity, and productivity. When you love what you do, it's difficult not to succeed.'
> **RICHARD CARLSON**

> 'Investors operate with limited funds and limited intelligence. They do not need to know everything. As long as they understand something better than others, they have an edge.'
> **GEORGE SOROS**

## TWO: *NICHE*

I cannot stress enough how critical it is that you determine your **Niche**. Without exception every millionaire I know can tell you in a couple of sentences exactly what it is they love to do that has made them so successful and rich!

Without a precise knowledge of what you do, your chances for success are greatly diminished. After all, it is extremely difficult to hit a target that does not exist or to win a game when you don't know exactly where the game is being played or what winning it means. Ask yourself the following questions:

- ☑ What am I trying to accomplish? What is it that I want?
- ☑ Do I want to make **Quick Cash**?
- ☑ Do I want to **Buy and Hold** assets for the long term?
- ☑ Am I looking to create **Cash Flow** (income streams)?

Keep in mind that your *Niche* can always be adjusted. You do not have to be *the* only expert of your particular *Niche* to be highly successful in it. If you decide you don't like the *game* you are playing then you can change your *Niche* and take your ball to a *game* you do like. After all it's *your* game. You are in charge.

## THREE: *LEVERAGE*

You need to become a **Master of Leverage**. You must leverage your own time and you must constantly focus on how you can access other people's skill, time, resources and money. *Leverage* is the most valuable tool available to the Level Five Active Investor for compounding investment returns and accelerating the process of wealth building. The use of *Leverage* accelerates the other Principles.

Mastering your *Leverage* of time will involve three main disciplines:

☑ Allocating at least 10 quality hours a week to concentrate on your investment strategies.

☑ Learning to prioritise your existing time in favour of the important and challenging tasks which bring you the most wealth (usually about 15–20% of what you do brings about 80% of the income). Do not get sidetracked by the easy and unimportant tasks.

☑ Learning the most efficient use of your prioritised time so that you get even more important work done in even less time. This will involve task delegations to other people who have particular expertise that exceeds yours, and systems streamlining.

'A little knowledge that acts is worth infinitely more than much knowledge that is idle.'
**KAHLIL GIBRAN**

'Our life is frittered away by detail... Simplicity, simplicity.'
**H.D. THOREAU**

'Information's pretty thin stuff, unless mixed with experience.'
**CLARENCE DAY**

Mastering your *Leverage* of other people's *skills* will involve assembling a team of experts who support and counsel you to assist you in meeting your objectives. You cannot be a successful Level Five Active Investor without the assistance and expertise of other people. For example, if real estate is your chosen investment, you will need a team including expert real estate agents, a solicitor, a tax adviser, contractors and handypeople. I cannot over-stress the importance here of the word 'expert'. There is little point getting the 'help' of people who cannot provide you expertise. You may have to search for these experts, for they are not a dime a dozen.

Mastering your *Leverage* of other people's *resources* and *money* is the key to removing what for you may have appeared to be your greatest barrier to investment success: the lack of money!

To be successful in Level Five investments you will often need to find investors willing to be your money partners. If you try to proceed without money partners you will either run out of money very quickly (the limiting factor that slows or stops the growth of most businesses) or end up exposing yourself to uncomfortable levels of risk. You must market your expertise and investment opportunity to worthy money partners.

> 'A young man is always faced with the job of bringing a tremendous number of variables under control. Hunches won't do. Simple rules of thumb won't do. These things may help, but what it really takes to achieve order and steady progress is system. The extension of his mastery over it – regardless of the level at which he works – is one measure of the young man's growth.'
>
> **HARVEY S. FIRESTONE**

## FOUR: *LATERAL THINKING*

**Lateral Thinking** is the art of looking at things from different points of view. You can make a lot of money by doing very simple things to *add value* in ways that other people have overlooked. In simple terms: ask yourself how could something be done better or what do people want that they are not getting now?

As a Level Five Active Investor, I apply *Lateral Thinking* by providing the opportunity for the average non-home owner (approximately 33% of the population, 75% of whom cannot qualify for a new home loan) to own a home. I, and my students throughout the world (including Australia and New Zealand), do this with *Vendor Financing* (sometimes called a *Lease Purchase* or an *Instalment Sale*).

> 'When creativity is regarded as a magic gift, there is nothing that can be done about it if you are not lucky enough to have the gift. But everyone can develop some skill in lateral thinking and those who develop most skill will be the most creative.'
>
> **EDWARD DE BONO**

I firmly believe that the best way to make a lot of money is to help a lot of people in a significant way. After all, there is a reason why heart surgeons earn so much. Think about it. Would you try to 'low-ball' your heart surgeon just before bypass surgery? Not likely! Far from it. You would probably want to pay even more money to have the best heart surgeon in the world flown in. The reason? You are in pain and you want the pain to go away. People in pain will gladly pay to remove or alleviate their pain.

That is what I do with real estate. I relieve the pain of not being able to achieve the dream of 'owning your own home'! And I do this without exploitation. Close to 25% of the population would like to own their own home but cannot through conventional financing means. I relieve their pain and provide them with a housing opportunity. This is an example of *Lateral Thinking* within my *Niche* of real estate investing.

## FIVE: *MARKET RESEARCH*

As you progress in The Game you will become a **Master of Your Market**. Keep in mind that although **Market Research** is important it is imperative that you understand that the only way to become a *Master of Your Market* is to actually be *in* the market.

'... getting the facts of a situation before acting is of crucial importance, and that getting these facts is a continuous job which requires eternal vigilance... '
**BERNARD M. BARUCH**

**Translation:** Jump in and learn as much as you can while playing The Game. The greatest confidence, skill and knowledge will come from doing, not theorising. Remember, if you need to know everything before starting you will never get started. You must avoid *analysis paralysis*.

## SIX: *EFFICIENCY*

One of the hardest things for poor and middle-class people to understand is that hard work and money have very little to do with each other. Mastering **Efficiency** depends very much on understanding the principle of *Leverage*: having people, time, resources and money working for you and not against you.

All successful Level Five investments feature streamlined operation and systems that allow the investor to accomplish more with less effort and less time. Ideally they are run so efficiently that they continue to run whether or not the investor is directly overseeing them on a daily basis.

The biggest difference between poor people (Slaves to Money) and rich people (Masters of Money) is this:

| | | |
|---|---|---|
| **Poor People**<br>**Work for**<br>**Money** | ← **Vs** → | **Rich People**<br>**Money Works**<br>**for Them** |

**This distinction is critical. Reread it. Reread it again.**

If **riches** are what you desire it is critical that you become efficient and develop systems that allow your money to work for you and not continue working the other way around. Remember, no one ever *earned* their way to wealth, they *invested* their way to wealth. **You *must* get into The Game!!!**

I cannot stress the importance of systems enough. My business and real estate investing is designed so that an 'average' person making A$10–$12 an hour could come in and run it indefinitely. I do however continually improve my systems by engaging exceptional people to run the show.

## SEVEN: *LAG*

The time-honoured principle of *Lag* is best described by the biblical theme that you 'reap what you sow'. In other words, if you follow the Principles outlined and persist you *will* be successful. The benefits *follow* the labour.

The 'reaping what you sow' theme has two meanings though, for it refers not only to the effort you make, but also to the character or quality of the effort. An element of 'What goes around comes around' is carried in the concept of *Lag*.

The mechanics of capitalism are predicted on this principle of giving first and getting back later. It's like rolling a barrel over a steep hill. It takes a lot of work to roll it up to the top, but rolling it down the other

'A constant hammering on one nail will generally drive it home at last, so that it can be clinched.'
**P.T. BARNUM**

'Let us not be weary in well doing: for in due season we shall reap, if we faint not.'
**THE BIBLE (GALATIANS)**

'Be not deceived; God is not mocked: for whatsoever a man soweth, that shall he also reap.'
**BIBLE (GALATIANS)**

'You must be good at one of two things: sowing in the spring or begging in the fall.'
**JIM ROHN**

side is easy. And there are The Nine Generalised Principles of Active Investing to help you get up the hill.

Life will provide you challenges and obstacles to overcome. The biggest difference between successful people and the average person is that successful people see upsets as chances to grow and learn rather than as failures. And they persist through them.

When handed a setback, rather than giving into fear and quitting, you must bolster your determination against the challenge and keep going. If your Principles are sound then all you have to do is make adjustments to your Rules until you find your own formula for success. Adjust your Rules until they are a good fit for The Nine Generalised Principles. In the next chapter, I will share with you my **17 Personal Rules of Active (Level Five) Investing for 20–100%+ Returns**.

Okay, so you might say that all sounds simple in theory, but becoming a Level Five or Level Six Investor is going to be a challenge. Absolutely! Remember that anything worth doing is going to be a stretch in one way or another. This is exactly why it is vital that you first become a Level Four Automatic Investor. Once you have laid the proper foundation you may, if you so choose, move onto the excitement and abundance available to the Level Five and Level Six Investor.

> 'If you think the game is worth it, you play the hand you're dealt.'
> **CHRISTOPHER REEVE**

> '... after all, this universe is not bankrupt – we are not sent into it to fight a losing battle.'
> **HORACE GREELEY**

I'll tell you this, playing The Game of the Level Five Active Investor is much easier than most people think it is. For most people it is their **belief systems** (or mindset) and lack of Principles and Rules that prevents them from playing The Game. Provided you have fully implemented **The 7 Money Steps of the Rich** (as a Level Four Automatic Investor), the transition to Level Five should be relatively painless: follow The Nine Generalised Principles of Active (Level Five) Investing and adapt your own Rules to suit The Game you find for yourself.

The universe, because of *Lag*, guarantees your success if you will just get in The Game and stay in there. Keep the faith and you will be rewarded. In the words of Garth Brooks: 'Life is not tried, it is merely survived, if you're standing outside the fire!' Yee–ha!

## EIGHT: *TIMING*

'Windows of opportunity' exist in every market. It is just a matter of using *Lateral Thinking* and *Market Research* to locate and recognise them, and of overcoming any fear you might have to enter the market when the right **Timing** beckons. So look around your market. Find the opportunities and jump in!

> 'A wise man will make more opportunities than he finds.'
> **FRANCIS BACON**

The key to proper *Timing* is to ensure that your *Niche* fits into the timing of your market. That you are not selling straw hats in the winter, only buying. Be prepared to modify or adapt your *Niche* if the *Timing* in your market is wrong for your first choice of strategy. Your *Market Research* will identify the Timing issues for you. Do not get hung up on the idea that there is only one way for you to be a successful Level Five Active Investor.

> 'Success does not come by chance. It is an opportunity that has been lassoed and organized.'
> **GEORGE W. PERKINS**

> 'Whatever you can do, or dream you can, … begin it. Boldness has genius, power and magic in it.'
> **GOETHE**

## NINE: *ACTION*

Rich people are **Masters of Action**. They understand that **Action** always beats *inaction*. They understand that the only way to find the right formula for success to win The Game is to participate.

Poor people are *Masters of Excuses* and laying blame on others and on circumstances. Their fears provide them with an endless babbling stream of seemingly logical reasons why they should not act and why they cannot act. I have often spoken with people who were willing to die defending and explaining how *no one* could get rich doing exactly what I have done to personally create millions of dollars.

> 'Compassionately accepting and taking responsibility for your present situation is the first and most important step in creating change. When you try to overcome a problem by pretending it doesn't exist, you are not taking responsibility for the problem – so you are not empowered to do anything about it.'
> **SUSAN M. CAMPBELL**

I refer to this negative chatter as 'Psycho-Babble'. I decided long ago not to argue with people who insist on being poor and refusing to do anything to help themselves out of whatever predicament they have set themselves in.

'First organise the near at hand, then organise the far removed. First organise the inner, then organise the outer. First organise the basic, then organise the derivative. First organise the strong, then organise the weak. First organise the great, then organise the small. First organise yourself, then organise others.'

**ZHUGE LIANG
(2ND CENTURY AD)**

To take *Action* it is critical that you take *responsibility* for your own financial situation. If you are not where you want to be, *justifying* and *laying blame* may sound good and may even temporarily bury some of the pain or frustration of your current situation, but it does your mid- or long-term financial success absolutely no good at all.

You and only you are responsible for your success or failure. Take complete *responsibility* for your own financial situation and change it by getting out there and into The Game. Take *Action*!!!

## CONCLUSION

The most important **Generalised Principle** for creating wealth is that you must *Do What You Love/Love What You Do*. So make sure to find a *Niche* with which you are very comfortable.

Apply **The Nine Generalised Principles of Active (Level Five) Investing** to your investment strategies and then move to the next step which is to establish *your* **Rules** to **The Game**.

---

## CHAPTER 24 ACTION STEPS REVIEW

1. Determine whether or not you are truly interested in becoming a **Level Five Active Investor**. If you are, start looking for an area of investing that motivates you passionately.
2. Apply **The Nine Generalised Principles of Active (Level Five) Investing** outlined in this chapter.

'Money is a living entity, and it responds to energy exactly the same way you do. It is drawn to those who welcome it, those who respect it.'

**SUZE ORMAN**

## CHAPTER 25

# John's 17 personal rules of active (level five) investing for 20–100%+ returns!

'The road to happiness lies in two simple principles: find what it is that interests you and that you can do well, and when you find it put your whole soul into it – every bit of energy and ambition and natural ability you have.'

JOHN D. ROCKEFELLER III

In the last chapter we learned **The Nine Generalised Principles of Active (Level Five) Investing.** You will recall that **Generalised Principles** apply to *all* situations whereas **Rules** are personal and are used to set up how *you* invest.

Let's begin this chapter by again talking about **The Game, The Money Game.** This idea of money being a game is an idea that links to the first and most important of The Nine Generalised Principles. To play The Money Game you must *Do What You Love/Love What You Do.* You must have the same enthusiasm and passion when playing The Money Game as you would when playing any other game. To be a successful **Active Investor** you must do something that excites you, moves you and thrills you. Without this passion for what you do, life's challenges and learning experiences can all too easily knock you off your path.

The concept of The Money Game can be broken down into practical steps that you can apply:

1. Discover an area of investing that you feel is a 'good fit' for you.
2. Apply The Nine Generalised Principles of Active (Level Five) Investing.
3. Develop **Your Own Rules to The Game**.

## RULES TO THE GAME

We have discussed applying The Nine Generalised Principles of Active (Level Five) Investing. After you have found your area of investment passion and applied The Nine Generalised Principles to it you must then apply **Your Rules to The Game**.

> 'If one advances confidently in the direction of his dreams, and endeavours to live the life which he has imagined, he will meet with a success unexpected in common hours.'
>
> **H.D. THOREAU**

> 'The life each of us lives is the life within the limits of our own thinking. To have life more abundant, we must think in the limitless terms of abundance.'
>
> **THOMAS DREIER**

Remember, it is *your game* and you can play it any way you want. Be like a little kid: if others won't play your way then just take your ball and go find others who will play your way.

Take a good look at the **Rules** (conscious or automatic) that you are currently using with regard to money and investing. Are *your* Rules empowering or limiting your financial success?

A typical example of how Rules can limit your success: I have met people who tried something and it didn't work the first time so they decided *never* to try it again.

Maybe this sounds familiar? The scenario might run something like this: you decide to buy shares based on a 'hot tip' you got at the water cooler. Of course, right after you buy (at the top of the market) the shares crash to an all-time low, wiping out half your money. You sell immediately and decide to *never* invest in the share market again because it is too risky. **For many this example may be all too real.**

The problem with your action is not that you bought the shares or that you lost money but that you decided to *never* invest in the share market again because of the loss. You made a Rule that will prevent you from *ever* making money in the share market.

And your 'rational' mind will constantly remind you of *Your Rule*. Regardless of how good the market is, you will not participate. When anyone ever questions you on why you will not invest in the market you will defend *Your Rule* to the ends of the earth with endless 'logical' reasons why one should *never* invest in the share market. This is your own 'intelligent' psycho-babble. The end result: **You lose because you are out of The Game!**

> 'Most people die of a sort of creeping common sense, and discover when it is too late that the only things one never regrets are one's mistakes.'
> **OSCAR WILDE**

> 'It is the glorious prerogative of the empire of knowledge that what it gains it never loses. On the contrary, it increases by the multiple of its own power: all its ends become means: all its attainments help to new conquests.'
> **DANIEL WEBSTER**

What you must understand is that there are

### *'Rules for winning'*
and
### *'Rules for learning'*.

In the example cited what you should have done is *learned* what you could do differently to enhance your probability for success. In the future you would: not buy impulsively at the top of the market; check the source of your information; do *Market Research*; use a stop-loss to limit your potential liability so you cannot lose so much, etc.

**Translation:** Add a Rule to never play that way again, not a Rule to never play The Game (invest) again.

*Every* day I learn new ways to do something or to not do something. I never quit The Game. I merely adjust *My Game* to incorporate what I learn. You should do the same.

## JOHN'S RULES  JOHN'S RULES  JOHN'S RULES

John Burley's **17 Personal Rules of Active (Level Five) Investing for 20–100%+ Returns**.

### 1. MY RULES

Rule number 1 is that I play by my **My Rules**, not the rules of anyone else. Level Five Active Investors know that they must have control at all times. Thus they cannot play by the rules dictated by others (such as so-called 'expert' financial planners, accountants, lawyers, tax planners, brokers and bankers who all too often play by the rules of 'It can't be done' or 'We don't do that here'). Level Five Active Investors design their own Rules and adapt the world to them rather than complying with and adapting to the rules of others.

**Note:** This does not mean breaking the law! All that I do, whether in the area of business, tax planning, entity strategies, or investing, is all completely legal and above board. There is no room in the business and investing world of the Level Five Active Investor (where your reputation is as vital as your skills) for shades of grey. There is no need. Everything I could ever want to do can be achieved using my own Rules, within the framework of exisiting laws, regulations and codes. I only do what is as 'white as the driven snow'. I strongly recommend you do the same.

### 2. THE NINE GENERALISED PRINCIPLES OF ACTIVE (LEVEL FIVE) INVESTING

Always respect and follow **The Nine Generalised Principles of Active (Level Five) Investing**. They are the blueprint upon which to build Your Rules.

### 3. INTEGRITY

It is my belief that the most important quality a person can demonstrate in business and in life is **Integrity**. If I find that the people I am playing (working or investing) with do not have integrity I stop playing (doing business) with them. I take my ball and go home. And I only play games (businesses and investments) which are compatible with and can be fashioned around my integrity beliefs.

I have learned the hard way that people with a lack of or questionable integrity will usually turn on you or let you down before the deal is done. Always remember: **The integrity of the other person is more important than any other aspect of the deal!**

Integrity must always be your starting point and your ending point. If you deal with people without integrity you will

> 'More men come to doom through dirty profits than are kept by them.'
> **SOPHOCLES**

damage yourself each time. Their association or short-term profit appeal is not worth the sacrifices you will invariably make.

I have read some wonderful passages over the years on the subject of integrity, written by great businesspeople, but none better than the selection I would like to share with you here.

Horace Greeley, the founder of the New Yorker in 1834 and coiner of the phrase 'Go West young man, go West!', once wrote in a speech on the subject of the 'true business man' the following passage:

> I close, then, with some suggestions as to what I consider the bases of a true business career – those which give reasonable assurance of a true business success. I place first among these, integrity: because I believe that there is to-day a good deal of misapprehension on this point. There is now and then a case of brilliant rascality known among us; and we hear of this, and talk of it; we are inclined, some of us, to admire it; but, after all, there are no cases, except very exceptional cases, wherein roguery has led to fortune. The rule is almost absolute, that our thrifty men have been essentially upright men. You will find few cases where the dishonest man has continuously flourished. There have been cases of his temporary, transient, meteoric success; but the rule is very uniform in its operation, that business success has been based on a broad platform of integrity.

P. T. Barnum wrote in an often delivered speech entitled 'The Art of Money-Getting' the following passage on integrity and its relationship to wealth creation:

> It is more precious than diamonds or rubies. The old miser said to his sons: 'Get money; get it honestly, if you can, but get money.' This advice was not only atrociously wicked, but it was the very essence of stupidity. It was as

much as to say, 'If you find it difficult to obtain money honestly, you can easily get it dishonestly. Get it in that way.' Poor fool, not to know that the most difficult thing in life is to make money dishonestly; not to know that our prisons are full of men who attempted to follow this advice; not to understand that no man can be dishonest without soon being found out, and that when his lack of principle is discovered, nearly every avenue to success is closed against him forever. The public very properly shun all whose integrity is doubted. No matter how polite and pleasant and accommodating a man may be, none of us dare to deal with him if we suspect 'false weights and measures.' Strict honesty not only lies at the foundation of all the success in life financially, but in every other respect. Uncompromising integrity of character is invaluable. It secures to its possessor a peace and joy which cannot be attained without it – which no amount of money, or houses and lands can purchase.

And finally from Samuel Johnson in *Rasselas* (1759):
Integrity without knowledge is weak and useless, and knowledge without integrity is dangerous and dreadful.

Integrity! Find it within. Follow it through everything you are and do. For without it you are incomplete and live without true meaning. One last thought on integrity. A very wise person once said, 'Once someone shows you who they are, believe them!' In other words, if someone shows you once in a business dealing or in general life that they do not have integrity... *believe them!* They will invariably continue on their path of deceit and dishonesty in their dealings with you until you no longer let them.

## 4. KNOW THE RULES

Before I play The Game I want to know four things:
A. **The Rules of the Market**
B. **The Rules of The Game** (based on my *Niche*)
C. The Rules to maximise ROIAT (Return on Investment after Tax)
D. My personal Rules.

## 5. BUY WHOLESALE

As a Level Five Active Investor, I know that to make a profit I must **Buy Wholesale** (or sub-wholesale) and then resell at *retail* (or just below). This is what all great investors do in one form or another, whether they are buying shares that are undervalued or out of favour, vehicles at below Red Book value or real estate at wholesale prices.

When I invest I need at least one of two aspects of the deal to be wholesale: I need either wholesale *price* or wholesale *terms*. Wholesale purchase price means that I can resell for retail and make a profit. Wholesale terms will produce higher cash flow to compensate for the higher-than-wholesale purchase price. Wholesale price *and* wholesale terms in the same deal is the Level Five Investor's nirvana.

> 'A professional investor never, ever, ever makes an investment decision based on tax deductions or future appreciation.'
>
> **JOHN R. BURLEY**

## 6. PROFIT AT PURCHASE

Make your money when you *buy*, not when you *sell*. When making a decision on how much to offer for a property, I make my decision solely based on the cash flow or calculated capital gains profit after expenses (not potential appreciation or negative-gearing tax benefits).

I *never* include tax savings or appreciation, for the simple reason that they are undetermined, constantly changing and not guaranteed.

Beware of salespeople cloaked as real estate agents or marketers, stockbrokers, financial planners, investment advisers, etc. All those fancy charts, brochures, and presentations are designed to fool you. Do not ever buy an investment based on 'projected yields' or 'future appreciation' or 'potential tax savings'. That is the 'game' of the Level Three Investor.

---

**Bypass promises and hype: stick to the 'Money and the Numbers'.**

---

Whenever these salespeople approach me with their investment schemes I tell them the following: I have an investment portfolio of several million dollars. I consistently make 50–100% annually on my investments. However, I am always looking to improve my return. At this point in the conversation the salespeople get very enthusiastic as they begin to go into their sales pitches, telling me how they can make me all this money. I ask them to send me a copy of their audited financial statements.

'Great estates may venture more,
But little boats should keep near shore.'
**BENJAMIN FRANKLIN**

'My ventures are not in
one bottom trusted,
Nor to one place; nor is
my whole estate
Upon the fortune of this
present year;
Therefore, my merchandise
makes me not sad.'
**WILLIAM SHAKESPEARE**
*(The Merchant of Venice)*

I tell them that if they are doing better than me (on return, not necessarily net worth) then they have got my money (to invest). I also ask for a copy of a statement showing how much money *they* have placed in the particular investment scheme.

Guess what? In all the years no investment salespeople have ever responded to my requests. The reason? They probably don't really know what they are doing and they probably don't have any of their own money invested in the products they are offering (nor any other investments for that matter).

**When it comes to investing I care about two things: the money and the numbers!** The *real money and the real numbers!* What is my *cash-on-cash* return going to be this year? If I cannot make money now, I am not interested in the deal. Full stop. End of story!

## 7. NO/LOW RISK IDEA

Presently, I only have at risk a small percentage (less than 1%) of *my* net worth in any one investment. I do this because even though I have never lost money on a real estate investment, I continue to eliminate the possibility (fear) of being financially ruined by a couple of deals gone bad.

However, when I first became an Active Investor I often risked up to 10% of my net worth in a single transaction. The reason was two-fold: I had a relatively small net worth; and I wanted to maximise *Leverage* to accelerate my wealth-building process. If I had taken a loss at that time, I was confident that I would still move forward. That was my mindset. Those were *My Rules*. Bear that in mind. For many people a loss would have resulted in a full retreat from ever investing again.

**Clarification:** When I say that I only have less than 1% of my net worth at risk in any one investment, I am not saying that I only have 1% invested in total. What I am saying is that I have used Level Five investment techniques (Principles and Rules) to limit my downside risk to just 1% of any given investment. I generally have at least 90–95% of my investment capital invested at any one time. Just not 90–95% of it at *risk*! I minimise my risk by following proper money management risk reduction strategies.

---

**Bottomline:** Never risk more than you are willing to lose and willing to persist investing without.

---

## 8.  OTHER PEOPLE'S MONEY

One money management risk reduction strategy is to use **Other People's Money (OPM)** to further reduce your risk. I have done this to the point where I have acquired more than 150 properties using none of my own money. (Many of my students in Australia and New Zealand have done the same types of transactions.) That's *Leverage with no money down*! Using OPM is part of Rule Number 7 because it is as No/Low Risk as it gets. If I have no money in the deal, I have no money at risk.

'If you are a competent person of integrity, it never ceases to amaze me just how much money people want to give you for investments!'
**BILL SHOPOFF**

In addition, *Leverage* allows me to do far more transactions than I ever could on my own. I often do transactions with partners because I know it is always better to have a *piece* of the pie than *none* of the pie.

My partners are willing to take on the risks for the capital invested and thus my risk in minimal. My integrity is what my partners rely upon over time, not on the basis of any one deal (although they are of course backing my business acumen as well). My partners are willing to risk their capital for good returns and I stake my expertise and my reputation for the opportunity of *Leverage* offered by their investment capital.

The relationship I have with my investors (money partners) has produced tremendous success over the years and we have *never* lost money on a real estate investment. In fact, I cannot even conceive of the possibility of losing money on real estate. My Buy Wholesale investment philosophy and my business systems are all designed to ensure that we do not ever lose money on a deal.

## 9. MONEY BACK

I structure my transactions so that if I have money in the deal I get all of it back in the quickest possible time.

Remember, one of the major objectives for money is to employ it so that it works for you. Once you retrieve your initial investment capital, your money begins working for you at a rate of return of *infinity* (which, by the way, is the best possible rate of return!)

I invest in such a way that my money partners and I get all the principal back within one to two years which means that we make 50-100%+ rates of return on each investment (each property).

## 10. 'DON'T WANTERS'

I buy from people who really *Don't Want* their property. This means that I generally buy my properties from highly motivated sellers (trustees of deceased estates or bankruptcies, liquidators, vacant houses, mortgagees in possession, foreclosures, etc.).

If someone does not want their property, they are much more likely to be flexible on their price or terms to dispose of it. You are entering the market on *wholesale price* and/or *wholesale terms* which will allow you to easily determine your *Profit at Purchase*.

In any market, no matter how good, somewhere between 2-5% of sellers are highly motivated to sell. Though these deals take effort to find, my students in Australia/New Zealand find them just as often as students in the United States and in other parts of the world. And when presented with written wholesale offers, these sellers will often respond in a way that allows the Level Five Investor to lock-up a *Profit at Purchase*.

## 11. CASH FLOW

Although I make a Quick Cash profit from the sale of a property and I often acquire properties intentionally to flip just for Quick Cash, I do prefer to generate as much of my profit as possible in the form of **Cash Flow**. That is *My Game* and what I love: *passive income*.

To achieve this, I acquire properties wholesale and then re-market them with *Vendor Financing* (owner financing) or a *Lease Purchase Agreement* (at retail).

I prefer the liberating power that comes from receiving a cheque at the beginning of each and every month whether or not I work directly for it. For me, wealth is Cash Flow, not cash. My problem with cash is that it has a tendency to get spent. Cash Flow continues ad infinitum.

## 12. 'LUNCH PAIL JOE'

Although I do use several investment vehicles, my main specialty is **real estate**. And with regard to real estate I primarily invest in single family homes that meet my **'Lunch Pail Joe'** definition:
A.  Priced 20% or more below the median (not average)
    price of the target area;
B.  3-bedroom/1 1/2 + bathroom
    (1,000–1,500 sq ft/100–160 sqm);
C.  Covered parking;
D.  Fenced garden;
E.  Livable condition;
F.  Acceptable neighbourhood;
G.  No more than 60 minutes away from my home or office.

I have found that by investing in 'average houses' in 'average neighbourhoods' where 'average people' live, I am in a position to profit whether the market is good or bad. The reason: people always need a place to live. And in regular neighbourhoods you always have a market because people are continually scaling up or scaling down where they live. For real estate investing purposes I greatly prefer 'average houses'.

## 13. NO EMOTIONS

When I invest, my primary concern is the Return on Investment after Taxes (ROIAT). In an investment what matters most is the bottom line: *the money and the numbers.*

I don't care what colour the carpet is or how pretty the garden. Just give me the *numbers* and I'll show you the *money!*

> 'If two persons equal in judgement play for a considerable sum, he that loves money the most shall lose; his anxiety for the success of the game confounds him.'
> **BENJAMIN FRANKLIN**

The *numbers* are the most important aspect of investing. Emotions should never play a part in an investment *decision.* I always tell students who contact me for assistance, 'Don't tell me about the house. Tell me about the numbers.' Be like the professionals. Don't get emotionally involved. Get rich instead.

---

**I want to make this very clear:** Level Five and Level Six Investors have no room for emotion while conducting business. The reason: if you become emotionally involved in the outcome of the deal, the odds dramatically increase that you will change **Your Rules** in the middle of the transaction. The usual result: DISASTER! Emotions such as fear, anxiety, panic and greed have a tendency to control decisions in relation to investing and cause you to sabotage your due diligence of the 'money and the numbers'.

---

This does not mean that you have no emotion attached to what you do. Make no mistake. If you don't have an underlying love for Your Game you are likely to fail or at best underachieve. If the deal stacks up you are allowed to 'feel good' about the 'Money and the Numbers'. This is not really an emotional reaction. Your response should be purely analytical, based on the deal satisfying Your Rules.

Be prepared to make some mistakes or errors of judgment when investing. Learn from them and leave them behind. Do not attach emotions to these experiences. Take the lessons analytically.

You love The Game, not any one deal or investment. Your future does not depend upon the success of any one deal or investment (at least not if you follow the Nine Generalised Principles of Active (Level Five) Investing). The *numbers* make the deal. Learn to love them too.

## 14. RIDE THE WINNERS AND CUT THE LOSERS

I have learned that most people 'cut their winners and ride their losers'. They often do this because of the recommendations of their 'professional' advisers.

Stockbrokers for example are trained to tell you to 'sell' when you make a small profit and to 'hold' shares that have gone down. Why would you want to sell an investment that was going up, or continue to hold on to one that had dramatically fallen in value, when there were better opportunities elsewhere?

Brokers are trained to give you this advice for two primary reasons. The first reason is that they understand that psychologically most people have a *huge* need to be right. They know that if you have lots of 'wins', no matter how small, you will feel good about yourself. You can tell all your friends about how you made money in the markets with your great broker. They also know that most people cannot psychologically accept losses and that is why they tell you to hold on to your shares that have gone down. For most people, not actually selling means they don't have to deal with the loss. They can pretend it is not really a loss because they fool themselves into thinking that the stock will come back some day (*not all shares come back!*). So, they just continue on their merry way constantly selling their good shares

'Though your emotions will invariably lead you astray when conducting business or assessing an investment, it is still a good idea to listen to your gut when assessing the integrity of the other deal participants. Sometimes the numbers stack up perfectly but there is something not quite right about the deal. Your instincts will tell you what is wrong if you listen to them. Just make sure you do not confuse these instincts with emotions caused by fear, anxiety, insecurity and greed. It may take practice to recognise the difference.'
**SIMON HALL**

'People have an overwhelming desire to be right... People want to take profits quickly and give their losses some room. This gives them the illusion of being right, but what they are really doing is "cutting their profits short and letting their losses run."'
**DR. VAN K. THARP**

far too early and holding onto the bad stocks for eternity. They 'cut their winners and ride their losers'.

The second reason this advice is sometimes given is because the broker wants to continue to make commissions when you sell and then reinvest (over and over and over again). This is called 'churning' and it generates a steady stream of commissions for the broker and the brokerage.

> 'Half the failures in life arise from pulling in one's horse as he is leaping.'
> **JULIUS CHARLES HARE AND AUGUSTUS WILLIAM HARE**

> 'Tis known by the name of perseverance in a good cause, – and of obstinacy in a bad one.'
> **LAURENCE STERN**

How often have you or someone you know sold an investment for a respectable profit only to see the investment continue to go through the roof? Do you know someone who sold Intel, Dell or even Commonwealth Bank five years ago?

Conversely, how often have you held on to an investment despite the fact that it was a 'dog' hoping that some day it would come back? How often has your dogged determination to be right cost you dearly?

Top investors **Ride their Winners and Cut their Losers**. They do this primarily through strict money management and tight control over their own investment psychology. You should learn to do the same.

## 15. INVEST LONG TERM

Most people look at far too short a time-frame in regard to their investments. They spend much of their time chopping and changing, running around looking for the next 'get rich quick' scheme or hot investment. The *reality* is that there are very few surefire and rapidfire roads to riches. Rather, the majority of 'get rich' investments take time to bring home large returns. Like the reality of the 20-year 'overnight success' in show business.

That is why when I invest, I primarily do so for the **Long Term**. I am not interested in 'spending' assets after short- or mid-term gains. I am looking towards my longer-term goals of wealth-building and stewardship of my assets. Most of the best investments carry with them the power of compounding and *Lag* and are not designed to be readily capitalised upon over the short term.

So when you assess an investment, be clear on your goals, your **Dividend Expectation Time-frame (DET)** and do not ignore an investment simply because you believe its benefits are not instantaneous. Check the numbers and understand the power of money invested over time. You are building wealth and this takes time. I invest for the Long Term.

## 16. OPEN MIND TO ADAPT MY RULES

Always be prepared, based upon your *Market Research*, to adapt Your Rules to a changing market to your own best advantage. Many businesses fail dramatically due to obstinate determination to stick to time-worn, but inflexible business practices or attitudes.

You must always keep an open mind in relation to the expectations and changes of your market. Nowhere has this requirement been more dramatically demonstrated in recent years than in the effects and market expectations for e-commerce on western-world businesses.

'He that will not apply new remedies must expect new evils; for time is the greatest innovator.'
**FRANCIS BACON**

'I do not believe I go too far when I say that in the future we will have trains of projectiles in which people will be able to travel comfortably from the Earth to the Moon.'
**JULES VERNE (1865)**

## 17. CONTINUING EDUCATION

Keep current on your *Market Research* at all times and practice your skills of *Lateral Thinking* to keep up with or anticipate the changes. I am constantly attending seminars, reading and learning. Throughout the world I seek out the best teachers and information I can find. I then pay to attend their seminars as a student to learn what they have to teach.

People ask me how often I attend other people's seminars and why? Well, in 1999 I attended 12 seminars as a student (and sometimes as a guest speaker). I paid many thousands of dollars for the seminars (and the additional books, tapes and manuals I bought at them). Why did I do this? Because you can never know

'How long should you try? Until.'
**JIM ROHN**

'Why sometimes I've believed as many as six impossible things before breakfast'
**LEWIS CARROLL**
**(Through the Looking Glass)**

'One should as a rule respect public opinion in so far as it is necessary to avoid starvation and to keep out of prison, but anything that goes beyond this is voluntary submission to an unnecessary tyranny.'
**BERTRAND RUSSELL**

enough and you can always learn more. Even if the seminar or material proves to be disappointing, I can always learn at least one new thing. Often there is considerable value in learning what is not important, valuable or legitimate, and thereby reinforcing what you already know.

I strive to continually learn more to improve myself, my relationships, my psychology, my business and my investing. By attending seminars, listening to tapes, watching videos and reading, I accomplish this. Education is an ongoing process and I strongly encourage you to continue your learning beyond your completion of the *Money Secrets* program.

## WINNING THE MONEY GAME

If you aspire to become a **Level Five Active Investor,** I recommend that you take a long hard look at how your **Principles** and **Rules** compare with those of top Level Five and Level Six Investors.

Reinforce those things you are doing right and learn from those things that you need to change. Make sure that you continually study **The Nine Generalised Principles of Active (Level Five) Investing** and review your own Rules to make sure that you are staying on top of *your* market.

I know that if you apply The Nine Generalised Principles and follow **Your Rules** that you will win **The Money Game**.

---

## CHAPTER 25 ACTION STEPS REVIEW

1. Write out your **Personal Rules of Investing** and how they relate to **Your Game**.
2. Review and apply all the **Principles** and **Rules** for investing outlined in the last two chapters.

## CHAPTER 26

# Making Quick Cash and positively-gearing real estate

'The brave man carves out his fortune, and every man
is the son of his own works.'

MIGUEL DE CERVANTES

In this chapter (which has three parts), I am going to introduce you to the exciting world of **Level Five Active Investor** real estate and three of the best real estate investment strategies.

- In **Part A: Buy and Hold**, I will show you how to Buy and Hold positively-geared rental property.
- In **Part B: Quick Cash**, you will learn the Quick Cash secrets that will allow you to buy and sell real estate *without* money for a deposit or the ability to get a bank loan.
- And in **Part C: Cash Flow**, you will learn techniques for quickly turning negatively-geared properties into Cash Flow machines. You will learn my powerful Cash Flow technique that provides a US mid-five-figure monthly income for myself and my family for the next 30 years!

My journey as a Level Five and then later a Level Six Investor began and remains primarily grounded in real estate. Because I was self-employed (from a lender's point of view: unemployed) and had little money to work with, I was unable to acquire real estate in the normal manner (i.e. put down 10–20% for a deposit and qualify for a loan).

Thus, I was forced to become creative. So creative in fact that over the last decade I have completed more than 800 real estate transactions. Among these I have acquired and *Vendor-Financed* more than 150 houses using none of my own money. And every one of these deals produced positive Cash Flow from the beginning. Understand that these are not theories or ideas that work in the US only. These are factual transactions that have actually been done by me and by my students throughout the world, including throughout Australia.

## INVESTING THEORIES

A lot of books, tapes and seminars are filled with *theories* on investing. The problem with people teaching theories is that theories often do not work. **I do not teach theories.** Everything in this book, and everything that I discuss at my seminars is actual data from actual transactions completed by me or by my students. No theory. Theory is for school, and as we all know theory often does not work in the real world. I only teach factual investment techniques that are being done in the here and now.

## CASH-ON-CASH RETURN

Before I explain real estate from the Level Five Active Investor point of view, let me make one more point about these types of investments and the investors who make them. Level Five real estate investors invest in real estate that makes them money now! When I say 'money now', what I mean is that they invest in properties that are profitable from day *one*. Not someday (hopefully) in the future. And let me be clear in what I mean by 'profitable'. 'Profitable' means that regardless of appreciation and without factoring in tax benefits, I make money *now*!

Let me show you what I mean by a 'cash-on-cash' return. If I was to put down a deposit of $10,000 on a $90,000 property I would have invested $10,000 (my actual out-of-pocket investment). If I was then to put someone into that property the amount of money above and beyond my expenses (excluding tax benefits) would be my factual cash-on-cash return (or loss). So, if in the above example at the end of the year my expenses were $8,000 and my income was $12,000 I would have made a $4,000 profit. I would then take the $4,000 and divide it into the $10,000 (my original investment) and I would come up with a first-year cash-on-cash return of 40%.

That is what Level Five Investors look for in a real estate investment. A factual cash-on-cash return. Any appreciation or tax benefits are just a bonus.

## THE ICE CREAM ANALOGY

Think of it this way. Most people like ice cream. Yet we all know that ice cream is better with chocolate sauce on the top, and even better with lots of whipped cream. The Level Five Investor looks at the real estate as the ice cream, any appreciation is the chocolate sauce, and tax benefits as the whipped cream. Certainly the chocolate sauce and the whipped cream make the ice cream taste better, but they are not the primary thought, just extras. If you get them, great, but if you don't you still have a bowl of great ice cream.

The problem with investing for appreciation and tax benefits is that these outcomes don't always occur as planned. Real estate doesn't always go up, does it? And if there is one thing we know about tax benefits: we know they can change at any time (as they just did in dramatic fashion from July 1, 2000 in Australia).

## NEGATIVE-GEARING

I know that many Australians and Americans have been led to believe that negatively-geared real estate is a sound investment. From a Level Five Investor point of view it is not. I do not know of any successful Level Five real estate investor (*not* a real estate marketer) who buys property with the primary motivation being potential appreciation or anticipated tax benefits. That is Level Three thinking and investing. I say this because appreciation and tax benefits are both completely unknown and absolutely not guaranteed.

## Tax benefits

Oh I know what the real estate marketing companies say: 'Negative-gearing is a good thing because you get tax benefits.' Think about this for a moment. What do you really get when you negatively gear? Today the top tax rate for most Australians is 30% (income level $20,001–$50,000). That means for a $1.00 deduction you would receive 30 cents. That means you lost 70 cents! It makes absolutely no sense. Yet people line up like lemmings to give away their *dollars* in order to receive cents. People earning between $50,001 and $60,000 (on 42% tax rate) lose 58 cents and people earning more than $60,001 (on 47% tax rate) lose 53 cents! Losses all around!

The advisers (who are not Level Five Investors), and the real estate marketers (who buy the properties wholesale and then often resell them to you for prices far above any realistic value) tell you that negative-gearing is a good thing. Yeah, good for *them*. Negative-gearing is not good, it is bad. Do not buy investments that are guaranteed to lose money. Especially when that is their main selling point. The clear cold investment facts are that you are buying an 'investment' that is designed to lose you money!

## Appreciation

The other incentive that people are given for investing in real estate that loses money every month is the claim that the property will go up in value, that it will *appreciate*. And most marketers pedalling negative-gearing schemes use the same hypothetical number. They say that real estate goes up by 10% a year, every year, like clockwork.

Let me ask you a question: Does real estate really always go up in price? Does it sometimes go down in price? And when it does go up, does it really go up 10% a year? Because if it was going up 10% each year that would mean that the property would double in value in just over seven years. Does most real estate double in value every seven years? Not according to figures from the Australian Bureau of Statistics. In a recent report it cites an average rate of appreciation across Australia of 3.6% per annum.

Yes, some areas do enjoy high appreciation for extended periods of time. This is not the norm though, and a Level Five Investor thus does not gamble on appreciation. They invest in cash-on-cash return.

(As an example of what I am saying, consider this: even in the sought after eastern suburbs of Sydney, if you had bought an 'investment' property during the last property boom in 1989 and held on to it through the recent boom in that area then sold it in 2000, your gross, not net, yield would not have topped 6% a year for those 11 years! Quite a risky (or at best uninspiring) investment proposition if appreciation and tax benefits were your main reasons for investing in the first place!)

## The problem with yields

Generally, when an unsophisticated investor is considering investing in real estate he or she is shown the great yield that the property will return. Sophisticated Level Five Investors know not to be fooled by 'yields'. The reason: the touted yield of an investment is usually completely made up. It does not exist in any way shape or form.

Marketers factor in tax benefits (now significantly reduced for many negative-gearers by the new tax rates) and appreciation (again almost always that mythical 10%) and then they determine your 'yield'. The Level Five Investor understands clearly that 'yield' means nothing. The Level Five Investor invests in property that is positively-geared and makes a cash-on-cash profit (for real). Do not be suckered into the 'yield' trap. Only invest in real estate that is properly valued and is positively-geared from the outset.

> Remember that it is always far better to pay taxes on profits than to have losses that provide tax deductions.

Think about, if you pay taxes isn't it because you just made money? You know, the reason for investing in the first place! And if you are left out of pocket every month to support a negatively-geared property aren't you actually *losing* money?

With all that said, I will now share with you how you can

invest in real estate and make money like so many of my students have here in Australia. There are three basic *Niche* strategies for acquiring real estate. All three can be done using little or none of your own money. The three strategies are:

| Buy and Hold | Quick Cash | Cash Flow |
|---|---|---|

My two favourites are the Quick Cash and the Cash Flow. These two techniques can be intertwined to produce a combined strategy. I have used these techniques in more than 800 transactions and shared them with thousands and thousands of people throughout the world at my 'live' and 'hands-on' seminars.

'What you have come to know, pursue by exercise; what you have not learned, seek to add to your knowledge, for it is as reprehensible to hear a profitable saying and not grasp it as to be offered a good gift by one's friends and not accept it.'

**ISOCRATES**

All of these examples are real. I do not believe in hypothetical transactions... all they produce is hypothetical money and theoretical success!

The examples are from a few of my US deals and some of my Australian seminar graduates who have successfully used all of these strategies and adapted them to local methods of buying and selling real estate.

**Bottomline:** All of these techniques are today being done successfully by my graduates in Australia and New Zealand. People who believe 'It can't be done' in Australia are the ones who are looking for excuses not to change their investment habits!

Where possible I have used Australian terminology, otherwise I have defined the nature of the transaction so you can understand the underlying strategy.

## FIND A *NICHE*

The first principle of successful real estate investing is to find a **Niche**. Your *Niche* is your investment purpose. It is what you are about. It is what you do. It is why you go to work in the morning. It is the *why* you do what you do. It is your investment passion.

If you do not have a *Niche*, you will constantly find yourself starting from scratch. You will have no focus to your efforts and will always be looking for a new way to do things. You will find yourself running all over the place trying every new concept without mastering any of them. You will in effect be running around in circles always chasing a 'deal', but not knowing what one looks like.

> 'When you want something bad enough the whole world conspires to help you get it.'
> **MADONNA (LOUISE CICCONE)**

Unless an investor determines a *Niche* and sets up a program that can be followed (replicated) over and over again, he or she is almost always destined for failure, or at best, mediocrity. And that's not why you are studying to be a Level Five Investor, is it? Of course not.

> You are here participating in this program because you desire to reach your financial goals. You want to be successful. You want to have the money to own the things that you and your family deserve. You want to be able to do what you want to do, where you want to do it, with whom you want to do it, when you want to do it, without any regard to cost. You seek the abundance that you so richly deserve. You desire to be wealthy!

For you to be successful in a big way, you must first identify *your* Niche, and then implement *your* strategy within that *Niche*. This will be your recipe for success that you can follow without having to reinvent the process for every new deal.

> 'Don't let life discourage you; everyone who got where he is had to begin where he was.'
> **RICHARD L. EVANS**

The first step is to decide what you are trying to accomplish. That will determine your strategy. I will share with you the strategies that I have found to be the most profitable. Then I will review the specific characteristics of each strategy and which is most effective in which types of markets.

My *Niche* is real estate investing. My strategies within that *Niche* are numerous, but because my main aim is to create passive income, my preferred strategy is the Cash Flow strategy.

## WHAT IS *YOUR* STRATEGY?

1. Are you looking to develop an appreciating portfolio (positively-geared, mind you) that others will pay you to own? This is the **Buy and Hold** strategy.
2. Are you looking to make some quick cash, say $10,000 or more, in the next 90 days? This is the **Quick Cash** strategy.
3. Are you looking to have substantial monthly income for the upcoming 30-plus years? This is the **Cash Flow** strategy.

All three strategies produce positive results, but where you apply them and the way you implement them are quite different.

'Nothing is more difficult, and therefore more precious, than to be able to decide.'
**NAPOLEON BONAPARTE**

As I introduce these strategies, you should be thinking about which *Niche* makes the most sense for you. You do not need to decide this instantly, though you should be thinking in general about which way you want to go. For many of you, the decision will be made before you complete this chapter.

I have used all these strategies at various times in my investment career. Which one I chose for a particular situation depended on what I wanted to accomplish at that particular time. To help you better understand the strategies, I will review transactions I have completed personally. I will also share with you transactions completed by Australian graduates of my Australian seminars. This should help you to make finer distinctions as to which strategy is best for you.

Let us begin our review in **Part A: Buy and Hold**.

# Part A: Buy and Hold

## THE BUY AND HOLD STRATEGY

This popular strategy has been taught in real estate books and seminars for many years. While it is applicable in most markets, I have found that it can be somewhat challenging to apply in certain regions of the country. Those regions where property prices are the highest will be the most challenging areas to implement this strategy.

The basis of this strategy is simple. Buy a good property, rent or lease it, and wait for the property to appreciate in value. It is the most common real estate technique of all time. And while it is still a viable option, I believe the **Buy and Hold** strategy is a little tired and was more effective in the past than it is today. That said, there will always be 'emerging' markets for which the Buy and Hold is a very lucrative strategy for people to follow.

Imagine if you had implemented the Buy and Hold strategy in Sydney in 1970 when you could buy a really nice house for around $30,000. Today that same house is worth well over $400,000. How many of those deals would you have needed to do? If you had acquired just a couple of houses a year from 1970 to 1980 you would now be a millionaire many times over. Where do you plan to be 10-20 years from today?

One of the keys to the Buy and Hold is that the incoming rents must cover the outgoing debt service and expenses. In the '70s and '80s that could be achieved in most areas of the country without too much difficulty. Today, in the centres of cities like Sydney and Melbourne, it is very difficult to get rents high enough to cover the expenses of the property. There are however many places such as Adelaide, Brisbane, Perth, Newcastle, the outer greater metropolitan areas of Sydney and Melbourne, and many other areas throughout Australia where you can still easily implement the Buy and Hold strategy.

The advantages and disadvantages of the Buy and Hold strategy are:

| The advantages | The disadvantages |
|---|---|
| ☑ Excellent long-term appreciation<br>☑ Steady, slowly increasing cash flow<br>☑ Great tax deductions | ☒ Heavy property management costs<br>☒ Cash-intensive<br>☒ Very long-term cycle |

Today, the challenges to the Buy and Hold strategy are obvious. In many regions, property prices have increased at a faster rate than rents. Expenses such as debt service, maintenance, repairs, and management costs have risen accordingly. In recent years, many investors have foolishly (in my opinion) become involved in properties with a negative cash flow.

As we discussed at the beginning of this chapter these properties are sometimes marketed as 'negatively-geared', whereby you can get a tax deduction when total property expenses are greater than total property income. Often though, 'investors' will bury large amounts of cash in a property for the purpose of reducing the payments so that the property shows a 'positive' cash flow. This sort of creative bookkeeping distorts the true value of property investment.

I do not recommend placing huge deposits as a solution to the negative cash flow dilemma. To me it is plain and simple. If the property cannot be bought in such a way that it will realistically carry itself from the outset then do not buy it. Ignore the highly publicised tax advantages. End of story. I never do *negative cash flow*. Never. I strongly recommend that you do not either.

> Let's get clear on this. If the property will not maintain a positive cash flow with a 10–20% (or less) deposit, with *realistic* market expenses applied, I do not acquire the property for a Buy and Hold.

What *are* 'realistic' market expenses? Over the course of hundreds of transactions, I have found that in addition to your payment (PIRI – Principal, Interest, Rates and Insurance), you can expect an additional 10–40%+ of your income to be eaten up by expenses. I have seen many investors put themselves in a difficult cash flow position by not properly planning for these normal yet often overlooked expenses.

I do not care how good a job you do managing the property. You *will* have expenses. Among these will be:

| | |
|---|---|
| • Vacancies | • General maintenance |
| • Legal fees | • Capital improvements |
| • Management fees | • Repairs |
| • Vandalism | • Council and water rates |

Over the course of time, I *guarantee* that you will not retain 100% of your projected rents. If it is a newer property in good repair, in a good neighbourhood, with good tenants, your expenses will run a minimum of 10–25%. If it is an older property or the neighbourhood is marginal, your expenses will rise beyond that mark. Keep in mind that for an older, tired property a 40–50% expense rate is not unheard of, or even rare.

OK, so we have accepted reality and moved into the real world of real estate. We have determined that we will not do *negative cash flow* or *negative-gearing*. Now the deck seems like it is stacked against us. What do we do now?

'If we are to achieve a victorious standard of living today we must look for the opportunity in every difficulty instead of being paralyzed at the thought of the difficulty in every opportunity.'
**WALTER E. COLE**

Do not give up hope. If you still want to use Buy and Hold, you can! The first thing to do is search diligently until you locate a property that will produce cash flow without a significant deposit. Depending on the region of the country in which you are investing, this can be a quick or a lengthy process.

Take comfort in the knowledge that the harder you have to look, the more profit you will make when you do find a good deal. For example, someone investing in Adelaide could buy a property for 80–90% (or more) of value (*instant $10,000 equity*) and receive positive cash flow from the property from the outset.

Conversely, someone living in Sydney (particularly close to the centre) would have to buy a property for 60–70% of value (*instant $60,000+ equity*) to produce positive cash flow. Obviously, the 60–70% properties are rarer and more difficult to find and thus the person in Sydney would need to look at far more properties to make a deal. However, the greater effort would offer a greater return. In the long run it all evens out. The investor in Adelaide finds more opportunities, but has to make a lot more deals to make the same money as the investor in Sydney, who must make more on each transaction.

**Warning:** Do thorough *Market Research* before considering buying a packaged investment through a marketer or developer. They are not all bad deals; however, be very wary and make sure to do full due diligence on those who offer real estate investment opportunities where:

- real estate, finance and property management are packaged together;
- guaranteed rentals are offered on the real estate for the first couple of years;
- free flights are provided to inspect the property;
- no deposit is required and the equity in your home acts as security for the loan;
- great tax advantages are offered through negative-gearing.

I find this often to be a very dangerous way to buy. I have had many people come up to me at my Australian seminars and tell me their horror stories of buying these properties for dramatically inflated prices and then not being able to resell or rent them out, after the rental guarantees run out, for anywhere near what was projected.

These types of real estate marketing schemes are known as "Two-Tiered Marketing" and are often targeted at investors in

Sydney and Melbourne who are used to seeing higher prices for investment property in their areas. The 'investment properties' are typically in less expensive areas (Brisbane, for

'The secret of success is constancy to purpose.'
**BENJAMIN DISRAELI**

example) and look 'cheap' by comparison. A local would think they were overpriced. Remember the Gold Coast-type schemes? Well, they are alive and well. So you best beware lest you be taken for a ride too. Do your *Market Research*.

If you do look at such packages, consider the following questions:

- What is the real market price of these properties?
- What are similar properties, not controlled by the marketer, being sold for?
- If they are part of a package, check the public records to determine what the marketer actually paid for them?
- Have they actually had an appraisal with comparable sales or is it just a valuation (opinion)?
- Is the financing competitive? Are there extra fees?
- Who is going to rent the property after the guaranteed rental period? And if it's such a great deal why do they have to guarantee the rent anyway? Remember that a rent guarantee is only as good as the marketer's ability to pay. Is the guarantee money in a trust?
- What happens to your budget if the tax laws change again?
- Are the properties really going to increase in value the way the marketer suggests? If not, how does that affect you?
- Have they applied realistic expenses for now and in the future?
- Are they pushing negative-gearing and appreciation rather than a sound and sensible investment?

**Bottomline:** Do thorough *Market Research* before ever investing. Especially where you are being 'sold' the proposed investment opportunity (rather than finding it yourself).

I have students throughout Australia (and throughout the world for that matter), who regardless of the house pricing of their region, are successfully applying the Buy and Hold strategy right now!

When you are looking to buy, there are many good sources to check:
- As always, newspapers, particularly your local paper and Saturday papers;
- For Sale by Owners, (street-front advertising or newspapers);
- Builders and developers (looking to off-load properties for wholesale prices);
- Internet sites (becoming very popular);
- Government Gazettes;
- The Department of Defence;
- The Department of Housing (state and federal bodies);
- Real estate agents (typically banks, liquidators and receivers use local real estate agents to sell 'mortgagee in possession' properties).

There are many other sources for obtaining housing price information and other valuable real estate information, none more convenient than those available through the Internet:
- Residex Pty Ltd, which has a large database of historical sales data, particularly for NSW, and is available through www.ozemail.com.au/~residex/;
- CPM Research, which provides a comprehensive collection of real estate sales figures and has free economic and property market statistics on 1800 351 180 or www.propertyweb.com.au;
- Investorweb, which has a handy research tool giving access to *The Sydney Morning Herald*, the Melbourne *Age* and *The Canberra Times* newspapers' historical price guides for a fee (of $39.95 for one postcode and $25.00 each for two or more postcodes) at www.investorweb.com.au;
- The Real Estate Institute of Australia for finding historical info re price movement in Australia at www.reia.com.au;
- Economic forecasting from www.bis.com.au;
- *The Australian Financial Review* property reports from www.afr.com.au/property/index.html;
- The Australian Bureau of Statistics at www.abs.gov.au;
- Australian information for public notices such as sheriff auctions in each state at www.ausinfo.gov.au;

- Property Guide to locate any property for sale anywhere, anytime www.propertyguide.com.au;
- Financial calculators on www.realestate.com.au;
- Information Australia on www.infoaust.com.au.

Let's now look at some examples of successful Buy and Hold strategy transactions.

## BUY AND HOLD EXAMPLE 1: BASCOM AVENUE, LOS GATOS, CALIFORNIA

Los Gatos is just outside San Jose, about 50 miles south of San Francisco. We're talking expensive. Some of the most expensive real estate in the world.

In case you are curious, as of June 2000, the median price for a house in the San Jose area (Silicon Valley) is US$550,000. That will get you a 30-year-old 115 square metre 3-bedroom, 1½-bathroom house on a small lot in a very basic neighbourhood. And you thought Sydney was expensive!

At the time, I was renting an apartment. Like many people I did not have the money for a big deposit to buy a house to live in. I was very frustrated paying rent. I felt like I was just flushing my money down the drain. I was sick and tired of it. (*Does this sound familiar?*)

> 'Experience is the child of Thought, and Thought is the child of Action. We cannot learn men from books.'
> **BENJAMIN DISRAELI**

I had purchased property for 'no money down' before and I was determined to do it again. I scoured the newspaper for two or three months. I made many phone calls and several written offers. I was actively pursuing an investment opportunity.

Then, on May 22, 1987 I struck gold! A dentist and his father owned a condominium in Los Gatos and were tired of the negative cash flow. They told me how the government had really given them a raw deal by changing the tax laws and taking away their depreciation and tax write-offs. They each made several hundred thousand dollars a year and because of tax reforms in 1986 they could no longer write-off their losses or depreciation in the current year. They could only carry forward their losses rather than write them off the same year as in the good old days.

**Note**: In 1986, the US Government, in essence with no warning, dramatically changed the tax benefits (negative-gearing) available to property investors. Although not as dramatic, similar 'reforms' in Australia have reduced the benefit of negative-gearing for individuals earning less than $60,000.

Incidentally, when this tax change occurred in the US, property prices plummeted, making a great buying opportunity for investors who wanted positive-gearing. Governments make tax law changes for many financial and political reasons – there is always the distinct possibility negative-gearing in Australia may disappear (its removal was attempted by the Federal Government in the late 1980s).

> 'Character and personal force are the only investments that are worth anything.'
> **WALT WHITMAN**

Anyway, the dentist and his father were tired of the vacancies and the property management hassles. They wanted out. They were just what I was looking for: a 'Don't Wanter'.

We agreed on a price of $119,000 (*the market value was about $138,000*). They suggested that I do what most Americans (and Australians) do. Put down a deposit of 20% and take out an 80% loan. Because they were 'Don't Wanters' they even offered to pay my closing costs (the Australian equivalent of conveyancing costs and stamp duty).

I told them that sounded great but that I had a problem: I didn't have the $23,800 for the deposit.

When they asked what money I did have, I told them the truth: that I earned a good living, about US$60,000 a year at that time, but that I only had a few thousand extra dollars in the bank.

They were disappointed because they were sure that we needed the deposit money to make the transaction fly.

Rather than just giving up I asked them what they were going to do with the deposit money when they got it. They said they were going to put it into term deposits paying about 7.5% (it was 1987).

I suggested that we create a 'note' for $23,800 at 10% (a 'note' is simply a short-term loan with various legal obligations). They would make more money, 10% versus 7.5%, plus Uncle Sam would give them additional tax benefits for providing *Vendor Financing*. They said, 'OK', provided their accountant and the son's wife (a lawyer) both agreed.

**Note**: Contrary to some people's opinions, *Vendor Financing* is quite popular in Australia and has been for some time. Think about it, aren't almost all farms sold with *Vendor Financing*? Isn't it commonplace for the seller to offer some sort of financing (to get the deal done) on commercial property?

While doing *Market Research,* I recently came upon a favourable 1927 Australian court decision (in tax court) in regard to *Vendor Financing*.

At my seminars around Australia I have met several people who specialise in *Vendor Financing*. I know one individual who has used *Vendor Financing* on more than 100 transactions. And another student of mine who has used it on more than 250 transactions.

> 'Let no feeling of discouragement prey upon you, and in the end you are sure to succeed.'
> **ABRAHAM LINCOLN**

> 'The way to secure success is to be more anxious about obtaining it than about deserving it.'
> **WILLIAM HAZLITT**

Make no mistake about it, *Vendor Financing* is alive and well in Australia.

Back to the story. I did my homework. I checked the tax law and did a comparison on the return over the next four years; it was a compromise, I wanted seven years, they wanted two. They talked it over, and to my utter shock and total joy... they agreed!

From there it was smooth sailing... right up until the escrow company decided that I could not provide the monies to the seller at settlement. In Australia, you don't have escrow companies, rather the real estate agent or conveyancer does this. In the United States the escrow company is a neutral party who receives monies from one party (usually a buyer) and on fulfilment of certain conditions, passes the money to another party (usually a seller). So in this example, Australians need to satisfy the deposit required under the agreement and give it to the real estate agent whereas I needed to satisfy the escrow company. Uh-oh!! They wanted to see the cold hard cash. This sweet deal had just blown up in my face. I did not have $23,800 and certainly couldn't get it in the required 72 hours.

It was over. I could not believe it. I had already moved in (on a rental basis just until the 'formality' of settlement). It seemed so unfair. Boy, did I feel sorry for myself. I can tell you I had quite a pity party for myself that night.

Late that night, I decided to stop feeling sorry for myself and to do something about my situation. The next morning I got busy. I called everybody I knew who could lay their hands on $25,000 in less than 48 hours. I offered them $500 interest for just one week. They did not even have to give me the money. The loan had already been approved. The agreement with the seller to return the money and carry the loan was already signed. All that was needed was a bank cheque made payable to the escrow company. They could not lose.

'Character is power; it makes friends, draws patronage and support, and opens a sure way to wealth, honor and happiness.'

**J. HOWE**

Guess what? I found a money partner, and he didn't lose. A week later he got his money back, plus $500!

This is how the cash flow deal worked out on a monthly basis:

| | |
|---|---|
| 1st mortgage with Southwest Savings | (665.65) |
| 2nd mortgage with seller | (198.33) |
| Body corporate fees | (97.12) |
| Rates | (119.93) |
| Total payment | (1,081.03) |
| Tax savings (918.00 x .33%) | 302.94 |
| Rent (2nd bedroom) | 450.00 |
| Total income/tax savings | 752.94 |
| Net cash flow out of pocket | (328.94) |

In the end, I was only paying $328.94 a month. The fair market rent was $525–$550 a month, and I had the master bedroom and the garage. Plus the big benefit, I was now in the business of long-term gain, or appreciation: the Buy and Hold strategy.

So I got the first part right: buying. I was living in a nice house in a great neighbourhood for an out-of-pocket cost of $328.94 a month. I had acquired the property with none of my own money for 87% of its value. Pretty good, huh?

Wait a minute though, because it gets even better. On January 23, 1990, just 29 months later, I resold the property for $220,000!

Talk about appreciation, from me *and* the condo! The property had appreciated an average of $3,483 a month! That is one of the great advantages of a fast-rising market. All you have to do is find the right deal where you can structure the cash flow and you have got it made.

At settlement, I had a bank cheque in my hand for more than US$93,000!

As you can see, even though they can require a good deal of work to acquire, properties purchased using the Buy and Hold strategy can be highly profitable.

## BUY AND HOLD EXAMPLE 2: DAN AND JANICE, MELBOURNE

On my first trip to Australia in 1997, Dan and Janice attended a seminar Robert Kiyosaki and I put on in Sydney (Robert is the author of the best-selling *Rich Dad, Poor Dad*). Dan is the principal of a foreign exchange company and his wife Janice is a securities professional. Both were extremely busy with their work but were very interested in the idea of acquiring investment real estate.

We spent some time talking and they decided to come out to my annual 'Level Five Advanced Investing Boot Camp' (held exclusively in Phoenix, Arizona with limited classroom size) where students from around the world come together and actually go out and buy real estate for real.

When they returned to Melbourne they set about implementing what they had learned. They had a unique approach. Because of their limited available time they employed a real estate agent to go out and make wholesale offers in the Melbourne market. The agent was instructed to keep making the offers until Dan and Janice acquired 20 houses!

And that is exactly what happened. For the last two years Dan and Janice have been the proud owners of 20 investment properties. All bought below market value. All positively-geared (after all expenses). And all enjoying the last few years of higher-than-normal appreciation in the Melbourne market. Congratulations to you two and thank you for your friendship and support on my many trips to Australia.

## BUY AND HOLD STRATEGY REVIEW

☑ **The property must be able to pay for itself.** The higher the price of the property, the bigger the disparity between the possible rents and the payments. Therefore, you are going to have easier success investing in areas where property prices are lower.

☑ **Stay Leveraged.** If you put down a large deposit your rate of return will be greatly reduced. Look for property that will produce cash flow with only a 10–20% maximum deposit.

☑ **No negative-gearing!** An investment that is guaranteed to lose money every month is not in my opinion an investment. It is a hope. Negatively-geared houses are Level Three investments that have been 'sold' to the Australian and American public. It is the marketing company which really makes the money here.

☑ **Remember realistic expenses.** Plan for your expenses being in the 10–40% range.

☑ **Make sure to properly check out the numbers.** When using the Buy and Hold strategy you really do make your money on the buying, not the holding.

☑ **Stick with 'average houses' in 'average neighbourhoods' where 'average people' live.**

Once you have found the right property you will make money every time. The only question remaining relates to the ice cream analogy: *'How long will it take for great appreciation to occur?'*

# Part B: Quick Cash

## THE QUICK CASH STRATEGY

The key to the **Quick Cash** strategy resides in the buying. You need to learn to act as if you are the buyer for a retail store. Your objective is to buy a product (*real estate*) and then quickly resell it for a profit.

You become the middle-person. You acquire properties for a price that allows them to be quickly resold for a higher price. That's why it is called *Quick* Cash.

Quick Cash properties must be purchased at *wholesale* or *sub-wholesale* and resold at, or just below, *retail*. Generally, you must acquire the property for no more than 80% of real (*not appraised*) value. By acquiring the property at this wholesale level, you are able to quickly resell the property and still make a good profit.

The advantages and disadvantages of the Quick Cash strategy are:

| The advantages | The disadvantages |
|---|---|
| ☑ Produces cash now! | ☒ High turnover |
| ☑ Short time-frame | ☒ Often cash-intensive |
| ☑ Few hassles | ☒ Often requires repairs or fix-up |
| ☑ Easily repeated | ☒ Income tax of up to 48.5% on profit if property held for under one year |

Here are examples of successful Quick Cash transactions completed by me and by my Australian students.

## QUICK CASH EXAMPLE 1: THE HOUSE ON PICKFORD WAY

My very first real estate transaction was in 1982. It was a Quick Cash deal. After reading a few popular real estate investing books, I had decided to try it myself.

I knew that I needed to find a really distressed situation because I did not have any money for a deposit. I needed to buy a property for *no money down*!

I studied the newspapers, called real estate agents and let people know that I bought real estate.

Several months passed and I still hadn't found a deal. It was very frustrating, but I considered I was learning a lot and I believed that if I persevered I would eventually find a great opportunity.

I was representing a small construction company at an energy conservation trade show when I found my first Quick Cash deal. I was talking with a guy who sold solar hot-water heaters. About 18 months earlier he had tried his hand at being a builder. He had acquired a 1-hectare plot of land and built a 170 square metre ranch house on it. It was a beautiful house. Brand new, complete, and just sitting there vacant. It had an appraised value of $89,000.

> 'The happiest time in any man's life is when he is in red-hot pursuit of a dollar with a reasonable prospect of overtaking it.'
>
> **HENRY WHEELER SHAW**

There was nothing wrong with the house. The only problem was the interest rate the new buyer would have to pay. In 1982, interest rates were very high: around 18% for a conventional loan. As a result, no one was buying houses.

Needless to say, the builder was feeling the pinch. He was having a hard time covering his construction loan payments. If he did not sell soon he would lose everything. He was a serious 'Don't Wanter'. He needed out!

Once he learned that I was interested in his house, and that I could qualify for a loan, he got excited. He told me he would do *anything* to sell me that house. And believe me, before we were done, he did.

He agreed to sell me the house for $75,000 and to pay all my borrowing and legal costs.

I told him that was great, but that I wanted to write up the sale for $89,000 with a forgivable $9,000 earnest money note to be held outside of escrow (this is just a loan between us which I never need to repay). I wanted to finance the house for $80,000 to receive a cheque (a buyer's rebate) for $5,000 at settlement.

He could not believe my offer. He could not believe it but he agreed to it

Here is how the deal played out:

| | |
|---|---:|
| Contract purchase price | 89,000 |
| Forgivable earnest money deposit | 9,000 |
| Loan amount | 80,000 |
| Buyer rebate | 5,000 |
| Total purchase price | 75,000 |

That's right, $75,000. Not only did I have $5,000 in my pocket, I also had an instant equity profit of $9,000.

Put $5,000 in *your* pocket as the buyer at settlement! Now that's what I call Quick Cash. I did not have to wait to resell the property. I just collected the money and moved in. What could be better than that?

The only drawback to the deal was the financing. The loan was difficult to obtain. Because of the high interest rates the loan had graduated payments (each year I would have to pay more to make up for paying less in the beginning) and it was negatively amortised (meaning I actually owed more each month than the original loan amount). It is incredible just how bad financing was in the early 1980s compared to today. Imagine, a fixed-rate loan at 18% a year. That was like buying a house on your VISA card or MasterCard. When I look back at the interest rates it makes me feel very good (all warm and fuzzy) about the financing that is available today.

This is how the cash flow worked out on a monthly basis:

'The nonconformist... can wear a green toga instead of a gray-flannel suit, drink yak's milk rather than martinis, drive a Kibitka instead of a Cadillac and vote the straight Vegetarian Ticket – and none of it will make the slightest difference.'
**J. PAUL GETTY**

'A man's true estate of power and riches is to be in himself: not in his dwelling or position or external relations, but in his own essential character.'
**HENRY WARD BEECHER**

| | |
|---|---|
| Principal and interest | (754.32) |
| Rates | (74.17) |
| Property insurance | (24.42) |
| Private mortgage insurance | (29.34) |
| Total payment (PIRI) | (882.25) |
| Tax savings (828.49 x .30%) | 248.55 |
| Rent income (3rd bedroom) | 350.00 |
| Total income/tax savings | 598.55 |
| Net cash flow out of pocket | (283.70) |

The end result of this transaction was that I paid a little less than $300 a month to live in a brand new house in the country on a hectare with a stream running through it.

Properties acquired for less than 80% of market value can often pay for themselves immediately. Even on a non owner-occupied basis they can often be financed or refinanced for 90% (or more) of your purchase price. In many cases, on an owner-occupied property, you can finance up to 100% of the appraised value!

One variation of the Quick Cash strategy is to purchase property for 50–75% of value (not uncommon at auctions of mortgagee in possession properties) and then refinance the property at full value. This enables you to quickly extract cash from the deal without *having* to resell the property. You can then resell the property with favourable terms, thus making even more money.

That is what I did with the house on Pickford Way. About six months after closing the deal, I advertised the property 'For Sale By Owner':

*By Owner. Desperate. I'm overextended and can't make my payments. Low Down. No Qual. Beautiful 3/2 Ranch House on 2½ acres w/creek. Call 555 2121.*

I put the house on the market for $89,900. Wouldn't you know it, a couple was moving down from a small mountain town in northern California. They fell in love with the house. They said they would take it. They paid $89,500.

They were not going to be able to move in for a couple of months, but did not want to miss out on their *dream house*. As per my advertisement, they were concerned about the monthly payments being kept up. So they offered to make the payments for three months while I continued to live in the house and look after it.

This is what I ended up making on the house:

| | |
|---|---|
| New deposit | 2,000 |
| Three payments by purchaser | 2,646 |
| Second deed of trust | 6,600 |
| Buyer rebate (original purchase) | 5,000 |
| Total profit | 16,246 |

Here is another exciting technique you can use for Quick Cash.

## EXCHANGE OF CONTRACT

**Exchange of Contract** is one of the best techniques available for Quick Cash. The technique is unbelievably simple! Advantages of the Exchange of Contract include:

> ☑ No need to ever take title to the property (you never own the property if you complete the transaction properly);
> ☑ No need to make any deposit;
> ☑ No need to fill out any loan applications;
> ☑ No need to fill out a credit report.

And yet, you still make money! If done right, *big* money! Interested?

Here is how this technique works:

1. You make an offer to buy a property and your offer is accepted (by way of *option* if stamp-duty provisions in your state apply to full value of the property).
2. You then sell, or assign your right (or option) to buy the property to another buyer (by various methods – see below).
3. When the other buyer settles, you receive a cheque for the exchange and/or the difference in the purchase prices.

Sound too simple? It actually is about as simple as it sounds. Do you think it can be done in Australia? Well, guess what, it can. Sure your laws are a little different than mine, but not that much different. Remember, both Australia and America have legal systems based on English common law. The *Market Research* completed by me and by my students has shown us that the biggest difference in real estate between Australia and the United States is the terminology, not the techniques (i.e. you call it a *deposit*, we call it a *down payment*; you call it *negative-gearing*, we call it *negative cash flow*; you have a *solicitor* complete a *conveyance*, we have a *title officer* complete an *escrow*.) The techniques are virtually the same, it's just the words that are different.

Yes, just like the United States, which has 50 states (and thus 50 sets of laws), Australia has laws and customs that differ between each state. However, the fact is that you can do the same types of real estate transactions in Australia and New Zealand that I do in the United States. My students are doing them here in Australia today! Why don't you join them!

Various transfer of interest techniques are used by investors in different states to comply with local laws or minimise the effects of state stamp-duty provisions. In South Australia, for example, you can assign the exchange contract and only pay stamp-duty on the original deposit or option amount, not on the full value of the property. Other state or territory stamp-duty provisions may vary from this. In the Australian Capital Territory, as another example, the stamp-duty on the transfer of an income producing property is tax-deductible, because you are transferring an interest in a leasehold (all property in the ACT is 99-year leasehold). In New

South Wales, if you secured your interest by way of deposit you would attract stamp-duty on the full sale price when you exchange, so the best investor method to 'control' the property in the first instance might be an option, not a deposit.

These variations again highlight the importance of conducting proper *Market Research* for your area (checking the local stamp-duty provisions, etc.), before undertaking the Exchange of Contract. **Level Five Active Investors** always do their homework before entering into a transaction.

The two main points to remember about this technique are:
1. You need to develop a database of buyers; and
2. You need to buy property sufficiently below market value to allow you to quickly resell for a suitable profit.

The easiest way to develop a database of buyers is to run ads asking for exactly what you want (*you will have noticed throughout this program that most successful techniques are amazingly simple*).

My ads always look something like this:

> **By Owner. I sell houses in western Sydney for 92% of value. Must qualify for a new loan.**

> **If you can qualify for a new loan, I will sell you a home for 92% of value.**

When people respond to an ad, I find out what they are looking for, and what their time-frame is. I ask how much money they have to work with and arrange for them to obtain approval for a loan through a lender. I often prefer to use a mortgage company in preference to a bank because I have found that since the mortgage broker is primarily paid by a commission they are often more aggressive in completing transactions.

You will be surprised how quickly you can create a pile of prospective buyers for properties you have not yet even found!

Then as your offers begin being accepted, you simply show the prospective buyers in your database the properties you have available. Instant resale. Instant Quick Cash!

## EIGHT KEY POINTS TO REMEMBER WHEN WRITING AN OFFER FOR AN EXCHANGE OF CONTRACT

1. **Your offers must always be *written*.** Most people will not seriously consider a below-market offer that is offered verbally.
2. **Always place the words 'and/or nominee' after your name.** This gives you the right to nominate, or endorse, the contract to another buyer (you may want to check the stamp-duty aspects of this with your conveyancer).
3. **Always include a contingency clause in your offer.** Include in your offer the words 'This offer is subject to acceptance and approval of the property and the financials within 72 hours of acceptance.' This gives you a legal and reasonable (ethical) escape if further *Market Research* reveals that the deal does not make (financial) sense to pursue.
4. **Always ask for sufficient settlement time.** Make sure you ask for enough settlement time to allow you to re-market the property within the settlement period (at least 60–90 days is desirable).
5. **Always request *(in writing)* the right to show the property to 'prospective occupants' in privacy.** It is important to use the term 'occupant' because this allows you to show the property to prospective tenants or buyers without having to disclose your intentions.
6. **Structure the transaction so there will be sufficient profit for you.** Example: Make written offers to purchase a $100,000 property for $80,000. You can then easily remarket the property for $92,000 to a new buyer who comes from your database.
7. **Do your *Market Research* and set up a conveyancer to complete the paperwork once you put the deal together.** Make sure that you have covered all your bases

going in to the deal, but do not think you have to handle all the minor details. Delegate the paperwork tasks to the professionals. *Leverage* your time and what you are good at – finding the deals – and let other people do their jobs too.

8. **With the GST changes came the $7,000 First Home Owner Grant Scheme.** For 'average houses', in 'average neighbourhoods' this represents a substantial portion of the deposit required by your buyer. This means that since you negotiated to buy the property sufficiently below the appraised value, your new buyer can then buy the property from you with little or no deposit money out of their pocket.

**What you can structure is limited only by your willingness to be creative. Use your imagination. Put it *in writing*. Take *Action* and get those *written* offers out.**

For this technique to work you are probably going to have to make many *written* wholesale offers. Take notice that I always place great emphasis on making *written* offers! You are going to have to fire offers every which way until you hit a 'Don't Wanter' who has a property that can be flexible enough to make the numbers work for you.

This is simply a numbers game. If you make enough *written* offers you will find sellers who are motivated to sell, *now*. If the offers are verbal almost every real estate agent and seller will say no. Once it is *in writing*, things are taken a lot more seriously. Most sellers will not be interested in your offer. That is fine, you are just looking for the highly motivated sellers who are interested. Many real estate agents will tell you 'It can't be done', or that 'We don't do it that way here.' Don't pay any attention to them. Just keep moving on and making *written* offers. If you do, you *will* succeed and become *rich*!

> 'The busy man has few idle visitors: to the boiling pot the flies come not.'
>
> **BENJAMIN FRANKLIN**

I have seen many people get started with investing by using the Exchange of Contract and Quick Cash techniques. I believe they are some of the easiest strategies for a first-time property investor. Particularly if you have no money, no credit, and no money partners.

'Over the years I have on several occasions been the recipient of the following statement from real estate agents returning with a wholesale offer accepted by the seller: "If I had known that they would have sold it for that (little) I would have bought it myself!" Such sweet words to the ears of a real estate investor.'

**JOHN R. BURLEY,
REAL ESTATE INVESTOR**

## EXCHANGE OF CONTRACT EXAMPLE

Many people use the Exchange of Contract to kick-start their Cash Flow careers. One of my Australian students, Steven Dover, did exactly that in quite spectacularly creative fashion. His story is truly inspirational, yet not untypical of the type of life-changing action we get from motivated people who are exposed to this *Money Secrets* information. Here is Steve's story in context so you understand the great strides he has taken in double-quick time:

'The easiest way for me to put all this into perspective is to just tell you my story.

I first went to John Burley's 'Automatic Wealth' seminar in May 1999 and then to the Boot Camp in November of the same year. John taught me to look at business and investing in a completely different way and without fear. Prior to May '99 I had a finance brokerage business turning over $80,000 a year, I was working from home and thought I was a legend. John's seminar shocked the life out of me and I realised that I was going absolutely nowhere, and fast.

I had car repayments of $890 a month; credit card debt of $6,000; home loan of $100,000; no savings; no residual income and no investments; but I did have heaps of *stuff*. I was the classic Level Three screaming pig and my pig squeals at the seminar were so convincing I thought I might win an Oscar nomination.

I really looked at my life situation hard after the seminar and decided to *get serious*. I developed my business and investing systems consistent with John's philosophies and went *ballistic*!!!

My situation today is vastly different and I just can't believe it is only a year and a half since I met John for the first time. My current business turnover for the financial year July 1, 1999 to June 23, 2000 is over $1.5 million dollars. I have moved to the Gold Coast and set up in a beautiful apartment and a very professional office. I applied the residual income Principles and Rules John taught to my business and I became a mortgage manager. I now have six staff.

My residual income is now $150,000 per annum and is growing by $25,000 per annum every month. I have absolutely *no debt*; a self-managed super fund; my office rent is prepaid for the next 12 months; and all my creditors are paid on time every time. Best of all I have legally minimised my tax exposure to around 16%.

I have now developed a way to incorporate the Cash Flow strategy into my existing business so that it is consistent with my day-to-day activity. I don't have to use any of my own money, and the investors and properties are in abundance. My goal is to complete 100 Cash Flow transactions by June 30, 2001. Below are the two types of transactions I have completed to date. I no longer have to do Exhanges of Contract, but they are what really got me started.

## My Exchange of Contract Deals

After the 'Automatic Wealth' seminar I realised I needed to cash up so I did some Exchange of Contract. I have completed 16 Quick Cash property transactions in total without putting one single dollar into any of the deals.

My first transactions were 12 townhouses that I bought from a developer who had a 38-townhouse complex in Brisbane. He was desperate to off-load the last 12 as they had been on the market for over six months without any offers. I negotiated to take four townhouses at a time for which I received a 15% reduction off the list price of $150,000. I adapted John's Exchange of Contract techniques to complete the transactions and assigned all of the properties to the end purchasers using their cash to settle.

The traditional way to do this type of transaction in Queensland is by signing the purchase contract on a standard REIQ contract with the purchaser being Steven Dover 'and/or nominee'. The only problem with this type of Exchange of Contract in Queensland is that the end purchaser is informed of my purchase price. To overcome this challenge I signed each contract with a 90-day settlement clause at the full purchase price of $150,000 and had a side (written) agreement with the developer to discount or rebate to me at settlement 15% of the purchase price. I also had another agreement in place with the developer that came into effect when

'Fortune sides with him who dares.'

**VIRGIL (PUBLIUS VERGILIUS MARO) (70–19 BC)**

I 'on-sold' a property. Once the property had been on-sold and was unconditional on finance, the developer would rip up the contract I had on the property and replace it with the new one. At settlement under our agreement I would still receive the 15% discount, which was made up of the standard REIQ commission, marketing and advertising fees, etc.

This type of transaction helped me in a number of ways including the following:

- I didn't have to buy or settle on any property so my closing costs were nil.
- The integrity of the valuations in the complex was maintained by signing contracts at the list price.
- The net returns to me on these transactions were on average $7,000 a property with an ROI of infinity.
- I on-sold and settled all 12 of these properties within three months through a network of real estate contacts that I have in Sydney and Brisbane. There were *significant* incentives for these contacts to sell my properties.

These were not my favourite types of property transactions though. Firstly, they were too exciting for me and secondly most people who bought my properties were investors and negatively-geared them. Today negative-gearing is not congruent with my business philosophies.

## Negative-gearing rescue package

I have adapted John Burley's Cash Flow 'Wrap' mortgage strategy (which he will explain in Part C of this chapter) and created a sausage machine system that I can replicate over and over again without having to put my cash into any transaction *ever*. This new system enables me to turn clients who are making losses on their investment properties into owners of positive cash flow properties. Here is a breakdown of my most recent transaction.

I managed to change this client's position from a loss of $4,684 a year into positive cash flow of $1,764 a year.

| Client's original position | $ | Comments/details |
|---|---|---|
| Investment property | 80,000 | Original purchase price |
| Original loan amount (including initial set – up costs and linked back to equity in own home) | 90,000 | The initial five-year interest-only period had expired and they had just started paying principal and interest |
| Yearly repayments | 8,193 | Interest rate |
| Yearly rates | 1,200 | 7.80% p.a. |
| Maintenance costs | 1,000 | |
| Management fees | 531 | |
| Total costs | **10,924** | |
| Yearly income (rent) | 6,240 | |
| **Yearly loss** | **4,684** | |

| Client's new position | $ | Comments/details |
|---|---|---|
| New 'Wrap' purchase | 110,000 | Set up as option to buy |
| Option fee | 3,300 | 3% of purchase price |
| New 'Wrap' loan | 106,700 | |
| Income | 10,302 | 9.00% principal and interest x 30 years |
| Management fees | 1,030 | 10% p.a. |
| Rates and maintenance | nil | |
| Yearly repayments | 7,505 | Refinanced the loan at $95,000 interest only at 7.90% p.a. which enabled the client to pay my fees without having to come up with extra cash |

| Yearly profit | 1,767 | 51% ROI |
|---|---|---|
| **New positive position** | **6,451+** | From a loss of $4,684 to a profit of $1,767 |

## My Income

Once you go over the figures below you can see why I am so excited about this Cash Flow 'Wrap' mortgage business. Because I am now a mortgage manager most of the income that usually goes to the bank stays with me. Listed below is the income I earned from this one transaction.

| **Up-front payments** Option fee | **$** 3,300 | **Comments/details** I keep the option fee for finding the purchaser and completing the contracts and advertising, etc. |
|---|---|---|
| **Up-front payments** 1% Brokerage Fee | **$** 2,100 | **Comments/details** I refinanced their home and investment loans totalling $210,000 |
| Commission from bank | 1,470 | Upfront commission of 0.70% |
| Insurance commission | 1,100 | I set up clients with income protection, bad-tenant, building and contents insurance |
| Bank application and processing fees | 650 | I am now a mortgage manager so these fees are paid to my company not to the bank |
| **Total upfront** | **8,620** | |

| Ongoing yearly fees | | |
|---|---|---|
| Management fees | 515 | I have set up an agreement with a property manager to pay me 50% of the management fee for business I introduce to her |
| Trailing commission from the bank | 1,050 | 0.50% loan management fee based on the loan amount of $210,000 |
| **Return in year one** | 10,185 | ROI of infinity |

The benefits of adapting the Cash Flow 'Wrap' mortgage the way I have are as follows:

- Easy to locate properties and investors (they have already bought negatively-geared properties).
- No property transactions.
- No cash in.
- No Consumer Credit Code issues.
- Don't have to worry about asset protection entities and structures.
- Off balance sheet.
- No limit to the number of transactions I can do.
- ROI of infinity.

As you can see, coming at it from a finance perspective certainly adds $$$ to the bottomline.'

Thanks Steve, and keep up the great investing.

# Part C: Cash Flow

## THE CASH FLOW STRATEGY

When I first began investing in real estate, I concentrated on the **Buy and Hold** and the **Quick Cash** strategies. I used the Buy and Hold because I wanted to develop assets for the future and, to be quite frank, I didn't know of any other way to achieve that long-term growth objective. I used the Quick Cash methods because, like many people, I needed the money ASAP!

Starting out, my initial plan was to use the Buy and Hold. My *Niche* consisted of buying properties and holding them as rentals. It didn't take me long to realise, however, after implementing my well thought-out plan, that the Buy and Hold was not for me. I did not like being a landlord for mediocre returns.

I did not enjoy investing my hard-earned cash in properties and leaving it there for at best break-even cash flow. I hated running around like a chicken with it's head chopped off, working for my tenants. I did not like doing repairs and was not very good at it. And I hated paying someone else to do those repairs even more.

I was at my wit's end. I was fed up with landlording and knew that I had to change *my* game. I *did enjoy* doing the deals, but the repairs and tenants were driving me crazy and making me broke.

I took a close look at what I had, what I liked and what I disliked:

✓ I had passion for and knowledge of real estate.
✓ I had access to a great supply of 'potential' properties.
✓ I was enthralled by the concept of long-term cash flow.
✓ I loved doing deals with little or no risk or money on my part.
✗ I did not like *owning* investment properties. I liked controlling them.
✗ I hated being a landlord, fixing and paying for repairs.

What I needed was a way to make the properties generate income without all the work. I learned that I did not really want to *own* the real estate. I just wanted the money. Let me repeat that:

> **I did not want to *own* real estate, I just wanted the money!**

So I applied *Lateral Thinking* to my situation. First of all I thought about why it is that so many people want to own their own home. For an American, owning your own home is the *American Dream*, just like for an Australian owning your own home is the *Australian Dream*. I found that in your country and mine about two-thirds of the population own their own homes. That means that about one-third of the population are the potential target market. And of that one-third approximately 75% would rather own than rent. So why don't they buy a house? Two basic reasons: not enough money for a deposit and/or not good enough credit to get a traditional bank loan. This means that about 25% of the people in your country and mine are locked out of 'the dream' of owning their own home.

I decided to help these people. What I started doing was acquiring properties and then remarketing them to people who could not buy a home in the traditional manner. And although I certainly did not invent this technique, it has created millions of dollars in passive income for me and my family over the last 10 years.

> 'Change is not made without inconvenience, even from worse to better.'
> **SAMUEL JOHNSON**

This **Cash Flow** strategy is often referred to as a **'Wrap'**. It works like this: You acquire a property, then resell it with *Vendor Financing* to a new buyer (obviously, you sell the property for more than you paid for it).

The buyer makes one monthly mortgage payment to the seller. The buyer *owns* the home. They take care of it. They

> 'Life is either a daring adventure or nothing. To keep our faces toward change and behave like free spirits in the presence of fate is strength undefeatable.'
> **HELEN KELLER**

do the maintenance. They pay the rates and insurance (on a pass-through basis to you, contained in the fixed monthly payment).

The seller continues to pay on any underlying loans and makes a profit by maintaining a difference between the underlying loan payment and the new 'Wrapped' loan payment.

This profit is known as the **spread**. In other words, all you do is collect the money and count the profits. You are not a landlord. You are a private bank!

The Cash Flow strategy provides the opportunity to develop a substantial monthly income without the burden of property management. I had modified my *Niche* and was now free from the headaches that accompany property ownership. I could now control the properties, for better cash flow, and resell the investment risks and maintenance responsibilities for the property to the new buyers.

The advantages and disadvantages of the Cash Flow strategy are:

| The advantages | The disadvantages |
|---|---|
| ☑ Immediate contract profit | ☒ Collections |
| ☑ Long-term cash flow | ☒ Short-term negative cash flow potential (due to vacancies or default) |
| ☑ Runs on auto pilot | |
| ☑ Reasonable tax treatment | |
| ☑ No renters | ☒ Take-backs |
| ☑ Nominal repairs | |
| ☑ Few hassles | |
| ☑ Great potential for early retirement | |

Today, I place a large emphasis on the principle of *long-term cash flow*. My company currently controls on average more than 100 properties a year producing average combined monthly positive cash flow in the US mid- five-figure range.

I prefer to acquire the bread-and-butter type of home in 'Lunch Pail Joe' (or 'Norm and Sheila') neighbourhoods. That is, a home priced at least 10–20% below the median price in a middle to lower middle-class neighbourhood. The type of property I invest in can be best described by walking you through some of my and my Australian students' Cash Flow properties.

## CASH FLOW ('WRAP') EXAMPLE 1: N. 68TH AVENUE, PHOENIX AZ

The first property I remarketed on a 'Wrap' was back in 1990. The property is a 105 square metre, 3-bedroom house on a cul-de-sac with 1 ½-bathrooms, a fenced yard and a two-car garage. The property has one unique feature: the back of the property is a triple lot. It is the pie-shaped lot at the back of the cul-de-sac. The house was built in 1978. The living room has a vaulted ceiling and a conversation pit area.

> 'The man who will win success is the man who is markedly different from the others around him. He has new ideas and can visualize fresh approaches to problems. He has the ability – and the will – to think and act on his own, not caring if he is dammed and derided by "the majority" for his nonconformist ideas and actions.'
>
> **J. PAUL GETTY**

I acquired the property as a repo (repossession) from the VA (Veterans Affairs – similar to the Australian Department of Defence) for a purchase price of $47,000 with monthly payments of $451 *(PIRI – Principal, Interest, Rates and Insurance)*. At that time there was no deposit required, just settlement costs. So, it was pretty exciting. My total investment was just $1,025.

The property was in pretty good condition. I switched on the utilities and checked everything out. Everything was OK. The heater and air-conditioner worked, the water heater was fine. (With foreclosures, you will often be unable to turn on power or water. In some cases, you will not even be able to get inside the house.)

I spent $348 for a handyman to paint a living-room wall and the bedrooms. I also re-wallpapered the kitchen.

I remarketed the 68th Avenue house a few weeks (after I had settled) for $63,900 with a deposit of $1,500 and monthly payments of $650. Boy, was that exciting! I knew I was on my way. A contract profit of $16,900, a monthly cash flow of $199 for the next 30 years, and no landlording!

And although to the uninformed $199 might not seem like that much, the **Level Five Active Investor** understands the value of small monthly payments working in their favour; $199 a month for 30 years is $71,640 of passive (positive) Cash Flow!

This $199 a month could in turn be invested each month (if it was not required for living expenses) in a compounding Level Four type of investment and keep growing (at 12% compounding it becomes $695,498 after 30 years!).

Incidentally, the people who bought the house told me that the first two things they were going to do were: tear down the wallpaper and repaint the house! I remember standing there thinking *'Great! There goes $350 flushed down the drain!'*

I learned an important lesson that day: most buyers do not mind doing a few cosmetic changes on their own to their new home. Particularly if they can buy the house for a low deposit. They usually feel that they are getting a better deal if the house requires a little touch-up work.

**Note:** In the US, investment property loans are generally for a period of 30 years. The 'regular' home buyer customarily uses a 30-year loan. Because I like to make things easy for everybody to understand, I generally remarket my properties with the customary owner-occupied 30-year loan. In Australia, I would opt for the customary 25-year loan.

When I am remarketing a property I pass on the interest risk that I have to the new buyer. For example, if I had a 25-year variable interest rate loan I would pass on to the new buyer a 25-year variable interest rate loan (obviously at a higher rate of interest and higher amount to be financed). I would tie their loan rate to whatever index my loan rate was tied to and add my *spread*.

In the US and Australia there are both *fixed* and *variable* principal and interest loans available for investment properties (this means you pay off some of the principal each month). Whenever possible my preference is to go with a fixed rate principal and interest loan. Although this makes my payment a little higher I am not that concerned because I am not limited to rental income. I receive the much higher 'Wrap' income. What this type of loan does do is offer me *security*. I no longer have the risk of interest rates going through the roof. I don't have to worry about the ability of my buyer to make payments on a much higher rate of interest. In addition, each payment provides me with equity build-up (just like my buyer) so that I will always maintain my *paper spread*.

The main difference currently between the US and Australia is the fixed period of time offered on a loan. Just a few years ago Australian lenders would fix the rate of interest on a loan for just a few, to maybe five years. That is all changing; the Australian banking industry has been going through some big changes to remain competitive with other countries' lending practices, particularly with regard to real estate. It is now commonplace for Australian lenders to offer 25-year principal and interest loans with the interest rate for the first 10 years fixed. However, many of my students, those who actually *asked* the lender and could provide either a solid financial statement or a track record, have received loans with fixed rates of interest for 15 to 20 years.

So, whatever loan you have, you pass on to your buyer (with your *spread*). If you have a 10-year fixed interest rate on a 25-year principal and interest loan that is what they get (plus your *spread*). Keep this simple. You do not need to set up some complicated formula that requires a degree in mathematics to figure out. I have found it is best to use basic standard amortisation tables so that everybody involved will understand the transaction.

Again, on the Cash Flow strategy I prefer to fix the rate of interest for as long as possible. I do not like *risk*, so whenever possible I do what I can to eliminate it. By fixing the rate I have one less thing to worry about.

## CASH FLOW EXAMPLE 2: N. 18TH DRIVE, PHOENIX, AZ

I purchased this property in December 1995. It is a normal 'Burley House'. Built in 1971, it is 115 square metre, 3-bedroom, 2-bathroom house. It is in a nice neighbourhood but the house was in need of a little fix-up at the time. It really needed re-carpeting and painting. Following my own Rules I did neither, and remarketed the property in 'as is' condition as a 'minor fixer'.

The purchase price was $68,900 with monthly payments of $490 (PIRI). I took out a 90% loan (we financed 90% of the purchase price) at 7%. My deposit plus settlement costs came to $8,184.

I remarketed the property six days later for $86,900 with

monthly payments of $825. I collected a deposit of $3,725. This gave me a contract profit of $18,000 and a monthly profit of $334; 30 years at $334 a month equals a whopping $120,481 of passive (positive) Cash Flow.

## CREATIVE REAL ESTATE MARKETING

Before we look at more examples of successful transactions, let me just share with you briefly how I remarket properties. Many people think the hard part would be remarketing the properties once acquired. Actually it is just the exact opposite. Remarketing the properties is the easy part. You will spend more time writing and presenting offers than you will remarketing your properties.

I use several low-cost approaches to remarketing. Here in the book we will cover the basic techniques.

I recommend you place ads in the local papers the week before you settle on the property. I have found that I get the most bang for my dollar advertising in my local papers like *The Pennysaver, The Shopper.* They are inexpensive and our target market reads them. You will have similar types of newspapers in your area. I also have good success running ads on the real estate day (usually Saturday or Sunday) in the major newspaper. Beware of the cost though, because major newspapers charge a lot. When you do use them, I recommend you ask for any specials they may have and stick to the real estate day only. In my experience, weekday ads rarely pay for themselves.

The purpose of your ad is to get the phone to ring. At our company it rings… and rings… and rings. It is not uncommon for us to receive an average of 30–50 calls every day requesting information on the properties we have for sale. Let me give you an idea of some of the ads that we run:

---

*By owner, $2,900 deposit, easy qualifying, nice 3-bed, $550 a month. Must sell now. Needs minor fix-up. 555 2121.*

---

*$2,900 deposit, owner financing with super EZ qualifying. Several homes available from $500 a month up. 555 2121.*

---

> *$3,650 total move in. No bank qualifying. Great starter home in a cul-de-sac. 3/2 with family room. Drive by 6405 W. Weldon then call 555 2121.*

We'll often put the low deposit amount in double- or triple-size font, the same thing for the 'easy qualifying' to get a little better pull.

> *Easiest qualifying in town, only $2,900 deposit, nice three-bed with pool, $795 PIRI. Call 555 2121.*

> *Owner will finance, only $3,500 total move in, drive by 7003 West Verde Avenue, low monthly payment 555 2121.*

> *Desperate! Minor fixer, only $2,900 deposit, must sell now. $650 a month, 7340 West Clarendon, 555 2121.*

> *Easy owner financing, only $2,900 deposit, low monthly payments 3-bed/2-bath with pool, needs paint 555 2121.*

## Six key points to Cash Flow ads:

1. Low deposit (down payment).
2. Easy qualifying.
3. Owner financing (*Vendor Financing*).
4. You are desperate, motivated, etc.
5. Minor fixer – most people believe this makes it a better deal.
6. Affordable (low) monthly payment.

Most people are more interested in the monthly payment, and how much it takes to move in, than anything else. The condition of the property, the total price, and the interest rate are secondary. So don't bog your ad down with the price and a bunch of other details (unless required).

Think of it like selling a car. When people buy a car from a dealer they only need to know three things. First, do I like the car? Second, can I come up with the deposit? Third, can I afford the monthly payment? If they can answer 'yes', they drive off in the car. Most people buy a house the same way. Keep it simple. Don't confuse them, help them achieve the Australian Dream of home ownership.

## Signs

Put up signs on and in the property. On the property, I use two types of signs. One is common and the other is unique. In the yard I use the standard metal sign (similar to real estate agents). It says 'For Sale By Owner' with the phone number. I also like to add the 'Low Deposit' and 'Vendor Financing' plates on the bottom. 'Vendor Financing' means that the owner (you) will provide the financing for the buyer to buy the property. You can get these signs at any real estate sign vendor. Check the Yellow Pages.

The other type of sign I use is unique. I designed signs that I tape to the inside of the windows. They're big enough to be seen from the street and say for example:

```
BY OWNER
$2,900 DEPOSIT
EASY QUALIFYING
555 2121
```

These signs are made out of corrugated plastic and I have them in various sizes, always big enough to fill the window. I always put one of these signs in the main front window. The lettering is large basic print, alternating line-by-line from red to blue. These signs really work well. I recommend you make some for yourself.

One last idea concerning signs. Buy yourself some bright fluorescent copy paper to make flyers. I use the same information I use on window signs:

---

**By Owner**
**$2,900 Deposit**
**Easy Qual.**
**555 2121**

---

Use these flyers around the local neighbourhood of the property, especially at major intersections. Keep them very simple. These will attract more attention than one would think.

## Door hangers and mail box stuffers

I will also often hire neighbourhood teenagers to either place flyers in mailboxes or hang flyers on doors. I cover every house in the area.

By getting the signs out, the property will have a tremendous amount of exposure. This is great because I often remarket the properties I own to people who already live in the neighbourhood, who are stuck in the rental trap.

By using the combination of signs I've described you will be able to remarket the properties much faster than by just running ads.

**Note**: Always check council and local ordinances prior to placing signs and flyers around the neighbourhood.

Let me show you one more of my examples before we share some of my Austalian and New Zealand students' examples.

## CASH FLOW EXAMPLE 3: W. SAN MIGUEL AVENUE, PHOENIX, AZ

I acquired this property in May 1998. It is a typical 'Lunch Pail Joe' house. Built in 1958, it is 110 square metre, 3-bedroom, 2-bathroom house. It had a swimming pool which required replastering (responsibility of the new buyer). The inside and exterior had just been painted by the lender.

It was a lender foreclosed property. The purchase price was $58,513 with monthly payments of $431 (PIRI). I took out a 90% loan at 7.2%. My deposit plus settlement costs came to $7,549.

I remarketed the property 16 days later for $74,900 with

monthly payments of $756. I collected a deposit of $3,656. This gave me a contract profit of $16,387 and a monthly profit $324; 30 years at $324 a month equals $116,740 of passive (positive) Cash Flow.

Let's take a look at the first year cash-on-cash return on this property. We do this by dividing our initial investment capital into the first year's income. The initial investment capital was $7,549 divided into $3,656 deposit plus $3,891 received as 12 monthly payments of $324 from the new buyer. This is $7549 divided by $7,547 = 99% first year cash-on-cash return.

A 99% first year cash-on-cash return! Doesn't that look a whole lot better than negative-gearing? In future years we will continue to receive the monthly profit while having received back all of our initial investment capital in a year and a few days.

The above examples were not special deals, or super-fantastic transactions. Actually, out of the hundreds of deals I have done, I selected these for illustration because they are very typical of the type of transactions we do on a day-to-day basis. Certainly, I have some 'Wraps' that make less than $200 a month. I have also done many that generate more than $400 a month.

## AUSTRALIAN AND NEW ZEALAND STUDENT EXAMPLES

Here are several case studies from Australians and New Zealanders who are applying the techniques you have just read about.

### KIWI CASH FLOW EXAMPLE

**Investor: Graeme Fowler from New Zealand.**

Graeme has been a very productive real estate investor over the last few years. A couple of years ago he invested in my real estate investment tape sets (*Secrets of Professional Investors, with Robert Kiyosaki; Blueprint for Success, and Fortunes in Foreclosures*). He put the information to good use.

In 1999 Graeme acquired 11 houses which he resold for Quick Cash. Many were on-sold before he actually bought them. Some had previously been on the market for several years. Using the creative marketing information he learned he was able to resell them within a couple of weeks making $10,000–

$15,000 on each property. Some he renovated and onsold at a larger profit. Graeme says, 'The key to all of them was buying at the right price. Walk away if you can't buy at the price you are wanting to pay.'

As of June 2000, Graeme had acquired an additional 17 properties. Eight of these are Cash Flow properties, with what Graeme calls a 'rent to buy' program. On his Cash Flow properties Graeme creates a contract profit of $10,000–$20,000, making him around $200 a month (for 20 years), in addition to an upfront $2,000 deposit. The other nine were a combination of Quick Cash and long-term Buy and Hold properties.

When acquiring properties, Graeme looks for properties that he can buy for at least $10,000 below 'true' market value. Some are mortgagee sales, some are properties that have simply been on the market for a long time. As Graeme says: 'There are many reasons why people sell well below market price. Generally I get about two out of 10 offers accepted. I never start at my final price either. Sometimes an agent will call after a couple of months to say a previous offer will now be accepted if presented again. I always make sure to contain the contingency clauses that John recommends.'

My congratulations to Graeme for his great successes and for showing all in New Zealand that you can do creative real estate transactions there.

## AUSSIE CASH FLOW EXAMPLE 1: GUILDFORD ROAD, PERTH WA

**Investors: Karen and Russell Dorlandt from Perth.**

We purchased this property as a 'minor fixer' in 1995 for $120,000. It was on the front of an 800 square metre block with a zoning that would allow it to be subdivided into three strata lots.

With high hopes for the future, we set about renovating the house. About $20,000 later we contacted a developer to talk about developing the rear of the block. Our hopes of building another two units were quickly dashed when the builder explained a few home truths about council by-laws. We settled on building one up-market 3-by-2 with a good-sized courtyard for about $100,000. The total cost so far was about $240,000.

Upon completion we had the two properties valued jointly at $265,000. A little ahead, but considering all the effort we put in and the time that had passed, it was little more than a learning experience.

We let the properties out for a joint rental of $1,300 a month. After expenses and vacancies we were breaking even at best.

After attending John Burley's *'Automatic Wealth'* seminar, the thought of being able to generate positive cash flow each month from these properties was very exciting. We immediately did the numbers and figured that it was worth a try.

Because this was our first deal we were a little apprehensive about success. The properties were also a little more up-market than a typical 'Norm and Sheila' residence, so we did not push the terms very high.

We followed two of John's recommendations – offer the property to the existing tenants using an Agreement for Sale and also advertise it in the local paper as 'Low Down, Easy Payments', etc.

Within a week the houses were both sold. One to a tenant and the other through the ad. We couldn't believe it. The tenant who bought the house was so happy not to be renting that she went out and bought some picture hooks so that she could hang up her own things immediately after the contract was signed!

As we were not aware of the 'Wrap' process at the time we renovated the properties, the ROI is not as high as it could have been. In hindsight we would not renovate again.

**Summary:** The combined Sale Price was $293,000 with an interest rate of 7.3% and repayments of $2127 a month. Our interest rate was 6.1% with repayments of $1463 a month. That is a monthly cash flow of $664, a contract profit of $28,000 and an ROI of 32% on our cash in the deal (cash-on-cash return).

Thanks Karen and Russell, keep up the great work.

## AUSSIE CASH FLOW EXAMPLE 2

Investors: Tony Barton and Max Gacitua from Maxton Properties in Melbourne.

We bought the house after finding and pre-qualifying the tenant. A 3-bedroom, 1-bathroom house with en-suite and off-street parking, about five minutes' drive north west of Ballarat in a suburb called Cardigan Village.

The tenant actually *chose* the property as she had lived in Cardigan Village for most of her life and loved the house. We were happy as long as the numbers worked!

Well, the numbers did work. We negotiated the purchase price down to $78,000 (written valuation from the real estate agent of $85,000; on the market for $89,000). The tenant has an option to purchase the house at $87,360. The tenant pays $180 a week, with a $2,000 option fee and a percentage of rent paid as equity into the property. Therefore the tenant can exercise the option to purchase the property, since she will have 20% equity in the property by the end of the eighth year.

The tenant pays council rates, insurance and water rates (as we are carrying the loan), 8% interest only for three years with a 17-year principal and interest loan following (although we have since found a better interest rate). First year cash-on-cash return is 41%. If the tenant exercises the option at end of the eigth year the cash-on-cash return will be 30% per annum.

All in all, both parties are happy with the deal and we will help the tenant qualify for a loan and the $7,000 First Home Owner Grant Scheme payment from the Federal Government!

Max and Tony have 'Wrapped' more than 30 houses in less than 12 months. Great going guys and thanks for your contribution!

## AUSSIE CASH FLOW EXAMPLE 3

**Investor: Melita Hunt from Sydney.**

Melita attended my Boot Camp in November 1999 and, following the 90-day plan, had three houses on her books before Easter! She has moved on from there and was invited back to Boot Camp as a mentor in April 2000. She recounts here some of the things she would not do again from her first deal and shows us how the numbers stack up. Congratulations, Melita, on the beginnings of a dynasty! Melita now has 10 Cash Flow properties.

After attending John's Boot Camp in November 1999, I was determined to get going on the 'Wrap' concept. Returning to Sydney though I got a little distracted by... well, Christmas! And to my shock/horror woke up one day in January with only one month left in the 90-day plan (given out at Boot Camp).

Like a mad tornado I set about catching up and within a couple of weeks had snared the first of several positive Cash Flow deals. I thought I would include the figures of my first deal (my worst deal) to show you the potential even when you are just starting out and really not too confident of what you are doing.

I made a couple of mistakes with this deal, like carpeting (at a cost of $1,200), putting a 20% deposit down and borrowing 80% (instead of 10% and 90%). Those old paradigms would not shift. Despite the errors, the figures still work in this deal.

Following John's advice to *Leverage* my time, I make written offers on properties I have not yet inspected. Then upon acceptance I inspect the property. If it does not meet my criteria, I invoke the Inspection and Approval (contingency) clause of the offer and cancel the agreement.

Thus I did not inspect this property until my offer was accepted. My agent said it was a good buy (a 3-bedroom, 1½-bathroom ex–Housing Commission brick with hardwood house with security screens, fences, carport and shed).

As you will see from the figures, the house was originally for sale at $70,000 and reduced to $65,000. I offered $55,000 and the owners countered with $62,000. I bought it for $57,000 (market value $65,000).

The new buyer pays $170 a week on a lease option basis (rental) and will pay $77,915 for the property if he takes up the option to purchase.

I talked to John and realised that I needed to amend my contract, and thus increase my *spread*, by making my tenant/buyer responsible for all outgoings including rates (tax) and insurance. Live and learn. Have a go!

Thanks Melita. Here are the figures from her 'worst' deal!

| Offer details | $ | Return on investment | $ |
|---|---|---|---|
| Asking price | 65,000 | Weekly rate | 170 |
| Real market value | 65,000 | Monthly rate | 737 |
| Offer price | 57,000 | Deduct PIRI (PITI) (460) | 277 |
| Loan amount | 45,600 | Annual spread (profit) | 3,320 |
| Rates (tax) | 1,106 | Deposit (down payment) recd. | 3,000 |
| Insurance (building and rental) | 400 | 1st monthly payment | 737 |
| Underlying interest rate | 7.40% | 10 months spread | 2,770 |
| Principal and interest (PI) | 334 | **Total** | **6,507** |
| PI, rates and insurance | | | |
| (PIRI or PITI) | 460 | Divide by initial investment | 42% |
| Expenses: | | Deduct deposit and 1st monthly | |
| Deposit (down payment) | 11,400 | payment from initial investment | 11,611 |
| Stamp duty | 1,268 | | |
| Closing costs | 1,580 | Divide into 12 month spread | 29% |
| Miscellaneous | 1,200 | | |
| Total initial investment | **15,348** | | |
| **Buyer information** | | | |
| Agreed purchase price | 77,915 | | |
| Option term | 7 years | | |

## AUSSIE CASH FLOW EXAMPLE 4

**Investors: Paul and Tracey Verschuuren and Mick and Jane Hagarty from Queensland.**

Paul and Tracey, and Mick and Jane are two couples who met at my 'Automatic Wealth' seminar in Brisbane in May '99 and their results as partners have been spectacular since. Here are four of their examples in their words showing various techniques revolving around the 'Wrap' concept.

## 1. Our first 'Wrap'

We bought a 3-bedroom, 1-bathroom, low-set brick home advertised for $65,000, for $50,000 (with 50,000 fleas!). We spent $3,000 in closing costs and $2,500 painting, carpeting and re-guttering the property making our total outlay, $55,500. The property was valued at $74,000 after renovations, and we obtained bank finance for $56,000 with repayments at $430. We then sold the property via a 'Wrap' for

$75,000 with repayments of $735 a month, producing a profit of $305 a month. Since our total outlay was only $55,000, and we obtained bank financing for $56,000, we ended up with *no money tied up in the transaction!* Thus we had a rate of return (ROI) of *infinity!*

## 2. Our second 'Wrap'

We found a house listed for $67,000 in poor condition. The owner was only 23 and wanted to go overseas with his friends. We offered him $48,000, he counter-offered at $55,000 and we settled on $52,000. A handyman painted the outside and half the inside of the house, fixed two large holes in the interior walls, replaced the shower screen, did some tiling in the bathroom and concreted a carport, all for $3,600.

We found an investor who funded the purchase and renovation of the property. Initially, we planned to sell the property using the Quick Cash strategy for $69,000 but ended up using the Cash Flow strategy and 'Wrapping' the property for $80,000. In order to cash-out our initial investor and make this a 'no-money down' deal, we obtained bank finance for $56,000 and borrowed the remaining $7,600 from another investor. After all expenses, this property turns a profit of $350 a month. Again, we accomplished this without having to tie up any of our own money.

## 3. Our rent/buy/'Wrap'

We purchased a very rundown 3-bedroom, 1-bathroom timber house for $42,000 and advertised it as a 'handyman special'. The only interest we had was from a couple on a disability pension who didn't quite qualify to service a loan. In Australia, pensioners who rent a house receive rental assistance from the government of up to $112 a fortnight (in addition to their disability pension). This additional income was enough to qualify them for the loan, if we could somehow sell the house to them whilst they were renting it at the same time.

We ended up selling them the house using a rent/buy for three years. Under the rent/buy they pay $175 a week in rent, of which $50 is consideration towards the purchase price of $58,000. After three years they will have $7,800 equity in the property and a proven ability to repay the loan. At this point either they will obtain bank finance, and cash us out, or we will refinance the property under a 'Wrap'. We make a profit of approximately $260 a month under the rent/buy and will realise a paper profit of approximately $10,000 upon the purchaser refinancing. A win-win transaction for all parties.

## 4. Our first rent/buy

By adapting the Quick Cash method into a rent/buy, we purchased a 3-bedroom, 1-bathroom house for $55,000, spending $4,000 on repairs whilst the house was still under contract, so that our purchaser moved into the house the day that we settled. We then sold the house for $80,000 using the rent/buy method over a four-month period. The purchaser pays $200 a week in rent, which is consideration towards the purchase price of the property.

This purchaser makes enough money to service a loan but does not have a deposit saved and therefore is not able to get bank finance to buy a home. By using the rent/buy we are able to help them save for a deposit by enabling them to build up $200-a-week equity in the property. Being first home buyers, they also qualified for the $7,000 First Home Buyer's Grant from the government. After the four-month period, they will be able to refinance the property with a bank loan, and we will get cashed out with at least $16,000 profit.

This is in effect a delayed Quick Cash, the difference being that we Buy and Hold the property while it is under the rent/buy, we don't get cashed out immediately, but we are able to sell the property at or above market value, rather than at a discount, increasing our profit by up to $10,000.

Thanks guys... spectacular job! Keep up the great investing!

And finally, here is an example and story from Steve McKnight, a very successful young man from Melbourne, who at last count had more than 40 properties on his 'Wrapped' books.

## AUSSIE CASH FLOW EXAMPLE 5

**Investor: Felicity Heffernan From New South Wales**

I first met John during his Sydney Automatic Wealth Seminar in August 1998 and it was here I heard about the 'wrap' cash flow concept.  Soon after the seminar I researched this concept and quickly realised it was going to be my niche.  This lead to me starting my business of wraps.

I live in a suburb in Newcastle, about two hours north of Sydney. My husband Greg and I have two beautiful young children, Laura aged eight and Courtney aged three. Greg works full-time and before starting my wrap business I worked part-time as a loans officer in a bank, as well as looking after my family.

At John's Automatic Wealth Seminar, I can recall shouting NEVER, EVER, EVER NEGATIVE GEAR EVER! I had two such negatively geared properties at the time, over half a million dollars of debts and going backwards by $500 each month. Yes, I was the typical level three screaming pig who did not want to admit to being one. After the seminar I was determined to make immediate changes. Greg and I set up our AIP and my sights were set on attending John's November 1999 boot camp in Phoenix, Arizona.

Greg had already made it clear to me that I could not spend any more money on seminars. So for me to attend boot camp we agreed that I had to do some deals with the knowledge already gained, and use the proceeds from the deals to fund the attendance of boot camp.

## My First Deal

The timing of my first deal could not have been better. I was at a work function with the bank one evening. At the time I had just purchased an investment property in the lower end of the market that had a positive cash flow. My colleagues thought it was quite comical that I would buy in areas that traditionally were not regarded as a good investment. 'There is no capital growth there,'... 'you will never get good quality tenants'...'blah, blah, blah.' I told them my intention was to 'wrap' the property and I went to great length to explain the concept. Most thought it sounded a good idea but something that could not be done.

Later that evening I was approached by one of my colleagues. He asked if I could explain the concept to him again. After doing so, he wanted to know if I would be prepared to fund his wife and he into the property. I agreed and we sketched out the terms and condition on a napkin and on the back of a bar coaster.

While I did not have a formal contract, I allowed my colleague to move into the property (something I would not have done without knowing him so well). I spoke to my local solicitor who said that he had done a similar contract called a terms contract back in the 1970s but was bemused as to why I would want this style of contract. I did not get the contract I wanted. However, my new buyer and I were happy with our original terms and conditions.

This was my first deal and the ticket to boot camp. I wanted to learn more and so far everything I had learnt at the seminars I was able to implement and do.

My husband's reaction was amazement - he could not believe someone was willing to pay extra to own their own home. Our research later discovered there were many people who found it impossible to get a traditional bank loan because they had impaired credit or an insufficient deposit to meet the bank's lending criteria. They were just looking for the opportunity to own their own home.

This table shows the numbers on my first deal:

| | |
|---|---|
| Purchase price for me | $133,000 |
| Purchase price for purchaser | $150,000 |
| Closing costs | $7,000 |
| Loan - 100% purchase price plus costs | $140,000 |
| My loan payment per month | $977 |
| Purchasers contract payment | $1260 |
| Created a monthly cash flow | $282 |

## How My Business Does Deals

My company locates and negotiates the purchase of a house and arranges the sale of it to a 'purchasing tenant' using an instalment sales contract. Property contracts are 'exchanged' and title transfers to the 'purchasing tenant' after they have made the last repayment.

We do not use any of our own finance or equity to purchase a house.

Rather, we use 'money partners' (investors) who qualify for bank loans. Under our direction they raise finance on the house we have selected for a 'purchasing tenant' and this loan becomes the underlying loan. We organise the sale of the house to the 'purchasing tenant' utilising the instalment sale contract. The 'purchasing tenant' pays instalments every month based on the price we sell the house to them and at an interest rate higher than the one paid by our money partner. We usually fix our loans for five years and pass the same terms and conditions on to the 'purchasing tenant' but always at a higher margin.

The 'purchasing tenant' is responsible for all outgoings, including such expenses as insurance, utilities and council rates. They are also responsible for all repairs and maintenance on the property.

## Why It Works For My Purchasing Tenant

Purchasing tenants are usually people who don't meet the traditional bank criteria for credit. They may be slow payers, previously bankrupt, self employed contractors whose income is irregular, or people unable to raise a deposit for a traditional bank loan.

Our criteria is that prospective clients must be working and have good current and previous rental references (this is paramount). So far I have not found these people to be big risks. I also ask for their credit report. Most people I deal with are hardworking Australians who want an opportunity to own their own home.

## Setting Up The Business

The essential but tedious part was building a good business team with people who shared my vision on wraps. The analogy is like a football team - when someone gets injured and cannot perform you have to replace them. We certainly had to replace a lot of injured professionals! The following professionals are considered essential:

- Solicitor - for drawing contracts and conveyance of properties
- Accountant - for structuring transactions correctly
- Insurance Broker - for properly insuring properties
- Mortgage Broker - for writing underlying finance
- Real Estate Agent - for finding suitable properties

We found a great mortgage broker who understood the concept really well and convinced a bank that it would be good solid business for them.

A real estate agent was located who was so keen to work with us that he shows our purchasing tenants through the house.

When we started the business we were very fortunate to find a purchaser that was desperate to own his own home. He was a single dad, renting his home and was sick of moving every 12 months. His motivation was so strong he demonstrated to his solicitor that wraps was a good thing. So we started sending all our new purchasers to that solicitor.

We basically established a business team willing to work with us and the system that we learnt from John.

The next part was to find good purchasing tenants. These were found mainly through small advertisements in the local newspaper real estate columns.

An example of an advertisement we use in the local paper is:

> **Owner Finance**
> **3 Bedroom Home, (Suburb)**
> **Easy Qualifying**
> **Deposit $3,500**
> **Repayments $200 p/w**
> **Phone: 4999 9999**

## Benefits For Me

I liked the idea that I could run this business from home and still be with my children. I have a message bank set up on my office phone and I have a mobile phone when I am out 'in the field.'

Sets up costs are relatively low for a business like this and I am able to use banking skills developed over 20 years.

## Hurdles

The largest hurdle was finding and building a good business team. Many professionals told me it could not be done, it was illegal, it would contravene the credit code and more!

We found solicitors that would not advise our purchasers on the contract, banks that did not want to lend a newly formed company structure with no trading figures, and real estate agents that thought what we were doing was illegal, and felt they may be tainted by having an association with us. We also had the New South Wales Department of Fair Trading breathing down our necks because somebody did not like our advertising.

We call all of these people S.P.O.s 'Sales Prevention Officers'.

## What Really Motivates Me

I like the money, however it is a little bit more than that. So many purchasing tenants are enormously grateful for the opportunity to own their own home and build equity, an opportunity the traditional banking market has not provided them.

> 'If you want to succeed in the world you must make your own opportunities as you go on. The man who waits for some seventh wave to toss him on dry land will find that the seventh wave is a long time coming.'
> **JOHN B. GOUGH**

Big hugs, tears and much appreciation are common when I hand over the keys to a house, often someone's first home and something they never dreamed they would achieve.

## A Recent Example

We purchased a 2/3 bedroom home (two bedrooms and a sunroom) with one bathroom, garage and carport on a traditional quarter acre block in the coalfields area of Newcastle. We sold the property to a first home buyer who used the Federal Government's first home owners grant as deposit for the home. We sold the house before we owned it.

The numbers for this deal were:

| | |
|---|---|
| Purchase price for me | $63,500 |
| Purchase price for purchaser | $82,500 |
| Cash in the deal | $10,160 |
| Deposit (First Home Buyers Grant) | $7,000 |
| Purchaser's weekly payment | $141.45 |
| Monthly cash flow | $223.84 |
| Cash on cash return | 95.34% |

Today I am involved with a business where we have over 30 property wrap transactions completed, with more transactions being completed every week, and using none of our money for the deals.

A big thank you to John for sharing this fantastic information.

Well done Felicity on your success and thank you for your contribution.

## CASH FLOW APPEAL

The reason I love the Cash Flow strategy so much is that it is quick and easy to execute, relatively trouble-free and provides substantial long-term passive income. The Cash Flow strategy best takes care of one of the biggest problems with money: our tendency to *spend* it.

Have you ever noticed that no matter how much money you make a month you always find a place for it to go? And what happens when you receive a windfall? Doesn't it just seem to evaporate? It doesn't matter whether it is $1,000, $10,000 or $100,000. It all gets spent.

For most people, the tendency to spend surplus cash is the major drawback with the Quick Cash and the Buy and Hold strategies. You have to keep going and repeating the transactions over and over again, because invariably you will spend the proceeds of each transaction on basic and extravagant living.

> 'Most people associate having wealth with having cash. True wealth is not cash! True wealth is *cash flow*! The best way to create true wealth is to control assets that are structured to create long-term cash flow.'
>
> **JOHN R. BURLEY**

Every time you do a deal you have to do another one to replace the money you just spent. And what happens if you hit a cold streak or get burned out? The money you worked so hard for will soon be spent and you will be begging your boss for your old job back.

This is why I like the Cash Flow or 'Wraps' strategy so much. 'Wraps' give me the opportunity to control all or part of every deal, not just control it to flip it onto someone else. I control the *asset*. It's mine. That is what *true wealth* is: controlling assets that other people then pay you to own themselves. This is how you gain financial independence, by controlling the asset over the long run and not just making a fee or a few thousand dollars for turning or flipping it to someone else to make *them* wealthy.

## SO LET'S GET WEALTHY!

As a **Level Five Active Investor** you can accelerate the process of becoming wealthy. I would like to help you get to where you have enough passive income each month for you to be able to quit your job. How much income is that? Do you need $2,000, $3,000, $5,000? Maybe you need $10,000 a month?

Let's shoot for $10,000 a month. I am not talking *some* months. I am talking *every* month. Just like clockwork. No landlording. No tenants. Just Cash Flow. Lots of it. Enough to live on for the rest of your life.

> 'Happy are those who dream dreams and are ready to pay the price to make them come true.'
> **LEON J. SUENENS**

> 'The conditions of conquest are always easy. We have but to toil awhile, endure awhile, believe always, and never turn back.'
> **SENECA**

At $250 a month, how many deals would you have to do to be able to tell your boss goodbye forever? How many do you need? Is it five deals, 10 deals, 20 deals or 50 deals? Several hundred dollars from each property each month adds up fast to substantial Cash Flow. Do the numbers. Work it out.

That is what I do. Lots and lots of little deals. As I said before, currently my properties produce positive Cash Flow each month in the US mid-five-figure range. Could you live on that? I would think so.

Well then, get to it! Stop playing *catch up*. Stop trying to make *just enough* to pay the bills. Play *leap-frog*. Make enough money on a Quick Cash transaction or two to leap past your short-term cash problems, or if you can afford to begin developing Cash Flow strategies from the outset, go for that and say goodbye to your money worries forever.

Whatever you do, you need to think long-term. Figure out what you have to do to handle your money situation once and for all. Develop your *Plan*, set your *Strategy*, find your *Niche,* and take *Action*.

## THE TWO PHASES OF CREATING WEALTH

**Phase 1** of creating wealth is the *work* phase. There is a lot of it and some of it will be hard.

You need to find and cultivate money sources (investors). You need to locate the properties. You need to create the loans (debt instruments) and remarket the properties. That requires work. It may take you six months or six years. Either way you can do it. There are people all over the world making this work right now. And I'll bet that it isn't anywhere near as difficult as the work you do right now or as exhausting as the idea of being a slave to a regular job until you are 65!

You are essentially no different from me when it comes to real estate investing. You are just a few years behind on your investment time-line. The principle of *Lag* has not had a chance to kick in yet. But it will, and when it does... look out! For it brings with it *Automatic* Financial Freedom!

> 'There is no failure except in no longer trying.'
> **ELBERT HUBBARD**

> 'The use we make of our fortune determines as to its sufficiency. A little is enough if used wisely, and too much if expended foolishly.'
> **CHRISTIAN BOVEE**

> 'One of these days is none of these days.'
> **ENGLISH PROVERB**

**Phase 2** of creating wealth is all about Cash Flow. **Cash Flow creates** *Automatic* **Financial Freedom.**

Cash Flow, not *cash* is the best source of wealth creation. When you are able to *retain* the Cash Flow from your deals, then you are well on your way to becoming wealthy. When you start *owning the Cash Flow* from properties, rather than *selling properties for cash*, you have begun to move into phase 2 of wealth creation: true **Financial Independence**.

Do enough deals and eventually the Cash Flow from your efforts will provide that $10,000 a month you wanted. You will have produced the Cash Flow to sustain yourself long-term. You will have the freedom to do what you want to do, when you want to do it, where you want to do it, with whom you want to do it, without any regard to the cost. That is true Financial Independence.

Find and develop your *Niche* for long-term passive Cash Flow. I recommend that you start now. Take a few minutes to *write down* what it is that you are looking for. What do you need? What do you want? The answers to these questions will tell you what your investment strategy should be.

Always remember that it is *Your Game*. You are in charge. You decide. What is your strategy going to be?

| *Buy and Hold?* | *Quick Cash?* | *Cash Flow?* |
|---|---|---|
| **The choice is up to you.** | **You are responsible.** | **Make it happen.** |

(For further information on my financial and real estate investment seminars in Australia/New Zealand and my 'Advanced Investing Boot Camp', contact Pow Wow Events International on 1300 550 240; in Sydney on (612) 9923 1699; through the Internet at www.powwowevents.com.au.)

---

## CHAPTER 26 ACTION STEPS REVIEW

1. Determine whether real estate investing is for you. If it is, determine your starting *Niche*. Determine your *Strategy* within that *Niche*!
2. Apply the information outlined in this chapter and start making *written* offers.

## CHAPTER 27

# 72 secret investments of the rich offering 20–100%+ returns

'You all have powers you never dreamed of. You can do
things you never thought you could do. There are no
limitations in what you can do except the limitations in your
own mind as to what you cannot do. Don't think you
cannot. Think you can.'

DAVID P. KINGSLEY

In this chapter I am introducing you to 72 different ways to
make 20–100%+ returns on money – even if *you* do not
have any money! And these investment opportunities are not
just limited to real estate, shares and other traditional
investment products. The examples I cite are all sophisticated
investment vehicles used successfully by the Level Five and
Level Six Investors of the world. Most people are totally
unaware that these non-traditional, low-risk, high-yielding
investment opportunities even exist!

**Note:** These investment opportunities are the ones that I have
discovered and am familiar with in the United States. And while

'Thinking leads a man to knowledge. He may see and hear, and read and learn whatever he pleases, and as much as he pleases; he will never know anything of it, except as he has thought it over... By thinking he has made it the property of his own mind.'

**JOHANN PESTALOZZI**

there are unique opportunities available in Australia that are not available in the US, there are also unique opportunities available in the United States that may not be available in Australia. Don't be discouraged by this, as every country has its own unique investment opportunities; you just need to be willing and able to find them.

Also remember that the Level Three Investors of the world will almost always tell you that 'It can't be done' or 'We don't do that here.' And you know that they are right! *They* can't do it... anywhere! But *you* can!

So how do you locate investment opportunities in Australia? Just as you do in any country! Here are some ideas.

- Read the financial press everyday, for example:

    Newspapers –

    *The Australian Financial Review*
    (weekday and weekend editions)
    *The Australian*
    *The Sydney Morning Herald*
    *The Age*
    *The Courier Mail*, etc.

    Magazines –

    *My Money*
    *Money*
    *Personal Investor*
    *Business Review Weekly (BRW)*
    *The Bulletin*
    *Dynamic Small Business*
    *Australian Business Money Making Opportunities*
    *Australian Property Investor*
    *Mortgage Magazine*
    *Shares*

- Scour the Internet for ideas. Search for specific investments that sound interesting to you.
- Mix with people who have similar financial goals to you. Join investor groups. The more you expand your network, the

more you will discover.

- Use an accountant and a lawyer who share your vision and have contacts and ideas. Use their network.

Many of my Australian students have adapted my investment opportunities for local conditions. They have also invested, after their research, in the United States, usually using a Nevada C-Corporation and limited partnerships as their preferred entity structures for managing and holding their investments.

This chapter is not designed to be an in-depth analysis of these opportunities. It is designed to expose you to a multitude of ways to produce **Level Five Active Investor rates of return** (20–100%+ a year). This chapter is designed to be introductory in nature.

> '...you will find that while expanding the intellect and the muscles, your enlarged experience will enable you every day to accumulate more and more principal, which will increase itself by interest and otherwise, until you arrive at a state of independence.'
>
> **P.T. BARNUM**

(For further information on how you can attend my 'Advanced Investing' seminars, covering this material in greater detail, you are welcome to contact Pow Wow Events International on 1300 550 240 or in Sydney on (612) 9662 8488, or through the Internet at www.powwowevents.com.au.)

---

**Level Five Active Investors** understand that there are two basic types of investment: those in which you *own* and those in which you *loan*. The *owning* types of investments (e.g. real estate, shares in a company, etc.) are known as **equity** investments. The *loaning* types of investments (e.g. bonds, loans, etc.) are known as **debt-based** investments.

---

With **equity** investments your profits are made in two primary ways: **appreciation** and **cash flow**. For example, a piece of investment real estate should appreciate (go up in value) while at the same time producing income.

With **debt-based** investments your profits are also made in two primary ways: **interest paid** and **discount at purchase**.

For example, you purchase a $1,000 bond that pays 7% interest. That is the interest paid. To increase your yield you would have to receive a discount at purchase. This would occur if you could purchase the same $1,000 bond for $800. Now your **return on investment (ROI)** would increase.

Here is my list of 72 highly profitable investments used by **Level Five Active Investors** and **Level Six Capitalist Investors** throughout the world.

## HIGHLY PROFITABLE EQUITY INVESTMENTS

- Auctions – buying and selling of personal property and real estate
- **Buy and Hold** real estate
- **Quick Cash** real estate
- **Cash Flow** real estate
- Foreclosure real estate
- Lease purchase (all property)
- Lease options (all property)
- Options (real estate)
- Commodities trading
- Futures contracts
- Hedge funds
- Index funds
- Leaps (securities markets)
- Managed funds
- Mobile homes
- Options (securities – puts, calls and warrants)
- Initial public offerings (IPOs) and pre-initial public offerings
- Short selling (inverse equity investing in securities markets)
- Share trading

When most people think of high rates of return they think of equity investments. Unknown to most people are more than 50 debt-based investments that can pay you 20–100%+ returns. The following list of debt-based investments is a small sample compiled from my own research and from public domain information available on the Internet.

## HIGHLY PROFITABLE DEBT-BASED INVESTMENTS

### Business-Based Debt Instruments
- Aeroplane/helicopter leases
- Bankruptcy receivables and reorganisation plans
- Commercial deficiency portfolios
- Commercial invoices (factoring)
- Commercial inventory (receivables)
- Commercial judgments
- Commercial leases
- Commissions
- Contracts
- Equipment leases
- Letters of credit
- Partnership agreements
- Property leases
- Purchase orders
- Royalties
- Sports contracts

### Collateral-Based Debt Instruments
- Aeroplane/helicopter notes
- Automobile notes
- Business notes
- Collectibles notes
- Equipment notes
- Mobile home notes
- Real estate mortgage/deed of trust notes
- Recreational vehicle and business vehicle notes
- Tax liens/certificates
- Vendor carry-back paper
- Warehouse inventory lines

## Consumer-Based Debt Instruments
- Consumer deficiency portfolios
- Consumer receivables
- Corporate retirement plans
- Credit card debt/charge-offs
- Inheritances
- Prizes and awards
- Probates
- Retail instalment contracts
- Time-share memberships
- Trust advances
- Unsecured non-performing debt

## Contingency-Based Debt Instruments
- Commercial judgments
- Consumer judgments
- Franchise fees
- Licence fees
- Royalty payments

## Government-Based Debt Instruments
- Farm production flexibility contracts
- Lottery winnings
- Military retirement and disability pensions
- Tax refunds
- Voluntary separation incentives

## Insurance-Based Debt Instruments
- Annuities
- Whole-of-life insurance policy trading
- Funeral purchase assignments
- Structured settlements
- Viatical settlements
- Workers' compensation awards

## SUMMARY

The above listed debt-based investments constitute a market of more than one trillion dollars annually. Right now, in the US, Australia, and throughout the world, people are conducting transactions with these instruments. These investment opportunities are little known to the general public. However, they are the 'bread and butter' of the Level Five and Level Six investors. In Australia, Investors have found their own *Niche* of debt instruments as well as looking globally for even more opportunities.

> 'First in little things, then in greater, then in greater still.'
> **JAMES ALLEN**

I personally know several individuals who have made millions from such investments. In some cases, tens of millions. And with a few, hundreds of millions of dollars from these types of investment vehicles. The opportunities are limitless. Follow *The Nine Generalised Principles*. Do your *Market Research* and get into *The Game*. Move forward and get a 'feel' for the market and a 'sense' of your place within it. Carve out a *Niche* for yourself in one or more of these areas and have fun.

---

## CHAPTER 27 ACTION STEPS REVIEW

1. Determine which areas of **Level Five Active Investing**, if any, are of most interest to you.
2. Conduct *Market Research* to determine the best opportunity available for you, at this time.
3. Get into *The Game* and carve out a *Niche* for yourself.

## CHAPTER 28

# Business and investment structures – the tax reduction and asset protection secrets of the rich

'Without a doubt corporations are one of the great secrets of the wealthy. They provide protection, privacy, and the greatest tax shelter possible.'

JOHN R. BURLEY

My sincere thanks to my good friend and mentor Bruce Whiting, chartered accountant and managing partner of MGI Wamstekers, for providing this invaluable information for the Australian reader.

In this chapter you will learn why and how Level Five Business Owners and Investors organise their businesses and investment assets into different entities. Deciding upon the right structure today, perhaps *before* you have created significant wealth, will save you much time, money and effort later on. Spend some time planning your entity structures now and you can avoid having to seek assistance from expensive accountants and lawyers to unravel a maze of business assets and investments not properly structured for tax, asset protection and estate planning purposes.

First we will cover the basics and then show you how you can structure your assets so you can minimise your taxes. I will provide you with enough information to grasp these basics and assist you in making an informed decision on the appropriate structure(s) for you.

**Note**: This subject is not a precise science and any structure decided upon is a compromise based on the relative advantages and disadvantages of each possible structure.

After the basics I will give you my tips to determine the best structure available to:
• legally reduce your taxes;
• protect your assets;
• assist with estate planning.

## TYPES OF STRUCTURES

There are four basic ways to do business or invest in Australia.

### SOLE TRADER (OR INDIVIDUAL)

In essence, as a **sole trader** you and the business or investments are one and the same entity. You are personally liable for the actions of the business entity and the consequences of doing business. This responsibility includes all debts and liabilities. You are offered neither protection nor privacy. As a sole trader, you are taxed at personal tax rates.

The advantages of being a sole trader or investing as an individual include the following:
• It is a simple way to operate.
• Capital gains tax concessions are greatest for individuals.
• There are no costs of establishment. You simply start trading.

The disadvantages of being a sole trader or investing as an individual include the following:
• Lack of flexibility to shelter income away from yourself. Top personal tax rates are 47% plus Medicare levy and if you enter the top tax bracket there is little you can do to reduce your taxes.

- No asset protection. All your assets are exposed to creditors in the event you cannot pay your debts or you are sued. This is not the most comforting situation if you want to sleep well at night.
- Businesses or consumers may not take you seriously. When marketing your business, you will probably not be viewed as a serious player if you are a sole trader.
- No succession. On death, unless you have organised estate planning, the business ceases. It does not run in perpetuity.

There is a common misconception that the registration of a business name offers additional status or protection for a sole trader or individual. It does not. A registered business name simply allows the sole trader or individual to trade in a name other than his or her own. And it offers some degree of intellectual property ownership of the registered name. That is all, nothing more.

## PARTNERSHIP

When you enter into business or acquire investments with another person or persons, you are acting as a **partnership**. Legally, partnerships are not treated as separate legal entities. Hence, each of the partners are jointly and severally liable for any and all of the actions of their business partners. This means that if one of your partners enters into a commitment, which the partnership cannot honour or repay, you and your other partners are equally responsible for that commitment. If none of your partners can afford to repay the commitment, then you may have to pay the entire debt on your own.

From a tax point of view, partnerships are deemed as separate entities. They have their own tax file number and a separate tax return is lodged for each partnership. Partnerships themselves do not pay tax. Rather, the taxable profit is split between the partners and disclosed in the partnership tax return. Each partner then discloses his or her profit share in his or her personal tax return. This means that partners pay tax on partnership profits at personal tax rates, making a partnership a less than ideal structure in most situations.

Every Australian state has enacted partnership legislation,

which defines the rights and duties of partners of a partnership, in the absence of any contract or agreement prepared by the partners. Five states also have enacted laws, which allow *limited liability partnerships*. These are taxed on the same basis as companies.

You will find that certain businesses, such as accountancy, architectural, legal or medical firms, where a group of accredited professionals operate under the one roof, are required by law to conduct their primary business – the provision of their professional services – as a partnership. This does not mean however, that for taxation purposes they can not structure other parts of their business (e.g. provision through a separate structure of administrative services, equipment or office leases).

The advantages and disadvantages of a partnership are very similar to those of a sole trader and an individual. The advantages of a partnership include the following:

- It is a simple way to operate.
- A partnership enables income splitting.
- If capital gains flow from the partnership to the individual's personal tax return, then those capital gains will be treated concessionally for tax purposes.
- There are no establishment costs. You simply start trading.

The disadvantages of being a partnership include the following:
- Lack of flexibility to shelter income away from yourself. Top personal tax rates are 47% plus Medicare levy and if you enter the top tax bracket there is little you can do to reduce your taxes.
- No asset protection. All your assets are exposed to creditors in the event you cannot pay your debts or you are sued.
- Businesses or consumers may not take you as seriously, although it is usual for professional firms such as accountants and lawyers to trade as partnerships.
- The removal, retirement or death of a partner can have serious capital gains tax implications for the remaining partners.

## COMPANIES

A **company** is certainly the most popular form of business structure. Companies have a constitution, which determines how they operate. They also have directors and other officers who are responsible for controlling and administering the company, and shareholders who own the company. The Australian Securities and Investments Commission (ASIC) currently has full responsibility under the *Corporations* Law to govern companies.

A company is a separate legal entity, both at law and for tax purposes. The most common type of company is a private company with limited liability (Pty Ltd), and my comments in this chapter refer to this type of company. There are other types of companies such as public companies, companies limited by guarantee, co-operatives and unlimited liability companies, which have specific purposes that we will not address here.

Companies lodge their own tax returns and pay tax at the company tax rate. Shareholders receive profits from companies by way of dividends. Where the company has paid company tax, dividends paid can be 'fully franked', which means the shareholder will receive a tax credit at the company tax rate for the tax paid by the company (at a rate of 30% from 1 July 2001). This avoids double-taxing of company profits. If shareholders are on higher tax rates than the company tax rate, they will pay the difference on their tax returns (e.g. 18.5% for the top tax bracket including Medicare levy). Conversely, as a result of recent tax law changes, if you are on a lower tax rate than the company tax rate, you will receive a refund for that 'overpaid' amount (tax credits) when you lodge your personal tax return.

Because companies are separate legal entities, shareholders are offered a high degree of asset protection. If a company is sued or there are creditors who cannot be repaid, the shareholders are not responsible to make good any shortfall of company assets except to the extent of any outstanding payments due on shares. However, directors be warned! There are some situations where a director may be held personally liable for outstanding debts such as:

- where a director incurs debts in a company and reasonably knew the company could not repay them;
- where the director continues to trade the company while the company is insolvent;

- where some tax debts are not repaid, particularly where they represent tax deducted by the company on behalf of employees (PAYG withholding) or reportable payments;
- where the director is held to have acted fraudulently or with gross negligence such that ASIC will be able to 'pierce the corporate veil' and hold the director(s) personally liable for their actions as directors of the company (note that the legal proceedings against Alan Bond as director of Bell Resources fell into the category of this still rather 'grey' area).

> 'Day in and day out, your tax accountant can make or lose you more money than any single person in your life, with the possible exception of your kids.'
>
> **HARVEY MACKAY**

It is a good idea, before you incorporate a company, to discuss these issues in some detail with your lawyer or accountant. There are various strategies available to reduce your exposure, such as establishing a sole director company, hence limiting the personal liability risk for debts to one person.

The advantages of companies include the following:
- There is a high degree of asset protection compared with other structures.
- Succession. Companies continue until they are wound up, so are not dependent on the longevity of particular directors or shareholders.
- Profits are taxed at the company tax rate, which is significantly less than the highest personal tax rate.
- Commercially, customers, suppliers and financiers view a company as a more professional organisation.
- They offer a wider range of superannuation opportunities for working directors.

The disadvantages of companies include the following:
- Establishment costs. Companies must be incorporated under the *Corporations Law*, which results in payment of incorporation and annual fees. It is also always prudent to seek professional advice before incorporation, so there will be additional fees for that advice.

- There are obligations under *Corporations Law* to maintain proper books and records, and lodge certain documents with ASIC from time to time.
- Directors have added responsibilities under *Corporations Law* and case law precedents to act in diligent and honest manners. They have higher duties of care and degrees of responsibility attached to their positions as company directors than private citizens do.
- Companies are generally more complex to operate than a sole trader, individual or partnership.

## TRUSTS

A **trust** is one of the least understood and most misused entities. A trust has a trustee and it has beneficiaries. The trustee has various equitable obligations, holds assets on behalf of (or in trust for) the beneficiaries, and deals with the trust assets in accordance with the trust deed.

A trust is not a separate legal entity at law, although like a partnership it must lodge its own tax return for tax purposes. A trust does not pay tax. Rather the beneficiaries include income or capital distributions from the trust in their personal tax return. However, there are some political rumblings suggesting the possibility of taxing trusts (other than fixed trusts) along the same lines as companies and thus will be subject to a tax rate of 30%. If this occurs, trust distributions would be treated in a similar way to company dividends.

The trustee is personally liable for the actions it undertakes on behalf of the beneficiaries, although trust deeds usually allow the trustee to use the assets of the trust with a fairly flexible level of discretion to meet those undertakings. Most trustees, particularly where a business trades as a trust, are also companies so they can take advantage of asset protection afforded by a company structure.

There are a variety of trusts, each with a different purpose. Here are the common types:

- **Family (or discretionary) trust.** The trustee has discretion to allocate income and capital among beneficiaries in any way it considers appropriate. This is a very common form of trust as it allows families great flexibility to distribute income and assets for tax purposes, the assets in a trust remain intact in the event of the death of a beneficiary (so a trust is good for estate planning), and using a company as trustee provides asset protection. A family trust is best used where only one family group is involved.
- **Unit trust.** Beneficiaries in this case hold a set number of units and the trustee must distribute income and capital in accordance with the number of units held, in much the same way as a company distributes profits to shareholders. Most managed funds operate in this way – when you invest your money you become a unit-holder. Unit trusts are also popular where different parties want to own a defined share in real estate or a particular business.
- **Hybrid trust.** An unusual trust, being a combination of a family trust and a unit trust.
- **Testamentary trust.** Created by will, not deed, a testamentary trust comes into being when the person who makes the will dies. It provides concessional tax treatment for children under 18 who are entitled to the tax-free threshold on distributions. A useful estate-planning tool.

I will now mainly be referring to **family trusts** when discussing trusts. The advantages of trusts include the following:
- Flexibility to distribute income and capital to any beneficiary. This means you can make trust distributions to a beneficiary who has a lower personal tax rate and thus reduce overall levels of tax.
- As you control but not own trust assets, in the event you are sued personally, creditors may not be able to claim those trust assets.
- There is a high degree of asset protection if the trustee itself is a company.
- Succession. Trusts continue for up to 80 years or until they are dissolved, so they are not dependant on the longevity of particular trustees or beneficiaries.

- Capital gains can be distributed to individuals, hence taking advantage of the capital gains tax discount available.

The disadvantages of trusts include the following:
- Establishment costs. Trust deeds must be prepared by lawyers, so fees will be payable. It is prudent also to seek professional tax advice before establishing a trust, so there are those additional fees as well.
- Obligations and responsibilities apply to trustee company directors, as mentioned in the disadvantages of companies.
- Trusts are not well understood and are more complex to operate than a sole trader, individual or partnership.
- The Australian Tax Office has historically not viewed trusts favourably and tax laws surrounding trusts are continually being reviewed and tightened.

## OTHER STRUCTURES

In addition to all these types of entities there are also *joint ventures, limited liability partnerships, incorporated associations, superannuation funds* and a few others. These have special uses and other than superannuation funds, which I have already covered in Chapter 16, are not too common. Your accountant or lawyer should be able to assist you if you think you require something along these lines.

## TAXATION RATES

Now that I have described the main types of structures, here are the tax rates for each of the above entities.
- Sole Trader (individual)

| Taxable Income | Tax |
|---|---|
| $0–$6,000 | 0% |
| $6,001–$20,000 | 17% |
| $20,001–$50,000 | 30% |
| $50,001–$60,000 | 42% |
| $60,000+ | 47% |

'Maybe death and taxes are inevitable, but death doesn't get worse every time Congress meets.'
**JOAN I. WELSH**

In addition to this tax, there is a Medicare levy equal to 1.5% of taxable income. Depending on your situation, you may also be entitled to personal rebates.

- Partnership. As indicated, while partnerships must prepare tax returns, the individual partners are taxed at their individual tax rates.
- Companies. Private and public companies are taxed at:
  For the year ending 30 June 2001                                    34%
  For the year ending 30 June 2002 and onwards                        30%
- Trusts. As indicated above, while trusts must prepare tax returns, the beneficiaries are taxed on their trust distributions at their individual tax rates.

## SELECTING THE RIGHT STRUCTURE

Congratulations! You now have an understanding of the types of structures suitable for business and investing, their advantages and disadvantages, as well as their tax rates. Now comes the tricky bit. Selecting the most suitable one for you!

The key to designing the right structure is to legally organise your financial affairs so you can:

1. derive income from businesses and investments and invest that income after paying tax at no more than the entity tax rate;
2. pay personal tax on the income you need to live on and shelter the 'excess' income in a structure that has a lower tax rate than your personal tax rate;
3. keep your investments and other assets away from potential creditors or litigants;
4. develop estate and succession planning opportunities.

The most suitable structure depends on what your current financial position is and, after reading the past 27 chapters, where you are heading. Here are the questions you need to ask yourself:

- Am I self-employed?
- Am I a business owner?
- What are my investments and what are they worth today?
- What investments will I acquire over the next five, 10 or 20 years?
- What is my *Niche*, and therefore what will I be investing in over the coming years?
- Do I need asset protection?

- What is my succession plan?
- Have I considered estate planning?

Many of these questions cannot be answered with absolute certainty, but you need to think about the *possibilities* before deciding on a structure that is suitable for you. Think about these possibilities for a few minutes before moving on to the next part of this chapter.

OK? Now you have pondered your future, I have set out below various scenarios and the structure that may be suitable in each case.

> 'Anyone may so arrange his affairs that his taxes shall be as low as possible. He is not bound to choose that pattern which best pays the Treasury. Everyone does it, rich and poor alike, and all do right; for nobody owes any public duty to pay more than the law demands.'
>
> **JUDGE LEARNED HAND**
> **(US SUPREME COURT JUSTICE)**

## WHICH SCENARIO BEST DESCRIBES YOU?

1. *I am a salary and wage earner who has just started an AIP with no investments or a small number of investments.* At this stage, it is more cost-effective for you to remain as an individual taxpayer. While you may be earning more than $50,000 a year and therefore paying more than the company rate of tax, unless you are earning significant sums from your investments (say $30,000), the costs and complexity of the different structures will probably outweigh the current benefits.

2. *We are married. One of us is a full-time salary and wage earner. We have just started an AIP with no investments or a small number of investments.* In this case, the AIP should be in the non-working spouse's name so that the income derived is taxed at (lower) personal tax rates. The first $50,000 of investment income will be very tax-effective.

3. *I am self-employed, married and we have just started an AIP. I have no investments and my spouse works part-time.* For asset protection considerations, a company structure may be the best option if you are trading as self-employed. If it is "personal exertion" income (i.e. produced solely by your labour), you will need to discuss with your accountant the taxation guidelines for deriving such income in a company. If asset protection is not a risk and the income derived is

not from your personal exertion, a partnership could be appropriate for income-splitting reasons, taking into account that if the combined income is greater than $100,000 you will not be able to shelter the income from the higher personal tax rates.

If the self-employed income is significant and you are able to invest heavily in your AIP, you may consider incorporating a company structure for your business trading and a family trust holding the shares in the company. That way, you pay company tax, then dividend the profits to the family trust, which uses the dividends to invest in your AIP. The advantages here are many. From a tax viewpoint, assuming you have a company as a trust beneficiary, you build up your investments after paying no more than the company rate of tax. That is a tax saving of nearly 20%, which provides you significantly more working capital. Plus you have commenced developing estate planning opportunities and strong asset protection.

You may ask: Why have the company and family trust? Why not just earn the money in the company and invest within that company? One of my rules is to never have investments in a trading company, as there is always the potential for customers, suppliers or employees to sue the company and if successful, have access to my investments. I prefer to keep my investments safely well away from any business trading.

Note that you will not miss out on the capital gains tax concessions available to individuals so long as you distribute such gains to an individual beneficiary. If your *Niche* is mainly deriving income with the remote (or long-term) thought of making capital gains, I believe investing via your family trust also to be the correct method.

If this style of structure interests you, I strongly recommend you discuss the concept in some detail with your accountant.

4. *I am similar to (3) but am single and likely to stay that way!* Other than the comments regarding partnerships and the potential to split incomes, I recommend the same structure as for (3). While you may not have an immediate family or dependents,

a family trust will still present you many advantages.

5. *We are similar to (3) but have a significant business.* Once again I would suggest the same advice as in (3). If the business has many assets either in the form of plant and equipment or goodwill, I would look at ways to protect these by selling them to the family trust (or establishing them there to start). This strategy offers asset protection advantages and the trust may even to be able to charge a licence or lease fee to the company for using those assets.

6. *Our investments are growing rapidly and we are well on our way to Financial Freedom. Both of us are salary and wage earners.* You need to consider your personal tax rates and what is likely to be your long-term salary or wage. If your yearly salary and wages are more than $50,000 each, you should seriously consider a family trust so that income derived will be taxed at no more than the entity tax rate and so you receive those other advantages associated with trusts. If your salary or wage is less than $50,000, you should hold your investments in the lowest salary or wage earner's name. You will also need to continually review your projected income from your investments and may consider a family trust as you creep past the $50,000 from salary and investment income.

7. *Our goal is to create significant wealth through finding our Niche and contributing to our AIP, but as yet we have not accumulated any investments.* This is a difficult one. If you are very committed and have absolute confidence you will achieve your goals in the short term, you may want to consider setting up a family trust now. If you are conservative, you can use the advice of (1) or (2) above and continually monitor your progress and develop a structure as you grow. The monitoring is important, as it is usually very costly to change your investments from one structure to another once established, because of capital gains tax and stamp-duty implications.

> **It may be advisable to now re-read the superannuation section in Chapter 16, as this may also be an appropriate structure for you.**

One of the most often-asked questions I get on the subject of entity structuring is 'When should we set up our structure?' The answer is: 'Just before you need it.' While this answer is not too helpful, it demonstrates there is no real answer to the question. As I have said before, getting the best structure is not a precise science and it depends on your specific circumstance and also the type of person you are.

If you are still in any doubt about the appropriate structure for you, I recommend you discuss your current financial situation and goals with an accountant or lawyer who specialises in this area. Make sure you understand all the advantages and disadvantages of the proposed structure before it is established. Don't forget that even when you do have the structure set up, you must continue to monitor it carefully. As your business, salary and investments grow, along with changes to tax and other laws, your structure may need to be modified or altered to suit those changes.

## FURTHER INFORMATION

If you want to obtain a greater understanding about tax and the different ways to organise your financial affairs there are many suitable websites. Here is a brief selection:

- Australian Securities and Investments Commission (ASIC) at www.asc.gov.au.
- Australian Taxation Office (ATO) at www.ato.gov.au.
- Institute of Chartered Accountants at www.icaa.org.au – this has  links to other sites, tax bulletins and tax media releases.
- Australian Society of Certified Practising Accountants at www.cpaonline.com.au.
- National Tax and Accountants Association at www.ntaa.com.au – this has tax tips and media releases.
- National Institute of Accountants at www.nia.org.au.
- Taxation Institute of Australia at www.taxia.com.au – this has free publications and tax news.
- School of Commerce at Flinders University at www.law.flinders.edu.au/tax - this has great links to other sites, a legal dictionary, news and information.

## CHAPTER 28 ACTION STEPS REVIEW

1. Understand the different types of structures available for business and investment, their advantages, disadvantages and tax rates.
2. Determine your financial goals and objectives and select the structure most suitable for you.
3. Look at the suggested Internet sites to further review the structures available and their tax implications.
4. Before taking action, always remember to seek assistance from an accountant or lawyer who is a specialist in this area.

**CHAPTER 29**

# Building your private financial library

'If a little knowledge is dangerous, where is the man who
has so much as to be out of danger?'
T.H. HUXLEY

'Knowledge enriches knowledge, and the more the variety,
the greater the enrichment.'
WILLARD F. ROCKWELL, JR.

Although *Money Secrets of the Rich* is designed to be a
comprehensive step-by-step program, I believe that it is
always important that you commit to your own **Financial
Intelligence** as a *continuous* process. Never stand by and allow
your Financial Intelligence to stop growing. You must continue
your education process to keep up with the ever-changing world.

Over the years I have spent tens and tens of thousands of
dollars on books, tapes and seminars. In fact, at my office I have
an entire room that has been converted to become my library.
The walls are filled from top to bottom with books and tape sets.
Although all have provided information, there are some works
that stand head and shoulders above the others.

Here is a list of the financial-related books that have had the
greatest impact on my life. This list is in no particular order, I just
listed all the books I could remember being influential in my life.

'Miss a meal if you have to,
but don't miss a book.'
**JIM ROHN**

'If a man empties his purse
into his head, no one can take
it away from him. An
investment in knowledge
always pays the best interest.'
**BENJAMIN FRANKLIN**

*The Richest Man in Babylon,*
  George C. Clason,
  republished Signet,
  New York.
*Think & Grow Rich,* Napolean
  Hill, Fawcett Crest.
'The Means and Manner of
  Obtaining Virtue', extracted
  from *The Autobiography
  and Other Writings by
  Benjamin Franklin,*
  Penguin Classics.

'The desire for knowledge,
like the acquisition of riches,
increases ever with the acquisition
of it.'
**LAURENCE STERN**

*Master Key to Riches,* Fawcett
  Books.
*Trade Your Way to Financial
  Freedom,* Dr. Van K. Tharp,
  McGraw-Hill.
*How to Make Money in Stocks,*
  William J. O'Neil, McGraw-
  Hill.
*If You Want to Be Rich & Happy
  Don't Go To School,* Robert
  T. Kiyosaki.

*Rich Dad, Poor Dad,* Robert T.
  Kiyosaki with Sharon L.
  Lechter, TechPress.
*The Cashflow Quadrant,* Robert
  T. Kiyosaki with Sharon L.
  Lechter, TechPress.
*Rich Dad's Guide to Investing,*
  Robert T. Kiyosaki with
  Sharon L. Lechter, TechPress.
*The 7 Habits of Highly Effective
  People,* Stephen R. Covey
  (Fireside) Simon & Schuster.
*The Millionaire Next Door,*
  Thomas J. Stanley, Ph. D.,
  William D. Danko, Ph. D.,
  Longstreet Press, Inc.
*Inc. & Grow Rich,* C.W. 'Al'
  Allen et al, Rich Life, Inc.,
  Sage International, Inc.
*Unlimited Power,* Anthony
  Robbins, Fawcett
  Columbine.
*The Magic of Getting What You
  Want,* David J. Schwartz,
  William Morrow &
  Company, Inc.
*Your Infinite Power to be Rich,*
  Dr Joseph Murphy, Parker
  Publishing Company, Inc.
*Infinite Power for Richer Living,*
  Dr Joseph Murphy, Parker
  Publishing Company, Inc.
*Don't Worry, Make Money,*
  Richard Carlson, Ph.D.,
  Hodder & Stoughton.
*Grow Rich With Peace of
  Mind,* Napoleon Hill,
  Fawcett Books.

*Success Through a Positive Mental Attitude*, Napoleon Hill & Clement Stone, Fawcett Books.

*Laws of Success*, Napoleon Hill, Kampmann & Co.

*Money-Love*, Jerry Gillies, Warner Books.

*The Businessman's Topical Bible*, NIV Honor Books.

*The Warren Buffet Way*, Robert G. Hagstrom, Jr., John Wiley & Sons.

*God Wants You To Be Rich*, Paul Zane Pilzer, Simon & Schuster.

*How to Master the Art of Selling Anything*, Tom Hopkins, Tom Hopkins International.

*The Prosperity Solution Volumes I & II*, Dr. Jonathan Parker, Gateways Research Institute (Audio).

*Seven Strategies for Wealth and Happiness*, Jim Rohn.

*Success Through a Positive Mental Attitude*, W. Clement Stone.

*How to Be Rich*, J. Paul Getty.

*One up on Wall Street*, Peter Lynch, Simon & Schuster.

*Beating the Street*, Peter Lynch, Simon & Schuster.

*Nothing Down for the 90s*, Robert G. Allen, Simon & Schuster.

*The Challenge*, Robert G. Allen, Simon & Schuster.

*Multiple Streams of Income*, Robert G. Allen, John Wiley & Sons, Inc.

'We shall not cease from exploration
And the end of all our exploring
Will be to arrive where we started
And know the place for the first time.'

**T.S. ELIOT**

*Influence, The Psychology of Persuasion*, Robert B. Cialdini, Ph. D, William Morrow and Company.

*Emotional Intelligence*, Daniel Goleman, Bloomsbury Publishing.

*How to Stop Worrying and Start Living*, Dale Carnegie, Vermilion.

*Don't Sweat the Small Stuff*, Richard Carlson, Ph.D, Hodder & Stoughton

*Wealth Without Risk*, Charles Givens, Simon & Schuster.

*Real Magic*, Wayne Dyer, HarperCollins.

*The Aladdin Factor*, Jack Canfiled & Mark Hansen.

*Chicken Soup for the Soul*, Jack Canfiled & Mark Hansen.

*The Nine Steps to Financial Freedom*, Suze Orman, Crown Publishers, Inc.

## SUMMARY

Remember to continue your commitment to **Financial Freedom**. I suggest that you commit to reading a minimum of one financial book each month. In the book *The Millionaire Next Door*, it is said that the average millionaire spends just over eight hours a month managing/learning about money. You do the same and remember to continually strive to increase your **Financial Intelligence**. This process should never stop, it is never complete. It is an evolution for each and every one of us.

---

## CHAPTER 29 ACTION STEPS REVIEW

1. Go to a library, bookstore, www.amazon.com, www.bn.com or www.pcug.com.au (which links to most Internet bookshops) and pick out at least one new financial book to read this month. Other financial information sites such as www.investorweb.com.au also have select online bookstores slanted towards investment themes. Make notes if you can and review those notes periodically/regularly.

'Formal education will make you a living; self-education will make you a fortune.'
**JIM ROHN**

**CHAPTER 30**

# Review III – The roof is on and the sun is shining

'It takes two to speak the truth – one to speak,
and another to hear.'
H.D. THOREAU

'After climbing a great hill, one only finds that there are
many more hills to climb...I dare not linger, for my long
walk is not yet ended.'
NELSON MANDELA

Congratulations, you made it! The final chapter on your journey to *Automatic* **Financial Freedom**. Over the last 29 chapters we have covered a tremendous amount of material. At this point your *Financial Intelligence* is easily amongst the top few per cent of the world. More importantly, if you have followed the instructions in this program, you have now made dramatic changes in your financial life. Let's review what you have accomplished.

## YOU HAVE...

- clearly identified where you are financially and what it takes to move up to becoming a **Level Four Automatic Investor** or higher
- set up an **Automatic Investment Plan (AIP)** and are now *Paying Yourself First (***Money Step #1***)*

## YOU ARE...

- *Reinvesting Your Investment Returns* to take advantage of the power of **Compound Interest (Money Step #2)**
- *Receiving Level Four Automatic Investor Rates of Return* by placing your AIP investment in a managed or other growth investment **(Money Step #3)**
- financially cognisant, knowing exactly where you stand and knowing *What Your Money is Doing* because you completed the **Income Statement** and **Balance Sheet (Money Step #4)**

## YOU HAVE...

- sold or donated all your unwanted or underutilised **passive assets**
- adopted the **powerful** *Automatic Money System* **(Money Step #5)**
- learned how to reduce your *cost* of living 20–50% without reducing your *standard* of living, by applying *Financial Competence (Intelligence and Responsiblity)* to your financial decisions **(Money Step #6)**

## YOU HAVE LEARNED...

- when and how to refinance your home and how to find the best home loan with the lowest interest rate!
- how to buy your next car for a 20–50% discount!
- how to cut your bank fees to the bone!
- how to increase your pay to the max!
- how to slash your insurance costs 20–100%!
- the 'truth' about life insurance and how to save big bucks!

## YOU HAVE LEARNED...

- to think like the Rich and become Money Attractant, not Money Repellant!
- **The Nine Generalised Principles of Active (Level Five) Investing,**
- my **17 Personal Rules for Active (Level Five) Investing for 20-100%+ Returns!**
- how to make Quick Cash and positively gear real estate in Australia and New Zealand (with case studies)
- about 72 Secret Investments of the Rich Offering 20-100% + Returns!

## AND YOU HAVE ...

- set up a plan to avoid debt and use the *Debt Terminator* to become **debt-free (including owning your house and cars) in 3–7 years! (Money Step #7)**
- learned about business and investment structures – the tax reduction and asset protection secrets of the rich
- begun building your private financial library.

**Wow! It has been quite an experience hasn't it! Exhausted? Excited? You have just completed a program designed to dramatically improve your financial life... forever!**

> What areas do you need to place more emphasis on? What **money steps** are the most challenging for you? And most importantly: What do you need to do to make sure you stay on track?

## FINAL THOUGHTS FOR BEYOND *MONEY SECRETS OF THE RICH*

Take the time to **Write out a Plan** for the next year and stick to it. Ask yourself what should you do next? What areas would be the easiest to improve? What areas are challenging you the most? Write this all out on your plan. Make this your personal hit-list for becoming rich! With what you have learned in the *Money Secrets of the Rich* program you now have all the tools you need to become very rich on your current income. All you have to do is follow the *Money Secrets* step-by-step plan and prepare and follow your own *written* plan and you will achieve ***Automatic* Financial Freedom**.

'Do not lose your red blood; whatever you are, wherever or however you are situated, keep your heart warm and your humanity at par. Push forward; be of good cheer. Believe in our people, in our methods, in our country, in your neighbor and in yourself; and remember, if you are going into business, that, after all is said and done – after your fortune is made, however great it may be – in the small hours of the night, in your heart of hearts, the thing you are really going to enjoy, take satisfaction in and be proud of – the thing that will carry you over the rough places – that will keep your heart strong and your brain clear, will be the thought of what you have done to help others – what you have left to a world that has offered so much to you.'

**GEORGE W. PERKINS**

Maintain confidence in yourself and your own abilities and in the reciprocal nature of abundant living that awaits you at every turn on this journey to **Financial Freedom**. Know that right now, you have the tools you need to make your financial dreams a reality. A reality that is yours to savour and enjoy each and every day.

And as you focus on your objectives, remember to take the time to enjoy the journey. For it is the day-to-day living by the **principles** and **rules** you learned in this book that will take you to your ultimate destination.

So *write* out your plan and focus on your goals. Start today and you will reap the benefits for the rest of your life. Come to know by experience that one makes one's own luck and that truly, as I have found, the essence of luck is 'the residue of diligence' when 'preparation meets opportunity'. Or as a Spanish Jesuit priest by the noble name of Baltasar Gracian once wrote long ago, in the year 1647: 'There is not good or bad luck except wisdom and foolishness.' So always keep learning.

And always guard your *Integrity* as you would guard your own life, for without it first and foremost in all that we are and all that we do, we are nothing.

In the Acknowledgments section I provide an insight into some of the qualities I have absorbed from remarkable people I have known over the course of my life. The positive influences that these people have had on my personal life, my philosophy, my spirituality and my business and investor skills cannot be understated. Daily I practise the essence of their teachings as tribute to them and perhaps to inspire others of the truth of the statement: 'Seek and ye shall find.'

In these final thoughts, I just wanted to say to you again to be kind to yourself along your journey. *You* are your most remarkable ally. Always remember to be your own best friend, rather than your own worst enemy.

Be kind to yourself over your mistakes or setbacks. There is much to be learned from one's mistakes, from the journey itself, that takes us ever closer to our destination. One has only to look closely, honestly and positively to find the lessons and the better way forward. I believe that the only real *failures* are in no longer trying, in refusing to see or bend to a better course, or in trampling or neglecting others along the way.

> 'We grow great by dreams. All big men are dreamers. They see things in the soft haze of a spring day or in the red fire of a long winter's evening. Some of us let these great dreams die, but others nourish and protect them, nurse them through bad days till they bring them to the sunshine and light which come always to those who sincerely hope that their dreams will come true.'
>
> **WOODROW WILSON**

> 'Man must be arched and buttressed from within, else the temple will crumble to dust.'
>
> **MARCUS AURELIUS**

The hard lessons I have learned at the hands of some less than scrupulous or less than honourable individuals over the course of my life, are always worth crediting. For perhaps without some degree of adversity, we truly learn little and taste only bland victories.

I certainly have never advocated that it was *necessary* for a person to have to 'fail their way to success' but I do acknowledge that mistakes are an inevitable part of life and that wisdom and expertise is often a tonic drunk from the well of 'life experience'. At least when one is making mistakes one is taking action and is not idle. Providing you are not making the *same* mistakes and are not damaging other people, I agree with George Bernard Shaw's sentiment: 'A life spent making mistakes, is not only more honourable but more useful than a life spent doing nothing.'

My aim in life has always been to gain as much wisdom as I

can from observing other people's mistakes and listening to their expertise. In doing this I have often learned as much from what I call my reverse mentors, as I have from positive mentors. By watching the failures of others, I have been able to implement *rules* and *systems* that have prevented me from making their mistakes.

'Invest in yourself – if you have confidence in yourself.'
**WILLIAM FEATHER**

'Everyone's got it in him, if he'll only make up his mind and stick at it. None of us was born with a stop-valve on our powers or with a set limit to our capacities. There's no limit possible to the expansion of each one of us.'
**CHARLES M. SCHWAB**

This has allowed me to avoid many difficulties in life. Of course my decisions have not always been right. Like most people, I have made my fair share of mistakes. My aim in this regard is simply to not repeat the same mistakes over and over, but rather to learn from them and move on.

As I have said, one of my primary motivations for creating *Money Secrets of the Rich* was to provide you with a step-by-step path to ***Automatic* Financial Freedom** without you having to endure the pain and hardship of reinventing the wheel. The path is a clear and easy one to follow and I have enjoyed sharing it with you.

So remember, as you complete this program, be kind to yourself and acknowledge *your* mistakes and credit them with the honour of bringing you to this place in time whereby you are able to now confidently move to *Automatic* Financial Freedom.

The power to effect change lies first and foremost in the courage to take full responsibility for one's own life. Remember what I said at the outset of the program, that you were exactly where you deserved to be financially! Now that you have completed the *Money Secrets of the Rich* program, the opportunity to prosper financially is right in front of you. What you do with this information is entirely up to you. I know many of you are already flying along. Others will have started but may lose momentum after a while. And some will be all intentions and no action. What is it that produces such differences in progress between different people?

What is it that *you* need to do to make sure you are one of the people who commits and sticks, who sees the *Money Secrets of the Rich* program through? Think about this, and then when you have decided what the difference is, take away anything that sounds like an excuse. What are you left with? Just you!

So please, do whatever it takes to move yourself forward. Success is a constant progress and it *does* get easier and easier with every positive step.

I have greatly enjoyed the opportunity to spend time with you over the course of the *Money Secrets of the Rich* program. I encourage you to contact PowWow Events International or visit my website to share your success stories. I would love to hear them. I also encourage you to teach others what you have learned, for it is in the act of teaching, that one is most able to learn.

I truly hope that one day our paths will cross while I am visiting the great Land Down Under or the Land of the Long White Cloud.

All I can sincerely say to you now, as one last encouragement to commit and follow through, in words that I wish could jump off the page in 3-D animation, is:

> 'In a sense, knowledge shrinks as wisdom grows: for details are swallowed up in principles. The details of knowledge which are important will be picked up ad hoc in each avocation of life, but the habit of the utilisation of well-understood principles is the final possession of wisdom.'
> **A.N. WHITEHEAD**

> 'Troubles are usually the brooms and shovels that smooth the road to a good man's fortune; and many a man curses the rain that falls upon his head, and knows not that it brings abundance to drive away hunger.'
> **ST BASIL**

**Have faith!**
**Take action! You *will* succeed!**
**You now have a do-able plan! Go forward!**

# Become rich!
### That's all there is to it!

I wish you every success, happiness and prosperity. This is John Burley saying Thank you and God Bless.

## CHAPTER 30 ACTION STEPS REVIEW

1. Review what you have learned in the last 30 chapters.
2. Spend some time reviewing and reflecting upon the *strengths* and areas to improve in your *Money Secrets* program.
3. *Write* out a plan for the next year and *stick to it*!
4. **Relax, reflect, resolve, review, respond, renew, revitalise and above all else take resilient *Action*!**

# Source notes

Jim Rohn, quotations from *Seven Strategies for Wealth and Happiness* (Brolga, Melbourne, 1994) and from *The Treasury of Quotes* by Jim Rohn, reprinted by permission of Jim Rohn International. Highly recommended work.

Richard Carlson, PhD, quotations from *Don't Worry, Make Money* (Hodder & Stoughton, 1997). Reprinted by permission of Richard Carlson. Highly recommended work.

Leo Burnett (1891–1971), corporate motto from Leo Burnett Advertising Agency.

Benjamin Franklin, quotations from various sources, primarily *The Means and Manner of Obtaining Virtue (The Way to Wealth from Poor Richard's Almanac*, 1757) and *Journals of a Voyage* (1726).

Norman Vincent Peale, *The Power of Positive Thinking* (Simon & Schuster, New York, 1953). Reprinted by permission.

Harvey S. Firestone, 'What I have Learned About Men' from *American Magazine*, April 1919.

Henry Ford, 'What I Learned About Business' from *My Life and Work* (Doubleday, Page & Company, 1922).

Benjamin F. Fairless, 'What Democracy Did for Me' from *American Magazine*, February, 1948.

Kahlil Gibran (1883–1931), *A Third Treasury of Kahlil Gibran* (Citadel, Secausus, New Jersey, 1965).

Henry Wadsworth Longfellow (1807–1882), 'Table-Talk' from *Driftwood* (1857).

John Train, *Dance of the Money Bees* (1974), *The Midas Touch* (1987), *The Craft of Investing* (1994).

Warren Buffett, *Warren Buffett Speaks* (1997); one was quoted in Judith M. Bardwick, *Danger in the Comfort Zone* (1995); one in Benjamin Graham, *The Intelligent Investor*, 4th ed (1973); one in

Peter Lynch, *One Up on Wall Street* (1989).

Thomas J. Stanley, PhD, and William D. Danko, PhD, *The Millionaire Next Door* (in USA; by Longstreet Press, Atlanta, 1996 and in Australia by HarperBusiness, Sydney).

James Allen, *The Mastery of Destiny* (Putnam, New York, 1909) and *As a Man Thinketh*.

Samuel Johnson (Dr Johnson, 1709–1784), various sources including *Of the Laws of Ecclesiastical Polity, Rasselas* (1759), and private letters to William Strahan, 27 March 1775.

Albert Einstein (1879–1955), attributed quotes and from *Out of My Later Life* (1950).

George Bernard Shaw (1856–1950), various sources including 'Maxims for Revolutionists' from *Man and Superman* (1903).

W. Somerset Maugham (1874–1965), attributed quotes and from *The Summing Up* (1938) and *Of Human Bondage* (1915).

Napoleon Hill, *Think & Grow Rich* (Fawcett Crest/Ballantine Books, reprinted 1983).

Suze Orman, *Nine Steps to Financial Freedom* (1997); *Take Care of Your Money* (Parade, 1997).

Lewis Carroll (Charles Dodgson,1832–1898), *Alice's Adventures in Wonderland* (1865).

Jim Jorgensen, *Money Lessons for a Lifetime* (1997).

George S. Clason, *The Richest Man in Babylon* (1926).

Anne Spencer Parry & Marjorie Pizer, *Below the Surface* (Pinchgut Press, Sydney, 1982; republished Angus & Robertson, Sydney, 1994). Reprinted by permission of HarperCollins Publishers, Sydney.

John D. Rockefeller (1839-1937), 'The American Business Man' from *Random Reminiscences of Men and Events* (first published Doubleday, Page & Company, 1909).

Tom Hopkins, *How to Master the Art of Selling* (Champion Press, Scottsdale, Arizona, 1982; republished HarperCollins, London, 1994). Reprinted with permission.

Jane Bryant Quinn, *Making the Most of Your Money* (1991).

Cecil B. de Mille (1881–1959), *Sunshine and Shadow* (1955).

Johann Wolfgang von Goethe (1749–1832), from *Conversations with Goethe* by Johann Peter Eckerman.

Giuseppe Mazzini (1805–1872), *The Duties of Man and Other Essays* (1910).

Victor Kiam, 'A Useful Tool of Self-Examination' from *Live to Win: Achieving Success in Life and Business* (William Morrow & Company, Inc., 1986).

Sir James Hardy, *An Adventurous Life* (Margaret Gee, Melbourne, 1993; republished Penguin, Victoria, 1995).

Stephen R. Covey, *The 7 Habits of Highly Effective People* (Simon & Schuster, New York, 1989). Reprinted with permission.

Andrew Carnegie (1835–1919), 'The Road to Business Success' from a speech on June 23, 1885 at Curry Commercial College.

Elbert Hubbard (1856–1915), *The Note Book* (1927).

Horne Tooke (1736–1812), quoted in Ralph Waldo Emerson, *The Conduct of Life* (1860).

Bertrand Russell (1872–1970), *The Conquest of Happiness* (1930) and *Sceptical Essays* (1928) 'Dreams and Facts'.

Jack Collis & Michael Leboeuf, *Work Smarter Not Harder* (Goal Setting Seminars, 1988; republished HarperBusiness, Sydney, 1995). Reprinted with permission of HarperCollins, Sydney.

Edgar A. Guest (1881–1959), *A Heap o'Livin'* (1916).

P.T. Barnum (1810–1891), 'The Art of Money-Getting' from *My Life Story*, and *Golden Rules for Money Making*, (1886).

Bertolt Brecht (1898–1956), *Die Dreigroschenoper* (1928) act 3, sc. 3.

Robert Herrick (1591-1674), *To the Virgins, to make much of Time* (1648).

Benjamin Disraeli (1804–1881), attributed to Disraeli, quoted in Mark Twain, *Autobiography* (1924) vol. 1, p. 246 and from a speech in 1870 and from *Vivian Grey* (1826) bk. 5, ch. 1.

Andrew Lang (1844–1912), quoted in A.L. Mackay (ed.), *A Dictionary of Scientific Quotations*.

Greg Easterbrook, *The New Republic*.

John Bunyan (1628–1688), *The Pilgrim's Progress* (1684) pt. 2, p. 231.

Michel Eyquem de Montaigne (1533–1592), *Essais* (1580, ed. M. Rat, 1958).

William Penn (1644–1718), *Some Fruits of Solitude* (1693).

Pliny the Elder (AD 23–79), *Historia Naturalis*.

Percy Bysshe Shelley (Declaration of Rights, 1812) article 27.

Winston Churchill (1874–1965), *My Early Life* (Macmillan, London, 1930).

Mark Twain (Samuel Clemens, 1835-1910), *Notebook* (1935).

B.C. Forbes (1880–1954), 'In Budgeting Your Days, Allow Time for Thinking' from *How to Get Out of Business* (Forbes Inc., 1927).

Sophocles (c.496–406 BC), Electra (418–414 BC) and *Antigone* (442–441 BC).

Thomas Alva Edison (1847-1931), 'They Won't Think' from the *Diary and Assundry Observations* (The Philosophical Library, 1948).

Stephen Leacock (1869–1944), 'The Perfect Salesman' in *The Garden of Folly*.

Merle Travis (1917–1983), 'Sixteen Tons' (1947 song).

Horace (Quintus Horatius Flaccus) (65-8 BC), *Epodes*, epode 2, 1.1.

Epictetus (2nd century AD), *Discourses*.

Edward De Bono, *Lateral Thinking for Management* (McGraw-Hill, London, 1971).

Bernard M. Baruch (1870–1965), 'My Investment Philosophy' from *My Own Story*, Copyright © 1957 by Bernard M. Baruch (Henry Holt & Co., Inc).

Clarence Day (1874–1935), 'The Three Tigers' from *The Crow's Nest* (1921).

Henry David Thoreau (1817–1862), *Walden* (1854) 'Where I lived and what I lived for' in *Writings* (1906 ed) and *A Week on the Concord and Merrimack Rivers* (1849) 'Wednesday'.

Josh Billings (Henry Wheeler Shaw) (1818–1885), *Everybody's Friend* (1874).

Horace Greeley (1811-1872), 'Success in Business' from a speech delivered in 1867.

Francis Bacon (1561–1626), *Essays* (1625): 'Of Ceremonies and Respects', 'Of Fortune', 'Of Discourse', 'Of Dispatch', 'Of Innovations'; and in *The Advancement of Learning* (1605).

William E. Gladstone (1809–1898), Diary, 31 December 1868 in M.R.D. Frost and H.C.G. Mathew (eds) *The Gladstone Diaries*, vol. 6 (1978).

George W. Perkins (1862–1920), 'The Modern Corporation' from a speech delivered at Columbia University, 1908.

Johann Wolfgang von Goethe (1749–1832), *The Power of Commitment*.

Susan M. Campbell, *From Chaos to Confidence* (Simon & Schuster, New York, 1995).

Zhuge Liang (2nd century AD), *Mastering the Art of War: The Way of the General*.

Oscar Wilde (1854–1900), *The Picture of Dorian Gray* (1891).

Dr Van K. Tharp, *Trade Your Way to Financial Freedom* (McGraw-Hill, 1999). Reprinted with permission of International Institute of Trading Mastery and Dr Tharp.

Julius Charles Hare (1795–1855) and Augustus William Hare (1792–1834), *Guesses at Truth* (1827), Series 1.

Laurence Stern (1713–1768), *Tristram Shandy* (1759–1767) bk. 1.

Jules Verne (1828–1905), *From the Earth to the Moon* (1865).

E.W. Scripps (1854–1926), 'Some Outlandish Rules for Making Money' from *Damned Old Crank*. Copyright © 1951 by Harper & Brothers (HarperCollins Publishers, Inc.).

Cervantes (Miguel de Cervantes Saavedra) (1547–1616), *Don Quixote* (1605).

Napoleon I (Napoleon Bonaparte) (1769–1821), *Maxims* (1804–1815).

William Hazlitt (1778–1830), 'On the Qualifications Necessary to Success in Life' in *The Plain Speaker* (1826).

Douglas MacArthur (1880–1964), quoted in Courtney Weaver, *MacArthur: His Rendezvous with History* (1955).

Washington Irving (1783–1859), from a report written in 1813 on the War of 1812.

J. Paul Getty (1892–1976), 'The Art of Individuality'. Copyright © by HMH Publishing Co., Inc. Reprinted from *How to be Rich* by J. Paul Getty (Berkeley Publishing Group).

Henry Ward Beecher (1813–1887), *Proverbs from Plymouth Pulpit* (1887).

Ben Jonson (c.1573–1637), *Volpone* (1606) act 1, sc. 1.

Helen Keller (1880–1968), *Let Us
Have Faith* (1940).

Seneca (Lucius Annaeus Seneca, The
Younger) (c.4 BC – AD 65),
*Letters to Lucilius* (c.AD 30).

Harvey Mackay, *Swim With the
Sharks Without Being Eaten Alive*
(1988) or *Beware the Naked Man
Who Offers You His Shirt* (1990).

T.H. Huxley (1825–1895), 'On
Elemental Instruction in
Physiology' (1877).

Virgil (Publius Vergilius Maro)
(70–19 BC) *Aeneid* (30–19 BC).

Willard F. Rockwell, Jr., 'The Hat of
the Student' from *The Twelve Hats
of a Company President*. Copyright
© 1971 (Prentice Hall/Career &
Personal Development).

T.S. Eliot (Thomas Stearns Eliot)
(1888–1965), *Four Quartets,* 'Little
Gidding' (1942).

A.N. Whitehead (1861–1947), 'The
Rhythmic Claims of Freedom and
Discipline', *The Aims of Education
and Other Essays* (New American
Library, New York).

Marcus Aurelius (AD 121–180),
*Meditations*.

Nelson Mandela, *The Long Walk to
Freedom* (Little, Brown, London,
1994).

# Acknowledgments

*M*oney Secrets of the Rich represents more than 20 years of my experience in the trenches of the business world. I could not have found my path and direction without the love, guidance and support of so many good friends and my family.

There are so many people who have contributed to the creation of this book that I would like to thank.

Before I thank these great people I would like to thank God for providing me with the motivation and tools to complete what has been for me a tremendous undertaking. Without his blessing and guidance I believe this work never would have been completed.

Thank you to my family. Thank you to Shari, my wife of 10 years, whom I love so deeply, for your love, strength and support. For standing by my side when I dragged you away from your California friends and family to Arizona to become a real estate investor with me. For working side-by-side with me during those fast-paced, hectic first few years when we completed hundreds of real estate transactions. But most importantly for always being there to listen and encourage me when I was down or the going got tough.

To my two best buddies, my son John, Jr. who always puts a smile on my face and in my heart, and my daughter Dani, who brings me so much joy and love and is truly Daddy's Girl. Thank you both. You provide me with the constant purpose behind being free (and not tied to a time-stealing job) and you provide the joy of one adventure after another! I truly am blessed!

To my dad, Bob Burley, who I have been fortunate enough to have work with me the past few years, I want to thank you for all you have done for me. For your love, your loyalty, your friendship and your advice. You are a great man who has taught me much about life, especially how to treat people. You have always believed in me and stood up for me when others have attempted to pull me down or convince me to conform. I'll always remember when I quit financial planning to become a real estate investor, everyone except for you and Shari thought I was crazy and a fool. But you believed in me and encouraged me. I am proud to call you not just my father, but my very good friend. I love you, Dad.

To my mother, Beverly Burley, I want to say thank you for the love you have given me over the years. For raising me and being there to talk with. You have taught me so many things, in particular: the joy of learning, to reach out and try new things, and to believe in myself. Thanks. I love you, Mom.

To my late grandfather, a naval officer who taught me so much about unconditional love, generosity, integrity, honour, true friendship, unwavering loyalty and the benefits of persistence and perseverance (the principle of *Lag*). I can never thank you enough. You taught me so much by your actions. You taught me humility and grace, and to always show compassion and the need to respect my fellow human beings whom you always so generously cared for and gave dignity to regardless of their rank or position in life. I do my best to follow in your ways. Grandpa, I miss you and not a day goes by when I don't think about you. I'll see you again in Heaven in due time.

To my co-author and good friend Bruce Whiting I would like to say thank you. First of all thank you to your family for allowing you to spend so much time on this project. And then thank you for your incredible knowledge, expertise and creativity in translating my techniques to application for Australia. It would have taken years to have even attempted to gain the information in your brain that was so critical in making this book the all-encompassing work that it is. I value your wit and friendship deeply. Thank you for everything, Bruce.

To my contributing editor, Simon Hall, the Aussie who between Sydney and Phoenix chained himself to various keyboards spanning a period of 18 months, day in and day out, without a whimper, at the cost of sore eyes, stiff shoulders and no social life outside my street. Who did this because he has a lifelong and passionate gift (*Niche*) for the written word and because he was inspired to bring out the best possible in *Money Secrets of the Rich*. Who added many personal insights to this book (including the bridging Chapters 11 and 21). I say thank you for enhancing and clarifying my thoughts. Your advice, research and gathering of information has proved invaluable in the creation of this work. And thank you for your determination, your patience, your extraordinary creativity but most of all for your friendship. I trust that this collaboration will be the first of many, Huck. You are a true wordsmith and compadre.

To Robert Kiyosaki, with whom I have had the pleasure of sharing ideas for many years. Thank you for the philosophical discussions (teachings) with regard to abundance, prosperity, business systems and creating wealth. Your insights into human nature, the education system and the power of the mind to construct its own future have enhanced my experiences and business/investing systems. Thank you.

I would like to thank all of my investors for their belief, trust and support over the many years.

I would like to thank the people of *integrity* that I am fortunate enough to call friends and do business with: Al Allen, Cheri Hill, Lou Freeman and the entire staff at Sage International for their wonderful support and professionalism over the many years (US corporation and limited partnership strategies); Don Wolfe for his many years of friendship, mastery training, mentoring and helping people to change; Dr. Van Tharp (psychology and investing), his wife Kala, his son Robert and his many students that I have had the opportunity to share experiences with and become friends; Jeffrey Taylor (real estate landlording); Eva Love and Will Noice; Loral Langemeier; Keith

Cunningham (business strategy and negotiations); Kevin and Sara of Insync (cover design); Mark Pratt (product production); Robert G. Allen (wealth training); Saul Klein (real estate); and to Scott Bell, Jerry LaFontaine and Mike Brooks for the opportunity to put on my first seminars.

My associates at Burley & Associates, Inc. who are much more than just co-workers but are friends, confidants and invaluable in my life, I give a special thanks. To Regina Redmond my ever-trusted manager who runs the day-to-day real estate operation, and our web business, and is always available as a sounding board for new ideas and strategies, my heart felt thanks. To Cindy Chapin my good friend who just happens to be the greatest logistics manager in the world, thank you for your dedication, hard work, loyalty, and creativity. You are truly a joy to work with. To Sue Holmes, the newest member of our team, thank you for taking so much of the load off everyone else. You have been a blessing.

To my great friends and Australian promoters, Suzi Dafnis and Peter Johnston of Pow Wow Events International, my deepest thanks for your trust and support in my work. Thank you for allowing this information to be shared with Australia. A special thank you to the entire staff and support teams of Pow Wow. You are without question the best in the business.

To my dear friends John and Debbie McCants (real estate investing and public speaking), thank you for always being there for me. Your friendship and support this last decade have meant so much to me. You are a big part of the success of the *Boot Camp* and for this I am grateful. I look forward to the many good times and adventures we will share together in the future.

To the many others who have supported myself and this work, thank you:

Dan and Janice Osborne, Michael Talarico, Erika Yeates, Melita Hunt, Felicity Hefferman, Steve Dover, Anthony Cordato, Max Gacitua, Tony Barton, Kelly and Anna Ritchie, the Downie Family, Tony Edward, Gordon Greene, Brad Sugars, Peter Aranyi and Pearl Sidwell, Graeme Fowler, Karen and Russell Dorlandt, Steve McKnight, David Bradley, Rad Williams,

Paul and Tracey Verschuuren, Mick and Jane Hagarty, Malcolm and Fiona Linsell, Dennis and Angela Perin, Tami Iredale and richard Portakiewicz, Craig Chandler, Richard and Veronica Tan, Bellum and Doreen Tan.

Joe Arlt, Hymer, Tyrone Thomas, Billy and Laura Harris, Marjorie and Dave Glowka, Jerry and Lisa Hoganson, Sylvia Lunsford, John Kellen, Perry and Darla Anderson, Stephanie Olsen, C.J. Matthews, Troy Arment, Marleen Geyen, Harold and Sunshine Croucher, Monica and Enrique Teuscher, Bill and Cindy Shopoff, Blair and Eileen Singer, Rolf Parta, Dr. Ann Nevin, Lane Bradford Leach, my pastor Bryan Fergus.

To all my thousands of graduates both past and present, thank you for your support and your continued success. Your accomplishments have made me so proud. Your enthusiasm vindicates all those long hours in the trenches.

My sincerest thanks and best wishes,

*John Burley*

I nitial impressions might suggest that to co-author a book is a relatively simple task. Enjoying, interesting and satisfying, yes. Simple, no. Many hours spent at the computer (in between the usual business and family duties) made me appreciate the many difficulties and challenges involved with putting a book such as *Money Secrets* together. Condensing many complex financial, business and investment issues into useful information that readers can enjoy learning, as well as act upon to their benefit, was no mean feat. To accomplish this I had a great crew assisting me.

Thanks to my business partner and friend, Hank Wamsteker, for educating me in his unique way about business, the importance of cash flow, to be passionate about helping clients and to not think like a stereotypical accountant all the time. And thank you to my dedicated staff who were the research engine behind much of the specific Australian information in the book.

I appreciate your help immensely.

To John Burley of course, who throughout our friendship has continually demonstrated the highest ethics and almost an obsession to teach people to achieve their financial goals. Also, for John's assistance in helping me with my money habits and putting me on the path to financial independence, I am very grateful. I have enjoyed our professional relationship and personal friendship very much and look forward to many more good times and satisfying projects together in the future.

To PJ and Suzi and their team from Pow Wow Events International for introducing me to John Burley and welcoming me into an active speaking role at John's Australian and US seminars over the last three years. This has allowed me to help many more people with financial education. Thanks PJ also for laughing at my jokes when I'm on stage. It's not easy to come up with new material all the time. I'm an accountant after all!

And to Yvonne and our three daughters, Lindzee, Kellie and Jamie, thank you for your support and patience and for allowing me the relative peace and quiet during the weekends I spent working on the book. I am sure we can now get back to spending more time together.

*Bruce Whiting*


My heartfelt thanks go to John for showing up at just the right time and connecting one of his big dreams with one of mine. And for his friendship, mentoring and barbecuing skills. Thank you also to his groovy family (Shari, the Bears – Bubba and Dani, Bob, Virginia) and to my dear friend Cindy and her family (Heather Feather, Jen and Bill) for putting up with me while I was chained to the computer in suburban Phoenix and not cooking any meals. Hey Hymer.

My enthusiasm for the written and the spoken word began early. Both my parents speak beautiful (self-fashioned) English and my brother and I grew up as the lead actors in a two-boy show full of complex comedic role-playing awash in a carnival of well-practiced accents and voices. We were a crack-up! Thank you three for giving me my countless opportunities. Thank you Mum (Marjorie) for having the purest, most generous heart and most unconditional patience of anyone I have ever met. Thank you Dad (Alan) for your persistence, cleverness and hard work and for being a textbook Level Four Investor. And thank you brother Jimmy (Jonathan) for being my anchor – my standard against which I measure the world. There is too much to thank you for here ... byiddy. Garhoy! Salutations to my other friends and family too.

For most of us the school years are lean for inspiring teachers who both recognise *and* nurture our unique talents. I consider myself lucky to have had five teachers along the way who maintained my momentum. They said the right things at the right time: Brian Jury; Len Nairn; Malcolm Lamb; and my two inspirational and gifted English teachers Tim Norfolk and Mrs Sheilagh Haines. You are all remarkable and insightful mentors. And through seven years of university, two breathtaking intellects: Dr Bowen-James from Sydney University and Dennis Harley from UNSW.

*Simon Hall*

# About the Authors

## JOHN R. BURLEY

John R. Burley has achieved what most people would consider impossible. Starting out with little money, a workable plan of action, and a lot of desire, John was in a position to retire by the age of 32. John has completed over 800 Real Estate transactions. Today, his investment portfolio includes well over 100 properties, stocks, businesses, and more.

Referred to as "One of the Premier Investors in America," on US National Television, John has also been named in Who's Who of American Business People and International Entrepreneurs. Prior to becoming a full-time investor, John ran his own successful financial planning company and has vast knowledge in the areas of finance, investments, corporate tax reduction techniques, asset protection and real estate.

John has shared his information with millions of people throughout the world and he truly believes that everyone can achieve a rich, full life, filled with prosperity and abundance. He teaches in a straight-forward, easy to follow step-by-step way that makes learning how to become rich fun and easy. In addition to closely managing his investments and running his businesses, John regularly tours Australia, the US and Singapore conducting seminars on wealth education and investment. Each year he himself attends dozens of seminars, listens to numerous tapes and reads forests of books on money, investing and financial education so that he can keep abreast of and decipher and navigate for others, all that the investment world holds out to market each year.

John lives with his wife Shari and his two children John, Jr. and Danielle in Phoenix, Arizona. He is a passionate and committed family man, a keen scratch golfer and avid fisherman.

John continues to earn and maintain the respect of the investment community because he is out in the 'real world' doing deals on a day-to-day basis. In other words, John R. Burley is a man who 'walks his talk'.

## BRUCE WHITING

Bruce Whiting is a Chartered Accountant and has been in public practice in Australia for 20 years. He holds a Bachelor of Economics from Sydney University and has practiced in diverse areas of accounting and financial consulting. His expertise includes operational and financial systems review, due diligence for mergers and acquisitions, public floats, financial reporting, and financial analysis and taxation.

It is in the area of private practice though, as Managing Partner of the dynamic and internationally represented accounting firm, MGI Wamsteckers, that Bruce has made his greatest mark. His passion lies firmly grounded in helping his private clients and his seminar students achieve dramatic improvements in their business, investment, taxation and financial lives.

Bruce has the experience at all levels of business to equip him with the knowledge, expertise and resource base to advise on most business and investment matters. And through many years of analysis, Bruce has developed keen insights into why some people enjoy much greater success than others. He combines these insights with his broad business, tax and financial expertise into clear, constructive information which greatly assists all who encounter it. He is always keen to ensure that people have the right business and investment structure to suit their own situations and objectives and to maximise their returns on their investments.

Bruce has presented at seminars in Australia and internationally and is himself an astute property investor. He has numerous successful business interests and is a director of many profitable private companies. He also has significant venture capital interests.

Bruce is married to Yvonne and has three young daughters, Lindzee, Kellie and Jamie. When not in the office or at home with his family, you are likely to find Bruce, a recipient of the Queen Scout Award, indulging his love for the outdoors, bushwalking and camping, or playing golf. He says he loves the simple things in life and this is how he makes so much in the business, investment and financial world so beneficial to those he advises and teaches.

## SIMON HALL

Simon Hall is a successful private investor whose passion for the written word and for assisting others to improve their financial education has led him to partner with John Burley to produce *Money Secrets of the Rich* and *The Burley Chronicles*. He holds both a Bachelor of Arts from Sydney University and a Bachelor of Laws from UNSW and was admitted to the roll of solicitors in NSW in 1993. He has significant experience in project management, contracts and tender formulation and evaluation and is a keen advocate of short-term contract or consultancy work as a great modern-day opportunity to achieving valuable and broad-based experience in the work force.

It is his passion not to be tied to a conventional working life that has enabled Simon to assist and inspire many people on their road to wealth. Outstanding results in the Australian share market and other business interests since 1997 have enabled him to amass capital and passive income sufficient to pursue common interests and projects in association with John Burley and other friends. Whilst he would always rather be snowboarding or travelling if given the option, it would not be at the expense of living debt-free and continuing to help others escape from the burdens of financial servitude and wealth ignorance.

His family and friends are of the utmost importance to him and above all other qualities he values those of integrity, loyalty and generosity. It is these preferences that have led him to work with John, Bruce and Pow Wow Events in recent years. Though born and bred in Canberra, Simon is also a long term resident of Sydney's eastern suburbs.

# Investors' resource materials

Thank you for reading *Money Secrets of the Rich*. On these pages are details of John Burley's unique learning resources that have been designed to give you additional investment education.

## Winning the Money Game

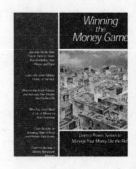

This live recording of a three-day seminar is the most revealing ever done on the subject of money. Information covered includes: The Seven Money Habits; The Levels of Investor; How the 'normal' person can become debt-free in 3–7 years (including your home and cars); Where to invest your money today and how to keep and protect your assets. Learn John's insider investment strategies. Develop a personal financial system designed to reduce debt and expenses while providing for long term financial security.

**12 audio tapes – $429.00**

## Make Fortunes in Foreclosures

This is how John acquired 152 properties using NONE of his own money. Each and every one of these properties produces Positive Cash Flow. Most experts agree that this is the #1 program for the real estate investor to begin their career. Recorded in the studio, this program teaches you the Eight Principles of Real Estate Investing. Learn the 'Nuts and Bolts' of how to invest and remarket foreclosures.

**4 audio tapes plus workbook – $210.00**

All prices are in Australian dollars and include GST.
Order now by calling **1300 550 240** or visit:
**www.powwowevents.com.au/burley**

# Investors' resource materials

## Blueprint for Success Real Estate Program

The success rate of students attending this five-day real estate training is four times greater than the industry average. It was this training that led Robin Leach of Lifestyles of the Rich and Famous fame to proclaim John Burley as one of the Premier Investors in America. Learn how to buy and resell real estate for Quick Cash (US$10,000+) within 90 days from completion of the training. Systems for developing long term cash flow are covered in great detail.

**20 audio tapes – $645.00**
**or manual (200+ pages) – $135.00**

## Secrets of The Professional Investor

Did you know nine out of ten investors do not make much money, if any? John Burley and Robert Kiyosaki show you how to be an unbeatable investor who wins consistently. In this tape set (recorded in Sydney), they speak frankly on how to make large sums of money with minimal risk. What□s more, they candidly reveal how much investors are lied to, often by people they trust. Get the hard facts on how you can get on the fast track to wealth... and if you want, retire early.

**16 audio tapes – $429.00**

All prices are in Australian dollars and include GST.
Order now by calling **1300 550 240** or visit:
**www.powwowevents.com.au/burley**

# Investors' resource materials

## Free Audio Cassette Tape

As a way of saying 'thank you' for reading this book and increasing your knowledge about financial success, we make available to you an audio cassette tape entitled:

*"Investment Strategies of the Rich"*

Please call 1300 550 240 to order your tape.

# See John Burley Live

John Burley visits Australia and New Zealand regularly to present his Winning the Money Game and Automatic Wealth programs. John is an excellent educator who demystifies the subject of money and investment.

For information about John's events in Australia and New Zealand, and his semi-annual Advanced Investing Boot Camp held in Phoenix, contact Pow Wow Events International on **1300 550 240** or visit:

**www.powwowevents.com.au/burley**

# Tell us what you thought about *Money Secrets of the Rich* and you could win the Ultimate Investors Pack!

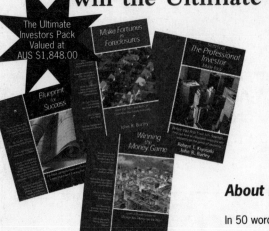

The Ultimate Investors Pack Valued at AUS $1,848.00

Go in the draw to win a complete pack of resources from John Burley when you complete and return the form below!

## About *Money Secrets of the Rich*

In 50 words or less, explain the value and benefits you have received from reading this book:

_____
_____
_____
_____
_____
_____

**The Ultimate Investors Pack includes:**
*Winning the Money Game* (12 audio tapes), *Blueprint for Success* (20 audio tapes, plus manual), *Fortunes in Foreclosures* (4 audio tapes plus workbook), *Secrets of The Professional Investor* made easy (16 audio tapes)

---

**About You** (Please complete legibly. Entry void if not legible.)

First name _____ Last name _____

Position _____ Company _____

_____

Address _____

Suburb _____ State _____ Post code _____

Country _____ Is this a ❑ work or ❑ home address?

Phone (W) _____ Fax _____

Email _____

Return to: Pow Wow Events International, PO Box 122, Rosebery NSW 1445  Phone: 1300 550 240
Fax: 1300 301 988  Email: burley@powwowevents.com.au  Website: www.powwowevents.com.au/burley

Privacy Notice: Pow Wow Events International does not sell or hire details of clients. We value your privacy. Winners are drawn quarterly and will be advised in writing.